Exchange is Not Robbery

More Stories of an African Bar Girl

John M. Chernoff

ISBN: 0-226-10355-2 (paper)

Cloth edition also available.

$22.50   £16.00

424 p. (est.), 2 maps, 6 x 9

Publication date: December 2004

For additional information, contact:

Peter Cavagnaro
Promotions Manager
University of Chicago Press
1427 East 60th Street
Chicago, IL 60637
(773) 702-0279
fax (773) 702-9756
pc@press.uchicago.edu

EXCHANGE IS NOT ROBBERY

Exchange Is Not Robbery

MORE STORIES
OF AN AFRICAN BAR GIRL

John M. Chernoff

THE UNIVERSITY OF CHICAGO PRESS : *Chicago and London*

JOHN M. CHERNOFF is the author of *Hustling Is Not Stealing: Stories of an African Bar Girl* (2003) and *African Rhythm and African Sensibility: Aesthetics and Social Action in African Musical Idioms* (1979), both published by the University of Chicago Press. Chernoff spent more than seven years in West Africa, based in Accra and Tamale, Ghana, where he also researched popular music and the music and culture of the Dagbamba people. His recordings of Dagbamba music include *Master Fiddlers of Dagbon* and *Master Drummers of Dagbon*, volumes 1 and 2.

The University of Chicago Press, Chicago 60637
The University of Chicago Press, Ltd., London
© 2005 by The University of Chicago
All rights reserved. Published 2005
Printed in the United States of America
14 13 12 11 10 09 08 07 06 05   1 2 3 4 5

ISBN: 0-226-10354-4 (cloth)
ISBN: 0-226-10355-2 (paper)

Library of Congress Cataloging-in-Publication Data

Chernoff, John Miller
    Exchange is not robbery : more stories of an African bar girl / John M. Chernoff.
        p.   cm.
    Continuation of Hustling is not stealing.
    ISBN 0-226-10354-4 (cloth : alk. paper)—ISBN 0-226-10355-2 (pbk. : alk. paper)
    1. Women—Ghana—Social conditions.   2. Women—Togo—Social conditions.   3. Women—Burkina Faso—Social conditions.   I. Chernoff, John Miller. Hustling is not stealing.   II. Title.

HQ1816.C47 2005
205.42′0966—dc22

                                                2004010381

For my wife Donna, my daughters Eunice and Eva,
and my sons Harlan and Avram

CONTENTS

ACKNOWLEDGMENTS

I would like to thank the Joint Committee on African Studies of the Social Science Research Council and the American Council of Learned Societies for a Postdoctoral Fellowship for African Area Research that helped me to develop some of the data for this book. I would also like to thank the following people for reading and commenting on drafts or for helping with various aspects of this book: Abraham Adzenyah, Emmanuel Akyeampong, Marianne Alverson, Kelly Askew, Deborah Benkovitz, John Berthelette, Willem Bijlefeld, Kenneth Bilby, David Brent, Alan Brody, Jason Brown, David Byrne, Amina Jefferson Bruce, Donna Chernoff, Harold Chernoff, Michael Chernoff, Richard Closs, Ben DeMott, Peter Edidin, Mark Ehrman, Kai Erikson, Steven W. Evans, Alan Fiske, Steven Friedson, Arnold Gefsky, Dawn Hall, Maxine Heller, Kissmal Ibrahim Hussein, Angeliki Keil, Charles Keil, Bruce King, Sarah LeVine, David Light, Rene Lysloff, Yao Hlomabu Malm, Michael Mattil, Leighton McCutchen, Will Milberg, David Mooney, Mustapha Muhammed, Steven Mullen, Judy Naumburg, Deborah Neff, Samuel Nyanyo Nmai, Timmy W. Ogude, James Peters III, Charles Piot, Dina Light Ranade, Marina Roseman, Eric Rucker, Nadine Saada, Philip Schuyler, Paul Stoller, Deborah Tannen, Robert F. Thompson, Richard Underwood, Christopher Waterman, Andrew Weintraub, David Wise. Betsy Morgan DeGory assisted with the research and contributed many ideas to the work. The following people provided technical assistance on writing the various languages in the text: Eric O. Beeko, J. H. Kwabena Nketia, Lilly Nketia, and Joseph Adjaye for Asante Twi; Kathryn Geurts, Kojo Amegashie, and Felix K. Ameka for Ewe and Mina/Gen; Beverly Mack and John Hutchison for Hausa; Philip Schuyler for Arabic; Paul Stoller and Jean-Paul Dumont for Verlan and French argot; Joachim Zabramba for Moore; Joachim Zabramba, Patricia Koutaba, and John Hutchison for Dioula. Also, of course, I would like to thank the woman who is called Hawa in this book and also all the people in Ghana, Togo, Burkina Faso, Nigeria, and other West African countries who helped me understand their world as they know it.

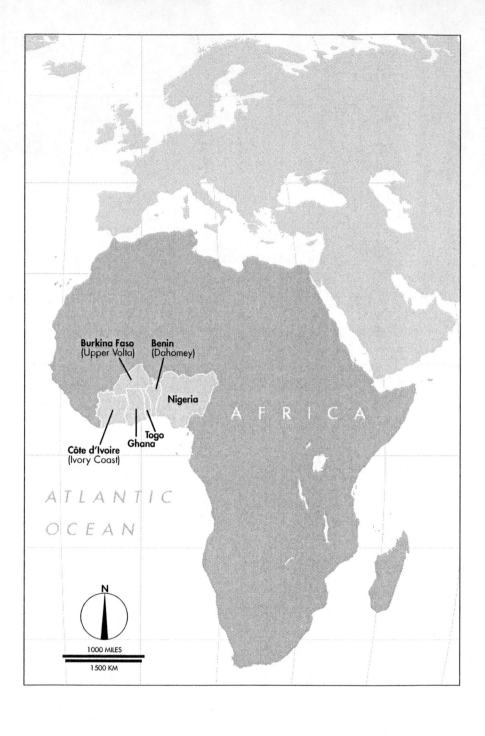

Burkina Faso
(Upper Volta)

Benin
(Dahomey)

Nigeria

Togo

Ghana

Côte d'Ivoire
(Ivory Coast)

AFRICA

ATLANTIC

OCEAN

N

1000 MILES

1500 KM

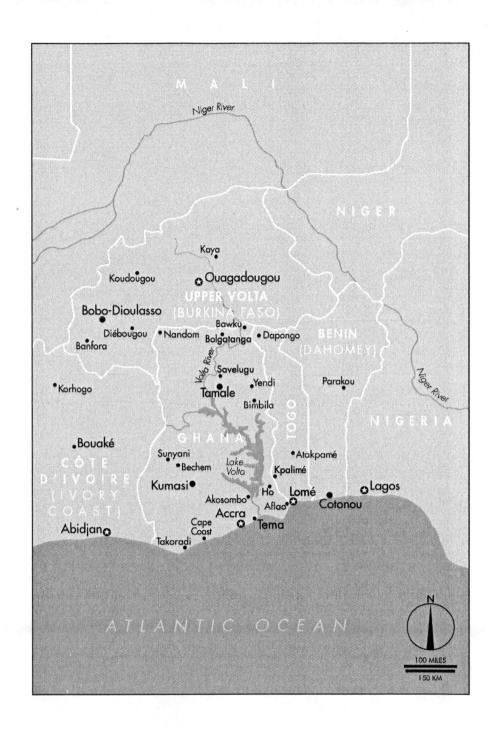

West African locations mentioned in Hawa's stories

The one who holds a rope knows its joining places and its weak points, but the one who wove the thread is the one who knows how long it is.

—DAGBAMBA PROVERB

PROLOGUE

Exchange Is Not Robbery is the continuation of *Hustling Is Not Stealing.*[1] Together, the two books portray West African urban life from the perspective
of a brilliant but uneducated African woman as she reviewed her experiences from her childhood into her twenties. Named Hawa in these books,
she was a virtuoso storyteller, but instead of narrating indigenous folk tales
on moonlit village evenings, she used her storytelling to entertain her
friends around the cooking pot and at the drinking bars with dramatized
anecdotes that resonated with their everyday lives. I met her in 1971 in Accra, Ghana, and I maintained our acquaintance after she moved to Togo
and then later to Burkina Faso. I recorded these stories during two periods
of intensive work with her in 1977 and 1979.

Exchange Is Not Robbery contains many flashbacks to Hawa's youth but
not a recapitulation of her circumstances. She was born in Ghana in the
early 1950s, where her family had migrated from Burkina Faso, then
known as Upper Volta. Based in Kumasi, her father worked on cocoa farms
and traded. Her mother died when she was three years old, and she was
raised in various homes within her father's and mother's extended families,
often moving from place to place because she rejected whatever she saw as
exploitative or abusive treatment. In the opening passages of *Hustling Is
Not Stealing,* she describes herself as a letter posted here and there. She was
given in marriage as a teenager to a man who had two other wives, but she
left her husband's house after quarreling with a senior wife. Her father refused to allow her to return to the family, and at the age of about sixteen
she began an independent life in Accra as an "ashawo," an unmarried
woman dependent on men outside of a family setting.

The Introduction to *Hustling Is Not Stealing* describes several aspects of
the postcolonial West African scene that present significant barriers to out-

1. *Hustling Is Not Stealing: Stories of an African Bar Girl* (Chicago: University of Chicago Press, 2003).

siders hoping to understand the cultural context Hawa portrays. What many Westerners know about Africa is still mediated by alienating mythic images, whether romantic, exotic, barbaric, or chaotic. Those images are further filtered and augmented by the publications of experts and scholars about the tangled processes of modernization. "Sleeping tablets for elephants," an educated Ghanaian friend called the publications; "They should be sold to zoos." The statistics are dismal, and the situations they represent everywhere seem to range from desperate to disastrous. Despite their frequently narrow focus, the scattered media reports, the fragmentary academic studies, and in their own way even the novels of the educated elite, all have ambitions to elevate generalizations about big social issues. It is difficult to get an idea of what life is like at ground level or to get a feeling for the experience of people who live there. As I noted in that Introduction, if one were able to read everything written about Africa, the only thing one would know for sure is that on the whole continent, nobody is having any fun.

For most of the 1970s, I lived and traveled in Ghana and nearby countries as a student of society and a musician. The West Africa I knew was the kind of cosmopolitan place that threw together many different kinds of people who might not otherwise cross paths. The national states reflected the gerrymandered borders of the colonial heritage, and their populations were drawn from dozens of different cultural and linguistic backgrounds. The social and economic scene reflected incredible concentration of wealth among expatriates and those who had power and those who managed or oversaw the Western-oriented institutions and businesses of the countries. The majority of the people had very limited access to the goods and the money that emanated from their country's development, but despite the disorganization and dislocations of African urban life, the people I knew were busy dealing with what was in front of them and making the best of it. Perhaps as a complement to my interest in music and community life, I was fascinated by the sociability, confidence, and cheerfulness I noticed everywhere in that social environment. Given the objective circumstances evidenced by statistics and compounded by analyses, the burning questions I asked were, "Why are people so nice? Why is there so much laughter?" I knew that the answers would be elusive.

Drawn to urban nightclubs originally through my love of African music and dancing, I also recognized that the nightclubs were full of cultural substance. I wanted to explore the experience, the values, and the mentality of the people there by looking at how some of the discontinuities and tensions of Ghanaian society were expressed in judgments about appropriate boundaries and behavior. I became friends with a broad mix of people who interacted inside and outside that unique kind of social space. Thinking about that convivial scene, I expected to highlight the optimistic spirit of young people in Africa. I thought that their personal stories would provide a way to get into their experience and to show how they talk and think about things. I would gather their stories — happy stories of strength and steadfastness, of tolerance and compassion, of good intentions and helpfulness to others, of generosity and cordiality, of courage and wit, of clear thinking and patience, of open-mindedness and adaptability toward new situations, and of playful management of unexpected circumstances.

In 1974 when I returned to Accra after an absence of several years, corrupt soldiers had taken over the government, and Ghana was in a steep decline that put formidable pressure on the people. During the 1970s, hundreds of thousands — even millions — of Ghanaians left the difficulties of life in Ghana and moved to other countries. The deteriorating conditions put stress on everything. The name of Accra, the people joked, was really I-Cry. Whatever anyone wanted was in short supply. The day-to-day worries of making do put people into greater contestation. The situation was demoralizing, and it was harder to see people at their best. A cynical friend characterized the mood in nightclubs as one of "desperate fun." Frequently there wasn't even beer available, one of the commodities I considered essential for my research, and the shortage of beer put a real constraint on the nightlife, too. People were hot, just a bit more on edge, and the nightclub ambience was no longer as cool. My friends and I still found ways to enjoy ourselves as things in Ghana unraveled, but some of the sweetness of life was missing. The particular nightclub I considered an ideal location as a research venue had closed. To my eyes, though, I didn't really need a nightclub context. Using one particular place as a setting would have been an accepted research convention, but I still had in mind a few people I considered good for the work, particularly Hawa. I had heard her telling stories within her circle of friends in Accra, and I had already thought of her as someone to work with, both as an example through her own life story and as someone whose stories might offer another way of articulating the qualities I wanted to convey about the people I knew. Indeed, Hawa had already been doing the same thing I wanted to do, closely observing her friends and associates and showing them in action as she described them and their problems in her stories.[1] Unfortunately, I didn't see her in Accra when I returned.

1. As noted in *Hustling Is Not Stealing*, I knew about two dozen of the people whose stories are told or who are mentioned incidentally in these books, including many featured characters.

In the meantime, holding my original idea in the back of my mind, I pursued my involvement with local music and musicians. One of the places where I studied music was adjacent to the border with Togo, and I often visited Lomé, where I ran into Hawa and quite a few of my other old friends from Ghana. When Hawa was in Togo, we talked about recording her stories about her life, but we didn't get around to it until several years later, when she had moved from Togo to Burkina Faso. By then, although I had tried some initial interviews with several other people I considered working with, it was more and more clear to me that Hawa was special. I traveled to Ouagadougou (Wah'-gah-du'-gu) to find her. During two periods of intensive work in 1977 and 1979, we sat and recorded her stories. She enjoyed the work and laughed throughout, finding something funny even in stories of apparent suffering. In their own way, her stories achieve everything I would have hoped for in my initial plan, and indeed, she covered a broader range of experience than I had expected.

Among the barriers to understanding I discussed in the Introduction to *Hustling Is Not Stealing* are the image of Africa, poverty and the social and cultural territory roamed by those at the margins of modernization processes, and the social dynamics of exchange with regard to gender relations and the position of women. I specifically described the ambiguous status of unmarried women who are on their own. Such women are sometimes known by the Yoruba word "ashawo," which has made its way into Pidgin and various local forms of West African English. I argued that although many people typically associate the term "ashawo" with prostitution, the social issues raised in pejorative judgments about such women are based more on the points that they are functioning independently of their families and they are outside of the institutional control of men. In the West, prostitution, as a direct exchange of sex for money, raises moral issues that reflect upon idealizations of love and marriage. In African contexts, however, it is not unusual for sexual relationships to be undertaken or understood at least partially in terms of exchange. There are intricate and varied inheritances of traditional mores involved in assumptions about love and exchange, and the women who hang out at bars share many of these assumptions with the office workers who ask their boyfriends to buy them things or pay their rent, the schoolgirls who sleep around to get money for school fees and supplies, the brides who require certain items of household property to be given to them when they marry, and the traditional wives who expect annual presentations of cloth or other things. The lines are awkward to draw, and relationships involving exchange and sexual behavior can be a matter of degree or temporary expedience. Hawa's stories were told before the appearance of AIDS, but the rapid spread of that disease into all segments of society at the centers of the pandemic indicates that the threat of infection is a reflection not only of sexual behavior but also of more generalized women's dependency issues. Since the time Hawa spoke to me, not much has changed regarding the needs and vulnerability of many African women. Rejecting traditional marriage options and cut off from family support, without formal education or means of advancement, Hawa is like many—amazingly many—women in Africa who depend on one another, on boyfriends, or on gifts from the men they meet in bars and nightclubs. Readers who are meeting Hawa and her associates for the first time in *Exchange Is Not Robbery* and who find themselves in difficulty getting past critical moral judgments might benefit from starting with *Hustling Is Not Stealing* and its Introduction.

Hawa's stories in *Hustling Is Not Stealing* and *Exchange Is Not Robbery* are satirical in tone, almost defiantly funny, particularly with regard to the irony that her insistence on being respected and treated fairly and her unwillingness to adapt to prevailing systems of exploitation had led her into a life of marginality and luck as a bar girl and into an identity that resembles the trickster figures of folklore. Refusing to see herself as a victim, Hawa embraced the freedom her lifestyle permitted. In *Hustling Is Not Stealing,* I described Hawa herself as a seeker, someone who in her life always sought to broaden her experience, someone who used her intelligence and personality to know as much as she could of available ways to live in her part of the world. I also discussed how her ability to retain and revisit her own experience in storytelling was a source of strength in her life. More than that, her life project was thoroughly coincident with her narrative artistry, an attribute that can be seen as a mark of integrity and genius. When she and I finally sat together with a tape recorder, she used that time as an opportunity for deeper reflection and indwelling, and she produced a very deliberate survey of her life experience. In the end, I realized that as much as I admired her verbal skills and saw her stories as a medium for intimate glimpses of how the people she describes understand themselves and interact, she saw me as a medium to extend what she had been doing all her life, and she saw our work together as a motivating challenge for a larger artistic and intellectual achievement. Two years after our initial period of work she sat again with the same concentration and energy to expand her stories. As much as I knew about her and her milieu, she also knew me and the type of cultural work I was doing. Can anyone really say who found whom? Usually it would be the literate researcher who helps maintain an overview of the work, but I believe that she saw a bigger picture than I did at the time.

Individually, Hawa's stories can be hilarious, shocking, or touching. As-sembled together, they comprise a sweeping ethnographic vision, a devas-tating critique of her cultural world.

In the Introduction to *Hustling Is Not Stealing,* I interpreted Hawa's sto-rytelling from several perspectives, among them literature, autobiography, and particularly ethnography. Hawa's portrayal of West African life re-verses many of the typical attributes of the literary genre of Western ethnography, the tolerant and somewhat jumbled intellectual field on which we base our claims to know what we know about African societies and cultures. Hawa's ethnographic project in these two books is the work of an uneducated illiterate produced without reference to the large body of Western ethnographic writings. Instead of presenting itself as another in-cremental contribution in the advancing program of understanding and development, it is lighthearted and funny, almost a science of relative fool-ishness, aimed at entertainment, acceptance, and coping. Instead of culti-vating comparative abstractions, Hawa examines moral ambiguities from a perspective of situational ethics. Instead of concentrating on a single place, she has a transnational scope that extends to an international population in four countries. Instead focusing on one type of local community, she moves among villages, towns, and cities. Hawa's ethnography is the work of an African who observes the behavior of Westerners in Africa. It is the work of a poor person in a multifariously stratified social environment. It is the work of a woman in societies dominated by men.

Although *Hustling Is Not Stealing* and *Exchange Is Not Robbery* should be read as one, the rationale for splitting Hawa's stories into two parts instead of cutting or condensing them was based on acknowledging the deliberate-ness and scope of Hawa's conception and thus on maintaining the full range of her chronicle. The divided configuration was made feasible by an apparently natural division in the stories, the change of location when Hawa returns to her native Burkina Faso, and by the greater degree of con-trol she has of her life there. Reading *Hustling Is Not Stealing* first might seem logical, but the episodic narrative structure of these books is such that a reader can probably begin anywhere. What remains constant is the com-plexity of tone, a mixture of explicit satire and implicit social criticism, in which a chronicle of exploitation is transformed by verbal art into an ebul-lient comic celebration of contestation and play. Dispelling myths with vivid examples, Hawa gives a panoramic view of contemporary society in Africa, encompassing towns and villages in several countries, featuring children, young people, householders, the elderly, the poor and the well-to-do. The scope of her stories ranges from nightlife scenes of sex and decep-tion, to outrageous witchcraft cases, to the mercurial relations in the venerable extended family, to the sweet and silly friendships of urban youth. Her cast of characters includes despotic stepmothers, degenerate expatriates, venal police, gullible optimists, predatory mooches, potheads, drunkards, con artists, party people, free-spirits, underdogs, victims, and dupes. Like anthropological artifacts or illuminated documents, they attract her interest and are absorbed into her narrative vision.

Apart from its Introduction, *Hustling Is Not Stealing* has five sections, each with several chapters. In the first section, after describing how she grew up and left her family, Hawa recounts some of the ups and downs of her life in Accra and Tema. In the second section of the book, she has a lengthy relationship with a British educator in Tamale, a provincial capital in northern Ghana, where she observes the life of British expatriates and postcolonial hangers-on. After her friend left Ghana, she lived in Accra again before moving to Lomé, Togo, where she stayed for several years in the early 1970s. The third section describes her return to Accra and her initial experiences in Togo, ending with a chapter describing how she endured a chronic sickness that was treated in an astounding manner by indigenous animist medicine sometimes referred to as "juju." The fourth section follows that experience more deeply into recollections about witchcraft in villages where she grew up in Ghana and Burkina Faso. She herself was born as the "child" of a shrine, and a full chapter in that section describes her relationship with the priest of that shrine from her childhood up to a visit to the shrine as a grown woman. In the fifth section, the stories return to her life with her friends in Togo and her experiences with German expatriates in a provincial town where she was imprisoned under bizarre circumstances for about seven months. Not long after her release from prison, she left Togo for Burkina Faso in the mid-1970s. For the reference of readers who are continuing from *Hustling Is Not Stealing,* I have attached the table of contents at the end of this prologue.

The Hawa we meet in Ouagadougou is the same playful and intelligent warrior as the Hawa we knew in Ghana and Togo. She is still active in collecting stories, both among her associates and in her village. She becomes more involved with her family and recalls more details of her childhood. She adds her observations of Francophone expatriates to her previous experiences with British and other Europeans. The first parts of *Exchange Is Not Robbery* in particular display Hawa observing and responding to a number of relationships. From the time she arrives in Ouagadougou in the company of her friend from Lomé, Mama Amma, her stories are almost a catalogue of various forms of love, abuse, betrayal, and heartbreak. In the first chapter she is annoyed at what she sees as the humiliation of her brother's divorced wife, and then she is provoked by the aggressiveness of her friend Woman toward her friend Limata. The examples multiply as she discusses the relationships of her close friends, witnesses the affairs of the French customers at the nightclubs where she works, and actually investigates the stories of acquaintances whose confidence she encourages. Later chapters continue the inventory as she describes the romantic predicaments of young people in her village, sometimes harsh and sometimes humorously naive, and the tenuous situations of Ghanaian and Togolese women living in Ouagadougou. With her mind on these examples, it is easy for Hawa to arrive at a clear-headed analysis of her options for marriage and having children, and she sees herself propelled toward even greater self-reliance.

Although Hawa is more in control of her life in *Exchange Is Not Robbery* than she was in *Hustling Is Not Stealing,* she faces new difficulties. Despite the presence of some very, very funny stories, readers may be troubled by what seems to be a darker tone. Hawa's efforts to stabilize her life appear surprisingly easy, but she confronts an ambience in Ouagadougou that in some ways seems more challenging—starker and less gentle—than the other places she has known. The moral ambiguities of The Life seem more intense. Hawa is looking at her prospects, seeing the casualties of The Life—from some of her friends to the greenhorn girls who are trafficked to Ouagadougou to some of the older women who are still hanging in it—and she is aware of its inadequacy as a long-range solution. She does not see herself growing old inside it, and it is clear that she would easily leave it behind. Yet she is also more sure of her antipathy to African marriage. She does not find her own provisional male friendships serious enough or interesting enough to be worthy of more than passing mention. She is not desperate and is still engaged with people, but she is feeling the need to be more tough-minded about her ashawo life. Despite her ambiguous position as an unmarried woman in her family, the image she conveys of the extended family displays additional intricacies of discord but also elicits nostalgia and indulgence toward her father and her siblings. She finds solace, shelter, and even renewal in her village. *Hustling Is Not Stealing* has a pervasive sense of youth, of passing through temporary difficulties into an open future. In *Exchange Is Not Robbery,* Hawa is back "at home" yet doesn't seem to see something—anything—for herself as she matures, and she is trying to come to terms with that reality.

Hawa's stories present a complex and constantly evolving moral document, a hard but uplifting account of what it can mean to be a woman on her own in Africa, in the underclass, fighting for herself from a position of weakness, aggressively exercising her intelligence, making sacrifices and choosing independence. Along the way, Hawa herself changes. It seems as if every time one meets Hawa in different settings or situations, one gets a different understanding or interpretation of what one has previously read or seen of her. Whatever Hawa's stories illuminate about many larger issues, I would invite new and continuing readers to dwell initially inside the stories, to take the journey with Hawa and with the many people who are involved in living their lives in the type of society she describes. It is an expansive, poignant, and illuminating journey. At the end, consistent with her continuing development from her vulnerable childhood in *Hustling Is Not Stealing* to the precarious dilemmas of her adulthood in *Exchange Is Not Robbery,* Hawa affirms her destiny with patience and good humor and grace, and she completes her narrative vision to the point her life has reached.

Hustling Is Not Stealing

PROCEDURES TO PROTECT IDENTITIES

Most of the names of people and places have been changed or switched. Sometimes I have simply deleted information that could indicate identity. Sometimes I have made up names, as with Tsukudu, the village supposedly near Kpalimé in *Hustling Is Not Stealing,* and also with some of the nightclubs in Ouagadougou. Rather than think up new names for every place, however, and given the unavoidable problem of substituting one person's name with another's, I have generally used names of actual places. Since the names given to people or given to enterprises such as nightclubs or hotels or businesses are part of the ambience of a place, I have relied on my knowledge of Ghana, Togo, Côte d'Ivoire, and Burkina Faso to create a sense of place by substituting actual names for actual names. Drinking bars in West Africa do not have names like Ryan's Pub or T.G.I.F. or Boardwalk or Graffiti or Electric Banana, for example, which are local watering holes in my town. I have my lists of bars and nightclubs in Accra, Lomé, and Ouagadougou: Las Palmas, Weekend-in-Havana, Kakadou, Watusi, Pussycat, L'Abreuvoir, Tropicana, Café des Arts, Mini-Brasserie, Level Two, La Camionette, Santa Fé, Rama Palace, Flamboyant, Bataclan, Dessambissé, Palladium, Cabane Bambou, Cascade, Don Camillo, Tiptoe, Silver Cup, Metropole, Lido, Apollo Theatre, Playboy, Keteke. And the hotels: Ambassador, Star, Avenida, Continental, Ringway, California, Aams, Paradise, Indépendance, Tropicana, Miramar, la Plage, la Paix, le Benin, Camion Vert, Sarakawa, Ricardo, Royal, Oubri. I have used these names interchangeably, sometimes switching them from one town to another but more often just switching them around within a town. The substitutions within a country are done on the basis of comparable factors, so that although the name of place or enterprise may exist and may seem likely as a venue, that particular name probably does not represent the actual name of the place or enterprise depicted in this book. Where I felt it acceptable though, I sometimes used the actual name.

I have followed a similar strategy with towns and villages. The switching has been done on several levels. On the first level, for example, the name of a medium-sized town that is a regional administrative center has been replaced with the name of a similar town. Atakpamé, Kpalimé, Bassari, Sokodé, Sansanne-Mango, Dapongo, Lamakara are names of small towns in Togo; I have switched names within that class. Similarly, the names of the administrative centers of Ghana's nine regions outside of Accra are Tamale, Cape Coast, Koforidua, Sekondi-Takoradi, Sunyani, Bolgatanga, Wa, Kumasi, and Ho; I have also switched names within that class. Because I am familiar with Tamale, for instance, I switched the location of the British club to that town so that I could use neighborhood and suburban area names. On that second level, neighborhoods and urban areas were also replaced and additional switches were made, as for example in Accra among Adabraka, Asylum Down, Kokomlemle, Kaneshie, Jamestown, Cantonments, Osu, Tesano, Kotobabi, Accra Newtown, Alajo, Airport, Labadi, Mamprobi. In Lomé, where necessary, I have followed a similar strategy with Tokoin, Hanoukopé, Kodjoviakopé, Quartier Casablanca, and Quartier Bé. The discussions should make sense within their new contexts, though in some cases they may not. In one particular case, that of the villages in Hawa's cultural area in Burkina Faso, the information is intentionally impossible; I have just chosen some village names from a wide general area to stand for the actual villages she mentioned. In such cases, readers may assume that Hawa is not confused but that I have tried specifically to make things confusing.

All of the names of people have been changed. I have used local personal names appropriate to the switched setting, such as Ewe names in Lomé, Ashanti names in Kumasi, Dagbamba names in Tamale, and British, French, German, and Arabic names as appropriate. Finally, African personal names have then been replaced with other names in their genre, whether Akan day-of-birth names, Muslim names, French or English names, or surnames. For example, female Muslim names are Fati, Amina, Abiba, Miriama, Alima, Ramatu, and so on; female Ashanti day-names are Akosua, Adwoa, Abena, Akua, Yaa, Afia, and Ama; female Ewe day-names are Akɔsiwa, Adzowa, Abla, Akuwa, Yawa, Afiwa, and Ama. After switches to confuse the identification of place or language of origin, the names of people were then switched within those groups or local contexts. Therefore, Afia (Asante and Akyem) might become Afua (Akwapim or Akuapem) or Efua (Fanti) or Afiwa (Ewe).

In short, I have done my best to confuse any potential effort to identify specific individuals or places, and readers should assume that any name in the text is *not* the name of the actual person or place described. No character is pictured on the cover. Any identification or attempt at identification based on the names of places or persons in this book will result in conclusions that are purely coincidental and unintentional.

A NOTE ON THE TEXT

Hawa spoke ten languages, but because she was uneducated and spoke English as a foreign language, her stories required a degree of editing to adjust her language for this book, particularly her use of pronouns and tenses. Despite extensive grammatical and stylistic adjustments, the text of this book still preserves many conventions of Ghanaian and Pidgin English.[1] Akan is the most widely spoken indigenous language group in Ghana, and it influences the English of many uneducated or semiliterate Ghanaians, including Hawa, who is not Akan but who was raised in the center of the Akan traditional area. Ga, the indigenous language of Accra, also influences Ghanaian English.

There are shifts and borrowings in both directions between English and indigenous languages. In Ghanaian English, some English words have a more limited meaning and others have a wider or extended range of meanings. When I have retained Ghanaian idioms, I have provided footnotes to explain the particular use of various words or phrases. The annotations explain the first use of a given term or idiom, and the definition is repeated in a glossary for easy reference if there are later uses. To accommodate readers who begin with *Exchange Is Not Robbery,* I have repeated the footnotes from *Hustling Is Not Stealing.*

In terms of syntax, particularly in speaking, there is a tendency to begin a sentence with an introductory noun or noun phrase, or sometimes an adverbial conjuction, that announces the presence of something. The phrase generally serves as an announcement of the main subject or object of the sentence, although sometimes it seems like a dramatic stage direction to focus attention on someone's speech or on what is to come. Such discontinuous sequencing typically establishes the main idea and then illustrates it. Occasionally the construction states the effect before the cause, indicating

---

1. Some of these conventions, with regard more to educated Ghanaian English than to Pidgin, are discussed in K. A. Sey, *Ghanaian English* (London: Macmillan, 1973).

the significance of the introductory phrase. The convention thus initially places a pointer in front, setting a basic idea or condition, something to keep in mind when hearing what follows. In preserving this aspect of spoken Ghanaian English, I have followed the introductory statement with a colon before the phrase or clause or sentence that elaborates the focus.

In general, Ghanaian English is quite clear, and Hawa's use of English is straightforward. Her speech lacks the verbose or artificial or even bombastic qualities that can characterize (and are often parodied among) educated English speakers in former British colonies. A mundane text that standardizes Ghanaian conventions would lose too much flavor and ultimately would lose its sense of place. As noted in the Introduction, I believe the text is not difficult, although it may seem a bit choppy before readers get into the flow of it. The first chapter or two are densely annotated and therefore offer a quick crash course in Ghanaian English. After that, the annotations thin out considerably, and I hope that the read will be smooth sailing. All in all, the syntax also preserves the style of a storyteller, punctuated with laughter and expletives and exclamations; thus, as it should be, the text is difficult to read faster than a person can talk.

I have used annotations sparingly to explain a few contextual details, but I have not used annotations to make connections beyond the text or to support the text. Readers who are familiar with West Africa either personally or through the ethnographic literature will be better able to recognize the references of some parts of the text that other readers might find surprising or questionable.

Regarding the pronunciation of African names and words, readers should try to pronounce all the vowels and consonants as written. For example, *kone* is pronounced as *connay*. In African or Pidgin words: *a* is short as in *bat; e* is like a long *a* as in *weigh; i* is like a long *e* as in *bee; o* is long as in *comb; u* is like a doubled *o* as in *boot.* The infrequent passages in African languages contain several phonetic characters: ɔ *is a short* o *as in* ought; ɛ *is a short* e *as in* bet; ɖ *is like a Spanish* r; ʋ is like a *v* pronounced with both lips; ã *is a nasalized* a; *Ɗ, ɗ, ƙ and ɓ are glottalized consonants. Doubled vowels simply extend the sound of the vowel. Regarding consonant clusters in Asante Twi,* ky *is like* ch; gy *is like* j.

Finally, in French, final consonants are often silent. Also, a final *e* does not make the preceding vowel long: the vowel preceding a final *e* is short, and the final syllable is often stressed, as in *Madame, camarade,* and *Cabane.*

PART ONE *The Life in Ouaga*

1 A STRANGER AT HOME

: *Love That Makes One Sick*
: *The Story of Woman*
: *Getting an Identity Card*
: *Virginity as a Fatal Disease*

: OUAGADOUGOU :

Love That Makes One Sick

The time I left Lomé,[1] my friend Mama Amma[2] and I traveled to Ouagadougou.[3] You know, I have a brother there. He is not my father's son; he's the son of my mother's big sister.[4] When we dropped at Ouagadou-

---

1. capital of Togo, the country to the east of Ghana

2. The name in Asante Twi would be Maame Ama.

3. (pronounced: Wah'-gah-du'-gu): capital of Burkina Faso, the country to the north of Ghana. Because Burkina Faso was known as Upper Volta when Hawa talked to me, I have retained the former name in the stories. Throughout this book, too, Hawa refers to the people of that country as "Voltaiques" instead of "Burkinabe." The term "Voltaic" remains in use with reference to cultures, languages, and peoples in the Volta Basin area.

4. Readers need note only a few points about Hawa's extended family system with regard to the terms used for relationships. Hawa's "brothers" and "sisters" would include Hawa's father's children from women other than her mother, and as might be expected, she addresses her stepmothers as "mother." In her culture, children remain with their father's family, and a father would have custody of a child from a divorced woman or of a child born out of wedlock once the child has grown past tender years. A major difference from Western kinship terms involves aunts and uncles. Hawa's father's brothers would also be called "father," or sometimes "junior father" or "senior father" or "small father" or "big father," depending on whether they were older or younger than her father. Similarly, Hawa

gou, we asked a driver at the lorry park,[1] and he showed us a Gurunsi woman,[2] and when we asked her, she knew my brother. She paid the taxi fare to carry us to my brother's place. Then we slept there.

And what got me annoyed: my brother was so gentle with his wife, and he was trying to play[3] some fucking things with us. Mama Amma used to laugh at me on this case, but I always used to be annoyed. The way my brother was with his wife: evening time, they would bring the

---

would call her mother's sisters "mother." Their children are "brothers" and "sisters." The words "uncle" and "aunt" refer to mother's brothers and father's sisters and their spouses. Hawa usually refers to her father's brothers and mother's sisters as such, showing their actual relationship to her, or as "uncles" and "aunts." In informal contexts, Hawa would generally call her cousins (even children of her "real" aunts [father's sisters] and "real" uncles [mother's brothers]) her brothers and sisters. People know their exact relationships, of course: the distinction of "real" mother or "real" brother is one way they might distinguish the nuclear part of the extended family. Thus, Hawa might say of a brother that he was the "same mother, same father" or "same father but different mothers," or she might call someone her brother and then say, "He's not my real brother; he's the son of my father's sister." When a particular distinction is relevant, it is brought out.

1. the station where various forms of transport arrive or depart. In large towns, there may be a central station, or lorry park, and various other stations at the outskirts for places on particular roads out of the town, each named for a main destination in that direction. The word "lorry" is used to refer to any motor transport, including passenger buses.

2. As she is from Hawa's cultural group, she is likely to know Hawa's brother and may be able to direct Hawa to his house. Hawa identifies herself as Gurunsi (also, Grunshi; French: Gourounsi). Gurunsi is a generic name covering many small but distinct cultural groups in northern Ghana, southern Burkina Faso, and northeastern Côte d'Ivoire. The name Gurunsi is actually a name applied to them by other groups, literally meaning "slaves." It refers to the time when people from these groups were captured or sold in disproportionate numbers because they were somewhat at the mercy or under the control of larger or richer centralized states in the Volta Basin. Most members of those larger states are drawn from a similar cultural background, and the Gurunsis are those peoples who were not initially conquered or assimilated into the larger states. They all share many cultural customs and they speak related languages, but each of the various cultural groups in the Volta Basin is more properly identified individually by the specific language its members speak. Until very recently, it was not considered particularly pejorative to classify the peoples of the smaller cultural groups together as Gurunsis, and both British and French maps mark their areas with that name. The classification of Gur languages is still being worked out. Linguists would classify Hawa's group as belonging to the Grusi subgroup of the southern branch of Central Gur, or to one of the Dagaari groups of northern Central Gur. Because her identity is disguised in this book, including her home village, her home area is only indicated as southwestern Burkina Faso in a range roughly circumscribed by the towns of Bolgatanga, Diébougou, Koudougou and Bobo-Dioulasso; a partial list of groups in that general area would include Nuna, Phwo, Lyele, Dyan, Winye/Ko, Sisaala/Debi, Dagara/Birifor, and Dagara/Wuli.

3. to do (something) to; also, to mess with, to bother; to be free with; to joke with

chairs outside. Then they would put their table in front of them. Then they would bring their television and put it on. And their children were also sitting behind there. Then she and the husband would start eating. Sometimes she would cut the food and put it in the husband's mouth.[1] They were always doing things like this. And we were all sitting outside to eat, you know. So I used to be annoyed. I used to heat![2] What is he doing all this for? When we are eating, we are eating. If we finish, they are together: they can do whatever they want. But not the time when we will all come around to eat.

And then there was another woman, the first wife of my brother. He divorced that woman. I used to feel pity for her. Then I used to be annoyed *more. Ha!* When he divorced her, the woman said she would never marry again in her life. She would stay in the same house and die there, because she had children, and her children were the first senior children for my brother, so she wouldn't leave the house and let the other bad woman come and treat these children in some way.[3] So she was there. They would give her chop money[4] like the other one. They would buy her dresses.[5] They would do everything for her. They gave her a place to sleep. So as they were doing that with the food, you know, it was like they were teasing that woman. So I used to be *annoyed!* You know, I used to take it sometimes as if I was that woman. *Ha!* I used to tell Mama Amma: "No! Shit! Even this kind of soup, which they play romance with, how can we eat it?" Then I would say, "Let's go out and eat." *Ha-ha!*

And at my brother's place, every time[6] he wanted to be giving advice to people — to be quiet, like the way he is, and he doesn't know how to drink,[7] only Coca-Cola or Fanta. He wanted to be —*shit!* I used to get fed up there. The first day when we arrived in Ouaga,[8] you know, the day when we went to his place, they gave us a room, with air conditioning. It was a nice place. Ask Mama. It had a bathroom, everything. And they had

1. To "cut" is to take or pull away a bit of the food. The "food" is the starch or grain, the bulky part of a meal, and one eats the soup or the stew or the meat "with" the food. People eating together normally eat from one bowl or plate, and traditional etiquette involves using the right hand to pull away a bite-sized amount of the food and use it to dip or scoop the soup or stew. The way the wife is feeding him would normally only be done by a mother to a baby.

2. I used to become hot (with annoyance).

3. in a bad way

4. money for cooking or food

5. clothes, any outer garment; applies to both men's and women's clothing

6. all the time; always

7. He doesn't drink alcoholic drinks.

8. short name for Ouagadougou

another section to the side, like a quarters,[1] for the children and the maid. But the way this man and his wife received me the first day, I wasn't happy. I told Mama, "Mama, as for me, I can't stay here."

Mama said, "Why? Hey, you have nice brother like this."

Then I said, "What kind of nice?[2] Don't you know Africans? If you see that an African man smiles a big smile, it's not in his heart. If you look at his eyes, you will know. As for this man, he is just making all this on face.[3] So I don't agree with him."

Then she said, "Oh, but they are nice." And this and that.

OK. The day we arrived, we were tired, so he let us sleep. We slept to the time when we wanted. The next morning when they took their tea, they put our own on a table, coffee and tea and bread and butter, and they took napkins and covered it. So when we woke up, the children said, "You people's coffee is here. Let us bring you hot water."[4]

But still I wasn't happy. Evening time, they had that *nyama-nyama*[5] television. *Ha!* The way you will see the Mossi[6] people inside, they sing like they cry: *wo-ee, wo-ee, wo-ee. Ha!* Then my brother and the wife wouldn't get tired and go inside the room. They would start doing something. So when I was seeing all this, I used to get annoyed.

So one night, I finished my bath, and I was outside to dry. I was dry, but you know, at that time it was starting to get hot,[7] so I was outside the house.

Then my brother was asking me, "Wouldn't you feel[8] to sleep yet?"

Then I said, "No, I don't feel to sleep yet."

Then he said, "Ah, as for us, we sleep early."

And I said, "Oh, I want to take a small[9] breeze outside."

1. generally a separate small building or rooms behind a house, for servants

2. (Pidgin): nice in what way? The phrases "which kind," "what kind," or "some kind" are usually meant to challenge something rhetorically by asking for specificity or an example, or to question something unacceptable or unknown, as in, "What kind way?"

3. showing a nice face without sincerity

4. The coffee is Nescafé, so the hot water is for either tea or coffee.

5. (Hausa): general word for anything of low quality or messed up; pathetic, lousy, cheap, poor, dirty, messy, run-down, worn-out, torn, nasty; literally, a pile or assortment of unrelated "stuff." The Hausa are the major cultural group in northern Nigeria; Hausa traders travel and live widely in West Africa, and the Hausa language is a lingua franca well beyond the Hausa traditional area.

6. largest cultural group in Burkina Faso, centered around Ouagadougou

7. It was getting into the hot season.

8. like, want, have a feeling

9. a little; a bit of

Then the wife said they were going to sleep, so if I'm going to lock the door, I should be sure that the door is locked. Then I said, "You can lock it."

Then my brother said, "Why should you answer like that? Why should you give her an answer that she should lock the door?

Then I said, "Yes, I'm not feeling to go inside. And I can't be sure the door is locked, because I haven't locked a door like this before. I haven't seen a door like this before in my life."

Then my brother said I was giving her cheek, and I said, "I'm not giving her cheek. She is giving me cheek, because she thinks your room is better than everybody's room. And she thinks I haven't seen a house like this before. That's why she's telling me to look at the door. She is not right to tell me I should lock the door. I'm not a child. I should know the door, where to lock it."

And my brother said, "Eh-h, you know, if you have a problem with my wife, you shouldn't make it with me."

Then I said, "Why did you ask then? If she does something, I can ask her a question. But why should you answer? Why don't you let her answer?"

Then my brother said, "No. If you want to get a problem with me, maybe if it's the way we used to sleep early, and you don't want to be sleeping at that time, just tell me. I will tell the people. When you come back, they will open the door."

Then I said, "If I want to go out, you can't tell me not to. But I don't know. I think I have been giving you respect, but I didn't know that you are somebody like that."

Then he said, "Hey, what are you saying?"

I said, "Yes, I'm talking something. I didn't believe that you would tell me this. I just came. I just arrived. Maybe I'm tired or something like that. But the day when I'm feeling to go out, I'm not afraid of you. I can tell you that I'm going out. If you tell me, 'If you go out, don't come back,' then I'll pack my things and go. That's all."

So he said, "Oh. Thank you very much. I'm going to sleep."

Then I said, "Thanks, too. But if you sleep also, you have to lock the door."

"So you won't stop?"

I said, "No, you have to lock the door, because I'm not — I'm not feeling like sleeping inside self.[1] I will go and sleep with the children over there."

1. (Pidgin): even

So he didn't lock the door. He just closed it. I also didn't go inside. I went and slept with our small[1] brother in the quarters.

Morning time, the wife was the first person to be talking about this case. They didn't say it in front of me. They just started making, *"Mm-hm, mm-hm, hm-hm."* Like that. Yesterday the door was standing unlocked, *mm-hm, hm-hm,* and that and this, *mm-hm.*

Then I said, "Hey, you people, if you are talking about something, you know that I am the one who did it. Say, 'Hawa, why didn't you lock the door yesterday?' Because I have told you that you should lock the door, that I am not going to sleep there, that I am going to sleep with the children. So it is not a palaver[2] to bring *hm-hm-hm.*"

Then my brother said I wanted to become a chief on them. *Ha!* I wanted to control them. Then I said, "No, it's not that I'm controlling you people. But if something happens, and you know exactly the person who did the thing, don't go behind. Just say it in front of the person. If she has an answer, she will give you. So I think, even, I think the way you people are, I think you have made your family house. So if you people don't like me, just tell me to go away. I don't want this. If you know that I am the one who did this thing, why don't you ask me? So I don't think we can stay together."

Then my brother said, "I'm not sacking you."[3]

And I said, "Yes, I know you haven't sacked me. I'm sacking myself."

You know, when we arrived, I had told them Mama's sister had run away from school to Ouagadougou, and when I was coming, Mama's mother said Mama should follow me and come to Ouaga and find[4] the sister. So I told them I was going to lead[5] Mama Amma to look for the sister.

Then I took Mama Amma and we went to a bar, Bar de Tante. We met a girl from Bolgatanga.[6] Her real name was Saana, but in Ouagadougou we used to call her Woman. Yeah? I knew her from Accra.[7] She was a

---

1. young
2. a problem, a case, a matter, a worrisome or troubling talk, a quarrel, an argument, a dispute. The word has a Portuguese origin, referring in one sense to public discussion between people from different groups, such as Europeans and indigenous persons, hence the common African association with misunderstanding.
3. telling you to leave; *sack:* drive away, make someone go away, fire (from a job)
4. look for; also, get
5. accompany, go with; also, drop off
6. town in northern Ghana
7. capital and largest city of Ghana

Frafra[1] girl. Woman. You know, she liked this record: "Any time I see my woman, yeah, any time I see my girl." She had a record changer, and she bought the record of that song, more than twenty — the same record. *Ha-ha!* The same record! So she used to play it every time, and everyone was calling her, "Woman, Woman."

So we met Woman at Bar de Tante, and we told Woman that we wanted a room. She said, "Oh-h, we have a room at our house. Only today the person left. This is the key the person gave me because I wanted to change to that room. And my room, some girl wants to take it. But if that will be the case, as she already has a room, and she just wants to move from her place, so I will give you people that room. As I know you, Hawa, it is not hard."

So I said, "OK, thank you."

She said we should wait for her. She was working in the bar. They closed at one o'clock. So we were sitting there up to one o'clock. We got *drunk!* People were buying us drink.[2] We were drinking. *Ha-ha!* Me and Mama Amma. So when we went to the landlord, he was a *nice* man. But he was fucking. He didn't ask for any money. He just said, "OK. Where is the key?"

Then Woman said, "Here is the key."

So he said, "Give it to them. Every month, you people will pay four thousand."[3]

So we just got the room like that. Then we went back home to my brother's house, and I told my brother, "Mama has seen her sister." You see? I didn't tell them the truth. Mama doesn't have a sister. I knew what made me come. I said it: I was coming to see my father. And the reason why I told them that Mama was looking for her sister was because I knew, by all means, if I say only that Mama has come with me, and then I go and hire a room to rent, my brother will ask why should I leave his house to go and rent a room. That's why I wanted Mama to follow me to Ouagadougou, so that I could get a room outside. Uh-huh. Then when I got the room, I came and told them that Mama had found her sister. So I

1. cultural group around Bolgatanga in northern Ghana
2. any alcoholic drink, generally hard liquor or spirits, but also beer
3. francs CFA, Francophone African currency indexed to French francs. CFA stands for la Communauté Financière Africaine. 50 CFA were previously equal to one French franc; in 1994, the currency was devalued to 100 francs CFA to 1 French franc, or 1 centime. In 1999, CFA francs were pegged to the euro at just under 656 francs per euro. In this book, U.S. dollar prices for CFA therefore directly reflect the prices for French francs. In the 1970s, with the dollar generally between 4 and 5 French francs, CFA varied between 200 and 250 to the dollar, only occasionally pushing 300 or above. Generally in this book, one can use 250 CFA per dollar to calculate amounts.

packed all my dresses that I wanted into Mama's bag, all together with
Mama's dresses. Then I said I would lead her to go to her sister and come.
But that day I didn't come home. I came the next morning, Sunday.

And that Sunday morning, when I came, my brother said, "Hey!" I
didn't mind him at all. I went inside and changed myself quickly, and then
I got all my bags from inside to the outside. Then he said, "Why?"

I said, "Ah, but I told you that I'm going today Sunday. I'm going to see
my father in the village."

So he said, "OK, I will take you to the lorry station."

So he took my things. He couldn't get a chance to talk to me, you know.
I just did something like — *Ha!* — I stopped his talking. He took me to the
station. He paid the lorry. He asked the driver how much, and he paid for
it. And he gave me ten thousand, that I can buy something on the road.
"OK. Bye-bye."

When I came from my village, I didn't go to my brother's house. I
dropped at Mama's place, where we took the room. You can ask Mama:
for a good three months, my brother didn't know that I was in Ouagadougou. *Pff-t! Ha!* It was my small brother who found me, and then the children of my brother: every time, when they were going to school, they
used to come to me to take money. Sometimes if they were coming from
school, they would pass to me[1] to eat. That was the way my brother got to
know that I was in town. When these children came home, they wouldn't
eat. They started beating the children: what did they eat outside? Then
they said, "Oh, no. We passed to Auntie's house, and we ate. She cooked
fufu, Ghana food.[2] She —" And *dat-dat-dat-dat.*

"Which Auntie?"

"Hawa."

"Ah! She is in this town?!"

So one day, they sent the younger brother with the children to know my
place. "Hey, why don't you come home?" And that and this. So one day I
said, "OK, these people, I will go to see them one day." So I went there.

---

1. pass by my place, come to me
2. Fufu is a type of starchy food, eaten with soup that is poured over it in a large
bowl for group eating. It is a staple food of Akan people. It is pounded with a heavy pestle in a large mortar. The ingredients are generally boiled cassava and plantain, but it can
be made with cassava alone; occasionally cocoyam (a small tuber) can be substituted for
plantain. Fufu can also be made from yam, and yam fufu is more common (and is preferred)
in savanna regions where cassava and plantain are not grown. African yams are not the
sweet potatoes normally called yams in America; they taste like potatoes but have a different texture. Generally two people prepare fufu, one pounding and the other turning the fufu
in the mortar.

My brother said, "*Mm-m,*[1] I know that you can rent a room. I'm not saying you haven't got money to rent a room. I know that you can get money to rent the room. But if there is a sickness, or if you have some troubles, what are you going to say?" *Ta-ta-ta-ta.* I didn't mind him. I went back to my place. When I went back, I made more than four or five months, and I didn't stop at my brother's house.

That time, I got work in a nightclub. You know, when I was in Lomé, I didn't work in a bar or nightclub. It was in Ouagadougou that I thought to get work in the bar. I preferred to work, because how I saw the country, and I thought that here, you know, sometimes I might meet some of my family, and if I'm living without any work, going up and down like the others[2] — I thought it was better to work. Then if I know this work, too, I could do it every time. I used to think that any place I go, if I could get that work, I would do it. It is better than to go around and go around, in other places. Sometimes you will go to some place, and you don't have work, or you start thinking, and you have problems. Anyway, this work is not any work. It is not good, and it's hard to do, but it's better than doing nothing, you know. Yeah, it's just — I think it's better than doing nothing. But anyway, by all means, people might talk about you if you work in a bar. But it's not too bad. People want to talk about you — especially sometimes — to me, I know that I am finished with my people, so even if they see that I am carrying shit, they can't say anything. By all means, some people used to go and give complaint, "I saw your daughter. She's working here." Or "Your sister." And sometimes, you know, some family doesn't want it. But to me, I decided that to work is better than going up and down.

The Story of Woman

You know, to travel — to go to some place — it's hard. You will see many problems. Somebody can be helping you, and you can see some things and that fellow will change. The time you are a stranger,[3] traveling-traveling, you will see problems. Even this girl I'm telling you about, Woman, she also showed me something[4] when I went to Ouagadougou.

1. Yes. "Mm" means "yes" in many Voltaic languages.
2. going around; going here and there, looking for money (from hustling)
3. not at home; also, visitor, guest. In many African languages, the same word refers to stranger or guest; you would call your visitor a "stranger" even if you knew him or her very well, and you would introduce the person to your friends as, "This is my stranger I have brought to greet you."
4. gave me an experience; *show:* teach; in some contexts, cheat, take advantage of

Look. I rented a chamber and hall[1] for me and Mama in that house, with Woman. We were there small,[2] and then Mama traveled, and I also went to Côte d'Ivoire. But Woman: the way she did, she treated me *badly*. Look, we were good friends. We were all in one house. Then Mama traveled, and one key was with Mama, and I locked the room and took one key to Côte d'Ivoire, because Mama was not there. When I came back, it was getting to night, and I went to the place. It wasn't there again. All the people had moved from there, and *all* the rooms, there were some different girls. I didn't know them. So I had to go to a hotel.

The next day I looked for Woman. I went to some girls, and one of them said, "OK, wait for two o'clock—I will take you to her house, because if you go there now, you will not see her. She's with her man." So at two o'clock the girl took me to Woman's house. It was in Dapoya.[3]

I was there about ten minutes when Woman came from the boyfriend's house. Then I said, "Oh, yesterday I came in the night, and I passed our place. Nobody was there. And my room, I think somebody's inside because I saw a new curtain."

Then she said, "Yes. The time when you went to Abidjan,[4] everyone left that house. Yes. And your room, they have stolen all your things inside. Even the bedsheet of you people, they have taken it. But this is what they left, and I packed it off.[5] So this is what you have." She said that the time when she was going away from our old house, Mama was not there, and I was not there. And she was the person we know much, so she had to take all our things to her new house. She carried all the things I had. But my special dresses, they stole all. This is what she told me. They stole everything and they left the bucket with the cooking pot and some small-small[6] things. I lost a small radio; she said they threw it outside, and the landlord took it.

Then the thing kicked me: I said, "No, but I must see him."

1. Generally in a compound house, the distinction among rental units is (1) a flat, which has a bathroom and usually a kitchen, (2) a single room off a courtyard, and (3) a chamber and hall, which has an entry hall or small sitting room between the outside door and the bedroom, or chamber.

Urban housing for most people is typically a room or two in what is called a compound house. The house itself is basically a series of rooms off a yard, or compound. The kitchen is outdoors, generally in a covered area at one end of the house or in a shaded area of the compound, and the cooking is done on an open fire fueled by charcoal.

2. a short time

3. section of Ouagadougou

4. capital of Côte d'Ivoire (Ivory Coast)

5. collected it; *pack:* gather, take and set down

6. a few

Then she said, "No. You know, these your people[1] don't understand. If
you see him, he will say that you have kept his room for five months. It's
five? And you rented the room and you locked it and took the key. For
five months. So three thousand times five: you can even buy two of this
wireless. So leave it.[2] This is your bucket, and all your things which you
can use. But the dresses, I think the dresses which you had, if you go back
to get them, you wouldn't want them again"— and that and this—"So,
if I'm you, I wouldn't go to this man and ask him for my things." So she
thought that if the house owner saw anything of mine, he will take it and
charge me money to get it back, and there is no need, because they have
already stolen from me.

So I said, "OK, it's a good idea." So I didn't go. But still I was not satisfied, you know.

So when she told me all this, she said, "You can come and stay with me
until you have a room in Ouagadougou here."

Then I said, "OK." So I told her that I'm in this hotel, and in evening
time, I will go and bring my things, but I have already paid for two days,
so we can go and get them later.

Then she said, "OK."

So I knew one man, one French man. We went to his house. We ate,
we drank, and we came home. I dropped her with the taxi, and then I
went with the taxi to the hotel at about eight or nine o'clock. I thought
to pack my things, because I thought I was going to get up from the hotel.
So I packed my things, but the time she told me she would come, she
didn't come.

So I said, "Ah, it's better I go and see her. If there's no chance for me
there, then I will rest in the hotel tonight, and I will find some other
place."

So the next day, I went to her place, and she said, "Oh, no. My man
came here. So you can take my little sister to help you. She is Limata." At
that time, I knew Limata, but it was not much. So we went to my friend,
the French man, and he took us to the hotel, and then this man carried
all my things in his car, and we went and put all at his house. From there
we passed La Tringle, and we drank a little bit. Then we went to Don
Camillo, then to Cascade, with Limata. And then we dropped Limata, and
I went with him.

The next morning I didn't come home. I thought I had some place to
keep my things, so I have nothing to do there. And I thought I am free

1. Voltaiques
2. let something be; also, stop doing something

where I am, so I stayed there for a day. The next day, I came. Yeah. *Ha!*
Oh-h, we were joking. Woman said, "Yesterday we cooked, and we left
some for you; you didn't come and eat. You must pay for this and that—"
You know, we were happy, so we were joking and all this. I had some
drinks I brought from Côte d'Ivoire, and I had some lavender.[1] I gave
everybody her share.

Yeah. I gave one lavender to Woman, and then I gave her one bottle of
Cognac brandy for her and her husband,[2] that I was thinking of them.
And I had one type of blouse, it had a rose flower on it; I had four of
them. And we were four: I was there with Woman and Limata, and there
was another girl called Mimuna. So these blouses, I shared them: one for
me, one for Woman, one for the other friend, one for Limata. I didn't
know Limata but I forced[3] to give her some dash,[4] because Woman told
me she is the younger sister. Limata is not the younger sister; it's just
how we Ghanaians[5] are.

So we were together nicely. Every time, when I wake up in the morning time, I will give one thousand five hundred to one small boy to bring
food and we would cook. I did that for about two weeks. Then Woman
said, "No, it's not correct. We are four. So if someone cooks today, somebody must take the charge."[6] Then I thought she was a good girl. She was
helping me, you know, but I felt that how I was a stranger and I was lodging with them, I have to do for them every time because it was forcing. If
I was in a hotel, I would pay one thousand a day, and I would eat outside,
and it would maybe be two thousand five hundred or three thousand for
the day—even that would be small.[7] So then Woman said, no, it is not
correct to pay always. So if I cook today, then the next day Limata will
cook, and the next day Mimuna will cook, and the next day Woman will
cook. We are four, so from this time we will share the cooking. Then I
said, "Ah, this girl is a nice girl."

So we were four girls in a chamber and hall. It was nice. Ending of the
month, the room was three thousand, and we shared the bill: I gave seven
hundred fifty, no? We paid that, and after, they brought the light[8] bill.
Then I said, "OK, I will pay this light bill. Next month somebody can

1. any eau de toilette
2. her boyfriend
3. tried hard
4. money; *dash:* a gift; also, as a verb, to give a gift
5. people from Ghana. Hawa is identifying herself as a Ghanaian because she was
born and grew up in Ghana, as described in *Hustling Is Not Stealing.*
6. They will cook in rotation, and the person who cooks will pay for the food.
7. That is, 2,500 to 3,000 would be a low estimate.
8. electricity

pay." And the light bill was not much — sometimes five hundred or something like that. So we were nice together.

Then Woman had somebody, so she didn't go out. Every time it was her man friend who took her out. But when we went out, sometimes Woman would close the door and go with the key. If we would go to work, then maybe her man would come for her, and she would lock the door and take the key. When you come from work, there is nobody there, and you have to sleep outside. *Shit!* With only your short dress, you will lie down like that because you are tired, and maybe you don't feel like to going to Cabane Bambou.[1] And sometimes, you don't have money to go to Cabane Bambou, to go with taxi and come back with taxi. Maybe you only had the money for taxi to bring you home from work. So you will lay down in the door like that, up to the morning time, and then you will wake up. *Ha!* And shake yourself. You shake yourself and put your hands in your eyes, and yeah, you see that it's morning time. You cannot sleep. You will walk around up to — some time, if you're lucky, twelve o'clock. Or sometimes at two o'clock, she will come home: "Oh, when did you come? Did you come? Why didn't you ask? This woman has a key. Why didn't you ask her to bring you the key? Sorry, I'm coming."[2] Then she will walk there, *kpo-kpo-kpo.* She will enter to that person's room. You wouldn't know what she's talking, and she will bring the key out and open the room. She means to show that she left the key with the person, but she didn't.

It's *AWAM!*[3] We knew all this, you know. We caught all this way. That's why Limata likes me. Limata was also suffering then. From the first, when she saw me and we started to be friends, and up to now when we stay together, too, it's from all this way that she likes me. We suffered together with this way.

I said, "Limata, do you think this girl went with the keys? Or she gave the key to this woman?"

Then Limata said, "No, I don't think, because suppose she gave them to her, in the morning time, this woman saw us. She said, 'Sorry, your sister took the key.'"

1. a drinking bar in Ouagadougou that is open all night, where one could wait till morning

2. I'll be right back.

3. (Pidgin): wrong-way, corrupt, lying, conspiratorial, bullshit. AWAM is an acronym for Association of West African Merchants, those produce companies that formerly bought cocoa during the colonial period before the establishment of the Ghana Cocoa Marketing Board. The Pidgin use of the word began when cocoa farmers staged a cocoa holdup and boycott in 1937–38, refusing to sell their cocoa to the AWAM.

I said, "Uh-huh. What kind of life[1] does she want to take us like that? She wants to take us that we are blind, that we don't see anything, or we are fools. So let her tell us the truth."

Then: Limata was afraid to challenge Woman, because they had stayed together for a long time, and they were good friends. So one afternoon I was annoyed, then I said, no. I went and hired a room at Zongo.[2] Then when I came back in the evening, I called this girl. I said, "Woman."

She said, "Yes."

"If you're fed up with us, if you're fed up with me, especially — when I say 'with us,' I am mistaken — but if you fed up with me, tell me, 'Oh, Hawa, I have, you know, I have much —' Even you can get some excuse to tell me. But this is not the way to keep[3] me."

Then she said, "Why?"

"Look, you are telling me that you are giving key to this woman, every time. And when you come, you go and get the key. OK. You give the key to the woman to do what with? This woman has to see me from morning time — from ten o'clock or nine o'clock, up to two o'clock, before you will come and pick[4] the key. Why? If you are fed up, tell me, 'I am fed up.' It's not force.[5] Or because we are friends, you don't want to tell me that it's not good between us —*oh-oh*. You can have something to say, with understanding, and then I will leave your place quietly. But this is not the way to treat us. So, I have got my own room: I want to move to my place."

Then she said, "No, no, no, you can't do that!" You see? If I leave her like that, it's a disgrace to her.

Then I looked at this girl and said, "Yes, you are a real killer. You can kill."

"What do you mean that I can kill?"

"Yes. How long have you been leaving me to be sleeping outside? Now I have my key to my room. That's why I want to ask you a question. When I am sleeping outside in the night, if the killers come to kill me, they would kill me. And if they don't kill me, then I'm still in life, and you try to boss[6] me so that I will sleep outside for your killers to come again. You won't get me."

---

1. way of living, lifestyle, character

2. (Hausa): a section of any town where people from other African cultures, generally savanna cultures, live; the neighborhood itself

3. take care of; hold; manage

4. take, collect

5. We're not being forced to stay together.

6. to talk nicely or gently to, sometimes but not always with a connotation of insincerity. Other meanings of the word are: to trick, to persuade or convince, to cool someone out, to calm someone.

Then she said, *"What!!?"* It was a big trouble! Ask Limata. This girl wanted to cut my throat. "I'm a Frafra girl. You don't know me—I swear, you will see." Yeah, she said the grandfather was the chief of Tongo,[1] and that and this.

Then I said, "Hey, when we talk about ourselves, we talk about ourselves. We don't talk about our grandfathers and grandmothers. Maybe your grandfather had Tongo, and maybe my grandfather had more than Tongo. Maybe I have the grandfather of Tongo."

Then this girl said, *"Aaach!"*

Hey! Then I said, "'You will see'? Ah! We are all human beings. If I will die, you will die too. If you make me crazy, there's no profit for you. If you kill me now, I have this mirror: it's for you." We were just talking like that, you know. *Ha!* And I told her, "All we are saying, it's nothing for me. You can kill me today if you like, but you will not rest; you will not rest in life. You will be dead too. And maybe you—if you force to kill me now, maybe my dead body will be nice to people. And maybe your own will be smelling, or something which people don't want to see. So, I'm very sorry. You are my good girlfriend. I will *never* be annoyed with you. But I'm just asking you that I want to take my things. Because I have my small roof, you know. So I want to live there, to be free even if—it's only a roof or it's not a better building. You have light here. I have no light, but I have a lamp, or I can put on a candle, so it is good for me. So I must leave. If I die there tomorrow, they will know that I died in my own place. The landlord has given me a receipt when I paid, so they will know that I had this room and I'm dead inside. But they wouldn't find me outside of the house when I am dead. I don't want it. So, I must go." *Ha! Shit!*

Then this girl said, "OK. You want to go?"

I said, "Yes."

"You want to go?"

"Yes."

"You want to go?"

"Yes."

Three times I said yes. Then she said, "I have nothing to say to you. But in night time like this, you cannot remove your things. Unless tomor-

---

1. small town five miles south of Bolgatanga, the major town for the Frafras. The chief of Tongo is a Frafra who has nominal control over the Talensi people who inhabit a plateau near there, where there is a famous animist shrine. According to the protocol of the shrine, people who want to visit the shrine first go to the chief of Tongo, who gets someone to accompany them to see the priest. In this context, Woman is threatening that she has access to the power of that shrine. The words "You will see" mean "You will see the result," that is, if she uses juju on . . . finished, Hawa will look at what has happened to her life and see the result.

row, everybody is to see your things, what you brought, and that is what
you are taking out."

And I said, "Thank you very much. You are a nice woman. Shake me."
So we shook each other's hand. "Thank you." Then I went to my room. I
went and slept without bedsheet, without anything. That day I had already bought a bed and a mattress to put on the bed, so I slept on that
mattress. I had two pillows at the first room, with Woman, and one mattress, but I didn't want to take it because it would make her hot.[1] So I
bought my own. Then I came and slept.

Yeah. You know, we were four girls in chamber and hall. They had one
mattress before I bought mine. What they had before was for Limata. So
when I bought my own, we put that one in the bedroom and put Limata's
in the sitting room. So I felt that they are three, so if I took this mattress,
the way I came to them, maybe we won't feel free. So I didn't take my
mattress. When I got my room, I bought a bed, with mattress, and I put
it inside.

Then I just had to come and carry my box, my big valise with my
dresses inside, and a small bag. And this girl refused. She said I must
carry it in day time to let people see. What I think, maybe she thought
that if I come to pick my things in the night, maybe I can steal from them.
This is the reason I think she said that I must take my things in day time,
for all the people to see the things I brought and to see that it is the same
one I am taking out. Or what did she think?

Yeah, she thought something like that: I can steal something from
them. So the next day, I didn't go. There was a small boy who used to
come to the house to help us. I used to send him for things, and I used to
give him dash, so he liked me. So when I got the room, I told the small
boy where I was, "Now I'm living at that place, so tomorrow you can
come there. I will send you." The next day, he came, and I told him, "OK.
You can go and tell Woman that, here is my key to the box. She can open
and see what is for her and see what is not for her, and take what is hers,
and the rest, she should give it to you, and you will take taxi and bring it."

Then I gave him the taxi fare, and this boy went. Woman just picked
one small bag, and she left the box, my big valise. The one she gave was
only blouses. She said I have to be there. So I didn't say anything. I had
this bag, with the bucket and some small things. But all my dresses were
there. I didn't say anything. The one the boy brought me, I said, "This is
what Woman gave you?"

1. annoy her

He said, "Yes."

So I didn't say anything, for about two or three weeks. Then I started going there. When I went there, you know what I would do? I would bathe in my house and go there and put my dress down, and then I would take another dress from the valise and put it on. And what I kept to wash and press, then I would go there and open the valise and put it inside. Always, I used to leave the key there. All my dresses were in the house of this girl. And I didn't take anything. So I was there, but I was not there. I didn't sleep there. I slept at my place, and then in morning time, after everything, I would go there.

Then Woman went to Ghana, and I went there to take the valise, and Limata said no, how Woman is, I shouldn't take the valise; I should let her come. And I said, "OK, I will leave it." I stayed in my room without this valise about two or three months. Every time when I bathed, I had to go there to change. Then one day I went there, and I said, "OK, I want to travel so I have come to take this valise, because I must put my things inside and go." Then Limata gave me the valise. And this valise was another problem.

When Woman came back, she asked who let me take the valise, and she said she doesn't understand why they gave me this valise. And Limata said, "Oh, she said she wanted to travel. And if somebody wants to travel and you have his valise, he must take it." Then Woman was hot on[1] Limata, that she took Limata like a small sister, and that and this. So wherever I went with this valise, Limata must find me to bring the box back.

So when I came back from traveling, I had to bring this valise back to Woman, because the way Limata talked to me, Woman was doing her rough[2] about why she let me take my valise. So I thought it's good to save Limata. I sent the valise back. For me, I don't want something like this problem: I don't like if there is somebody I don't know — I didn't know Limata well, eh? We were just meeting, to know each other a little bit — and she will have this trouble from me. Woman said Limata has to bring this bag back. Maybe I stole something, or I owed her, I don't know. You see this case, this is what I thought. And as for me, first time[3] I thought — *Pfft*, she feels the valise is nice, or she feels there is something inside. OK, every time I will go there and change the dresses, and I would leave the valise with her. *Ha!* But the time when I wanted to travel was the time I went to get the valise. And then, when I got back to Ouagadougou, *oh-oh,*

---

1. annoyed with, bothering
2. quarreling with, hassling, making things difficult for her; also, *make rough*
3. at first

Limata had a big case with Woman, and Woman was saying all these things, that why should Limata let me take it, and that and this. OK?

You know, the first time I was there together with them, Woman also had a valise that was stolen. She had a big valise, a portmanteau like the size of mine, but not like mine; it was a black one, and they put a zipper around it. So the time when we four girls were there, they came and stole Woman's valise and my wireless. I had another wireless, too, apart from the one they stole; they stole that other one, too. We were four girls. Limata didn't lose even her headscarf; the other girl also didn't lose anything. The wireless they stole from me, it pained me, and I was not happy. Woman was also not happy.

So Woman said we should go to a maalam.[1] *Ha!* The maalam told us to bring one goat, and after two weeks we will have our things. I said, "OK, let's go and buy it." So we bought it, and we took it to the maalam with three chickens, one black, one red, one white: we took all to this maalam. *Ha!* The maalam killed the meat and chopped it![2] *Huh?* He ate well! Then, *ah!* Three days passed. One week. Two weeks. These things were not coming. How these things were not coming, how could we make it?[3] So we lost our things, and we shared that debt too.

Then next, Woman said she went to another maalam, and that maalam said it was a friend of mine who came and took these things. Then I said, "Oh? A friend of mine? Is it a boy or girl? Because since I am in this house, not any boy has come to me. And not any girl has come to me. There is only one girl who came to me one day, in the day time. That time we were cooking, and we all ate together. And the girl brought groove[4]— we all went inside with you and grooved together, and we ate."

Then Woman said, "Yes. It's that girl, because the way they showed the girl, she is a little bit short, but she's tough[5] more than you and she's pure black, and —"

So that girl was called Zorro. I said, "It's Zorro?"

She said, "*Aha!* The man — even the man called that name — her name."

"OK, we will find Zorro. It's not hard for us to find Zorro, you know." So when we found Zorro, the place where we saw the girl was for herself.

1. (Hausa): Muslim scholar or cleric
2. The maalam slaughtered the chickens and ate them. *Chop* (Pidgin): to eat, consume, use, spend; also, to get money from; also, to have sex with; also, to kill.
3. What could we do?
4. also, *grooving*: marijuana; as a verb, to smoke marijuana; *groover*, or *groovier*: a marijuana smoker; *groovy*: high
5. heavily built, heavy-set, thick and large-framed; strong

And this girl had no wireless. There was a valise: she hadn't got many things inside, because she had two places. She put all the night dresses at her man's place, and then at her place she kept the ones she used to wear in the house.

Then Woman told me, "Let's forget about this, because even, in my valise, there are not nice things inside. I had only my old dresses inside. I am very sorry for you. Your wireless is lost. And this girl, the way I saw her, she is not the one who took it." So we forgot about this. OK. We finished that palaver.

But this girl, Woman, the way she came to hate me, I don't know. But why? She said that Limata has given my valise to me, and this was the trouble for Limata now. Only Woman had lost her valise the first time. My own valise was inside the room. Limata things were inside. Mimuna's things were inside. And they knew that this wireless, maybe somebody just fucked me and gave it to me; it's not costing me any penny. But then: Woman took it together to make an excuse, that if Limata can give me this valise the time I traveled, then Limata has to pay for the valise Woman lost the first time. *Ha!* Have you seen this before? Woman!

Then I said, "OK, Limata has nothing to pay. OK. Take this thing with all that I have inside. And leave Limata free. Because I don't want to worry somebody's baby. I have no baby, and I don't worry people's babies. I don't know the way the mother suffered to get her. And maybe she hasn't got problems like this before. Now because of me, she's going to get this problem? Take it."

Then Woman said, "No-o-o." She didn't say that she wants the valise, and that and this. And she started, you know, bringing some stories about the way she came to Ouagadougou here, but I am Voltaique, and now, because of her, I am now resting well, and that and this, and she is also all right in Ouaga.

And I said, "No. If — suppose you were resting well, you wouldn't do all this. See this valise: the way you see it's shiny, maybe you think the inside is also shiny, but the inside is black like charcoal. It's not shiny inside. But if you see the color of the valise, you think something better is inside. There is nothing inside, my friend. If you like, I will open it and you will see all that I have. The same dresses you used to see me with, it's the same thing inside. You don't see the way it is."

Then she said, "No, we don't have problems like that."

And I said, "No, before, you told me that I have to come and take my things in day time. Like the way I brought them. And I didn't come. I sent some baby to you to bring it to me. And you told the baby that this is what you can give him. So I thought, it's two times. Maybe you like the color of the valise. If you feel it, tell me. You are my friend; I can take my dresses out of it and leave it to you."

"Yeah, you know, I'm very poor. You don't feel for me." Then she started talking about her troubles: "The way my family is poor, it's the way they looked after me when I was growing up, and it's the same way I am keeping myself, too. I don't feel to take people things."

Then I said, "OK, why? I came and took this valise when I was traveling because you were not there. And I told Limata all my problem. When you came and Limata told you, what did you tell her? You said: why should she give me this, because you lost your valise. And you are the one who told me that in your valise there was no real thing inside. All that was inside is nothing for you — nothing, because it's old dresses. Are you not the one who told me this?"

Then she said, "Yeah, but it's — it's not nice. When you brought the valise, Limata didn't know you. Because of me, you came to the house. You came to the house because of me. If you come to take the valise, if I am not there, you shouldn't take it."

Then I said, "What? Even my father who borne me,[1] if I go and put something in his bank, where he saves his money, and I want to travel, if he's not there, even if I break it and take what I want inside, it's for me. The valise is for me. If you like, you can take me to anywhere. But don't trouble this girl. This girl didn't do anything. She was here. I came, and the room was open. I saw my valise — it was not inside of some cabinet. It's the same way I put it there. And I wanted to travel. You are not there, I cannot waste my time to wait for you. You must know that if I am traveling, I don't take my family. I can be with them. Sometimes, I used to be with my father, when he was working in this cocoa,[2] then I will just wake up[3] and take my bag. I will say I am going to market; they will hear that I'm at Accra. And so how much about you? You are a friend; you were a good friend to me. But after all that you have done, it is not good for me now. I'm fed up with you. You were fed up with me a long time ago — you didn't tell me. But today I'm going to tell you: I'm fed up with you."

Oh-oh! I put this palaver into fire. This girl boiled up:[4] "Is this the way the world is? When you help somebody, he must throw you down. This time, when I see any girl suffering, I won't help her!"

---

1. gave birth to me. The idiom is used for both men and women, and it is normal for a man to say he has borne his children.
2. cocoa farms in Ghana
3. get up; stand up
4. to become furious, to become very angry

Then I said, *"Ey!?* Don't say I'm suffering. You saw me in hotel. If I'm not a rich woman, I cannot stay in hotel. Can you tell me that since you came to Ouaga, have you slept in hotel before? I was rich: that's why I rested in my hotel. Even the time when you asked me to come back with you, the first day you asked me, did you see me coming back? If you didn't follow me and beg me[1] again, I wouldn't have come. *Abi?*[2] *Na me I be tough-o.*[3] Don't be sorry for me at all. And don't pity me. Never, never in your life, if see somebody like me, don't feel pity. How can you pity for me? *Ha! Shit!"*

Then she said, "Yes, you can tell me shit."

You know, I was boiled up too, because the way she was doing with Limata, I was feeling pity. Limata was telling me every time that she didn't take this case seriously, but the day I saw Limata, the way she looked, then I didn't feel happy. So: I can talk to Woman. I know Woman is strong and everything, but I don't fear her. As for me, if you say something to hot me,[4] I don't fear. Even if you are a tiger, I can eat you, you know. I can just open my eyes in different kinds, eh? If I am serious, you will see my eyes, and you wouldn't know that I know how to laugh, eh? If I am joking too, people will think that there is not any foolish person like me. Yeah. So we can do all of these things: she can say what she wants, and I can say what I want and shit her.[5] So then I said, "Look, you know, you have come to Upper Volta here. If you like, tomorrow I will take you to my village. And I don't know, but I haven't heard a story like you people's story. Now you are here bluffing[6] in the nightclubs with your dresses. When you go to your small village, you are going to put your dresses down, and put on small leaves.[7] *Shit!"*

Then she came and held me! *Ha-ha!* She came and held my dress! *Ti-ti-ti-ti.* And people said, "Oh, Woman, don't do that!"

1. ask me; *beg:* to apologize, to ask forgiveness. "I beg" means "Please."

2. (Yoruba, also Pidgin): or. The word is used for emphasis, like saying, "Or what?!" or "Isn't it?" or "It's true, or am I lying?"

3. (Pidgin): Or what? As for me, I'm heavy. The -o at the end of a word adds emphasis.

4. to make me annoyed

5. dismiss; also, get rid of, ignore, snub

6. taking yourself high; *bluff:* to boast, to present oneself as better than others

7. Hawa is abusing Woman as a Frafra, that Frafras don't wear clothes. Formerly (and still for some older villagers) the common attire for those who could afford it was a triangular cloth that covered the private parts and was tied around the waist with strings; some women would wear beads around their waists to which they would tie a cloth between their legs. The Talensis have an annual festival that sustains this notoriety, when even young women wrap their upper bodies with a small towel or cloth, leaving their buttocks revealed.

Then she said, "No, what this girl wants to say is what? She is Voltaique? I can beat her. I can even kill her." And that and this.

Then people say, "No, Woman, leave her, leave her."[1] And they separated us.

When she held me, I didn't do anything. I just made my arms loose. I said, "You can kill me? *Kill* me now! *Abi na you be tiger?*[2] Finish me now, then I will see that I have finished in the world."

So the people begged her and she left me. I went to my house, and she went to her house, too.

About two weeks, then Woman sent Limata to me. Woman said that Limata should tell me that we have all been friends for a long time. I shouldn't take something like this to be serious, that we won't talk to each other. And that and this.

Then I said, "Limata, no. As for me, I am not satisfied with that. If you are satisfied with that, we will go to her house. I will see her."

So we went to Woman's house. Then I told Woman, "You told something to Limata to tell me. But I don't understand. I want to listen to you yourself with your tongue. Because maybe Limata can boss me." And Woman said the same thing that Limata said.

So then I said, "Look, if you go to your Bolgatanga, you're going to your uncle you told me about.[3] So if you have gone to Ghana before you're coming to talk all this, if he told you that if you are friends with me, you will get me, you will never get me in your life. Never. And so I don't want you to be around tomorrow. We are not friends. If you see me, see me like somebody you know: 'Hello, hello!' If I see you, I can say hello to you. But we can never be like the first time. And you will never get me in this way. What your father has told you, or your uncle told you, I have an uncle like him, too. If you make your juju[4] and come and catch me: *e no go fit-o. Abi? Me I no believe for this thing.*[5] And what you are thinking, to go to Ghana

1. let go of something or someone; also, let someone be free. "Leave me" means "Let me go."

2. (Pidgin): Is that it? You're a tiger?

3. Hawa is referring to Woman's claim that her grandfather is chief of Tongo, that is, that Woman could go to her relatives to get medicine from the Talensi shrine (to use against Hawa).

4. make a sacrifice to an animist shrine. The word "juju" is still commonly used by indigenous people to refer to non-Christian and non-Muslim (animist) religious activities, or to the medicine given for herbal or magical treatment of sickness, or for animist religious or superstitious practices, or for the diety or spirit itself, or for the shrine of that spirit. It is no longer generally used by anthropologists because it has derogatory connotations, like the associated word "pagan."

5. (Pidgin): It won't work. Or I lie? I don't believe in your juju.

before you will come and beg me, I won't answer you. We are friends still, but not like before. When I see you outside, I can greet you. Any time you are passing my house, if you feel like seeing me, you can enter and greet me. Any time when I am passing your place, I can greet you. But we cannot be like the first time. To be close like the way we were before? No. You have fooled me many times from Dapoya to here. So you cannot fool me again."

So you know, when we finished these problems, from that place, this girl was nice. She saw me everywhere, she greeted me, and I greeted her. But we didn't have the way we used to talk from the first time.

And then after, when I left, Limata's problems also started. If somebody came to Limata, Woman would say, "Yeah, when I was in Ouagadougou here before you came, this boy was my boyfriend, and he is that and this, and that's why I left him." And Limata would get fed up: she would leave the house and come and sleep with me in my room. And then I got Limata a room in my house, and she came to stay with me.

And Woman was asking people where Limata was living. And some people told Woman, "Yeah, I used to see her with Hawa." And every time when Woman saw me with Limata: *pa-pa-pa-pa*, that no, she's not happy when I walk with Limata.

One day we went to Cabane from work. We saw Woman there, and Woman said that I want to spoil Limata, the friendship between her and Limata. She started to talk to people, that I am a *konkɔnsa* girl;[1] she was living with Limata for a long time, and Limata hadn't got any problem with her. But since I came, it wasn't one year, and now Limata doesn't listen to her.

And then I said, "Yeah, as for me, if I am a man, I will feel for a woman they are jealous on." *Ha!*

So whenever Limata and I went to Cabane, if we saw Woman, Woman would sit down. Then I would say, *"Ah-h, chérie, chérie Limata. Mais qu'est-ce qu'il y a?"*[2] Then Woman would turn and pass, and her face would be tied:[3] she wouldn't want to see us. Up to now, she doesn't like to see us at all. It's funny. It's very funny.

So when you travel, you see some things. Yeah. And this case, I saw it

---

1. (Asante Twi): *Kɔnkɔnsa* refers to talking about people, often in a manipulative or distorting way, or to gossip that causes trouble between people. *Gossiper: kɔnkɔnsani* (singular); *kɔnkɔnsafoɔ* (plural).

2. (French): Ah, my dear, dear Limata, what's up?

3. She would be grimacing and not looking. To "tie" one's face is to tighten one's face, to put on an unfriendly expression, to look annoyed.

from my own friend, not a stranger. I stayed with a friend, and when I was going out from that friend, it wasn't good for me. Before, Woman was a good friend to me, but after, I don't know the way that she saw me. Maybe she was fed up with me, or she had another best friend more than me.

Getting an Identity Card

You know, I told you that when I left my brother's house, I didn't go back there for about four or five months. And what made me go there: I didn't have papers. Yeah, before having my papers, the way I suffered, this is what I'm going to tell you. I went to Banfora.[1] When I was coming back to Ouagadougou, I didn't have a *carte d'identité*.[2] I didn't have any papers. Police people asked me for my carte d'identité, and they arrested me on the train and took me to the Railway police station. So I had to make a telephone call. I said I was going to my brother, that I was from Bobo-Dioulasso[3] going to see my brother. But I had a Banfora ticket. *Ha-ha!* So then they said, OK, did I know my brother's house? I said, yeah, I know his house and I know his workplace. Then they said, can I see him at this time of the night at his workplace? I said, No, but if they can let me telephone his house. So when they asked for the telephone number, I gave it to them, then they telephoned, and they gave me the telephone. Then I told him that they had detained me. *Ha!* It was about twelve o'clock in the night. He was talking on the telephone: "Y-y-you see!" If he's talking, he makes like that. "A-a-a-a, you see? Y-y-y-you see all this? Y-you have — I can't sleep. Y-you have — I was telling you to come home. Y-you don't want to come home!"

Then I was thinking, "Oh, shit!" *Ha!* You know, when he was saying all this on the telephone, in my heart I said, "Look. Shit. You won't put this fucking thing down? Come and get me out. You are making heh-heh-heh, talking all on this way."

So he said he was coming, and he came and met the inspector.[4] He was a *good* friend to him. The inspector said, "Oh, I didn't know. Suppose I knew she is your sister, I wouldn't have booked it."[5]

1. small town in southwestern Burkina Faso
2. (French): identity card
3. major town in western Burkina Faso
4. An inspector might be the senior duty officer at a neighborhood police station.
5. entered it in the record. He is apologizing because once the matter has been entered, he cannot remove it and help her brother avoid the fine.

Then they said, never mind. And my brother paid, I think, two thousand five hundred or something like that. Then he took me in the car and started again: *tat-dat-dat-dat, tat-dat-dat-dat-dat.* I knew what I was going to do, so I didn't mind him and all that he was saying: "Eh-heh, you come and sit down, and y-you don't want to sit with me, and then you see these troubles. To come and wake me, at this time, and you know that tomorrow I'm going to work." And that and this. "E-even if y-y-you are here in the house, if you are doing something, I will know. But I don't know you are in town, and then you start causing trouble in the police station, to write all your name there, to know that our family is that and this. You see? This is why I wanted you to understand yourself, to don't do all these things."

I didn't say a word. *Ha-ha!* I didn't say a word. I just kept quiet like that, looking at him. So the next day, I was a *good* girl, you know. Trying[1] in the house, playing with the children. When they were cooking, I said, "Oh, I know how to do it. Come and let's make the tuwo."[2]

So then my brother said, "Ah!" He called his wife: "Put your hand in this T-Zed and see. This is the real T-Zed. But as for you, if you do it —"

So he was trying to mess his wife in front of me, and all this. He was telling the wife how to make the tuwo. You know? That day I was doing good work in the house, so he also wanted me to be happy. And he thought he had his intelligence, and I thought I also knew what I wanted.

So in day time, when they went to work, I ran away to Mama Amma and told her all the problem, that she shouldn't worry. I'm in danger, now, so I must be in the house as a good, quiet girl. Oh, eight o'clock in the evening: I will sleep before the children. *Ha!* I am in my room. I lock the door. I'm in the air conditioning. Then I will get groove: I will smoke *good!* I do it inside. All the room[3] is sealed. And there's air conditioning inside. I sleep. So I didn't have a problem with this at all. At seven o'clock, I will lock my door. Three days. The fourth day, my brother told me, "Uh-huh, if you are a good girl like this, is it not better? When you were — ah — what do you want? Anything you want, you should tell me."

Then I said, "Brother, but you know, one thing I have to tell you. I think that as I have come home, you know, there are some others who

1. helping
2. staple hot food of the savanna region, a paste-like starchy food made from boiled flour of sorghum or occasionally other grains, eaten with sauce or soup. T-Zed is a conversational acronym for T-Z, which is Hausa for "tuwon zafi," literally, a linked form of "hot (zafi) food (tuwo)." The Hausa term, shortened to "tuwo," is also commonly used by people throughout the region.
3. the whole room

don't want to come home. And so I have tried my best to come and see you people. So, I'm living here. But now I'm living like a slave, without papers. I can't say I'm Voltaique. I can't say I am Ghanaian. I haven't got any kind of papers. And it's my father who made it that way.[1] If it wasn't so, the time they arrested me on the train, if I had my Ghanaian passport, they would have taken me as a Ghanaian."

He said, "What?! Why should you get a Ghanaian passport?" *Dat-dat-dat-dat!*

Then I said, "Yeah, because you people are not serious. OK. My father took my passport from me, and then look now. They have detained me on a train. I didn't — I'm not a thief, I'm not anything. Because of papers. And you people are here. Just to say that 'you are my brother' or 'you are my sister'?"

Then he said, "Because of this, you are worried? Wait. I will make it[2] for you."

Then, oh-h, that day he did a good thing. That day when I told him, he didn't say anything. The next day, early in the morning, about seven-thirty, he woke me. He said I should come and take my bath and have my coffee so that we will go to town. The whole day, he didn't work. We went to make my papers, from there to there, from this office to that office. They wanted two people to stand and sign the papers, but he was alone. OK, I should wait there for him to go and get another friend to come and sign the papers, and all this. Then he got all my papers correct. OK. And how foolish I am: I didn't wait to get the carte d'identité. It is these papers you take to get the carte d'identité. But I didn't have time. They went to work, they came, they didn't meet me at home. *Ha!* I flew. I flew again.

Then I got a man. These people who are taking the tax — their big man, their chief — what do they call them? I think in Upper Volta they are from the *gendarmerie*,[3] or something like that. I had a man from there. This man had been following me. He was a Busanga.[4] And we Gurunsi people and Busanga people, we are like Nzema[5] and Ashanti.[6] You know?

---

1. See *Hustling Is Not Stealing*, chapter 4, in which Hawa's father seizes a Ghanaian passport she obtained, claiming it inappropriate for her because she is Voltaique.

2. get it; pay to have it issued

3. (French): barracks, police station; barracks or administrative offices of armed forces militia or armed police

4. cultural group in southeastern Burkina Faso

5. cultural group in southwestern Ghana

6. cultural group in central Ghana

Nzema and Ashanti: they used to joke with each other.[1] Somebody told
me this man was a Busanga man, but I knew what I wanted from him,
so I didn't want him to know where I was from.[2] Every time, I used to
give him a promise.[3] Any place we met, if he said, "Let's go," I would say,
"No." I would give him maybe tomorrow, or the day after tomorrow to
meet me at some place. And he wouldn't see me. So when I got my papers, one day we were at a bar — African Bar — just near to our house
at Dapoya, and this man came there, and I told him, "Oh, now I have my
papers, but it's left with the carte d'identité."

So this man took me to the photo shop, and they took my photo for
the carte d'identité. And he collected all my papers from me. OK: then he
was not bringing these papers back to me. And any time when I saw him,
when I asked him about the papers, he would say, "Let's go to my house
and get your papers. I have made the carte d'identité but it is in my house.
I forgot. I thought maybe sometimes I won't meet you, so I can't carry it
in my pocket every day."

Agh! What kind of case is this? So then I was trying to get my papers.
This man also said, "Unless my home." So I was fed up with him. If the
papers are lost, they can be lost. He can keep the papers. When I would
see him, I didn't ask him anything again. If he wanted to joke with me, I
wouldn't joke with him again. I was serious.

So one night I went out and he met me at some place, and he said,
"You, you are annoyed with me, isn't it?"

Then I said, "Yes? Why shouldn't I be annoyed with you? Do you know
that I shouldn't be annoyed with you? Or I should do you something,[4] and
you will get me? So it's your luck. You can go, because you have got all
my papers. Because of this paper, even if I needed you or if I loved you, I
wouldn't say anything, because you think that because of this paper you
are going to get me like that. But this paper is nothing. I can go and make
another one. So you can carry it. So if you want somebody, it's not that
you should show him something like that, a hot time[5] like that, before

---

1. It is not uncommon for two cultural groups to be "playmates" and have such an
understanding of their relationship. Such relationships are often modeled on special family
patterns like those between grandparents and children, usually based on stories of histori-
cal origins. The "playing" can involve trickery or joking that should be forgiven.

2. Hawa wants the man to focus on the papers, and she doesn't want the man to feel
free with her to try to change the relationship.

3. an appointment, a time to meet

4. do something to you

5. difficult time

you will say that you can love the person." So when I said this, you know, something came to his head and he went home and brought all the papers to me, the ones I had given him, all. *Ha-ha!*

Yeah, you know, these papers are what you are going to give before they will give you a carte d'identité. You see? That gendarme was lying to me that he had done it, but he didn't do it. So the day when I talked to him seriously, I think he was ashamed or something like that, so he went and brought the same papers to me.

When I got my papers back: *hey!* I was happy. But still, I was still looking for the carte d'identité. Then I went and saw one groove seller. He also was a good friend. I used to buy groove from him. He was Voltaique, but I think he was born in Ghana. Even he had a big problem in Ouaga, and he has run to Ghana. He is wanted because of groove. They locked the wife for seven or eight months before they left her, too.

We used to buy our groove from this groove seller, maybe two thousand or three thousand. So we were good customers to him. He liked us. He used to converse with us, and all this. His wife was nice. When we went there, if her husband was not there, she used to serve us grooving to smoke while we waited for the husband. So one day we went there, and I brought all my problem, because, you know, I had spoiled my way at my brother's house, so I wanted a brother in town to help me. How I saw the man, I thought that he will be a nice soul brother, so if I put my problem on him, as he was popular in the town, maybe he could help me in some way. I thought I would get a cheap[1] brother. So I told him all my troubles. I told him that, I had a problem, but I didn't know what to do, because all my families[2] were in the village. I didn't tell him that I have a brother in Ouagadougou. So I had all my papers, and they said until my father comes before they will make the card.

Then he said, "What? They lie! You have all your papers?"

Then I said, "Yes."

He said, "Do you have them here?"

That time, I used to carry them everywhere. So I showed him, and he said, "OK. Let's go to police station." Yeah. He said he had a friend who was doing this, that the friend was the chief there, for the carte d'identité.

So he took me to Central Police Station. The man there took my papers. More than two weeks, I didn't see him. *Agh!* Police chief. *Ha!* Two weeks! Every morning I went. Afternoon time, three o'clock, I was there.

---

1. easy to get
2. the families in the larger extended family

I didn't see this man. Any time when I went and I asked of him, they said that he has gone out. And my papers were with him. So now I didn't know what to do. Mama Amma had been leading me, and she got tired. If I said I was going to police station, she would say, "OK. Go. Go and come."

So I thought: ah! What should I do now? Or — should I go and tell my brother? If I go and tell him, he will abuse me. *Ah! Ah! Fucking!* So I knew the time when he was not in the house. I went there. I saw the young one, the small brother. He was about eighteen years old.[1] I said, "Come." He came. And I said, "Let's go out. The children are there."

He said, "Yes?"

And I said, "Come." I took him to our place, and I told him, "Look, somebody lied to me that he would make my carte d'identité for me. Then I gave all my papers to him, and he went and gave them to the Commissaire of Central.[2] Then the Commissaire, every time, when I go, they say the man is not in. It's two weeks now."

So he said, "So you didn't get your carte d'identité?"

I said, "Yes. And I'm afraid to go and tell big brother, because he will abuse me."

Then this boy said, "Oh, but this one is cheap. I can make it." A small boy, huh?

Then I said, "Ah? You can make it?"

He said, "Yes, let's go to police station."

We went to the police station. We asked the man's name, and the man was not there. Then he said, "OK, I will wait at the police station here. You should go home. If the man comes, I will come and call[3] you."

Then I said, OK. I left him in police station. He came home about half-past three. He said the man had come. He didn't ask for the man, but somebody showed him this is the man. Then he just came and called me, because maybe if he goes and talks to him, before he calls me, the man will go out. So when we went, the man was going out, and we met on the road.

"Ah, *Mademoiselle Hawa, comment ça va?*"[4] I looked at him like this. He said, "Tomorrow morning, come and take your carte d'identité."

I said, "No, I don't want a carte d'identité. I want my papers."

1. In American terms, he was about seventeen. Age is counted from birth, so that a baby is one during the first year, two during the second, and so on.

2. the commissioner at the Central Police Station

3. come and get

4. (French): Miss Hawa, how are you?

"*Ça va pas, non?*"[1]

Then I said, "*Oui, ça va pas. Et ça va chez toi?*" You see? I told him, "Me, I want my papers, then you are telling me that 'You are not correct.' And you are correct!?"

Then he said, "Oh, is this trouble?"

I said, "No, it's not trouble. It's not trouble. When I come, I come with a smile, that I want my papers. I can't wait for tomorrow again."

"A-ah, if it's not this police station, there's not any place where they can make these papers."

Then I said, "Shit. I don't care about that. You give me the papers. Even if you people don't make my carte d'identité that I'm not Voltaique, it won't pain me. Even I don't want to be Voltaique." *Ha!*

Then he said, "*Cette fille là!* This girl!"

I didn't mind him.

Then my brother said, "What did this girl do? *C'est normal, non?*" This small boy told him that it is normal to me to say that, because he has taken these papers for a long time. So if I'm annoyed, I'm right to do that.

So he said, "*Petit, c'est ta soeur?* Small boy, is she your sister?"[2]

Then my brother said, "Yeah."

"So you are following her to come and take her papers?"

He said, "No. Our big brother is annoyed that he gave her the papers to go and make the carte d'identité and bring the papers, because these papers, they don't leave them with us. They keep them with the family, because maybe we will lose our papers. We are careless. So my big brother has been abusing me every day. I told him, 'I gave the papers to police.' He said he doesn't believe me. So if the papers are there, you should give me the papers. I will go and show to our big brother. Then he will know that they have the papers there, but they didn't make her carte d'identité yet."

This man said, "OK, you are right. What you say is true."

So we went into the office and he brought the papers to us. And the boy told me that, "Come, we will go to the carte d'identité office."

They took my measurement, then they said, OK. Then the boy said, OK, I could go home now. So I was in the house when he brought my carte d'identité. This small boy! It's wonderful!

1. (French): You're not well (all right)? In this context: Is something wrong with you? Are you out of your mind?

2. (French): *mon petit* (masculine), *ma petite* (feminine); literally, my little one; a form of address to a young boy or a young girl, or occasionally to an adult; in this context: my child, kid

Virginity as a Fatal Disease

So, you know, he is a funny boy. He is called Yisifu. First time, when
Mama Amma and I came, he said he liked Mama Amma. OK, when
Mama Amma went away, then I was walking with Limata. Limata became
my good friend in Ouaga. At our first place, Limata was also staying there
with Woman. It was from Woman's house that Limata and I started to become friends, up to now when we stay together. Then when Mama left,
this boy said he liked Limata. This time, when he comes to our house, Limata calls him her darling, and Mama Amma calls him her darling. So
now he's ashamed. You know what he calls them? *Camarades:*[1] my
friends. *Ha-ha!* Every time he used to come to me. Sometimes when he
doesn't come, Mama Amma and Limata used to ask me, "Why? Why
doesn't Yisifu come? Why doesn't Yisifu —?"

Then I'll say, "Ah. I don't know why."

But every time he used to come to our place, and he's somebody who is
jovial. And he is very clever. Then you know, one day he came and gave
me a funny story. Look how the world is going on! This boy came and
told me, "Sister."

I said, "Yes." I thought he had something serious to tell me.

Then he said, "Can I see you?"

Then I said, "Yes, you can see me."

He said, "No, you have your friends here, but I want to see you in the
room."

So I went inside the room with him, and he brought his story. He said
he has been sick, going to the doctor — and the doctor told him that —
that because he didn't go with a woman, that's why — he didn't make a
love to a woman, that's why he's sick. So he's begging me, if I can give him
one thousand to go and find a woman. *Ah!! He-he-he-he!*

I looked at this boy. I said, "Huh?"

He said, "It's true. Don't you —"

At that time, you know, I thought he just wanted this money for something. Then I said, "Look, you are my small brother, isn't it?"

He said, "Yes."

"I can't show you a way to find a woman. When it was my age to find a
man, it was not somebody showed me. So I can't show you this way. If
you need money for something, I can give you. But this kind of money

---

1. (French): mate, friend, comrade

you are asking me, it is foolish. From today it is your first and last time to tell me this! What are you thinking?!" *Ha!*

Then he said, "Oh no, sister, you know — it's only — you are — my problems, it's only you I used to talk to. I can't talk to our big brother, you know? If I said something bad, or I made a mistake, you should forgive me. Don't be annoyed too much."[1] *Ha-ha!*

Then I didn't mind him. That day, I saw that this boy had become lean. I thought maybe he was sick. Even when he came, I told Limata, "Oh-h, you people, your husband has become lean; he is slim. And I don't know, maybe he's sick or something. That's why he doesn't come to us."

So I made up my mind that if he was going, maybe I would find about five hundred for him. Even if I had one thousand, I would give him. But that day, when he said this to me, I was annoyed, so I didn't give him anything. It was Limata who gave him two hundred to take a taxi. And he went. When he went away, for about one month, he didn't stop at my place. So I went to the house. I knew exactly the time when my big brother was not there. Then I called this boy. He came. Then I said, "Why don't you come to me?"

He said that what he has done, when he came home, he thought about it, and he was ashamed, and what and what. That's why he stayed away. He was feeling that if he comes there, he would be ashamed.

And I said, "Were you ashamed before you said that to me?"

He said, "No. The time when I was going to say it, I don't know what I had mixed up in my brain. Because the doctor told me that if I don't do this thing, I will die."

Then I said, "OK. Have you done it now?"

He said, "No."

Then I said, "Why didn't you die by now, then? The doctor gave you how many days?"

He said, "No, the doctor said about two months' time." *Ha-ha! Hee-hee-hee-hee! Shit!*

So I said, "OK, forget about it. This is a past thing, so you can come to me." So we went together.

And that time, the mother had asked him that she wanted a big table. So he and I went together to the market, and I bought the table for him to take it for her. And I gave him five hundred francs. He was happy. So the next day he came again, and that day I gave him only one hundred francs. I didn't give him a full taxi fare. So then when he went, he didn't come

---

1. very much. "Too" as a modifier normally means "very," without implying comparison or excess.

again. In about three days' time, he came. I didn't give him anything. I was keeping him like that about one week. Every day when he came there, I didn't give him anything, for about one week. Then I went and bought him material to make a trouser and shirt, up-and-down.[1] Then I took him to the tailor, and they measured him and they sewed it for him. And I bought him shoes. And the day he took the dress from the tailor to go out with it, I gave him two thousand. And you know, from that time for one month, my small brother didn't come to my place again. He had his up-and-down and his shoes: he was a Yankee boy in town. He didn't have time, even to see the sister.

You know, it was very funny. For one month's time, I didn't see him, and then he started coming. He would come once, then maybe three or four days, then once, then three or four days, then once. It was about two months' time, and he came and told me, "Sister, I want to ask you a question. I don't want you to be annoyed with me like that day."

Then I said, "What kind of question?"

"Will you be annoyed?"

Then I said, "No."

"But I beg you, don't be annoyed."

Then I said, "No, I'm not going to be annoyed."

He said, "Eh-h — you see — I want to ask you — if you know the tablet which can cause abortion. Because I have a problem."

Then I said, "Oh, what kind problem do you have?"

He said, "Don't you see? This time I don't come here often. The time when you gave me this dress, I started going out. So there is one of my classmates, and she had been bluffing me. But this time she used to agree with me." Then he told me that she said her time for menstruation was passed. So the girl said she was afraid: if this boy didn't find medicine for her to make an abortion, she was going to tell her father. And he also knew very well that if this girl goes and tells her father, and the father comes and tells our big brother, then our big brother would just sack him from the house. *Ha!* This our big brother is strong, eh? *He-hee!*

Yeah. So then I asked him, "Who told you to come and ask me this? Because you have seen that I have no husband, so I'm an ashawo,[2] so that I

---

1. an outfit that uses the same material or cloth for blouse and skirt, or shirt and trousers

2. a "loose" or "free" woman who is dependent on men outside of a family setting. *Ashawo* is a Yoruba word that literally means "money-changer." Money-changers are not only currency exchangers at borders but also are people who keep track of money at social events and markets. At social events in many cultures, for example, people give money to dancers and musicians, and there will be an elderly musician to change money into

know all these medicines? That's why I don't conceive,[1] or that's why I don't have a baby? This is what I take? Or who told you to ask me this?" *Ha!*

Then he said, "Oh, sister, but I have talked to you not to be annoyed."

I said, "Yes, but you are telling me foolish things. This is a foolish question you are asking me. You are educated. You are at the school, isn't it?"

He said, "Yes."

"So you don't know the medicine which will cause an abortion? Haven't you read something about causing abortion?"

Then he said, "Even if I know it, but how can I get it?"

"How can you get it? How did you manage to get the girl?"

He said, "No, but that girl, the father is rich, you know. She doesn't ask for money."

Then I said, "OK. The father is rich. She doesn't ask for money. Then ask her for the money to go and buy the medicine, because the father is rich. If she doesn't want the family to know, then why should she say that she is going to tell the father?"

Do you see? This girl just saw this boy that he hasn't known a woman. I think this case was something like that. She just wanted to take this boy in some way to catch him for nothing, to get money that she is going to cause abortion. And this boy also feared to ask me for the money, so he asked me if I know a medicine which can cause abortion. So I said, "OK, let her go and tell the father. And if big brother sacks you from the house, you can come and stay with me here."

So he went away. Then every time when he was coming to me, he didn't give this complaint. I was waiting up to three months. And one day he came to me, and I called him, "Yisifu, come." Then he came. And I said, "Let's go inside."

And he said, "Why, sister?"

I said, "No, let's go inside my room." So he came to me. Then I said, "Sit down." He sat down. And I said, "What about the girl?"

He said, "Oh, the girl, she lied. She didn't conceive. One of her girl-friends came and told me."

Then I said, "So why didn't you tell me?"

---

smaller bills and coins. At market, an older person will handle the money while some younger assistants help package or load goods. Applied to women, the appellation suggests a person who is keeping track of a relationship with an eye firmly fixed on its exchange value. For a fuller discussion of these issues, see the Introduction to *Hustling Is Not Stealing.*

1. become pregnant; also, make someone pregnant; as a noun, the pregnancy

He said, "You know, sister, some things like this, when I want to talk to you, you know, I don't feel like talking to you on this way."

So then I said, "You can't talk to me on this way, but when you want the medicine to cause abortion, you talk to me. And when you want the money to go and find a woman, you talk to me. And so what? It's a shame more than to tell me that the girl was lying. Is it not?"

And he said, "OK, then forgive me. She was lying, because her girl-friend came and told me that this girl said this boy thinks his eyes are open[1]—he has a sister who buys him clothes—and he will come and bluff in town—"

You know, my brother is also foolish. I think he used to boss the girl that he has a sister who is rich. All the clothes: I can take him to the tailor to sew him clothes, then he will know his way. He can buy a label and put it on the clothes with a needle, and he will say this is from home. You know "home"? They don't buy it; it's already made. He brought it from Europe. His sister has a husband, a white man. They used to order the things from Europe to give to him. *All* the girls thought it was true. So they—*jigaa-jigaa*[2]—*ha-ha!*

Yeah. You know, they just wanted the boy like that. Everybody at the school was trying to catch him, because he was always changing his dresses. Mama Amma bought him trousers and one shirt. And Limata has given him a watch. So he is a Yankee boy, you know. In the school, he is a big boy. Every time they see him changing his clothes, and he is telling them that he has a sister who came from Europe, and she used to order things from Europe for him, and that and this. So the girls thought it was true. So: *ha!* Everyone who wants to catch this boy, maybe she thinks that I used to give him money, and if she catches him, she will also catch the money. So: *ha!* They had been trying for nothing.

So as for him, he's funny. He plays football.[3] He has about six or seven girls he's training; they used to make practice. He doesn't train boys. All girls. The girls he was training to play ball, I think they are seven or six, and they made a group to take a picture, with their ball, with their shorts, with their everything. He hasn't shown me this picture. It was one friend who was telling me about it. So once, when I told him that I was going to Ghana, he said, "If you go, you should get me a Yamaha."[4]

1. he has experience
2. tussle, with the connotations of reacting with physical force, embracing and tumbling with someone, or preening oneself with an arrogant demeanor
3. soccer
4. any motorcycle

Then I said, "Ah! What do you want a Yamaha for? You haven't got a motor,[1] as number one. You don't ask me for a motorbike, but you are asking for a Yamaha." *Ha-ha!*

Then he said, "No, but a motorbike, maybe if you give me money, I will buy it. But they say Yamaha is cheap in Ghana."

Then I said, "There are no things like that in Ghana. Nothing. You can't find this in Ghana."

He used to borrow the friend's motorbike and come to the town with it. So he thinks it's for him now. And so now if he has Yamaha, he is a big man. *Shit.*

2 WORKING GIRLS

: OUAGADOUGOU :

Working at La Tringle

Yeah. I said it was when I went to Ouagadougou that I decided to get work in the bar. You know, when Mama Amma was in Lomé, she was working at Watusi.[2] And it was not quite some days when that woman in Mama Amma's house killed somebody — I told you about it[3] — and they came and arrested Mama Amma and all the other girls from the house. So from there, the nightclub closed, and Mama Amma didn't work again. She was just going to Pussycat.[4] But first time, Mama was working in Lomé. I didn't work there, but when I got to Ouagadougou, I thought that if I work it would be better.

1. in this context, a motorbike like a Mobylette; also, motorcycle
2. discotheque in Lomé
3. See *Hustling Is Not Stealing*, chapter 15.
4. discotheque in Lomé

So how I got this work: when I reached Ouaga, I was just feeling like going to a nightclub which is a nice nightclub in the town, to see inside, how it is. So the first nightclub which was good there was La Tringle. After La Tringle: La Fesse Folle. La Fesse Folle was for one white woman. But La Tringle was for one African woman, and any time there were people there. If we were going out, then at about eleven o'clock we would take a taxi straight to La Tringle. But the first time when we went to La Tringle, Mama stopped at the gate, and I went inside to look, and that day, there was only one French man, a young man. When I saw that, oh, shit. So I went to go out. Then the man called me, "Did you want to have a drink? One drink with me?"

Then I said, "No, I'm not alone. I'm walking with my girlfriend."

He said I should call her. So I called Mama, and then we had this drink. We were going to have one drink, but, oh, we drank a lot there. We drank more than twenty thousand that day. That was the first time we went out, so we must do what we could do, you know. So we were drunk. And when the man was going to pay at the counter,[1] we were following behind him. The man was paying his money, and the manager of the nightclub said that they should dash the man some drink. She was a woman, an ugly woman. Then he said he was not alone; he was with two girls. So she said they should give all of us drink. So we were there.

Then the woman called me. She asked, where was I from? I said, "Well, I am from here, but I was born in Ghana. So I have just come back."

Then she said, "Can you speak French?"

Then I said, "Oh, small-small."[2] I spoke a little bit from Lomé, you know.

Then she said, "Wouldn't you like to work here?"

I said, "As what?"

She said, "You know, La Tringle, first time, the girls didn't serve. But this time, they make all the nightclubs in Ouagadougou for the girls to serve. That's why. First, it was boys who serve. The girls who are on the counter are there. If the boys come and order the drink, the girls are serving the boys to give to the people. And the girls who are with the people, their own is for dancing and to talk to the men and let them buy plenty of drinks, and that and this. And we are on the counter. If people come and stand at counter, where the people are serving there, then you will talk to the person nicely. You know how to —"

---

1. the bar; *on counter, in counter:* behind the bar; *counter girls:* girls who serve from behind the bar

2. a little

So it was a school I went to. Then I said, "Ah, but—so it's not that I'm going to serve with tray or something like that."

She said she liked me. I can be in the counter here with the girls. Then I said, "Anyway, but you know, I will think about it. But also, I am not alone. We are two."

Then she said, "Oh, you can bring your girlfriend, too."

So I called Mama to greet her.[1] Then I said, "OK, if that will be case, we will think about it."

They were paying twelve thousand for the month. But if you got people to buy you many drinks, then they would add. All the drinks had their prices: somebody will buy you maybe one tot[2] or one beer or one Coca. If you got cognac, the special brandy, if you drink that one, it's one thousand francs. If you drink a drink of one thousand francs, you get two hundred. If you drink a drink of five hundred, you have twenty-five francs. Look at the foolishness. A thousand, you get two hundred: instead of a five hundred drink and you get one hundred, they wouldn't give it to you. Twenty-five. It's because she wants you to drink something which is costly. If you are going with the champagne: one cup is thousand five hundred. You will get three hundred. You see? If every time you drink two champagnes a day, it's more than your pay for a month.

Yeah. The time I was in counter there, I said, OK, I know the way. I used to take Sprite to make Champagne Sprite. You will pay thousand five hundred, but it's Sprite. *Ha-ha!* I will put it in a champagne bottle, so I will use the cup for champagne. If you want one cup, then they have the open one in the fridge. They just bring it and shake it and pour it. Eh? You see that I am drinking champagne. *Aboa!*[3] You think I will get drunk? I'm drinking Sprite.

So we were there, and this woman was asking about the work, and I said, "OK, we will think about it, and we will come and tell you."

When we finished that drink there, then this French man said we should go out. We went out to La Fesse Folle. When we went to La Fesse Folle, Mama Amma said she was hungry. So I said, "OK, we will go and find some kebabs[4] and go and buy, because we don't know where to find the food now."

But instead of telling this man that we were hungry, so maybe he would

---

1. introduce Mama to her
2. one shot
3. (Asante Twi): an exclamation of contempt or scorn, literally, an animal; comparable to the French expression, "Ta gueule!" or the English "In your face!"
4. Kebabs are sold by roadside vendors, mainly at night when sit-down eating establishments are closed.

buy us food, we didn't tell him. We told him that we were going to see one of our sisters. We said we are three, and one of our sisters is at someplace. As we have the key, maybe she will close [1] and go home, and we won't come, and she will be waiting for us there. So we are coming. We are going to give her the key and come back. So he gave us one thousand to take a taxi. So we got our one thousand and went our way. We went to our house and slept.

This madam had told us that we should come and see her morning time. So when we went home, we were thinking. I said, "Mama Amma."

She said, "Hm."

I said, "This work, as for me, truly, I will do it, because of my brother. What he is doing, I am annoyed, so even if I don't have anything to do here at all, I will do it."

Then Mama Amma was asking me, can she do it. I said, "Yes. Why not? Don't you think it's better than what we are doing?"

Mama said, "For me, true, I haven't done work like this."

Then I said, "But you were doing some in Lomé, isn't it?"

She said, "Yeah, but here life and Lomé life is not same-same." [2]

I said, "If you don't want to do it, tell me the truth. I will go and lead. I will do it. But I feel that we are two, and we have come together. If I leave you alone and go to work, and you are alone in the house, you won't be happy. So if you like, let's try it. If you don't like it, then we will leave."

So she said, "OK."

So the next morning, we were preparing to go to the nightclub to meet this woman. And you know, in Ouagadougou I have one brother, a taxi-driver: he is not my brother, but he is just a kind of brother. He is also a Gurunsi man. That morning, around eleven o'clock, he came to our house to see us. We were dressing, and he said, "Where are you people going?"

I said, "I'm going to see Madame Colette at La Tringle." The woman was called Colette.

So he said, OK. He took us to La Tringle, but they said she didn't come. Then this taxi driver said, OK, he knows her house; he will take us. Going to the house, he met her car coming to town. So we turned the taxi and followed her to the nightclub, and we went and saw her. Then she said, OK, we should come to work at half-past nine. About eight o'clock we were there!

At that time, Palladium was there. We went to Palladium and drank and drank and drank. Oh, before we went to work: fine! [3] We had our

---

1. finish work
2. the same. The word is doubled for emphasis.
3. an affirmation: yes

small grooving, too, so we grooved nice. When we were coming from Ghana, I had a lot of groove. I bought it in Kumasi: four cups. I had a bag — oh, that bag, it pains me! It's lost. A dungaree bag, eh? I bought it from Lomé from *buroni-wawu*.[1] Inside this bag, it had about six pockets. And I made more pockets too. I just sat down and tried, then I took the ganja,[2] put it inside, and cut somewhere and made a pocket. So all the length, I made pocket, pocket, pocket, inside. I can put everything inside, and you will see the inside of the bag: nothing. This is how I made it and took this groove.

So that time we had good groove. Every time when we would go to the work, if you see us, you will *like* us. We are *happy*. We worked for this woman about three or four months. Then she said that people don't buy drinks from Mama Amma, so she sacked her. *Ah!* Then I left the work. I said, "If you sack Mama Amma, I won't work too."

So then she came and said, OK, if that will be the case, we can come and work here. I can tell Mama Amma to come back, that we will work.

And I said, OK. So we went back to work, two weeks.

Mama Gets a Boyfriend

Then, every Sunday we didn't work, and we would go to another place to dance. So one Sunday we went to Cabane Bambou. You know, Cabane Bambou: there is a drinking bar outside, but first time, the inside was having a nightclub, too. The musicians were playing there. Cabane Bambou was also for that woman, and her law was if you are working with her at one place, if you are at another bar of hers, you are working there. When I go to Cabane Bambou, and somebody buys me a drink, they will mark[3] me over there, and she will give me the same amount which she was going to give me at La Tringle. You see? So I told Mama, "Ah, if it's here, and we drink, it's nice."

We went to Cabane. That was our first night to meet Christian. We saw him with his group; there were four or five who came. Then I said, "Mama, let's go and ask these people for dancing, so that they will buy us drinks. If we drink and our eyes are good,[4] then we will go to other places."

1. (Asante Twi): second-hand clothing from overseas; from *Oburoni w'awu*, literally, "White man, you died." *Buroni-wawu* is the noun form. The pronunciation is "broni-wawu."
2. (Jamaican English, from Hindi): marijuana
3. make a note about; also, recognize, note
4. In this context, we get satisfied; we get a buzz.

Then Mama said, "Oh-h, me, I can't go. Oh-h, me, I can't."

So I and one girl, we went forward. Then I asked Christian to dance. He got up and we danced. Then I said he should buy me beer. He bought me one small beer, and I went to sit with Mama. We took half of this small beer: I took half and gave Mama half to drink. We were sitting down and Christian came and called me again to go and dance. So when we finished dancing, I said I wanted another beer. Then he said he was going to come[1] before he would buy me a beer. I was annoyed. So I was abusing him to Mama, "These buroni-wawu white people[2] who don't have money, they say they will come to a nightclub."

You see? I asked the boy for a drink the second time, and he said he was going to come before he buys me a beer. So when they went out, then I said, "Oh, *pfft,* there are no better people here who can buy us a drink. Let's go to the bar. If we have one hundred francs, we will drink there, and then we will go to another place. Maybe we'll get a good place." When we came outside to the bar, one Ghanaian man called me to sit down, and asked what will I drink. Then I said beer, and he gave me the beer. And we started drinking.

So this Christian, you know, he doesn't respect anything. The first day I got to know Christian was that day. Mama Amma didn't know him at all. I was sitting with that man and he just came —*po-po-po*— then he said, "We go?"

Then I said, "What? We go where? Where did you know me?" I was sitting with the African man, so I just wanted to abuse Christian that he is a foolish white man, you know, to say that he's going to come when I asked for the beer. Then when he comes, too, I'm sitting with somebody: if he comes, he should say "Good evening" to the man, but he just said, "We go? We go?"

So: "Where are we going?"

Then he stood and looked at me. He didn't say anything. He and his group left. When they went away, I didn't see him again. You know, he was living in a village.

So the next Sunday, too, we didn't work. We woke up from sleeping, and we were hungry. So there was one restaurant near to our house, Africana: they make a nice salad there, and kebab, a nice one. Sometimes if we didn't cook, we would eat this salad. So that Sunday, Mama Amma and I went there to eat salad.

We ordered and we were sitting there, and this Christian and his

---

1. He would go and do something before coming back.
2. useless white people (because they have been sent to Africa)

friends were sitting behind us. They were three. And that time, I didn't know that he was Christian, that he was the one I had abused, you know. I wasn't drunk the night I met him, but I didn't look at him much to know him. So Christian came and called Mama Amma that she should come and sit with him, and Mama Amma told him, "Ah, but I can't sit here with you. I can't sit alone here with you people, and leave my sister there."

Then Christian said, "This your sister is not good. That day I went to Cabane Bambou, she asked me to dance. I danced with her. I bought her one beer. The second time, I came and danced with her, I told her I was going to come, then we would go home, and then I would buy her a drink so that we would go home. When I came back, she was sitting with a big African man, and she was trying to abuse me. So I can't call her on my table. But don't tell her anything. If you want, you can ask her if she wants to drink something or she wants to eat something, you can serve her, and then I will pay."

Then Mama Amma came. She didn't tell me what the man told her. You see? She told me, "This man says if you want to drink or if you want to chop something, you can take it. Then you should bring him the receipt."

Then I said, "Tell the man, 'Thank you very much. If I didn't have money, I wouldn't come here.'"

Mama Amma said, "Oh, why? Are you annoyed?"

Then I said, "Ah, Mama Amma, I'm not annoyed."

Then she said, "Why?"

I said, "No. When this man came here, he didn't say 'Hello' or 'Good evening' to me, and he just came and called you to come and sit down. I don't know how you people talked before you asked if I need something to eat. Why don't you tell me 'good evening'? Somebody who wants to give something to somebody, he can say 'hello.' But we are sitting together. Then he comes and calls you alone. And then, after, he is sending me food or — I'm not coming here to wait for somebody before eating."

So when they brought the salad, I let them put Mama Amma's salad, with the drink she ordered, on the table of Christian, and I took the receipt and paid and ate and drank my beer. I paid for me and Mama. All that we ordered, I paid for it. But I let the people send it to their table there. Then I went. I left them and went home.

So I was in the house, and Mama Amma came and searched for me. Mama Amma told me that Christian said he wanted her to know his place, so she was going to see there and then come back. I was in the house up to eleven o'clock that night, Mama Amma didn't come. She had a key, so I also locked the door and went out and went to town. I came back at two o'clock. Mama Amma hadn't come. The next morning, Mama Amma came and told me that when she went with Christian, Christian gave her five thousand. And he said they should go to Kaya.[1] He was working at that village. Then I said, "OK. Go with him."

They went to their Kaya for two weeks, and then they came back to town. When they came back, Christian said that Mama Amma told him that I was her senior sister. Then he started to joke with me: "*Toi, tu n'es pas gentille.* You, you are not nice."

And then I said, "Why?"

He said, "Eh-heh, that day, I was sitting, and you came and called me nicely to have a dance with me. I bought you a beer. After, I told you I was going to come, and you didn't wait. I came, and you just talked some rubbish talk like that to me."

Then I said, "Yes, because I don't look for small boys like your type."[2] *Hee-heh-heh!*

Then he said, "Hey! Hey, Mama Amma, *tu vois? Tu vois?* Mama, do you see? You see? I told you that your sister is not a good girl."

You know, when he started all this, then I knew, "*Ah-hah,* this is the boy." But if he hadn't said that, I wouldn't have known he was the one. But he started, and then I said, "Yes, this is what." So that was the place when we came to know each other much, to become friends, you know.

So later, one time Mama went to Lomé, and she hadn't come, and Christian came. He brought me groove. Oh, it would fill up this glass. He brought it from his place. Then I said I didn't know when Mama would come, but she would come. That time I was working in Zé Bon. He came to Zé Bon. We danced. He bought drink. We drank. And then this boy told me that he didn't have a place to sleep. So I said, "OK, if that will be the case, I can give you my bed to sleep, but I will sleep on the ground, on the floor."

Then when we went to the house, he was trying to do something, you know. So I fucked him off,[3] and I let him take his car about three o'clock to go away. I sacked him from the house. So: you know these French people, how they are fucking? He brought this grooving for me, that he was giving me. But morning time, when I looked for the thing, I couldn't find it. *He-he-ha! I couldn't find it!* I was *thinking* and thinking and thinking. I said, "*Ah!* Christian can't take this thing. I don't believe that he's the one who took it."

1. small town north of Ouagadougou
2. your age, your standard, your size
3. sacked him, made him leave

But in about two or three months' time, when Mama Amma came, when I saw him, I asked him. He said "*Mais c'est normal:* but it's normal." It's normal that he should take it because what he wanted from me, I didn't agree. Why should he give me all this? Look-o! *Ha-ha!* But when he brought the thing for me, he didn't tell me anything about wanting something from me. He just said, "Oh, test this thing and see how I planted it, whether how it's growing is nice or not nice, and what. So I have brought some for you to test. I know that you, you know this grooving much, because you stayed in Ghana."

But that night, this boy became full because of this grooving, and he wanted to do something. So when I sacked him, he stole the grooving. But it's wonderful: how this boy saw where I put the thing. Yeah. The time when I sacked him to go out from the room, then I was standing outside. I said that in five minutes, if he doesn't come out, I will let people beat him here that he's a thief. So when he was inside putting on his dress, he just took the thing and put it in his pocket, and then he was leaving, "Oh, *mais j'veux pas palaver. J'veux pas palaver. J'veux au revoir.*" He doesn't want trouble. He's going. "Thank you very much. Thank you." He doesn't want trouble, huh? He's going? Do you know that he carried this thing? And thanked me on top. "Thank you, I have my things."

So the next time, when Mama came, when I saw him in front of me, I didn't say anything to Mama. But the time when it was left small for him to go away, then he was together with Mama again, and we went to drink at some place, and I was telling him, "Christian, what you did last time, is it good?"

He said, "What?"

I said, "The grooving, the one which you gave to me, and then after, when I sacked you from the room, you had to take it away?"

That was when he said to me, "*Mais c'est normal.*" So: these French people. It's normal, huh? *Hee-hee!*

: BANFORA, BOBO-DIOULASSO :

The Village Nightclub

Yeah, you know, when Mama Amma got Christian, then she started going to the village with Christian. So she left work, and then I was working in La Tringle. And then they came and closed La Tringle.

You know, Madame Colette: that woman was another woman. She

liked money proper.[1] If the money went to her pocket, to take it out: never. So she had trouble with the income tax. They came and closed the bar down. We were waiting up to two months, and they didn't open it. Then I said, "Shit." I traveled to Bobo[2] and Banfora. Do you know Banfora? You will pass Bobo before getting to Banfora. So I was at Banfora, and Mama was in Kaya. We kept our room in Ouagadougou. Sometimes we would come to meet in Ouaga, and we would make a weekend. Then everybody would go his way.

Then Mama Amma told me that I should come and meet her on the seventh of the month, and we would go to Lomé for a visit.

And Banfora, too, I had worked two months, and I didn't take my pay. I was working in the nightclub there, and they gave me a room to stay in, with water, electricity, everything. It was the manager who was paying for it. So I didn't have much problem with money. I thought that if I leave my pay with our manager, then before I collect it, it will be big money. He was a nice man, too. So I was two months without collecting my pay, and I came to Ouagadougou, and Mama Amma told me that we should travel. So I said, "OK. I will go and collect my money, and we will go together."

So when I went to Banfora, it was on the fifteenth, and the manager said I should wait till the ending of the month, then he would give me my three months' pay. That man was a very nice man. I haven't met any master like that. Look: I could work two or three weeks in the month, but he would pay me a full month. I used to just trouble him like that. I will be working today, and something will come to me that I have to go to Ouagadougou. When I go to the house, I don't sleep. I will sit down. I'm grooving and grooving and grooving. And drinking. That place, every time, the customers were buying me Heineken. When you see my table, I packed them like that. I couldn't drink all, so I used to bring some home. Sometimes before I would go home from the nightclub, maybe I would have about five or six Heinekens in my bag. I would drink up to the morning time before going to join[3] the train. I wouldn't tell anybody that I was traveling. Evening time, if they opened and I didn't come to work, they would take a motor to go and look for me in the house. It's dark. Before I would come back from Ouagadougou, it was maybe two weeks or one week. Then I would come and give the manager a *nice* story. And he would believe me. He was a nice guy. The wife was also good. If the hus-

1. really, well, a lot; generally used simply to emphasize a verb
2. short form for Bobo-Dioulasso
3. board

band wanted to be annoyed, then she would say, "No, you know this girl. She's a good girl. She works correctly." And sometimes, he also used to bring himself and say, "Ah, as for you, Hawawu,[1] even if you can work with me at all, almost, in one month, even if you make one week or two weeks, I like it."

You know, Banfora is a village. Eh? It's not big. So when I went to work there, the way these village people are, I am from the village too, so I know their life very well. You know, some of them just used to come: you will see them dirty, and you are smelling them. You don't need them. But you need them to buy the drink, isn't it? Some girls used to bluff: "Hmm! This one didn't take a bath." Oh, I would close my eyes. I don't hear anything. And my nose, too. So: *ha!* I will try to force you, and you will buy. You will buy and buy champagne, and we will drink together.

And then, there is some kind of way how I used to get the Voltaiques. They will say, "Oh, let's go home." I will say, "Look, you know, my country,[2] in Gurunsi, in my village, they don't see a woman for one day. We don't press to see a woman. We are not making quick[3] to see a man for one day, or a woman for one day. If it's true that you like me, I am not like Togolese[4] or Ghanaians who say that they come to look for their money. No. I want somebody who will respect me, because here is our country. So I can't see you today and follow you." I had many people to tell them this lie, and then be chopping them. *Ha-ha! Hee!*

You yourself, if you are Voltaique, if they tell you this, you will believe it, because you can't get a girl in the bar like this in Upper Volta, in one day like this. No. Voltaique girls, they are very strong a little bit. So if I give you this lie, you will believe me. And every time, you will think, if you are coming to entertain me well at my nightclub, maybe one day I will be happy to follow you. You will be doing that and get fed up and go away. But I will just talk these topics to you, and then that and this, so that you will be happy, and every time when you come: "Hey! Hello! Hawawu! Hawawu!"

So the girls I worked with used to be annoyed. Some of them said I made juju for people to like me, to be buying me drink. Look-o! I have juju, and I don't make people to be giving me money? I will make juju for people to buy me drink? Is this not foolishness? So they will be talking every time, *"Ho-oh."* But me, I don't care. Some girls used to say, "Eh?

1. diminutive of Hawa
2. her traditional area or her hometown or village, that is, in her culture
3. in a hurry
4. people from Togo, the country to the east of Ghana

Hawawu? If you go with your boyfriend, and this boy comes to the night-club and Hawawu says 'Good evening' to him, it's finished for you." Hey look-o! Look at the way I suffered: these girls don't know. Because of the people who buy me drink, they are annoyed.

But the village people, you know, if you know their life, you can live with them very nicely. As for me, I don't fear anything of theirs. Look, I used to serve some boys. They were fitters.[1] And you know, as they are living in the village, they get their money, and then after that, they don't care about changing their dress before coming to the nightclub. They can come to the nightclub with their fitter clothes. I don't care. I have my clean dress. If you ask me for a dance, we will dance. So every day, when these people would come to the nightclub, sometimes they would come two, sometimes they would come three, sometimes one would come: even if they didn't spend, I could get about twenty thousand from drinking with them alone. They used to chop money like that. Yeah. I would drink with them very well.

And then after all that, it was their manager who liked me. When I would get off from the work, he would go and drop me at my house with his motor, and he would give me one thousand. But I don't need to go with him, because I'm Voltaique. I'm looking for somebody who is seri-ous. If he's serious, I'm going to know. He said he's serious. Then I said, "OK, if you are serious, you will see some time."

So he was following me for about three months: he didn't get me. So he got fed up. He started falling in love with one girl, in the same nightclub. *Ha-ha!* So I said, "Eh-heh." So when he would come and this girl would go and sit there, then I would also go and sit down. He will be buying drink for me, he will be buying for the girl. *Ha-ha!* I'm not annoyed. Every time, I'm not annoyed. Sometimes, the way he used to have the girl, when we would close, he doesn't want me to know anything. And I wouldn't ask him anything, too. I didn't ask him, "This girl is your what?" or some-thing. No. He would let the friends drop the girl at his house, and then he is going to drop me. He would give me my one thousand, and then he would go and sleep with the girl.

So one day the girl came to the nightclub. They called her Ayi. She said, "Hawa — my big sister."

Then I said, *"Mm."*

She said, "True, there is something which you are doing, I'm not happy. So I'm going to tell you. You are my big sister. I shouldn't hide any-thing from you."

1. mechanics

Then I said, "What?"

She said, "Eh-h. I don't understand my boyfriend. Every time when he comes, you come and sit down there. I don't know why. And any time, when you sit down with him up to the closing time, he will send his friend to take me to his house, and then he is going to drop you before coming. Is he your — is he something for you?"

So I said, "Ah, why don't you ask the man?"

But the girl couldn't ask the man. They were three new girls who had come, this girl and two others: I brought them from Bobo to work. Then they left our nightclub and changed to another nightclub. My *patron*[1] also had to see the patron of that nightclub, because he gave the transport[2] to go to Bobo and bring them. So they had a problem. And always it was Hawa's problem: "Hey, Sister Hawa, if you were not the one who brought me here, I wouldn't see all these things."

Then I said, "Ah. What do you want me to do now? I brought you to work."

Then she said she didn't want the work again. "This time, we won't work at this town. So tell your master to let us go back to Bobo."

I said, "*Oh-ho!* You tell my manager."

So I didn't mind them. My manager was dealing with them for about two weeks. That other man from the other nightclub was a Lebanese man; he was fed up, too; so he sacked them. Then they came and begged our manager to take them back again, and our manager also refused. I told the man that if he takes them, I would leave the work. *Ha!*

So they were just at Banfora. You know, Banfora was not a big town. It was a very small village. They had only one taxi. But this time they say there are many things there. That's where they are making the sugar in Upper Volta. They have many sugar cane farms, and they are making sugar, and I think now many people are there. Maybe now they will have taxis. But before, only one. And that taxi, if you wanted to stop him, you had to run after him. If he was near to the market, if you saw him to call him, you would chase him before he would stop. You would start stopping him from here, and he would go and stand far down the road. Maybe he would stop at a drinking bar: you would be chasing him and he would run away and go inside the bar. And he didn't work in the night time. Only day time.

1. (French): owner, manager, boss; also a form of address: sir, big man, boss; *patronne:* mistress

2. money for transportation; also, a vehicle or truck

So if you were working at the nightclub, and your house was far from the nightclub, you would suffer. Our manager had a flat for the girls, with three bedrooms, with one hall, bathroom, kitchen. If he had three girls there, then if other girls came, he would look for a room for them somewhere.

So that time, Banfora was a village. But as for me, you know, when they closed La Tringle at Ouagadougou, then this woman let me promise not to work with somebody. And that time, I was feeling her work, because she was a good woman. So I always used to take it that, OK, this woman said she didn't want me to work at any nightclub in Ouagadougou, unless her place. When she closed the nightclub, those two months, sometimes when I used to meet her in town, or I would go and greet her, then she would say, "Oh, Hawa, come and take five thousand." Just like that. So I liked her. So when she said, "Don't work anyplace," I thought it was better if I go to see other places before coming back. That's why I went to Banfora, Bobo, to know the other countries, too.

When I went to Bobo, this woman had a hotel and nightclub in Bobo. I was lodging in her hotel. I didn't work. I just went for some few days like that. But Banfora, I went to work. When I was in Bobo, I went to the nightclub to have a small look, and I met the brother of the manager of the nightclub at Banfora.

When he first saw me, he said, "Can you serve me?"

Then I said, "I'm not working here. I'm a stranger."

So he said, "Oh, sorry. Sit down with me, and we will have a drink."

I sat with him, and he called the girl to come and serve us. Then he said, "Where are you from?"

Then I said, "I am from Ouagadougou."

He said, "What are you doing here?"

I said, "I just came yesterday. I just wanted to know Bobo, to see Bobo."

Then he said, "Would you like to start work here in Bobo?"

Then I said, "How I see the place, I don't think. But I will think of it. I don't know yet. Only yesterday I came, so I don't know how the town is."

Then he said, "Suppose, if you don't want here in Bobo, I have one brother who has a nightclub in Banfora. He's looking for girls. Have you done work in a nightclub before?"

Then I said, "Yes."

And he said, "Where?"

I said, "I have been in La Tringle before."

Then he said, "Oh-h." The boy had been working with this Madame in La Tringle. "But why?"

Then I said, "They closed it. Because of that, I don't want to be work-ing at other places. So if I go out of Ouagadougou to work at another place, it is not bad. The time when I hear she is open, I will go back."

Then he said, "If you want, I will telephone my brother tomorrow." The answer he would get, he would tell me. Then he wrote his office ad-dress and gave it to me, so that tomorrow I would come to his office. Then I said OK.

Their office was for the people who had the big-big trucks, the truck tractors, for the people who are making the roads or who are making the farms. He was working there. I went to the place at twelve o'clock, and he told me that he had telephoned the brother. The brother said, OK, he will come tomorrow and see me. I was in the hotel about seven-thirty the next evening when he came with the brother. The brother said that if I want to work with him, he would be happy for me to work with him, because his brother had told him that I had been working with Madame Colette. His brother had also been working for her, so he knew Madame Colette. If it was a girl who worked with Madame Colette, she would know the work proper. If you were working with Madame Colette, if you were very slow, she wouldn't like you. So he wanted me to work with him. But he wanted to ask, Madame Colette was paying me how much?

Then I said, "Well, Madame Colette started with me at twenty thou-sand, but if we drank, we had something more from the drink. This is what Madame Colette started with me."

Then he said, as for him, the place is a village. So he can't talk about giving me something from the drink. But he will give me twenty-six thou-sand for a month. He wanted me to work. Whether I drink, whether I don't drink, I will have my twenty-six thousand for the month.

So I said, "OK, but I think we can make this contract for two months."

Then he said OK. So at two months' time, then I said I wanted to go.

Then he said, "Why? Because the money is not plenty?"

Then I said, "Yes, because in Madame's place, when I go, it's twenty thousand, but before ending of the month, I know how much I can drink with people. You know? So I know how much I can get for the month. If I come and stay here, I'm wasting my time. Sometimes I will come to the work, I won't get a lift. If you are not in town, if you travel, I have to walk from my place to come to the work, and then close and walk back there. So I think it's better I go back to Ouagadougou."

So he said, "OK, don't go. I will increase your pay."

Then I said, "Then you have to say it and let me hear."

So he came to thirty thousand. Then I thought, ah, in Ouagadougou even, what I was taking, together with my drinks, I wouldn't get thirty thousand for a month. So I'm going to relax here. *Hee-he-he!* I'm going to *relax!*

So I had to go to Ouagadougou and tell my people that I was going to relax in Banfora. I got work for thirty thousand. At that time in Ouagadougou, you couldn't get nightclub work for thirty thousand for a month: "*Ah!* Who are you?"

Then this man gave me two hundred thousand to come and get girls for him. How I chopped the money! *Pfft!* Ask Mama Amma! *Ha!* We had our room. Then I said the room is hot. I dey[1] sleep for hotel: air-conditioned. All his money, I chopped it! Two hundred thousand. I got seven girls for him. And seven girls from Ouagadougou to Banfora, I think maybe first class might be three-thousand-and-something, to pay for seven people. All the rest, he didn't get balance[2] even one penny. I didn't give him. I said, "Ah, you know, these girls, when you meet them, you know? You have to talk to them, buy them a drink, try to boss them. You meet them at their business place. All the girls."

So I tried, you know? And he liked it, because all these girls were working in Ouagadougou. I went and disturbed them, and they left their work. I would just go to the nightclub. If I see you are nice, I will say, "Come and serve me." You will serve me and drink something with me in the nightclub. Then: "You know, it's business I'm going to talk to you. We have a nightclub in Banfora. You know, this time they started working the sugar factory there, and in that town there are many white people who don't get nice girls. If you go there, you will make money more than in this Ouagadougou here. As for Ouagadougou here, this town is spoiled. There are many girls. So if you want, my girlfriend, hurry up. How much do they pay you here?"

She will say, "Twelve thousand."

I'll say, "What is twelve thousand? This man can give you twenty thousand."

You will see the girl is shaking. You see? *Ha!* Just looking at me. *Koo!?*[3] I have bossed! I will say, "Look, this man." Then I will show her. I will open my bag. She will see that the money is full up![4] I will say, "Look, all this money, this man gave it to me. Why? I don't know him; he doesn't

1. (Pidgin): used by itself or with another verb to denote being or existing in a condition or activity. *I dey:* I'm here; I'm all right.

2. change

3. (Asante Twi): or *Ko,* a nickname for a "guy," short for Kofi; also used as an exclamation, like "Hey, man!" A "guy" is a person, man or woman, who is modern and who can fit in with the other young people in a place.

4. The bag is filled with money.

know me. We are not family. He trusts me. He doesn't care about money. So if you want, let's go."

So I just made this way, kalabule way,[1] then I got —*hee-hee!*— seven *nice* girls. When I took the girls there, when he saw the girls, he was happy. He didn't ask of the money. He kept one as a girlfriend, and the wife came and attacked me in my house, saying that I am from Ouagadougou, and I brought the girlfriend for the husband, that the husband doesn't come home. I said, "Eh? Is that so?" *Ha-ha!*

So he liked me on this way. When I got those girls and put them in the nightclub, I had nothing to do. I would work for two weeks, then I would spend my holidays for two weeks in Ouagadougou. They would pay me the full thirty thousand for the month. So I was in the train: Ouagadougou, Banfora, Ouagadougou, Banfora.

Sometimes I used to tell him, "Patron, you know, here they don't have food." I used to make myself that I don't know how to eat African food. So I would say, "Here, there's nothing good, so I would like to go to my shopping in Bobo."

Then he would say, OK, if that will be the case, he will give us a small fridge to put food inside, a nice one, in our house. So sometimes I would go to Bobo or sometimes I would go to Ouaga. When I was coming, I would bring cabbage, potatoes, everything, and put them in the fridge. Sometimes I used to give them to people as a gift, and when the food was getting finished, then I would say, "Hey, Patron, you know, here I can't find my food, so —"

But these things, really, I didn't eat these things I used to buy from the traveling, you know. This cabbage and other things, I used to eat them, but not much. I used to dash them to people, because if my food was finished, I would have to go and find my food. I used to chop T-Zed *fine,* but this man didn't see me with the T-Zed. And I don't know if it was my luck or his luck: any time he would come and meet me, I would be eating these things. If I was eating salad, then he would ask me, "When you are eating this kind of leaves, are you going to satisfy?"

Then I would say, "Yes, it's good."

Or sometimes he will come and meet me with *ragoût,* the stew, when you make the soup and then you cut the potatoes inside. Then I will put

1. corrupt, lying, trickish, bullshit. The term "kalabule" was current was current in the 1970s particularly with regard to the economic arrangements consistent with the black marketing, smuggling, and shortages discussed in the Introduction of *Hustling Is Not Stealing;* it could also refer to off-the-books and under-the-table dealing in the informal economy.

cabbage and some things like that, some carrots, and I used to mix them like that. So if he would come and see me, then he would say, "If you eat these things, did you used to satisfy?"

Then I would say, "Yes."

So he thought every time that this is the kind of food I used to eat, you know. But I ate fufu and other food more than he himself, but he didn't know. If I just opened the fridge and showed him that the food was finished, then he'd say, "OK, you can go and come." Sometimes, he used to be good. He'd say, "OK, I think the month is far,[1] so can I dash you small money?"

Then I'd say, "Hey, Patron, if you do that, then you will be a good man."

Maybe he would put his hand in his pocket: five thousand. The time when I brought this girl, he loved the girl. *Hey-yeh-yeah.* I chopped him! *Ha!* When I went to Ouagadougou, ten thousand; he would give me, as a gift, to go to Ouagadougou and come. Sometimes I used to boss the girl, "Let's go to Ouagadougou and see what Patron will do." If I was going with the girl, he wouldn't give the money in the girl's hand. He used to give me and say, if she gets the money, maybe she will stay in Ouagadougou, and she wouldn't come back, and that and this. I should take care of her and bring her back. So maybe thirty thousand, he would give me, and he would say I should take care of the girl. Yeah? When we get to Ouagadougou, I would tell the girl, "Let's go and find something, some dresses to buy."

Then she would say, "I haven't got money."

I would say, "OK, I'll pay for you." *Ha!* "I'll pay for you. When I go home, Patron will pay me."

You know, it's a way. *Hee-hee!* So then I would get her something. I would pay about three thousand. All the rest of the money, I would chop all. And when we went back, I would tell the man all that we have spent, and I have bought some dresses for her, about six thousand. You know? This girl didn't hear[2] French. *Ha!* And this man didn't hear English. *Ha! He-hee-he.* I was the *interpreter! Ha-ha!* When the girl tells me something to tell the man, when I see that the thing is not good, I will change it. You see? *Hee-hee-hee.* If the man tells me something to tell the girl, when I see

---

1. the end of the month. Workers are normally paid once a month, and the month has not advanced far toward the next payday, so she needs more money to reach the end of the month.

2. understand; also, speak

that what the man will tell the girl will bring a trouble, I will tell something different to the girl, too. So they were just — oh, both of them, they
liked me. The girl liked me and the man liked me. They didn't know
anything.

But then they transferred the man from Banfora to Bobo, so he sold
the nightclub to Lebanese people. Then I said, "What? Me, I no go work
for Lebanese man-o." I started my life with them, so I don't like them. I
won't work for a Lebanese man.

The Lebanese man said, "*A Yallah,*[1] I go pay you like your master is
paying you."

I said, "Yes, I don't want it." You know, there were only two nightclubs
in Banfora, and that guy was challenging our manager too much. The
time I went to Ouagadougou and brought girls, he also went to Bobo and
brought girls, that he wanted his place to be better than our place. You
see? But every time, our place, we had *many* people more than there. At
our place, we had a restaurant for food, and then we had the nightclub inside, so we used to get people more than him. The girls he used to bring,
every time they didn't keep[2] about two months, then they went back.
When he was going to bring you from Bobo, he would say, "I have rented
a house. You will live there. It is not that you are going to pay. I'm going to
pay everything. Ending of the month, I will pay you twenty thousand."

Ending of the month, maybe you won't get even ten thousand. He
will say the room is costing this — he cut that day you didn't come to
work — and that day you came to work, but you didn't wait to the closing time, and you went away. He will do all this account on you. So all
the girls he brought, in two or three months, they would go away. So he
was bossing me, "Yeah, I know you. You worked for Haruna. Haruna
likes you. He is serious with you. You are a businesswoman. I can pay
you thirty thousand."

I said, "No. I don't want it."

Then I left Banfora. The time when Mama was going to travel to
Lomé, then I told her I was going to come. That ending of the month,
my manager said that I should wait, then they will pay me for my three
months. So I waited, and he paid me for three full months before I came
back to Ouagadougou. But Mama had gone to Lomé. She left Christian,
and she had another boyfriend —Jeremy — so she had no time to waste
for me. They went to Lomé.

1. (Arabic): Oh, God.
2. stay; take (time)

: OUAGADOUGOU, KAYA :

Mama Amma and Her Two Boyfriends

Did I tell the problem of Mama when she got to Ouagadougou? She had two boyfriends: one American man and one French man. The French man was Christian. And that American man — he was Canadian — was called Jeremy.

And Jeremy: Mama liked Jeremy because she used to get grooving from Jeremy. Jeremy was Peace Corps, the Canadian one. Christian also was a Peace Corps, French Peace Corps. You know, the French people also have Peace Corps. They call them volunteers. So Christian: Mama got more money from Christian than from Jeremy. Jeremy didn't have enough to give, but if he got groove, we would have it.

You know, Christian was working at a village, so sometimes Mama used to travel with him. And when Jeremy would ask me, then I would lie to him that I had sent her to my village. *Ha-ha!* Shit! OK. That passed about two or three times, and I was lying. The fourth time, one of the girls who stayed in our house told Jeremy that I was lying. It was Woman. Yeah, that time we were staying together with Woman.

So Woman told Jeremy that Mama has a French boy, and the boy is nice to her, and she is serious with the boy. So that is why every time when she goes to this boy, I used to tell him that I have sent her to my village. So Jeremy just came one day. He had a big motor. He said, "Ay! Ay! Hawawu!"

I said, "Yes."

"Are you there?"

I said, "Yes."

"What are you cooking today?"

I said, "I have nothing to cook with, because I haven't got money."

"Hey, what about Mama?"

I said, "Mama didn't come here."

He said, "Is she still in your village?"

I said, "Yes."

Then he said, "Here, look: Hawawu, I want to tell you something. Tell me the truth. Where are you from?"

And I said, "I have told you where I am from. I come from the road of Bobo."[1]

---

1. road to Bobo

Then he said, "I have seen Mama in Kaya yesterday." You know, Kaya is not at our side;[1] it's on the other road.

And I said, "What?! Mama in Kaya?"

He said, "Yeah! I have seen her with some fucking small boy. He's Christian. They came to the bar to buy drinks. I was talking to her; she didn't mind me."

I said, "What? It's not true."

So I was serious, you know, because I didn't want this man to get the lie. And he too: somebody told him, but he was very clever to say that he had seen her by himself. So I said, "Ah, as for that one, I don't know. I know that — all I know, I sent Mama to my father to get me something. Because this time, she doesn't want to work. I have been going to work, so I don't have time to go and get it. That's why I sent Mama."

Then he said, "Look, I know you love Mama. If you were a man, I think maybe you would make love with Mama, or you would marry her. But try and tell me the truth. Mama has a boyfriend, a French boy, OK? Right?" *Ha-ha!*

I said, "I don't know."

He said, "No! Say 'Right!'"

Then I said, "How can I say 'Right?' You cannot force me to say 'Right' because I don't know anything about it."

He said, "No. The first time Mama went to this boy to stay one week, you told me she went to your village. The second, two weeks. And this is the third. And still, she's going to your village? And what problem do you have at your village, and you won't go to see it for yourself? But you are sending Mama like that?"

I said, "Oh, but Mama is — I just take her like a small sister to me. So anything which I have to do, if I can't, Mama can do it."

Then he said, "No. You know, Woman has told me that Mama has a French boyfriend. And Mama went to him at Kaya. I haven't been to Kaya, but Woman told me, and I believe what Woman said."

Then I said, "OK, if you believe Woman more than me, then go there and ask her. Don't talk to me again."

So OK, then we had this problem and finished, and then this man went away. It was not quite thirty minutes when Mama came with Christian.

Then I thought Jeremy had gone, so I told Mama, "Ah, Jeremy has just left here. It is not quite thirty minutes. But he was telling me that Woman told him about your travels and all. So I had to be a liar to Jeremy now. So

1. near us, in our direction

I am ashamed even to talk to Jeremy. I have talked to him. He couldn't wait, so he went out."

Do you know: I think when they are coming, Jeremy saw them in the car, and he went and stopped at some place to take his Coca and come back to the house. He came and met Mama and Christian. He called Christian, "Christopoo." When he came, he said, "Mama, welcome! How are people in Kaya?"

Then Mama said, "They are all right."

Then he said to me, "You see? You said she was in your village, but she was in Kaya." *Ha-ha!*

So that day, I was *very shamed!* I couldn't say a word, you know, because things like this used to make me ashamed. *Ha-ha!* Then he said, "Mama, can we go and have one beer?"

And Christian said, "Mama, *faut acheter les bières.*" Jeremy wanted to go out with Mama to take one beer, and Christian also said, "Mama, go and buy the beer so that we all drink, because you have come and met your sisters."

OK. Then I was telling Mama in Ashanti, I said, "Take the money of Christian and go and buy the beer. If you think this Jeremy is a good man, he just asked you, 'Mama, let's go and take something.' But he knows that we all can drink. So get the money from Christian and go and buy the beer."

So she got the money from Christian and then she went and brought six bottles of beer. There was one girl with us, called Natalie. We gave one bottle to Jeremy, and one bottle to Christian, and other ones were for us.

You know, at Kaya, Christian was doing agricultural work there. When he was coming to the town, he used to bring many potatoes, big onions, and all these things. So when he and Mama came, they brought these things, and he started to get them from the car. Then Jeremy was sitting and said, "Look, Mama. So because of this food"—*ha-ha!*—"because of this food you are always with Christian? Yeah, he is a good farmer. I cannot farm, but I can eat all that he has." *Ha-ha!*

Then Jeremy said, "You know, Mama, I don't know why. I don't used to follow girls. I just follow you because I like your way. You know, I don't have much money to give you, but I think to be happy, you know, is better than to follow money."

So Mama was annoyed. And Mama said, *"Tsk."* Then she said in Ashanti, "If this man doesn't go away, I will fuck him off right now."

You see, Christian also was speaking a little bit of English. And you know, Christian was afraid of Jeremy, because Jeremy was big and tall, but Christian was a short man. He was not fat. He was a very short man, but he was very smart[1] when he was working. You would never see Christian sit down for five minutes. Never. But if Jeremy came to our place and met Christian, Christian would go to bed *straight*. He would fall down sick. He didn't want to say a word. *Ha-ha!* And Jeremy also knew it. Jeremy knew that Christian was afraid of him.

But Mama spoiled herself. Now Christian has finished his work; he has gone. But Christian was ready to go with Mama to France. From France, they would go and work in America. He wanted to work in America. He was good at acting, and he could draw a picture just like that. He said he was going to do that job in America, and that when he finishes his work, he's going with Mama.

That was the time when he gave money to Mama to go to Ghana and make her passport.[2] And Mama also—Mama is another fucking girl, eh? At that time, I didn't know what Mama did, but now she has told me what she had done, the way she spent the money. She told Jeremy. Jeremy was about to go to Lomé and Ghana. So Christian was going to take Mama to Bolgatanga with his car. So Mama told Jeremy the day she was going to leave Ouagadougou, and then Jeremy went and waited for Mama in Ghana. When Christian dropped her in Bolga,[3] she took transport to meet Jeremy in Tamale.[4] Then they went together to Lomé. So Jeremy was with Mama. She was doing all their cooking and everything. She was telling Jeremy she was just seeing this boy, Christian. He is a foolish boy—he has money, but he doesn't know how to spend it, so Jeremy shouldn't be jealous, and that and this. And then the money Christian gave her to make her passport, she spent the *whole* money in Lomé.

You know what made her tell all this to me? Limata had an American man as a friend, and one day we were in the house, sitting with him, and Mama came, and Limata greeted her. Then the man said, "Ah, is this the Mama from Jeremy?"

Then we said, "What Jeremy?"

He said, "A Canadian—he was a Peace Corps here." By that time, Jeremy had gone to Canada.

Then we said, "Yes."

He said, "I wanted to talk to her, because the man was telling me about her every day, but I didn't know her."

---

1. fast, quick; fast-moving, on top of things; also, hip
2. get her passport
3. short name for Bolgatanga
4. (pronounced Tah'-mah-lee): major town in northern Ghana

Then he was talking to Mama, and Mama asked him, when he went to his country, did he meet Jeremy? Then he said he had met one of the friends of Jeremy. He said Jeremy was getting married.

So it *hurt* Mama! She said, "Jeremy! God should *punish* him! If I did not suffer with Christian before I got that money which we ate together, then I will believe. But if I suffered — I was suffering with Christian in that village. Kaya. I followed him to the garden. I followed him to the farm to look at his things, before I got that money. Then we spent it together, and Jeremy lied to me and went even without writing."

You know, she said Jeremy had told her that she shouldn't mind about the money that Christian gave her to make a passport. If he goes back to America, he would send her money, and then she could make a passport. Then he would send her a ticket. And she was *sure* of Jeremy, that Jeremy would take her, so she didn't mind Christian. So when she spent the money finish,[1] then Jeremy also went away: no letter, no anything. She was waiting in Ghana, suffering. She didn't have anything. So she had to come back to Ouagadougou. When she came back to Ouagadougou, Christian also was preparing to go, because he had finished his work. Sometimes if Christian came to Ouagadougou, he used to come to me to ask of Mama. And I used to boss him every time.

So the day when Mama came, I was happy. Then when Mama had made three days in Ouagadougou, we went to see Christian. We took a car,[2] and we reached Kaya about seven or half-past seven in the evening. We met Christian with two friends, together with one African girl. So they were three whites at the table, eating. That girl, it was Christian who went to Côte d'Ivoire and brought her from Abidjan.

So when we reached there, *hey!* That day Mama cried there. Oh! She cried like a baby. I went to sleep. Mama didn't want me to sleep. "Boohoo. Boo-hoo."

"Ah! Mama, why?"

She said, "No, nothing pains me, but that I have brought you here and we didn't get a good place to sleep."

Then I said, "No, if it's for me, don't cry. I'm all right." *Ha-ha!* "I'm all right the place I am."

You know, these fucking people. The French people. I don't know how they think. OK: you know this girl doesn't know anybody in this town.

---

1. and finished all of it. The word "finish" at the end of a phrase signifies the conclusion of the action.

2. transport; a taxi or minibus

Because of you she has come. OK: you have a new girlfriend with you. OK? But you can let the new girlfriend to understand that, "Well, anyway, this cannot spoil our chance. She was my girlfriend. She traveled; she didn't come back. That's why I have you here. But as they have come, I can't send them away in the night, because they can't get any car. So we will give them a good place to sleep."

This man didn't do so. He just said to me, "Hawa, you know, if you people wouldn't mind, I have this camp bed." He had that type of canvas bed, one. Then he was telling me, "Eh, if you wouldn't mind." So as for Mama, he thinks she wouldn't mind. When Mama was here, she used to take the mat outside and sleep and take the breeze. So I can have this camp bed, and the Mama will put the mat in the sitting room because they haven't got many bedrooms. They have only two bedrooms. And there are two white people who live in that flat. The other man will take the other bedroom, and he is with the girl in the other bedroom. So he can't give us a place in his room, but we can sleep in the sitting room.

So: whew! I didn't say anything. Then I said, "OK, can we get some cold beer here to drink?"

He said, "Anyway, we haven't got cold beer, but in the bar we can get some."

So I gave Mama one thousand to buy beer. We bought our own beer. And then this boy came and drank some. It pained me! Ha-ha! We bought the beer, and then we sat down there, and they were eating, and we were carrying on with our beer. Then he got up from the table and brought his glass, and just pulled one bottle and poured some of the beer into his glass, and started talking to me, you know. And I also was answering him. But I was annoyed.

Then I said, "Well, as for me, even outside here, I can sleep on this chair where I'm sitting. I can be sitting here or I can sleep on this chair, up to the morning time, the time I will get a car to go."

Then the other man with them was a doctor at Kaya. So this man was seeing that the way I was talking, maybe I was not happy, or I was thinking of something. Then he said, "Oh, never mind. I have — my wife will come, but she hasn't come yet. I just have my flat — four bedrooms — so I can spare one to you people to sleep inside."

So they took us in the car and dropped us at that man's place to sleep. That was the place where Mama was crying for the whole night. And morning time, five o'clock, I got up and then I woke Mama. Then we took our bath. About five-thirty, this man came. He called us to take tea. We went and drank the tea with him.

About six, he took us to Christian's place, and Christian said, OK, that they used to pay them on the fifteenth, these French volunteers, so now they haven't got anything, but he can give us five thousand to make our transport, and that and this.

Then I said, "No, thank you very much. We have our transport. We just came to see how you are. If you are all right, there's no problem."

"Oh, no, if you refuse that money, it means that you are annoyed."

I said, "*Mais non.*[1] I can't be annoyed with you. I'm not Mama. If — suppose you were my boyfriend, I would know what to tell you. But I'm not — I just know you. You are nothing for me. If Mama cannot be annoyed, I can't be annoyed. So you just ask Mama to forgive you. It's not me. I'm not annoyed with you. But I don't want the five thousand. And I have transport from here to Ouagadougou."

So he called Mama and talked to her too. I don't know what he told her. And then we left. We took transport and came to Ouagadougou. And Mama: hey, Mama wasn't happy. So we were in Ouagadougou. And Christian said that he would come to Ouagadougou in three days, and he would come and pass at our place. Three days' time, we didn't see him. About one week's time, he came with the girl. He wanted to take the girl to France because Mama was not serious, so he was taking the girl to Abidjan to get her passport. So they passed at our place. Christian didn't drop down from the car. He told the girl to drop and come and see whether we were in the house. So the girl came. Then we were there. Then he told us that they would go to Côte d'Ivoire tomorrow, but evening time they would come and see us. Evening time they didn't come. The next day they were going to Abidjan, so we didn't see them. When they went to Abidjan, Christian came back alone.

Mm-hm. They went to Abidjan, and this girl also had a boyfriend, an Englishman. So first when Christian had just come from Ouagadougou, maybe he showed the girl some small respect or some small money. The girl thought she would get it every day, so she left that man in Abidjan to follow Christian. Then she came and suffered a little bit in the village. So when they went back to Abidjan, they took a hotel, and they were in the hotel. She knew the country. And Christian, too, in day time, he used to go to the friends and go around. And this girl just left Christian. One day Christian went out, and she took Christian's suitcase, a nice suitcase which he had brought from France. Uh-huh. She got that suitcase and

1. (French): Not at all.

packed everything of hers inside. And Christian was having forty-three
thousand, and he said when he went out that day, he took eight thousand.
So the amount that was left was thirty-five thousand. The girl collected
that thirty-five thousand and the suitcase. Then she went away. And
Christian too didn't know her house. He had just seen her in the night
time. They were friends; they were nice with one another. Then they
came together and stayed about two months in Upper Volta. Then they
went back. The girl didn't show him her house; she didn't show him her
family. She said, "My family is living in village." So the girl just got lost
like that. And Christian came back alone. Then the day when he came
back, he came to where we were working. That time we were working at
Triomphe.

There was one girl who was also working there. She was called Lydia.
When Lydia saw Christian, she saw a white man, *ko-ko-ko-ko*. And Mama's
heart was beating! You know, I saw Christian come and greet me at the
counter, then I said, I'm coming. Then Lydia went quickly and served
Christian. So I told Mama to go and sit with Christian. Then Mama said,
no, when Christian came, he didn't greet her, so she wouldn't go and sit
there. You know, she liked the man. I think she liked the man, or something like that. But every time, she wanted to bluff: she wanted the man
to come forward. But the man didn't want to come forward. And it used
to pain Mama. So Mama was bluffing. Then this man took that girl away,
Lydia.

Then Mama came to me: "You see! You see! I will show Lydia. For me,
I'm not a bad girl. But this girl alone, I will show her. I told her that Christian is my boyfriend. Did you see? Did you see she has gone with—"

Then I said, "We didn't close yet. How can she go?"

She said, "She has gone!"

And true, when I looked for the girl, her bag was not there. I knew she
had gone. So the next day, I went to Lydia's house straight. And I told her,
"This white man you followed yesterday is for Mama. Apart from today, I
don't want to see you with the man."

"Ah-h, but the man himself, he said he was going to Kaya today. He
said if I want, we can go to there."

Then I said, "OK, then pack your things and follow him. But we won't
work together."

So when I came home, I said, "Mama, I went and saw Lydia. This is
what Christian told her," and that and this.

Yeah, so I sacked that girl from the nightclub. Oh, yeah, as for me,
every nightclub I have worked, there is this thing. Everywhere I work, we

have many Ghana girls, or Togolese. OK? Sometimes I will meet the girls there, and *all,* they will sack all of them, and they will leave me alone. They will start bringing new girls. And those new girls, I will be the director for all of them. Anything you say, anything you do, even if you don't do something bad, I can go and lie to the manager that this girl is that and this. They will sack her. This is how I do my work. *Ha-ha!* Every nightclub I go, I have to be the champion, you know. Because there are some girls, sometimes they used to talk foolishness. Some people make trouble with the clients, and all this. And there are some — especially Ghanaian girls — I used to get them like porridge, you know, *koko?*[1] She's talking English, and it's *ta-ta-ta-ta,* and they will call me: Who is speaking English and French? So at that place, I will get my chance, you know. Then I will become an interpreter. And sometimes, if I don't like you too much, what you say, I wouldn't say the same thing to the manager. So you won't come to work tomorrow. *Ha-ha!*

So from Lydia's place, I came and told Mama. Mama should wait. If Christian comes to the nightclub, if this girl follows him again, then this girl won't work there again. That night, Christian didn't come, and the girl also don't come to work.

Then I said, "Fine!"

Do you know? Christian had gone alone that day. But I didn't know. When I didn't see the girl at our work and Christian also didn't come there, I was sure that the girl had followed Christian. Maybe they went out somewhere. So that was why she didn't come for work. Then I asked the manager, "Why? Is it that some girls are working, or we all are working. If some people want to ask permission, you tell the people to wait up to the closing time. And you allow the other girls to go, without it being time to close. What's that mean?"

Then he said, "Which girl went?"

Then I said, "Lydia. Yesterday, when Lydia went out from here, it was not yet twelve o'clock. And even today, she didn't come to work. So who is going to work for her? If all of us do that, is it good?"

You know, the time when Lydia went with that white man, the manager didn't know anything about it. So when I told him, this man took it seriously. The next day, Lydia came. They paid her off in an envelope, that she had to stop her work. So: *ha-ha!* They sacked Lydia. And we didn't get Christian. OK?

1. get them easily, get them cheaply. Porridge (Hausa: *koko*) is an inexpensive and commonly sold roadside food in the mornings.

Yeah, Lydia was funny. She used to call me a Japanese woman.[1] If she saw me, "Hey! Japanese!" Then I would say, "Shut up! With your big mouth!" *Ha!*

So then it was about three to four weeks' time, and Christian came back to Ouagadougou again. He came to the nightclub again. When he came, then Mama came to me. "Hey, Hawa! Hawa, Christian has come."

Then I said, "Did you say hello to him?"

She said, "No."

"*Why?!* Go and say hello to him."

She said, "No."

Then, "OK, wait. Come and stand at my place in the counter. I will go to say hello to him." So Mama came to my place, and I went to Christian.

Then he asked me, what am I going to drink. If I work in the night-club, I used to drink champagne. So: "I will drink champagne."

Then he said, "OK, go and get your cup."

So I took one glass of champagne. And Christian took one beer. Then I said, "Christian, what did you do that day?"

He said, "No, the time when I came back to Kaya, you know, and then, when I came here, I came to greet you at counter. You didn't come to me. I was afraid that if you saw me, you would abuse me, you know, or something like that."

Then I said, "What kind of abusing you? You are not my baby. If you don't love my sister anymore, that's not any of my business."

"No, it's not that I don't love her. That's why I came, you know. It's just left with about two weeks, and I'm going away, so I think that what I have done to her is not nice. That's why I have come to apologize. And, you know, the day when you people came there, I know I didn't do anything good. But after, this girl deceived me. I took her to her place to get a passport. She stole my valise with my thirty-five thousand and went away. I don't know where she's living. So I'm coming to see if Mama can make a passport, then we can have our understanding, because I have sent all the photos of Mama to my mother."

You know, he took a colored picture of Mama, too. When he washed it,[2] he sent it to the mother, and the mother sent it to him. So: "This photo I took of Mama, my mother has sent it back, that she has seen it. And now this girl has also disappointed me. If I go, it's a very big shame for me. That's why I'm coming to see you. I know that, as for Mama, she hasn't

1. because of her light color and the shape of her eyes. The word is used to refer to any Oriental person, including Chinese.
2. developed and printed the photo

got much experience.[1] But as for you, you have experience. So I think if I see you, maybe you will talk to her, and she will get understanding."

And I said, "OK, if that will be the case, you will wait for us until we close."

"Oh." Then he said, "Ah! I have some groove in my car." He used to do this thing himself in the village. He used to get the seeds from me and plant it.

So OK: it was not yet closing time. Then I went and told Mama, "Christian is waiting for you at closing time. Go and sit with him."

"*Tsk!*" she said. "Oh, *medea gyaa no!*" You know, Mama used to like bluffing. *Ha-ha!* She liked bluffing. "*Medea gyaa no! Sesɛe na w'a ba!*"[2]

Then I said, "Oh, Mama, you go and sit down with him. Just go and sit down with him. At closing time, we will get him to the house. I know how I will talk to him."

So Mama got up and went and sat down there. And he asked her what she would drink: beer, beer, beer. That day, Mama drank six Heinekens — six. Six thousand. The man paid it. Then we went home. The next day, they were nice. The second day. Then the third day they went together to Kaya, and the man packed all that he didn't need to take to his country, to give to Mama. And Mama thought she would get money again from him like the first time, you know. He asked her: can she make her passport? And she said, "Yes, if you give me money, I can make a passport."

So this man said, "OK, if that will be the case, I will go home and send you your money to go and make a passport. Then I will send you the ticket."

Then this man also went away: no letter, nothing. We wrote him two times. *No* reply. *Ha-ha!* Then one of his friends told me that this man is working in Abidjan now. He came back to Abidjan. He doesn't want Mama to know where he is. So he didn't give any reply. Maybe he has made another girlfriend there. Maybe. And then, you know, I asked the friend that, will he give me Christian's address from Côte d'Ivoire? He said no. I said, "Why? I just want to write him.[3] We are friends."

He said, "No, the man said he doesn't want Mama to know where he is."

So he just ended it like that. And Mama lost her chance.

So the time when this American man was trying to talk about how Jeremy had made a wedding, then Mama said, "Yeah, this is the Jeremy who

---

1. sense; also, ideas, intelligence, wisdom
2. (Asante Twi): "Don't mind him! It's now that he has come!" Mama is saying to leave him alone, because it's only after all that happened that he is thinking of her.
3. communicate by mail. She would dictate, and someone would write it.

let me lose my hope, you know. If it's not so, suppose I made my passport in Ghana, and came back, maybe by this time I'm in somewhere. Even if I'm not in Europe, maybe I'm not in Ouagadougou here."

So every time if things come to Mama like this, it's: "Jeremy: God will *punish* him! God will punish Jeremy! And the way I suffered with Christian and got this money and we ate it together. Jeremy bossed me for him to eat this money with me in Lomé. And then when he goes to his country, even to write a letter to say, 'How are you?' No."

And the time Mama was in Lomé, it is very funny. They finished this money. And Jeremy came back to Ouagadougou. OK? And you know that this French man is waiting for you. Just write him: "OK, I have some difficulty in Lomé, so I have spent my money. So send me money to come."

Mama didn't do that. She wrote to Jeremy. And that was the time when I also came from Côte d'Ivoire. I had some Canadian dollars. Then I asked Jeremy to change them for me. So Jeremy said, "Didn't you get a letter from Mama?"

Then I said, "No, I just came back about three days ago."

He said, "I have a letter from her. She wants me to send her money to come. But Mama, she doesn't know. If she wants the money, she knows that fucking French boy is rich. He has money. Why doesn't she write a letter to him to send her money? So, if you wouldn't mind, I can use your dollars to change and send it to her. If she comes, I will take the money and give it to you."

Then I said, "What?! What do you mean? To take my dollars and send to Mama? If Mama comes, then you will boss her and get the money from her to give me? Then what about — do you think I can't send her money too?"

"No, because she didn't write to you," and that and this.

I said, "No. My dollars are not moving. Even the thing I am going to do with it, it is not sufficient: it wouldn't reach. So I can't send Mama money."

"But can I write Mama to write a letter to Christian to collect the money?"

Then I said, "Yes. Why don't you write to her back, that 'Mama, I have nothing. You have to send for that your stupid man to send you the money.'"

Then he said, "What do you mean to say, 'stupid man'?"

Then I said, "Yes! You take him as a stupid man, isn't it? If you don't take somebody as a stupid man — he has given money to the girl. You can go and eat with her. You people finished the money. And you say that she should write to that fellow to give her money again. So he is stupid."

He said, no, when I'm saying this, it means that I'm going to be abusing him, because we had some problem a long time ago, but I shouldn't take that seriously, to be talking this.

And then I said, "Hey! If you can't change my dollars, you give them back to me. You are not the only Canadian man here. I know many of them, but I just asking if you can change it. This is not a problem."

So he said OK, he would go and ask one of the friends tomorrow and change it for me. Before I got my money, he took my dollars for *four* days! I was boiled up! *Ha-ha! Agh!!* When I thought, I said, "*Ah!* Ah, this man wants to what? This man wants to take this money like that or what? Or does he think he's what?"

So every time he used to go to Cabane Bambou to drink. Every day I would go there, and he didn't come. He had one *ugly* girlfriend. If you saw the girl, *whew!* Some —*ha-ha!* I don't know what. She may be American, or Canadian, or what. But she could also speak slang like that. But the girl was very, very, very *ugly!* I haven't seen it before. She was straight like this. She hadn't got any waist;[1] she was very *slim,* you know. And her shape — she didn't have anything. If you see her coming, especially when she is wearing a full dress — ha-ha — you will say that this is — some kind of toys which they used to put in Africa. We used to have this kind of toy. They put thread on it. They used to make them dance. *Ha-ha!* So when she was coming to Cabane Bambou, then all the people who knew this man, you know, all the girls, you will see that one will say, "Hey, Jeremy is bringing this ghost." Then one will say, "Yeah, you know, they say the ghosts used to be *tall.*" *Ha-ha!* So everybody would start looking there. Jeremy. *Ha!*

You know, how Mama was feeling, I think Mama liked Jeremy more than Christian. She liked Jeremy because of grooving. But Christian: the way she liked Christian was because Christian was cheap for her. When she asked him for money, he would give her. She used to go to the village with Christian. Maybe sometimes one month, or three or four weeks before they would come back to the town. In two or three days, they would go to the bush.[2] She always used to do that. So I think maybe she also liked Christian in some way.

I think Christian was good for her, you know. Why Christian was good for her was because he used to be afraid of Mama. Mama used to shout on him like a child. Yeah. Then this boy would just get up and do what Mama said. He had *a lot* of hair on all his body. He had a beard before Mama

1. hips and lower back
2. in this context, the village; *bush:* any wild, uncultivated, or uncivilized area

knew him. And Mama said, "I don't want to see this tomorrow." So he cut all. *Ha-ha!* So he was very funny boy. Once, this boy took his bath and came back, and Mama asked him, did he bathe with a sponge?[1] You know, if he was somebody, he would say, "Yes, I bathed with sponge." But he wanted the truth every time. So Mama said, "How many minutes did you spend in the bathroom?"

Then he said, "It's five minutes."

Then Mama said, "So you mean that in five minutes you bathed with sponge?"

Then the boy said, "Oh, but I have bathed this afternoon about four o'-clock, so I don't need to bathe with a sponge. I just bathed with soap."

Then Mama said, "Go quick and do it and let me see!"

And this boy just got up and took a bucket and fetched the water. We haven't got a shower at our place. Then he went to the bathroom and started bathing with the sponge.

And I said, quietly, "What?! Hey, Mama, why?"

Then she said, "Oh, no, Hawa, I respect you. I don't want that. If I have a problem with Christian, you should shut up, because, you know, he used to sweat by heart,[2] so if he doesn't bathe with sponge, it's not good. Let him go and take his bath." Yeah! This man just got up quickly to the bathroom and took his bath nicely. And then he came to ask Mama, that she should smell him and see whether he didn't take a good bath.

But Jeremy, Mama couldn't do that! *Hey!* Jeremy. He will shout on Mama and Mama will start shaking! *Ha!* But this boy, Christian, she got him cheap. So that's the way she liked the boy, you know. Any time, anything she said that he should do, he would do that. Even to go out, if this boy asked, "Mama, where should we go today?" Mama will choose the place. If Mama said, "We won't got out," they won't go out. You see? That's why Mama liked that boy so much.

But she used to treat him badly. Sometimes Christian would come home with Mama. Mama would leave Christian at my place, and then she would tell him that she was going to my big sister's house, and so he should go home and come for her at some time. Then maybe she wouldn't come early. Sometimes Christian would wait for Mama, and Mama

---

1. a round ball of dried grasses used to scrub the body, like a washcloth. In houses without running water, the "bathroom" does not have a toilet but is rather an enclosed area with a place for water to run outside the house. One bathes from a bucket, using a smaller container to wet oneself, then soaping oneself with the sponge, then rinsing oneself with the remaining water.

2. for no reason; also, senselessly, roughly, carelessly, without sense of purpose

wouldn't come, and Christian would go home and sleep. Morning time Christian would come and meet Mama in the house. I would have to lie and say, "Ah, when they came I was asleep, so I didn't have time to tell Mama that you have come here, that you have told her to come home. So the fault is from me, so you should just forget about it." Ah! Yeah, I used to suffer with my friends.

You know, Mama, if you see her, you will think she is young. She is very slim and all this, like a young girl. But Mama, her age never comes on. She doesn't want to tell me her age. You know, when we were in Lomé, she told me that she is twenty-two. OK, when we came to Ouagadougou, to go and make a carte d'identité, she said she's twenty-two again. Yeah, every day she's twenty-two, huh? She never came up.[1] So if she has to get a new carte d'identité, she has the old one but she will say it's lost. Then she will call the other age. And they put twenty-two. So every day it's twenty-two. She never comes up from twenty-two. *Ha-ha!* Mama is still there in Ouagadougou. She's working at Zé Bon now.

Limata and Her Old Man

And you know, I had a problem with Limata and her husband, too. Limata, my girlfriend. You know, she had an *ol-l-d* boyfriend. But first time, she knew somebody from Zé Bon, and then that man went to his country. The man said they were making films. Every year, or every two years, they would come to Ouagadougou. So the time he left, then Limata found the old man.

Then this man who was making the films came back to Ouagadougou, and he went and asked at Zé Bon, and they told him if he goes to La Tringle, he will see one of the girlfriends of Limata who will direct him to Limata. At that time, I was working at La Tringle. When they came, they were three. They asked for Limata, and I said, "Well, Limata used to come here, but she hasn't come yet, so you can wait." They waited up to half-past twelve in the night. Then they said if she comes, I should tell her where they could meet her tomorrow. So I said, "OK, if that will be the case, you should come to Oubri,[2] Hôtel Oubri, at six o'clock. I am going to bring Limata there."

The next day I went to Limata's house and told her that this man had come. Then Limata came to my place. At that time I was living near to

1. got older
2. small hotel in Ouagadougou

Oubri. So we went together at six o'clock to Oubri. This man had bought some things to give to Limata. OK? So Limata also told him her problem, "Anyway, since you left, you know, I have a man. He is the one who takes care of me, doing everything, paying my room and everything. So this time I am not free like the first time."

Then the man said he would like to invite us to go and eat. So Limata gave him another day, for him to meet her the next day at Oubri about seven. OK?

The next day I went to Limata's house, and then the old man came. So Limata had made a way with the old man, but she didn't tell me where. She just took the old man inside and talked to him. Then when they came out from the room, the old man told me, "OK, I am wishing you a long life." But I didn't understand why he said he was wishing me a long life. Do you know that Limata lied to the old man that I was having — my birthday party! So I have invited her. So if the old man can excuse her for today — ha-ha! The old man just came out and said, "Long life!" Ha-ha! "And Happy Christmas to you!" Hee-hee-hee-hee!

So I also answered, but I didn't know anything inside it. Then the old man dropped us at my place. That time was about six-thirty. And these people were going to come at seven. So when the old man went away, then I said to Limata, "Hey, the old man said 'Long life' to me. What does that mean?"

She said, "Ah-h, I told him that you are having your birthday party, so you have invited me."

So these people came to Oubri about seven o'clock. I was taking my bath, and Limata went and saw them. They were four, three men with one woman, one white woman. Then Limata came and told me. I finished my bath, I got on my dress, and we went there. So these people invited us to go and eat someplace.

We came out from Oubri to get a taxi: *voilà,*[1] the old man! The old man met us on the road. We were two African girls with four whites. The fourth one was a woman, so we were three women, three men. So when we saw the old man's car, I said, "Hey, Limata, today your luck is not good. Go and see the old man."

When she went to the old man, he said, "No, no, no, no, no. You can go. I know that those white people — No, no, no, no. In Ouagadougou there are many whites. So you can go and search for another one. I know that I am old. You have got the young ones, so you can go with them. It is finished."

---

1. (French): there! In this context: There he was, the old man!

So the old man just pissed off like that with his car and he was gone. And as we had met the old man and Limata went to the car, then the other man also lost hope, because he was with two friends and one woman. So he was feeling shy. Then Limata came back and told the man, "Yeah, that was my man, one I was talking about. Even because of you, when he saw us walking, he said it's finished between us, and he wouldn't come back to me. Don't mind him. Let's go."

But in that place, the other man also had a shock. You know, when he saw the old man and how the old man went away, he didn't feel happy. You see? Limata told him that the old man said it was finished between him and Limata, so she should go with this man. And this man also knew that he was not staying in Ouagadougou to work. He had just come for a few days. So he wasn't happy. When we went to the place to eat, we ate and finished, and then he told Limata that he is not going to stay here, to say that he can take care of Limata, and he doesn't want anything of Limata's spoiled because of him. So Limata should go home, to go to her old man and beg the man.

So Limata said, "No, leave him. I won't go anywhere."

Then the man said, "If that will be the case, I am going to sleep, too."

So they came and dropped me and Limata at La Tringle. I was working at La Tringle, and I had to come to work.

The next day we were waiting for this old man. He didn't come. The second day, he didn't come. Hey? So the old man was serious? The fifth day, the old man came there with an African man. The African man was his friend, and he had rented a room in that man's house to Limata. So the old man went and told this African man that he didn't like Limata again, so the man should come and take the balance of his rent money from Limata and sack Limata from the house. OK?

And that time, Limata didn't have any money with her, so Limata told him tomorrow. And the next day, Limata didn't find money. Then I said, "Look, all this is a problem. OK, *camarade,* if that will be the case, how much is the cost?"

"It's thousand five hundred."

"OK, take the thousand five hundred and go and pay the man, and go and bring your things here. We have a big flat, so you can take one room." At our place, Mama had one bedroom, and I took one room. So Limata went and packed her things and came. And Limata wrote a letter to the old man that, suppose, if she's dead, the man shouldn't cry, because he knows that he is the one who is killing her. OK?

So when this man got that letter, he came back to the house to say, "I'm not killing you." She is killing herself, because she has got young ones, and he's an old man. So it's finished. He wouldn't mind anything. People have been telling him that Ghanaian girls are not good. He didn't mind them. He also tried it, and he's sorry. Even if he were somebody who understands much, he wouldn't be with African girls again, because he has already got one at his house, and she is also troubling him—he had a Malian: the girl came from Mali, and he had one baby with the girl—so if he's somebody who understands much, he wouldn't follow African girls again. So it's finished.

So then I wanted to talk to the man, and he said, "Shut up! Don't talk to me. You said you are having your birthday party. Then you bring your boyfriends, and they are friends to serve Limata, too. You people can take Limata. I dash her to you people. Yes." *Ha-ha! Hey!* He is dashing Limata to me.

Then I said, "OK. It's good. I wish that Limata's mother, too, will tell me this, you know. As you are the boyfriend, you are telling me you are dashing Limata to me. If suppose the mother was saying this to me, I would be happy."

Then he said, "What do you mean?"

I said, "Yes. Because if somebody will dash a child, or you dash a person—you know, it's your mother or the father who can take you and dash somebody. But as for a friend, a boyfriend and a girlfriend, to take her and dash me, I don't see any profit in it. So I wish, suppose you can write to Limata's mother to dash me Limata: I will like it." *Ha!*

So then he told me, "Eh, every time, you used to bluff me. You used to talk topics. You think you know more than everybody. If it's not that Limata is foolish, I think Limata has more sense then you."

Then I said, "I haven't got sense. Don't you see how I am? Don't you see how I am big and tall?[1] The sense I haven't got: that's why I am like that. I'm so stupid. But to dash me Limata? It's better you write to the family to dash Limata to me. I don't want your dash. If you want to dash me a person, bring your fucking baby from the house and dash me!"

Then he said, "Which fucking baby?"

I said, "That baby, your black-and-white." *Ha-ha!* "Your black-and-white."

So he got annoyed and went out and went his way. Then you know, Limata was blaming me that I made the old man get annoyed and go away. *Look-o!* She took two or three weeks: she didn't talk to me in the house. But she was talking to Mama, "Eh, suppose when the old man

---

1. She is short, so she is being sarcastic.

came, suppose Hawa had made jokes with the old man, then maybe the old man would be all right — but then she started to tell the old man foolish things — so the old man is annoyed with me — so now, Hawa has put me into a problem — I have a room for five thousand — who will pay for it?" And this and that. So she was telling Mama, and Mama was telling me.

So then I called Limata. I said, "OK, *camarade,* you know, I can't pay for your room, because I can't pay for my own. But if you like, the old man said he is leaving you. If I were you, I wouldn't wait for some man to tell me, 'Leave your work and stay with me.' OK? I am staying with you: if a small problem comes — eh? — you cannot leave me like that. You bring my landlord to come and ask me for his money? It's not a correct way. So if you like, you can take this old man to the gendarmerie. He will come and pay you some amount. He's the one who let you to leave your work at the nightclub. You stayed with him for one year and some three or four months. And then a small thing happens like that, one day, and then he tells you to piss off. It's not correct. You can take him to the gendarmerie. Or if you don't want that way, too, let's go and work. At our place, if I ask my Madame to take you today, then today she will take you."

So when I told this to Limata, then Limata said, OK, if that will be the case, she really won't take the man to gendarmerie. She will leave him for God. She wants the work. But she said that one time she came to our place, and the manager asked her to work, and she said no, her husband didn't want her to work. So if I take her to the work now, there is shame in it a little bit.

Then I said, "Oh, this woman is not so." So that day, when I brought Limata to the nightclub, the woman didn't come that day. And the brother told me that the woman had traveled to Bobo. So I said, "OK, this is my girlfriend. She wants to work."

Then he said, "OK, she can start work. When my sister comes, I will tell her."

So Limata came to our place and we were working together. *Mm-m?*

Then one day the old man came to our house and told Limata that he was going on leave. He would be going in three days, on Monday, but Sunday afternoon he would come and say bye-bye to Limata. So Limata was happy a little bit. On Sunday we didn't see this man. On Monday, he went away like that. OK. So what do we do? We were working.

Then one day we were in the workplace when this man sent a card. He didn't know Limata's address, but he knew that I was working in La Tringle, so he sent it in care of me to give to Limata. It was a card — that he is in France — he is going to spend two months — this is a picture of their village, and that and this. Then when this man was going to come, he wrote a letter a week before and showed the day he was coming.

So then Limata was pressing, "Let's go. Let's go and meet him at the airport!"

I said, "You *shit!* To spend all this two hundred for taxi to go airport to meet this man? *Don't go.*"

So Limata said, "Hey, *camarade.* But, you know, as he has written me that he's coming —"

Then I said, "You don't go. You wait. Let him come. Let him bring himself. Don't bring yourself."

The day this man came was a Monday, but it took him four or five days before coming to our house to see Limata. Then he asked her why she didn't come to the airport. So I said, "That day, Limata told me that you were coming so we should go to airport. But I didn't have money, and Limata didn't have money, and I thought there was no need to walk from here to the airport and walk back home. That's why she didn't come."

He said, "Yes? Are you a lawyer?"

And I said, "No, I'm not a lawyer. I'm just saying the problem about why we didn't come, you know."

Then he said he was asking Limata. So I said, "OK, *camarade,* it's your time to talk to your man."

You know, this man just didn't like me. The first time, he liked me more than any other girlfriend of Limata. But because of my party, when I got Limata to my place, and he saw her with the men: hey, that thing spoiled us. But now we are all right again.

So when he came, then he got into the room with Limata — *tn-tn-tn-tn* — he had brought some colo[1] shoe. I think that that shoe, Limata didn't even wear it. A red shoe, with white lines, with thread. He brought it from France to come and boss Limata. So then, Limata put it on. Then the man called me: "Come and see Limata! Is this nice?"

When I went, I said, "Anyway, it's nice, but the time for it has passed. I have one; it is old. It is old —" *Ha-ha!* "It's an old thing. So the time has passed. I think this is cheap in France, isn't it?"

Then — *ha-ha!* — then he said, "*Tu racontes trop.*[2] You know too much. Go!" Yeah. So: "Go!"

So I went my way. Then when he left, then I said, "*Camarade,* if suppose it's me, this shoe, I won't take it. The way I will make my face, even

1. colonial, old-fashioned
2. (French): You talk too much; you gossip too much.

if—you yourself, you will fear to give it. This old thing: didn't you see my own in the room? I don't wear it again. Do you see girls wearing this type again? He went and carried this from buroni-wawu to come and give to you here."

Then Limata said, "Ah, it is not that, you know. He is a good man. As he can remember me and bring me something, it's nice."

So then I said, "Uh-huh."

So this man was back from his leave for about three months, and then Limata said she wanted to visit her family in Tamale. Limata is from Tamale, and I told Limata I would also go there with her. Then Limata said that the old man said he spent all his money in France, so she was afraid to tell him that she was going to Ghana, and then maybe the man would say he didn't have money. So I said, "OK, if you like, I will talk to him. I'm not afraid of him. You are afraid of him, but I'm not afraid of him. He is your man, so you know your man. And that's why you are afraid of him."

So one day, this man came. I was sleeping. He used to call me *"La Grande"*: somebody who is tall. He said I am very tall. *Ha!* So when he came: "Hey! *La Grande!*"

I said, *"Oui patron."*

"Allez hop!" Every time he used to say, *"Allez hop. Allez hop."* So if he was coming to the house, "Hey, *allez hop.*" That was the way he did. Then he said, "We go and take *un peu*¹ at Oubri?"

Then I said, "OK." It was about twelve-thirty. We went to Oubri and we were talking. Then he said he wanted to go to Ghana.

I said, "When?"

He said, oh, maybe in about one month's time or two months' time. He hasn't known Ghana. Many people were going to Ghana from France, and—

So I said, "Oh, but I am going at the ending of this month."

Then he said, "Ah! Very early like that?"

Then I said, "Yes."

Then he said, "Limata, too, is going?"

Then I said, "Ah, I don't know. I can't tell Limata about my going because I'm afraid of you now. Maybe you will say that I'm going to serve Limata to my friends. So I didn't tell her anything. Even Limata doesn't know that I am going."

Then when he saw Limata, he asked her, "Why don't you go with Hawa?"

---

1. (French): a drink

Then Limata said because she wasn't ready to go yet.

Then he asked her, "What are you going to be ready with?"

She said she hadn't bought the things which she was going to give to the mother, and this and that.

Then he said, "If I give you twenty thousand, can you do that?"

Then I asked him — you know, he used to go shopping by himself, because he didn't trust the girl he was living with — I asked him, "Twenty thousand can do?"

He said, "Yes."

"To buy all the provisions she is going to give to the mother, and the rest of the twenty thousand to join a car?"

Then he said, "Ah, they say that Ghana money, if you have one thousand francs, you will get plenty of cedis.[1] They say even one thousand can bring Limata here and go back."

1. Decimal currency was introduced in Ghana in 1965, replacing and phasing out the Ghanaian pound that had replaced British West African currency in 1958. One New Cedi is one hundred pesewas, or ten shillings. The New Cedi was aligned with the U.S. dollar but has been progressively devalued. The old or Nkrumah cedis were originally valued at eight shillings and fourpence; for ease of calculation, the New Cedi was introduced in 1966, valued at ten shillings, with two New Cedis being a pound.

The devaluation of the cedi proceeded slowly in official trading, radically in black market trading. Eventually, the currency was floated under a "structural adjustment" program of the World Bank. For people using hard currency converted at the black market rate, prices and inflation were somewhat consistent with the world market, but because the government did not devalue the cedi to reflect actual value, the currency became seriously overvalued. The actual value of the cedi, and by extension the actual cost of goods in hard currency, could only be known via the black market rate.

In 1970, the cedi was trading at 1.15 to the dollar officially and 1.50 unofficially. Major problems developed during the regime of General I. K. Acheampong and became progressively worse. In 1974 a dollar bought 1.80 cedis; in 1976, 2.80 cedis; in 1977, when many of the interviews took place, a dollar bought 4.00 to 4.50 cedis; in 1978, 7 cedis; in 1979, when additional interviews were conducted, the figure was 12–14 cedis. By 1981, a dollar bought 38–40 cedis; in 1982, 75 cedis; in 1983, 130 cedis; by 1988, the number had risen to 200 to 300; in 1996, a dollar bought 1,600 cedis; in 2000, a dollar bought more than 5,000 cedis; in early 2001, a dollar was about 7,500 cedis.

In 1971, when I knew Hawa in Accra, a bottle of beer was fifty-five pesewas; an orange was threepence; a bus ride across town might have been sixpence; a short taxi ride from one area to another cost two shillings. In contemporary Ghana, the costs would be in the thousands of cedis. Now nobody can dream about dealing with pesewas or pence, let alone shillings or single cedis. The result is that the prices Hawa gives will seem absurdly low, with things thirty years ago appearing to cost thousands of times less than current prices.

With regard to the high levels of both inflation and overvaluation, one therefore has to think about the cost of goods and services in hard currency terms such as dollars. The following inflation factors indicate the turn-of-the-millennium value of a dollar from the time period of this book: 5 in 1968, 4.5 in 1970, 3.6 in 1974, 3 in 1977, to 2.5 by 1979. For

Then I said, "Eh?"

So I didn't say anything, because I didn't know whether Limata would like me to talk to this man. When we went home, then I asked her, "*Camarade,* but what was that man talking about this twenty thousand?"

She didn't say anything. Then she said, "Eh, *camarade,* you know, you have to talk to him, you know, because I am afraid of this man's ways, and so on this case, you have to talk for me."

So I said, "Ah, to talk *for* you? Sometimes I think that maybe you don't feel[1] the way I used to talk to your man. Because the last time he came, I was trying to joke with him, and you were giving a complaint to Mama that I was the one who sacked the man."

Do you know?! From there she made a quarrel with Mama that Mama was kɔnkɔnsa, and why should she tell Mama something and Mama will come and tell me? *Ha-ha!*

So in evening time, this man came. Then he said, "Are you sure that you are going?"

Then I said, "Yes."

Then he said, "Then I think I will borrow some twenty thousand to give Limata, and then she can go. I will come and meet her."

Then I said, "Limata is not going to take twenty thousand now and follow me, because if Limata is getting twenty thousand here in Ouagadougou to go to Ghana, all her expenses will be on me."

He said how did I know?

I said, "Because I know. I have been in Ghana many times with Limata."

Then he said, "So what do you think?"

I said, "Look, this time in Ghana, they have nothing. So everything is costing. So if you really want that Limata should go with me, to me, I think if you give her two hundred thousand, maybe it will take her for a month. One month, not two months." *Ha!*

Then he said, "Ah! It's true. *Tu es une bonne patronne.* You are a good manager. Two hundred thousand!"

Then I said, "Is it much?"

Then he said, "Two hundred thousand? If you carry this money in Ghana border, a thief won't catch you?"

---

a rough calculation of cedi values, one can divide the black-market value of a dollar in cedis into the inflation factor. For example, in 1974, a dollar bought 1.80 cedis, and a 1974 dollar would be worth about $3.60 in 2001, so a cedi was worth about two 2001 dollars. By 1977, in 2001 terms, a cedi was worth about seventy-five cents. From the late 1960s to the early 1970s, one cedi would be equivalent to between two and four dollars, after adjusting for inflation.

1. like

I said, "Who will catch me? So don't you think the girls who are here in Ouagadougou, some of them used to pass[1] the border with a million?"

So he said: no, anyway, he knows that we women are dangerous, but he can't get two hundred thousand for Limata. So if I can help him to make economics for him — you know — now we have become friends — so he will beg me — whatever how much I will spend on Limata, when we come back, he can pay it — but he will give Limata one hundred thousand.

So OK. But Limata played foolish. I don't know why my friends, if they see money — I know we all, we don't have it — but if they see small money, they used to shake. You know? This man lied to this girl and gave her seventy thousand, and said he would send her thirty thousand by post. Limata didn't tell me anything. We were in the car, then I told her to change her money, that to change for cedis at Ouaga side is better than to take it to Ghana because maybe you wouldn't get the same price there as in Ouagadougou. So then she said, "Even the money, the one this man gave to me, I have spent some, and then this is what is left — forty thousand."

Then I said, "What did you do with the one hundred thousand?"

She said, "He didn't give me all. He gave me seventy thousand, and he said that he would send the thirty thousand in the post."

"How? Even if it was one hundred thousand, if you take some out of it, I don't like it. Carry your money. But why should you do this? Why didn't you tell me, too?"

Yeah. The man promised to give her one hundred thousand. If she had refused the seventy thousand, the man would have given her the one hundred. Don't you know that? Yeah! He would have given it because he promised. Me, I said two hundred thousand. He said two hundred thousand was much, so he would give her one hundred thousand. OK? It was a promise which he had made. He shouldn't have come to see her alone and lie to her to give her the seventy thousand, that he will send the rest in the post. What?! She should have had that one hundred thousand, then she would write and say, "I am short of money, so you have to post more money for my transport." Maybe he would post her another thirty thousand, so she would get one hundred and thirty. But she would get one hundred only. Maybe.

Then we were in Ghana, and she gave me a complaint that the sister was going to give birth in that month, and then when she brought this money home, she didn't know that she had played foolish with it. So she wanted to write to the old man, whether the old man could post her more than thirty thousand. I said, "He won't post you more than thirty thou-

1. cross

sand, because you have already spoiled your chance. You should have taken the full one hundred thousand. OK, when you come here, you would write to him that, 'You know, this is the problem which happened to me, in Ghana. So please, will you send me a little bit of money?' Maybe if he doesn't send you thirty, maybe twenty. Then you would have profit. But this time, if you write to him, he will bring the same thirty thousand to you. If you like, you should mark it.[1] I think you will get the same thirty thousand. He won't give you more than that."

This old man, too, was very clever. He wouldn't give more than that. He was French, but he had kept long[2] in Africa. I don't know how old he was, but he was old. He had stayed in Africa for a long time. I think he was in Cameroon and some other places. He didn't have white hair. He had nice hair, with no white hair inside. But he was old anyway. You know, some people can grow old and then they still look nice. He was a very short man. He was not bad, but he was old. He was working at the border. If somebody was coming with something from Europe, you know, they are the people who are at the border to collect tax and all this. As the people bring cars and other things, to get them and to pay the tax and all this, he was a broker for that. This was what he was doing in Ouagadougou. But he had kept long in Africa. He said he was eighteen or nineteen years in Africa. He got Limata cheap.

You know, the boyfriends of Limata used to like her because she is cool. Every time you are cool, cool, cool, cool. But sometimes too much cool is foolishness. Sometimes Limata can be cool, and sometimes she can be smart. But she always wants to be cool.

You see? Limata was always thinking about this old man, that he was keeping her. But I told you this old man had a wife. Anyway, he didn't marry her, but he had an African girl he was staying with for about twelve or thirteen years. They had one baby. When he got to know the girl, the girl already had one baby, with one white man. And that other man left her with the baby and went away. And when the old man came to know the girl, she kept the first baby with her, so both the two were with them, his own baby with the step-baby. He was sending both of them to the school, paying their school fees. And the girl was with him, too. Her name was Zuweratu. She was from Mali.

And she and the old man were not all right. You know, this Zuweratu, the family was Muslim, but when she came to Ouagadougou, she became Catholic. OK? And then he was getting fed up with the girl because that

1. note it down; remember this point
2. stayed a long time

time, she used to sing the songs of the church and start crying, falling down, crying out that it's God who has come to her, and that and this. So every time, the man used to come and give the complaint, that he thinks he is getting to the last of the girl. He said he had built a big house for the girl in her country. I think he said he spent two million or three million CFA! And every time, he had problems with the girl. So he was going to send her back to her county, to Mali.

But you see? He was deceiving Limata that he would like to divorce with that girl, you know, so that he would keep Limata in her place. And Limata too, she was sure that this man would do that, but *I* was sure that this man wouldn't do this. So he got Limata in a cheap way. Do you think that if he got this girl in this same way he got Limata, he could build a big house for the girl? He can't. He wanted to look for a cheap way. But Limata was sure in him. Every time, I used to give her this advice. I said, "Look, this kind of people who you are with, you shouldn't be cheap for them."

And Limata used to say, "Maybe he had a problem. Maybe he has spent his money."

"What? Is it your look-out? If you want something, you should just ask him. If he hasn't got it, he will tell you he hasn't got. But every time he says that he has a problem, and that and this. And you don't have a problem? You have three children: they are with your mother. Your mother, an old woman like that, is still working, government work, to feed your children. Is it nice?"

You know, Limata doesn't know how to talk, to boss people. Look: she had this old man. OK? This old man was keeping Limata as a permanent girlfriend. He didn't want to miss Limata any time. And he told Limata, "Don't work." *Hm?* Whatever she wanted, she should ask him. And any time, he would bring one thousand to Limata for chop money. But sometimes he could make three days without coming. How can she manage to eat? You see? So sometimes, maybe Limata would go out and meet somebody who was good. But she thought that maybe as he built the house for that woman, maybe if she followed him slowly, she too would get something from him. But that's not the way that Malian girl followed this man to get that house. If you saw the girl, you could know that she was a strong woman. She was very slim. *Agh!* She was a very strong girl. She didn't give the man chance. Look, once, we met the man in the market. Then he said he can't stop because the wife is following behind him with the motor. So he can't talk to Limata. So you think if Limata was also strong like that girl, he would be afraid to talk to Limata in front of the girl? He didn't marry this girl. He didn't marry Limata also. So the girl was stronger than Limata. She was stronger than the man, too. *Yeah*. The man was afraid of the girl. Anything she asked the man, he used to give her. But Limata wanted the man himself to come to her and say, "OK, Limata, take this." But these French people, they are not like that.

You know, you can see these people. Sometimes, if you work in the nightclub, you can see the different ones. A white man can come, and he will ask you to dance. When he finishes dancing, then he will say, "Oh, come and drink something with me." He knows that you have danced. Maybe you will feel like drinking. Even French people, they have that kind of people, but truly, the French, few of them are doing that. Many of them, they want if you *ask*. They don't want that they will give you for their pleasure. They want you to ask them. Yeah. It's their life. Every time, they want you to ask them for something. But not to say, "Oh, today, I think maybe is not good for this girl, so I should give this to this girl." No. If you don't ask, you will be waiting and waiting and waiting, for years and years. They are like that.

But Limata was taking the English life. Even she could see what the old man was doing, and she would still say, "No, maybe he will change."

And when this man came back from leave, he said, "Oh, *pfft*, this Malian girl won't come back again." So Limata used to go there. Maybe for one week she wouldn't come home. We all, we didn't mind. Me and Mama, we already had heavy everything at our place, so we didn't give a damn about this. The day Limata would come, she would come and change her dress — oh, packing her things, her dresses which were dirty, to go to give the cook there to wash, and then sleeping in air conditioning every time.

One night I was going out, and I met them coming. She had packed all her things in the car boot[1]. She said that the man said that the Malian girl was coming tomorrow. Then I said, "You see? But you told me this man said the girl won't come. I said the girl will come. You see now?"

She said, "Eh-h, the man said he made a telegram to the girl to bring his baby for him and go away." And he told Limata that after the Christmas, the girl would go away. She wouldn't come back to him. But I knew all this was a lie. He was just lying to Limata. Limata is not a small baby, but she doesn't have a long sense. *Ha!* She doesn't think long. She doesn't have a long experience. Anything the man told her, she used to believe him.

Me, I don't believe anybody. I don't. I don't believe. I don't believe myself, even. How much about somebody? I don't believe myself. *Ha-ha!* Oh

1. trunk

.0.yeah! For me, if you say something to me, until I see it. If I see it with my eyes, *uh-huh,* then I will know it's true. But to tell me this and that? No. *Jamais.*[1]

: KORHOGO :

The Short Big Man Who Liked to Dance

When I left Banfora, I came back to Ouagadougou. That was the time when Mama had gone to Lomé with Jeremy. When she left the room, before I came, thieves had broken our door and packed everything inside the room. So at that time, I didn't feel like working in Ouagadougou again.

So I was hanging for about two or three weeks' time, then I got someone who was from Korhogo, in Côte d'Ivoire. He was a manager of a nightclub, and he came to look for girls to work in the nightclub. Then I decided to go to that place and work, because in Ouagadougou, I was fed up. They had broken my door, packed all my things. So I decided to go with this man. This man said I should find him more girls. I got Limata: Limata accepted that she would go, but at the *last* moment, she said, "I'm not going again."

Then I got another girl. She was a South African, Georgina. She was working at Ricardo. And one girl from Cameroon: she was called Laura. She had two names: she was called Agnes in Cameroon, and in Upper Volta she was Laura. When she got to Côte d'Ivoire, she was Joyce! *Ha-ha!* So we three went to Korhogo.

The nightclub where we were going to work was for one minister in the government of Côte d'Ivoire. He was staying in Abidjan, but the nightclub was at his own village. They made it as someplace, if some ministers or ambassadors came to that village, they would drink there. So we used to get these big-big people to sell drinks to them. Even I met the Ghana ambassador, from Abidjan, in that nightclub. That day, when he was coming to that place, they put *all* Ghana flags, everywhere. They came to our nightclub, danced well, and they were playing all Ghana music, and we were serving them champagne, champagne.

But that place was nice. Sometimes, if you got that kind people, before you close, maybe if you got ten thousand as *cadeau,*[2] it was small. Some people could just give you a five thousand note: it's a *cadeau.* So if they

---

1. (French): never
2. (French): gift, tip

came like that, we girls who worked there used to be happy. So we stayed five months there.

OK. The five months, what made me to say that I wouldn't stay again: both these two girls I brought, they bluffed. They bluffed themselves, because they thought they were from far. South Africa is very far away: you can't find any South African girl like that in a nightclub in these places. So she wanted to be *too* much. And she was not beautiful too. She was a very *ugly* woman! If you saw her from the back, you wouldn't think she was a woman; you would think she was a man. Even her face didn't resemble a woman. But she could *bluff!* Georgina: *God!* This girl had a mouth. If you tell her something, *tsk,* you will go and poison yourself.

The manager for the nightclub was a Senegalese man.[1] You know, this minister didn't have time to run this nightclub, so he had some Senegalese people as managers. They looked after the girls and all the workers. These people got fed up with this South African girl. And she was a tight friend to me. She bluffed people, but as she didn't bluff me —*Ha!*— I was all right with her. So I liked her.

So the manager sacked the two of them, Joyce and Georgina, that they had made trouble, that they were boxing inside the nightclub. So the next day I went and begged these Senegalese people, and they took them back to work again.

OK. The next problem. This South African ugly woman: there was a — what they call it?— like a D.C., like a District Commissioner in Ghana, they have it in Côte d'Ivoire — at that place, the D.C. of Korhogo. He was very *short!* I don't know, but I think he used to wear guarantee shoes,[2] small-small guarantees. I don't know his height. Maybe he might be the same size as me, or I would be passing him[3] a little bit. I don't know. But when he comes to the nightclub, you know, he has his guarantee shoes, with his big tie: he's a big man. A very small man! And every day, he's happy. Every time, night and day, if you meet him, every time he's showing the teeth. So he was a very funny guy. I *liked* this guy, and he *liked* me. He used to call me his sister. But this guy could dance with you to *Hell.* He wouldn't ask you even to drink a glass of water with him. He wouldn't buy a drink for you. And every night he was coming there to the nightclub. He doesn't buy drinks for girls, but he was holding the girls to dance with them. And you know, we girls who are working in the nightclub, we have interest for dancing, but we have not much interest to dance as we

---

1. from Senegal, Francophone country on the far western tip of Africa
2. a thick-soled shoe or platform shoe; high-style shoe. The shoes are called "guarantees" because the soles will not wear out.
3. more than

want. But if you are dancing with the people, that's the place they will start to buy you a drink, then you will also be happy. But if you have been dancing, dancing, and the fellow doesn't want to tell you, "Take something with me," then you used to be *annoyed*. We used to get annoyed from that kind of people.

So one night this man came to the nightclub, and he came and asked this South African girl, "Let's go and dance." This girl didn't want. Then I stepped on her foot. Then she got up and went and danced with the man, and then she came and sat down. The second time he came and asked her, and she wanted to refuse. Then I said, "Hey, this man, you know, they say he is the D.C. in this village. And we are strangers. We have to know — we must know the way we will entertain these people before we will get to know their character." So she shouldn't do that; she should dance with him. So this girl danced the second time with this man. And the third time, this man came and danced with me. OK. The fourth dance he went back to this girl again. That time I was also dancing with somebody. So the girl refused to dance with him. And then he said, why should the girl refuse to dance with him? What is she here for? Then the girl said, "I'm here to make the people happy."

"But why don't you make me happy then?"

She said, "I have made you happy a lot. If somebody's making you happy, you must make the fellow happy, too."

He said, "How?"

She said, "Yeah, you have been dancing. I was coming to serve you your champagne and you were drinking with your girls."

You know, he had a group. Every time when he would come, he could bring about four girls, or six girls. He wouldn't dance with anyone! It was only the girls who were working in the nightclub he would be dancing with. And he would be buying drink for these girls to be sitting down and drinking. And then when he finishes dancing with you, he will leave you at the place and he will go back to these girls and they will be drinking, talking, joking, laughing. And you, the girl who has been working in the nightclub, he just takes you like a *slave*. You see? So this girl was trying to tell this man the truth, that "I have been dancing with you. You never say to me to take even one Fanta or Coca."

Then this man said, "Hey!" Why should this girl say so? He doesn't like a girl who will ask for drink. But he used to dance with the girls. If you are a nice girl, you won't ask him for anything. When he is going, he can give you a gift. He can dash you something.

Then this girl said she is not here to be making people happy, then the time when they are going, to take their gift. She is not here waiting for people to be dashing her. She wants somebody who gives himself respect.

Then this man said, "Hey-y! What? You mean to say that I don't give myself respect? Who are you and what are you? Where from you?[1] Which country did you come from?" Then this man was shouting. And you know, at our nightclub, we used to get many white people, so all the white people started going out, one by one. Then this man: "No! No! No! No! No! No no no! What kind of woman?! And where from her?! To come and say this! That I don't respect myself? Even if you are from here, from Côte d'Ivoire, I will send you back to your small village there."

Then our manager came. This short man was talking quick-quick-quick, because he was annoyed, so he didn't give this girl a chance to talk. So he was saying that they had to deport this girl. Then our manager said, "Oh, she is a South African. She is a stranger. Take patience. Maybe she doesn't know."

He said, "No no no no no! This girl won't sleep in this town today!" They have to deport this girl. Even if the government does not agree to deport this girl, even if it's — how much does the plane cost to go to her place? He will rent it, and he will send this girl back to her village this very night.

By that time, it was about two o'clock in the night. We were boiled up. This small fucking man, eh? There were many *big* people who were coming to talk to him: "*Oh grand frère, vous pouvez pas faire ça.* My big brother, don't do that."

But this man just went, "No, no, no, no!" They must deport this girl. And he was drunk. Yeah, he drank good champagne. So then our manager rang telephone to the big brother of our owner, the minister, and the big brother came to the nightclub and took this man somewhere to boss him. So when the problem came, we had to close work.

When we went home, then Georgina said, "*Pfft!* I don't care — they can deport me. That fucking man like this, small fucking idiot like this — every time he will come and trouble you — dancing, dancing, he won't buy a drink. You people — when you — and I said — and you, Hawa, you dey make yourself like somebody who doesn't — whose eyes are not strong. But sometimes you used to make some things like your eyes are strong.[2] Look at this! You were pressing me to go and dance with him. Tell him! He can't kill you! Only to send you back to your country."

1. (Pidgin): Where are you from?
2. who has pride. In this context, Georgina is saying that Hawa presents herself as someone who isn't serious or who doesn't mind being pushed around, but that Hawa also sometimes tries to advocate for herself or to advise others to stand up for themselves, so Hawa should agree that Georgina was right to refuse the man.

So we were having this talk in the house, you know. I was giving her advice, but she didn't want to listen to me. You know, I think if you travel to another country, you have to be easy, to be quiet, to know the people of the town before bluffing yourself. But this girl didn't want to understand me on that way. So she didn't care. In her country, she didn't eat stones or grass before she came here. If they send her back there, it's the same thing she was eating that she is going to eat there.

Then I said, "Then what brought you?"

So—*ha!*—then we got palaver between the two of us, you know. *Ha!* She said that I'm afraid of these people because they are that and this. Then I said, "No."

So the next day, they went and begged for this girl, and this matter finished a little bit. And he still used to come to the nightclub. But this time, if he's coming, he won't come with any girl. He will come alone. He will come and sit down nicely. Then he will call me. He called me *"Ma petite."* You: you are a small man, and I am also short like you. And you are calling me your "small one." He will just say, *"Ma petite."*

Then I will say, "Yes, Patron."

He will say, "Come and serve me. Bring me one bottle of champagne."

Then I will bring him one bottle of champagne. I will serve him.

Then he will ask me, "Are you drinking something?"

Then maybe I will say, "Yes."

As for me, if I am sitting with you, if you are drinking champagne, I won't drink champagne. I will order a different drink. If I'm drinking the same drink with you, they won't mark me. But if I'm drinking a different drink from yours, that is in my account. This was the way of that nightclub. Maybe you will be taking a beer: then I will say I will drink champagne. Then if we buy one bottle of champagne, we can drink it together, that is in my account, because I have served you your drink first. But for my own, if I just go and get a glass and drink with you, I haven't got anything inside. It's just like some dash that I'm dashing the nightclub, and I don't want to be dashing to the managers. They have their money to open their nightclub.

So if he comes like that, sometimes I will take Heineken or beer to drink with him. And we will be sitting. And you know, from that time when this girl did this, I think many people were talking to him, that the way he was doing, he didn't respect, or that's why this fucking girl could tell him this. So from that time, he didn't dance again. He had to be cool. Every time, he will sit down, drinking with me. He will be talking, asking me many questions. That what do I—I am a nice girl, a nice small girl— why don't I marry? Why should I work in the nightclub? It's not a good work. If I can change, or if I need some work, if I know some work, I should tell him — he can try to find me some work. This work is not good for me, and this. I'm too young to do this work, and that.

You know, he was a nice man. *Heh!* He used to give me this advice. And I don't want that kind of advice. You know? Yeah. But he thought that he was trying his best. Any time, when he comes: "*Où est ma petite?*: Where is my little one?" I used to tie my face. I didn't like it at all. I knew that every day he will say the same thing. Every time, he will buy me drink. Even I could drink about six or seven thousand. He doesn't care. He will buy it for me. Then for the last show he will say, "You see, this time you are drunk. It's not good for a woman." *Ha!* "A young girl like this — you are going to spoil yourself with this alcohol. It's not good. You serve — this is fucking work — it's not good work for you. You are too nice to do this work. Why? You don't have somebody who will ask you to marry you?"

Then I will say, "Ah — because I don't have somebody who will like to marry me."

"Then if I say I will marry you, are you going to agree?"

Then I looked at this man. How he is — *eee-e-e* — small like this, like me, how can we walk together? How can people respect us? *Ha!*

So: every time he used to call me and buy me drinks, and he didn't mind Georgina. Then at the last minute, Georgina came and had a problem with another D.C. from another village. So all the people got fed up with her, that the first time when she got the trouble from this short man, the short man was not correct, but this girl, she is just coming here to show them that she's from South Africa, and she can fuck[1] the big people in Côte d'Ivoire free. So as she got the first case, and they left her, then she started with the second one, too. So they wouldn't allow. They sacked Georgina from the work. And you know, I was very sorry for her. So I said, "Tsk, if this girl is going to leave this place, I'm going, too. I can't stay."

Then our manager asked me, "Why? Did I do you something bad?"

I said, "No, you didn't do me anything bad. I just don't feel it, to be staying here alone." You know, I told you I came with Georgina and Joyce. And first, a long time before all these problems, it was Joyce who had a problem, and they sacked her. So Joyce was no more working there, but she was in town. She used to come to the nightclub. She didn't work. But the second time, when it came to Georgina, then I thought that the third one might be coming to me, too. So I couldn't stay. Then this man was

1. verbally abuse

trying to boss me all the ways. They had already increased me more than all the other girls, but they would increase me again. Then I said, "No, I don't want it."

So I'm very stupid, you know. I used to think of Ouagadougou, how they used to ask for the carte d'identité in the night, so every time I had my carte d'identité in my bag. So: this man wasn't happy, and he went and took my carte d'identité. He thought that if I don't have my papers, I can't go back to Ouagadougou. So he took my carte. Whether he threw it in the toilet or what, I don't know.

So I had given them a time. I told them that I was going on the fourth. So on the second, I went shopping and bought a valise and all this, packed my things and everything. When I finished packing, all my papers were in one side. I took them out, and I was looking for my carte d'identité. I didn't find this carte d'identité. *Wow!* I went and asked this man, our manager. You know, I didn't used to go out with my bag in day time. I wouldn't go anywhere with my bag unless I was going to the work. I used to take the bag only because of my cigarettes and my key. So the man said, ah, as for him, he didn't see any carte d'identité, but I should wait, he would ask the brother. So I was annoyed. Then the brother said he didn't see the carte.

OK. So I said, "It's nothing. Now I have lost my carte, I can't go on the fourth."

And they thought I would be working up to the time I would get my papers. And every night, I didn't go to work. Day time, they would come and *beg* me. They will *talk:* papapapa! I will say, "Oh! Evening time, I will come."

Evening time, I won't go. But I was still in the house of the manager. He was paying. I was not paying. I didn't care. *Ha!* I'm not going to the work, but I'm lodging there free, too. It's a hotel—ha! Morning time he will come again: "Oh, but we were telling you to come—"

I will say, "Yeah, I'm going to come. Today I'm going to come. Yesterday I had a problem, that's why I didn't come. But today I will try to come." Night time: I won't go. I was doing that for two weeks.

Then one boy showed me an inspector. He was a *good* friend with these Senegalese people. And he also grooved: he was a groovier. But I didn't know he grooved, and I didn't talk to him before. So I was afraid. But this boy said, "OK, if you want, he is my friend; I will direct you to his place."

So this boy directed me to his place, and I told him about my papers. Then he said they couldn't make a carte d'identité for me here. If I wanted to get a carte d'identité, I had to go to Abidjan. We had an ambassador at Abidjan. But it was not difficult: they could make me a *laissez-passer*.[1] So I said OK. Then he said that I should go and buy a stamp at post office.

You know, all this time, Georgina was waiting for me. All this time I was wasting, she was waiting for me. We were living at the house, the same house which the manager had rented for us. We didn't pay. We were living there, cooking, eating, bathing the water. And now we knew that we were going to leave, so we were spoiling many things in the room. *Ha! Hee-he-he!* That was so the next person would meet all this the same way we had met it, because we had repaired the lights, and there was some place the fan was not good, and all these things, we had brought people to fix them. So we tried to damage everything that we had repaired in the house. *Ha! Hee-he-he!* So me and Georgina, we went to post office and bought the stamp: one was hundred francs. We bought two stamps for two hundred and took them to the man's office. Oh! In about five minutes he finished everything.

Then we went and had vaccinations. We used to go and get these things: we wanted to have a full health card for when you are going to travel. Yeah. If you go to do it, they mark your card. You will go about four or five times before you get all. So we were trying for that, because Georgina said she would stay about six months in Ouaga, then she would be going to her country, South Africa. And I was about to go with her to South Africa. So we were doing everything correctly there. OK.

Then, when I got my papers, I passed straight to the manager's place, just to tell him that because I was a stranger, he wanted to teach me.[2] "*Voilà-voilà:* that's it. I'm going. You can chop the carte d'identité. Tomorrow I'm flying. You think you are what?" I just insulted the manager. You know, he was a fucking Senegalese man, so we could just abuse him. We didn't take him as our manager. We used to take him as a friend, a jovial friend.

And he was owing me three thousand, that manager. And he hadn't given me. And that time, with all what I was doing, I didn't press to take it. But the same day when I got the papers, then I went to give him full attack to give me that three thousand. So I said, "You give me my three thousand." So he went inside and brought five thousand. And I said I didn't have balance. Then he said I have to go and find the balance. So I said,

---

1. (French): a paper issued by police to allow someone to travel or to cross a border; literally, allow-to-pass

2. cheat me; show me experience by taking advantage of me. The idea of teaching is opening one's eyes to something the person didn't think about or know about.

"OK, I'm going to look for the balance. Georgina, let's go. If I have the balance at home, I'm going to go and pick it and bring it for him."

So I just chopped his five thousand. I didn't give the two thousand balance. *Ha! Ha-ha!* The next day, I packed all my things in the taxi, and we went to pass to the nightclub. You know, this nightclub was a *big* place: they had a room for the manager to sleep. So I went to the manager. I said, "*Voilà.* This is the key to the room. And your two thousand: you come to Ouagadougou and get your balance of two thousand, OK?"

He didn't say anything. *Ha-ha!* Then we went away. You know, when you are from Korhogo, you have to come to some village before you can get a train to Ouagadougou — ah, shit, what is this fucking place's name? Ferké![1] — yeah, but we didn't get a quick car to go to Ferké. We came to Ferké about eight o'clock in the night. No train. All the trains had passed to Ouagadougou. So we had to hire a room. They had something; French people call it *campement.* I think it's a rest house, a government rest house. So we got to this *campement* and took one room. And there, too: no water. OK. To go to toilet: no toilet inside. They have to take you to the other side to go to the toilet. And when we got there, about eight o'-clock, we were *hungry.* And we didn't know the town, so we asked them, are they serving food here? They said, yeah, they are serving some rice with groundnut[2] soup. So we bought the rice. We couldn't eat it. "Hey! Georgina!"

Then Georgina said, "Hawa, you know, we are fools. Suppose we had slept at Korhogo, then we would have *nice* food to eat. Then the next day, we could get up early in the morning, we would get a car, the morning one. We could drop at Koudougou.[3] Evening time we would get a train to go. But it's too late."

Then I said, "Yeah, it's too late. So what can we do?"

Mosquitoes! We couldn't sleep that night! *Whew!* The room: they had mosquito net, but I think there were some holes in it. We covered it, but it didn't seem as if there was a mosquito net there. It was hot. The mosquitoes were biting us for the *whole* night. We woke up about four or half-past four, in the morning, to take our baths and do everything and bring all our things out to the station.

From the rest house to the station was not far: it was just near. Then we were sitting there, waiting for the train, and we were talking, talking, about how if we meet this Senegalese man in Ouagadougou or some place,

1. short name for Ferkéssédougou
2. peanut
3. medium-sized town between Bobo-Dioulasso and Ouagadougou

how we are going to show him, how he thinks—*pfft!* Somebody opens his nightclub and he tries to become big inside. The day when we meet him at Ouagadougou or some country, how we are going to show him. You know? And we were conversing this, so we had mind to write a letter, to post from Ferké to that fucking man, to abuse him. So—*Ha-ha!* We wrote a letter: how he's fucking, how he's such an idiot, and all this. We just wrote this letter in the train station. *Ha!* If we meet him, what we are going to show him. He should pray to God that he shouldn't meet us at some place apart from Korhogo. *Ha!* And we posted it to him! *Ha-ha!* And since then, we didn't meet the man, huh? It's true. I think he's afraid. We didn't meet him. We didn't meet him again.

PART TWO *The Human Face of Neocolonialism*

3 FUCKING FRENCH PEOPLE

: *The French Nightclub*
: *The French Ashawos*
: *The Godfather*
: *Not Crazy, Just Stupid*

: OUAGADOUGOU :

The French Nightclub

When I came back from Côte d'Ivoire, La Tringle had opened, and my Madame Colette said I should come and work again. And that time, I thought I was a bit all right. And the way I was in Côte d'Ivoire, working all the time for about five months, then when I came back, I wanted to be free a little bit in town. So when she told me to come and work, I used to say, "Tomorrow" or "After tomorrow."

Then some people opened another nightclub: Zé Bon. That nightclub, first time it was called Le Bois Bandé. It was one African man who opened it. And when I came back from Côte d'Ivoire, Le Bois Bandé had closed down, and these new people were coming to open it as Zé Bon. They were trying to decorate inside, to change the plan and everything inside, the chairs and all, before opening it.

Yeah. But when I first came back to Ouagadougou, I was just wasting time in town. Then when they opened Hôtel Oubri, I worked one night there. But they had many Togolese girls there, and the same day when they opened the place, these girls started making a show, fighting. One girl tore another girl's dress, and you could see her breast, and all this. Then I thought, "No, if I'm here, one day they will do me the same thing." So that same day I left the work. You know, that day, when they were going to open, we went there at four o'clock and finished in the morning at half-past two. They made a party from four o'clock to eight o'clock. And everybody they invited was drinking free. After eight o'clock, the party was finished, so if you were still there, you had to buy with your money. So we were workers, and we had to continue up to the time when they were going to close. But because of this fighting which the girls started do-ing, everybody started running away, so they had to close. So when I went and slept, then I said, "No." I thought, "Suppose this comes on me? No. I can't help it. It's fucking. Tomorrow I won't go to the work."

Then: Limata had said that she wanted to work in Zé Bon. I told her, "I don't want to work at Zé Bon. But if you want, I can take you there." At that time, Limata was not speaking French well, so I went and asked for work for Limata. I didn't say that I wanted work. I said I had brought my friend.

Then they asked me, has she already worked in a nightclub? Then I asked Limata, "Did you work in a nightclub before?"

Then she said, No, she didn't work in the nightclub before, but she had worked in a bar before.

So they asked me, can she know all the names of the drinks?

Then I asked Limata. Then Limata said she can know some but not all.

So then the manager said, "OK. Is she your girlfriend?"

Then I said, "Yes."

"As you speak nice French and you know all the names of the drinks, why don't you work with her? If you work with her, we can take her. But as she doesn't speak French well, we also don't speak English. But if you are with her, we will like it. You people can work together." You know? This manager was charming us like that. *Ha!*

So then I told Limata, "You see, as for me, I said I don't want to work here, but this man also said, if we are together, he will take the two of us. But if it's you alone, as you say it's not all the names of the drinks you know—"

Then she said, "Oh, *camarade,* but forget about that mind. Let's work together."

You know? So I was not all right. We went there about nine o'clock, and they said we should start work. Then I said, "As for me, truly, today I can't start." So Limata started that night. I stayed there to talk to her up to the time she closed, and we came back home together. I did this for four days, and then I told her, "OK, *camarade,* let's do the work."

The first time Zé Bon was good, eh? When I was waiting for Limata, she started at ten o'clock, and they closed about four o'clock in the morning. And Limata had about six thousand as dash. She said, "Look, *cama-rade,* this work, even these tips, even if you are a fool, you can make this card."

Do you know this card? You know, there is a man who used to go around the houses. All the Ghanaian girls, if they want, that's how they save their money before going home. They don't take their money to the bank. This man will give you a card. Every time when he comes, he writes it down, how much you give him. Some people save one thousand a day. Some people can do five thousand a day. Some people do five hundred a day, even two hundred a day. He is just like a banker. If you are making five thousand a day, at ending of the month, you know, if the month has thirty days, you will have one hundred fifty thousand. And he will get five thousand out. He takes one day in a month. If you are saving five hundred a day, he takes five hundred a month. Yeah. That's for him. And he will be keeping your money all right for you.

So Limata was telling me that as today she had six thousand, even if she's a fool, tomorrow if this man comes, you can just make rough and give him two thousand to keep. Two thousand a day for the month is how much? And ending of the month you will also get your pay. So she was confusing me with these things.

And I told you I was about to travel again. I didn't want to stay in Oua-gadougou. But Limata was always talking this to me. She worked four days. I used to go with her on time at nine o'clock, but I didn't work. I would go just to sit down. If they asked her for some drink, then she would come and tell me. If she didn't understand, I would go with her and ask the person. Then I would come to the counter and tell the server to serve that drink for Limata to give to the people.

So: four days. Then the manager called me, "Ah! Why? Don't you want the work?"

Then I said, "Oh, yeah, I will do it, but you know, I have some problems I have to—"

He said, "What kind of problem? It's a money problem? If it's a money problem, you tell me. I can give you some advance. If you want some money, I can give you some money. And then you will start work."

Then I said, "Oh, no, it's not a money problem. I just have some family problems. I don't want to start work now."

Then he said, "OK. You know, there are many girls coming here to ask for work, but I don't want to take girls who haven't got understanding. But I think you are a nice girl. You have understanding. I want you to come and work with us. So you give me the day you will be free to start the work." *Ha!*

Then I said, OK, if I come back tomorrow, I will tell him the day. When we went home, I said, "Ah, Limata, why is this your manager troubling me?"

Then Limata said, "Oh, Hawa. You, too: come! Let's go and work. It's better."

"But I said I want to travel."

Then Limata said, "Oh, let's work for three months. I want to travel with you." You see?

Then I said, "OK." So: I will have different company. As Mama Amma was not there, then I have got somebody in Mama Amma's place to go and travel with her. So I agreed. We went and started work. The next day, I told the manager, "OK, I will come." That day was the twelfth, and I told him that I would come on the fifteenth. So on the fifteenth, we started work there.

The man was good. Look. I started work with him on the fifteenth. At the ending of the month, he paid Limata fifteen thousand and he paid me fifteen thousand, because he knew that I wasted all these days with Limata. I used to come and sit down. I was taking the orders, and Limata was carrying the drinks. So he was a nice man.

When we started working there, the first time in Zé Bon, there were no African people who came in there. *All* white: white women and their men. So every time, they gave us our table. When you go to Zé Bon, this is the table for us girls. Every time you have to be sitting quietly there, and then you shouldn't joke and laugh loudly, you have to talk slowly, and that and this. You will see somebody: you just say, "Sh-h-h." You know? So we tried to learn to be gentle. And every time they used to have problems with some girls. But Limata and I didn't have any problems with them.

So: we were working there about one month to two months. It was good. Then from two months' time going, there were some kind of people who used to come there, and we hadn't seen this kind of life before. It was our first time to see these things. They would start to break bottles and glasses and cut each other. So at first, when they started these things, we used to run away from the nightclub. Whether it's time for you to close, or you didn't close, you will just take your bag and go. If it was a problem like that, we used to want to leave the place. But how we saw them, for some months, we saw that any time they have their problems, they know that Africa is Africa. They are not in their country; they cannot do the same thing with the Africans. They used to do with each other. There was not any girl or any boy, African girl or African boy, who was working there whom they wounded. So you had to understand that place. When there were some things like that, we used to watch them.

And the way they used to do to get their problem: I think it's easy for them to find the way — or it's their habit.[1] Their habit is for the women and the men; they all have the same habit, you know. Maybe you are a married woman. And maybe you have a boyfriend. Well, even in Africa here, people do it, but they used to fear; they hide it away from the husbands. But those people, they don't hide it. They used to take it out, you know, plain-plain. Sometimes.

And they are so stupid that some friends will come together, as friends. Maybe you are with your friend and with your wife, and your friend is with his wife, and you people have come together to the nightclub. Then you know, at first when they come to sit down, you will see that they respect. They are gentle a little bit. But when they start drinking, drinking, drinking, you will see that the way has changed. The one woman will accept to be at the other man's place, and then the other woman will accept to the friend. Yeah, they change. And they are dancing. You know, it's from the dancing. When they are going to start this, they don't change at once like that. OK. As you have all been sitting down, maybe you sit with your wife. Your friend is also sitting with his wife. And your friend will get up first to ask your wife for a dance, or you will ask the wife of your friend for a dance, so that your friend also will take your wife to dance. OK?

And maybe — I think — you know, as for me, I don't blame the men too much. Maybe it's from the women. You know, we women, sometimes a woman will lie to people she doesn't want. She wants the husband to be jealous, isn't it? At that time, the husband will ask the other girl to dance, and then when they dance and finish, then his wife will be sitting with the friend. Yeah. So they will be starting — *ta-ta-ta-ta* — like that.

But it's very funny. Sometimes, they will come and call for their drink at the counter. Maybe we girls, we serve them and go away. When they finish their drinks, maybe one man will come to the counter, or one woman will come to the counter, to say that they want this kind of drinks at this table. They will show which table they are sitting, whether it is right or left or the third table or the fourth table. So when they come and give this order at the bar, the manager can call anyone, any girl, if you are near: "OK. Hawa, take this drink to that table."

And sometimes, eh? You will go with the tray and you will start asking people, "Is it here I'm going to put this?" And they are busy with each other: they will start kissing. They won't mind you! Maybe you will take the drink to another table, and then they will shout, "Oh, no no no! It's

1. character, way of living; also, culture

for us!" At that time, they have time for you! "It's for us here." Then you will go and serve them.

That time, too, you know, we didn't know much about their life. We used to think that maybe they were friends, that they were not married people. But the time when we got to know that they were going with the friend's wife, or the friends were taking their wife, it was the time when they started boxing. Maybe somebody wouldn't like that way, or somebody would like the way for one day but not for always. And some woman, maybe she would go and taste the other man; maybe he is sweeter than her husband. Then every time she would want to do this, and the husband used to get annoyed. You know, only the men used to fight. You will never see the women fighting there.

So when we started seeing them like that, then we knew that we were blind. The French women — look, African girls who don't have husbands, they go to the nightclubs. *Hm?*— but the real French woman who has married, who has a husband, at night she doesn't sleep. She will go around to every nightclub before she will sleep. So before we knew that they used to go with each other's wives, we were blind. We didn't know that these women were their wives. We took all of them to be the ashawo white people. All of them: we thought they were ashawo women. But when the fighting was going to start, then we understood the inside of all this.

The French Ashawos

There was one woman we called Mama Amma's sister. Once this woman wore some kind of dress, you know, and the breasts were just like Mama Amma's ones. So we used to say, "Mama Amma's sister." She liked to wear tight dresses. She was very slim. She had a nice stomach, and then she had this kind of breasts, like Mama Amma, hanging up. She had two children with the husband. But the first time, we thought that this woman was ashawo, eh? So the husband used to get night duty. If the husband was on day duty, every time they would come together. But they would come about one week, and then you wouldn't see the husband again. She started coming alone, flirting with anyone. So we thought she was just a woman. We didn't know that she had a husband with two children. So one day, the husband went to the night duty, and maybe, you know, there were some friends who were watching the people, and they went and told him. I think somebody told the husband what this woman was doing in the town. He came to Zé Bon about half-past twelve in the night. He didn't meet the wife. And he asked the manager, "Where is my wife?"

You know, our manager was a nice handsome boy. He was called François. A nice boy! *Très beau!*[1] So the manager said, *"En tout cas,*[2] your wife was here about ten minutes ago, but I don't know the time she went out."

Then he asked the manager, "Who did she go out with?"

Then the manager said, "You know, I'm always busy to serve the people. I cannot see who is going out."

Then he said, "No! Give me one bottle of champagne."

And the manager brought a bottle of champagne. And you know, this man was going to cause trouble. So he said, "OK, open it." Then the manager opened it. Then this man said, "Where is your glass?" And the manager brought another glass. Then the man told him, "Serve you yourself and serve me." The manager served him first. Then the man said, "No. Serve yourself first! So this is your glass? Put it front of me, eh?" The manager gave him the glass, and then he said, "OK." Then this man took the empty glass of champagne and said, "Serve me." So the man served him.

And you know, the man was shouting. We all, we thought that he was drunk. But I think he was not drunk. I think something was worrying his heart. Then he said, "OK. Cheers!"

Then the manager took his glass: "Cheers."

And the man just: *kss-sss!* He *knocked* the glass strongly, and the glass broke, and all the drink was in the face of our manager! Then he said, "You say you opened Zé Bon! It is your work to find the wives of others for your customers! You have been finding our wives for people. I've heard it, but when I come here, I don't want to show it. I'm good with you. But tonight, if you don't bring my wife, I will show you who I am. Unless I get where my wife has gone — you are a good friend with me — any night and day, you can come to me. And if I get night duty and my wife comes to your nightclub, I think you will take care of her. My wife cannot go to any place without telling you, because she knows that we are good friends. So you know where my wife is." *Ha-ha!*

And you know, our manager was afraid of *anything* in this way! He didn't want any fight. *Hee-hee!* Even you can give him a slap, then he will start to beg you. So he just started talking: "Oh, no. Don't bring this, my friend. You know, this is — a woman is a woman. I also have a wife. But you must understand, French women — OK, if your wife is — your wife, she understands you. OK. You work in the night. Why should she come out to this place? I am here. But I haven't got time to look at the people. I

1. (French): very handsome
2. (French): anyway

have to serve the drinks from the counter. Everybody comes and asks for their drink, and I am the one who gives the receipt, and all this. So I don't usually see your wife — the time she has gone out."

Then this man said, "No. You have to find my wife for me."

He was shouting, so many people had to come to the counter and say, "Hey? What is happening? What is happening?" And this man said he was looking for his wife.

So there was some stupid idiot, he just came in there like that. He said, "François!"

Then François said, "Yes."

"So this woman: is she your girlfriend?"

"No."

"She is your what?"

He said, "Oh, the husband is my friend. I used to visit them; they used to come to me. We are friends."

"But why should he force you and take you out from your office?" You see? This is his office. Because he works in the nightclub, he is in his office.

Then the manager said, "Ah, no. We are friends, so we should under-stand each other."

Then the woman's husband took his champagne and put it straight in the eyes of François. "To say that you are a friend to me!? How can you be my friend? From selling my wife?" So he was saying that François is something like a pilot, like in Accra, the pilots, those boys who find the girls for the men.[1] And to me, the way that man was asking François these questions, I thought that he already meant this man.[2] So he put champagne in François's eye not to talk something stupid, like that he's a friend to him.

So then the other man who came and was asking François questions, then he had to blow[3] this woman's husband. He just knocked the man: *ka! ka! ka!* Then the man went down. The husband didn't know that this man would fight him or anything, because this man was talking to François and not to him. You see? The man didn't ask any question. He just gave the blows straight. Then he said that he was not there when the husband broke the glass and all the drink went and wet the face of François. But he was talking to François when the woman's husband

1. a man who directs another man to a woman; the reference is to a pilot who brings a ship into port
2. intended to do something to the man
3. to give a blow, to hit; also, a punch

threw the drink on François, so he took it that the husband threw the drink in front of him to show that the husband doesn't care if somebody will come to be in back of François. So he just wanted to show the husband that he has bones, that he alone can beat the man, without François. Then he said that the husband had lost his respect. If it was not so, at the time when he was talking to François, the husband shouldn't have put his drink in the face of François. So just when François said, "We are friends," this woman's husband was annoyed and he took his glass of champagne and put it to his face, and then the other one who was standing behind just started blowing the man who put the drink in the manager's face.

So the husband went down, and he was crying, "My wife is not *bagatelle*."[1]

Do you know *bagatelle?* What do they say? "Prostitute," or something like that. In French, *bagatelle* is meaning many things. You know, this word, even the French people used to say that it is many, many things. *Bagatelle* can mean somebody who is careless: he is a careless person; he doesn't know how to keep his things. But it comes to many things. And as Ghanaians say *ashawo,* the French people also say the same thing, *bagatelle.*

So: "*Ma femme, c'est pas une bagatelle. C'est ma femme. J'ai fait marriage avec elle.*[2] I have married my wife in the family. We have made a wedding. We have two children." You know? "Every time I used to hear things, but I didn't believe! I believed you, François — as my friend — so I didn't know that you could do something bad like that. But now this time, even at twelve o'clock when I go home, my wife used to do something — she used to give me some face which is not — I thought maybe she has somebody outside. So even if you bring your people to be killing me or —" and this and that.

So when this happened, people went there and separated them. And then this man, I think that he didn't know that the other one was going to blow him. He didn't catch himself, so the blows went into him. So he was bending down, and then the people asked him, "Can we take you to hospital?" And he said, "No."

So that one passed. OK. We had another French woman. This woman could *dance* rock! I haven't seen anyone. I have seen the rock in the cinema. This woman, too, if she could make a cinema with her rock, she

---

1. (French): a trifle, a flirt; in this idiom, an easy or loose woman, a woman who sleeps around
2. (French): My wife is not bagatelle. She's my wife. I have married her.

would get plenty of money. And if you saw her, you would never believe
that she was a madame[1] who had a daughter, a nine-year-old daughter. We
thought that maybe she was eighteen years old. We didn't know. But she
was very nice! If you saw her hair you would think she was a *young* girl.
She had *plenty* of hair. And she had a kind of colored hair, too. I think she
used to dye her hair. She didn't have black hair or brown hair. She had
something like silver hair. And it was *long* hair. Down to here. If she put
on jeans and you saw her, you would like her. We were calling her a girl;
we didn't know that she was a woman. She could come with about four
or five people — men. They would start dancing rock. Do you know this
woman: the husband was a soldier, one of these French soldiers who were
training the Voltaiques. *Ah!* The day when we saw the thing, we all wondered. That's the way we said, "Ah, these French women, they are proper
ashawo." *Ha-ha!*

So: the husband came to the nightclub. That night the woman came
with three people. You know, if she came, she wouldn't sit down. She was
always at the counter. And you know, the wonderful things she would
do: every nightclub where she used to go, the husband had a bottle of
whiskey or a bottle of something. People used to buy like that in the
nightclubs. If they drank, then what remained, the manager would write
the name on it and put it on the shelf. So if the wife came, she would
take the bottle of the husband. She was with a group, but she wouldn't
drink with them. They could go out together, they could go everywhere:
but everywhere she would go, she would bring the bottle of the husband,
and these people would buy their own. Maybe after, she would take the
bottle of the husband and serve them and finish the bottle and put it back
empty.

So I think the husband got to know that the wife used to do all these
things. He came to Zé Bon about three times. This woman didn't see him.
Sometimes the husband would sit down outside and send one of the girls
to serve him. Then he would ask us whether that mademoiselle[2] with
plenty of white hair was there? We would say, "Yes." You know, we didn't
know that he was the husband: he used to call her "Mademoiselle," so we
didn't know anything.

The fourth time when this man came to the nightclub, he was ready to
come and *fight!* He was sitting outside. He drank four whiskeys. He had
a bottle inside, but we didn't know him, because every time, when he
would come inside, he didn't sit down. But outside, we knew him. So he

---

1. (French): a married woman
2. (French): girl, young lady; an unmarried woman; Miss

drank about four whiskeys, and then he asked for the bill. I gave him the bill. Then he paid. He had a balance of eight hundred. Then I said I was going to bring the balance. You know, as they were giving him balance, they didn't finish quickly, and when I took the balance, then I saw that this man was entering. So I went to him with the balance, and he just pushed me! I didn't fall completely. And these small coins, some of them dropped. And our place to sit was just there, so I just came and I sat down like that. Then he went and passed me.

Then Limata said, "Why? You have—?"

Then I said, "No, it is the balance I'm going to give him. He is the one who has the balance which they were giving me now."

Then Limata said, "Hey, find his balance. If not so, today he will do something to you."

But he just went straight. When he pushed me like that and I fell down a little bit, he was already going away. And Limata was talking-talking. We saw that he was holding some man with the wife. This woman and the man were dancing, slowly; they were having a slow dance in the darkness. So this soldier just took this man, on the left side, and got the wife on the right side, and took them both like that, outside. He just picked the woman and picked the man, together with their slow dancing, to take them out.

Then our manager, how stupid he is! All of you people are French people. Maybe you know that this woman is the wife of that man. So if this woman is the wife, if there's something happening like that, it's not the time for you to go and beg. But he just went to the man, straight, and said, "Why should you do that? You want to spoil my nightclub? Why should you hold people like that?"

Then the man said, "Hey, *ta gueule, toi!*[1] *Ta gueule!* Shut up, you! I don't want to hear a word from you."

Then our manager was coming back. Then people were asking, "François, what is happening?"

He said, "I don't know." So everybody was asking him, and he was just shrugging his shoulders. Then everybody started laughing, and people started going out.

So when the soldier took these two people out, he started fighting with the man. He left the wife behind. So—*ha!*—but this was something: I think the wife knew the husband. The way he just took this man out and gave him—*boop! boop!*—then this man went *buup!*—like something was

---

1. (French): the mouth of an animal; *ta gueule:* shut up; an abuse similar to "in your face" or "your stinking mouth"

in his stomach, *"Ugh!"* And then he fell down. And this woman ran. She took a taxi. She was going in the taxi, saying *"Vite! Vite! Vite! Vite!"*[1] I don't know where she was going, whether she was going to the house or what, but this woman just ran and left the husband.

And then all the people were coming outside, saying that they should get this man to hospital because he was completely — you know, he was just like dead, so they thought that this soldier killed him or something. So the people were saying, "Oh, let's take him to hospital."

And some people said, "OK, if you take him to hospital, what are you going to say? The man who beat him, he is the one who has to take him to hospital."

And you know, they found more troubles in that. So this soldier man said, "Who said that the man who beat him has to take him to hospital? That person should carry the man and bring him to the car."

So you know, French people, they don't take it that, "I have been going out for pleasure; if there's some trouble, I don't want to see it." The other man said, "Yeah, I am the one who said it. It's right. We all are white here. You can be French, you can be Swiss, you can be German, you can be American: we all are white. You wounded him. You have to take him to hospital. He's not yet dead. Even if he is dead, you have to take him to hospital. Because even if you knock somebody with your car without knowing, the car should take the person. So this one is like, you have come here, you just killed some boy and put the trouble for all of us. So you have to take the man."

Then the trouble came between the soldier and that man. And that man also was drunk. He was not a strong man. He was a little bit old. Then this soldier man just came to make *kpom-kpom!* And this man also fell down. So now he killed two people! You know — *ha!*

Hey! That was the time: you know, in Africa, I have been in Ghana, I have been in Lomé, but I didn't see people who were trying to act something like karate before that time. This man just said, *"Heey!"* And he shouted and he jumped! A heavy jump! And he will make so and make so, with his legs and all this. And then he will stand, and he is *ready!* And he was looking: the eyes were not one place. He was turning around, to see all the people. Yeah, he wanted to show them the soldier way, you know.

So they had to leave this man, because he was wild. And they were afraid. So they all had to drop back and then beg the manager of the night-club, "OK. This is your work. You have your nightclub. People have wounded themselves. You should know where to take them."

1. (French): quick, that is, go quickly

So this manager came out and took the two people to the hospital, and this man went away. Then for two or three weeks, this man and the wife didn't come there again. We didn't see this woman; we didn't see the husband, too.

So then that woman whose husband who had a blow for nothing, the first time, it was her time again. The man who used to work nights, that woman came back again.

The Godfather

When that woman came to the nightclub, she was just like a chief. Many people knew her. When she was there, she used to get many people who could buy her champagne, champagne. And our manager liked her way, because she could make people spend on champagne for her. With the husband she drank whiskey, but when she was with other people: champagne. So she was there like that.

So: you know, in Upper Volta, we have many Lebanese people who are naturalized as Voltaiques. There was one man who had naturalized as a Voltaique, and what I heard of him, they said he was born in Upper Volta, he grew up there, and then he was living there all his life. He was a very old man, too. He was called Hussaine. He had one nephew who was a very big ruffian. They called him Shahin.

This Lebanese boy was a *ruffian!* All the medicine for him was Voltaique boys.[1] But with French people, he was a Lebanese boy. He was a very *small* man, eh? It's only in the nightclubs he spends his life, because the uncle is rich. I told you the uncle had lived in Ouagadougou for a long time and was naturalized. Yeah, the uncle knows even the President of Ouagadougou.[2] So any problem this boy has in Ouagadougou, or if this boy brings any trouble, he's cool. Only African boys can fight with him. When he knows an African boy who can fight with him, he will get all of them in a group, to make friends with them so that he hasn't got any problem again. If it was not so —*oh!*— one African boy beat this boy very well before! He brought about twenty of the friends. But if you people make a group and beat this Lebanese boy, he wouldn't fear. *Huh?* He will get up and make friends with you people. Then he will be walking with you people. So if he has trouble, he wouldn't try to understand. He has all the Ouagadougou crooks, the bad boys, with him. But every day, he is in nightclub, and he is paying his way. But you know, this time that boy is

1. The only people he needed or who were good for him were Voltaique boys.
2. the head of state

coming cool. I don't know why. I think maybe somebody hurt him. Yeah, I think so, because this time he's cool. Ha! So I don't know why the boy is cooling down. Before, in Ouagadougou, you would hear the name of Shahin. He made rough — too much.

And do you know: Shahin was going with this woman every time. OK? Shahin would come to the nightclub every time this woman was there. This woman also liked dancing rock. Sometimes if this woman didn't come, he used to ask us, the servers, that did we see this woman? We would say, which woman? He would say, the woman who likes to talk much, and she used to sit at the counter. Then maybe we would say she didn't come yet. If you said that she came and went away, Shahin wouldn't stay. He wouldn't drink anything. He would go back. And then in two or three minutes, he would come back with the woman. OK. So they were nice like that.

So this woman and the Lebanese boy, the day for them was coming but the day hadn't reached yet. The first one, I think maybe this woman had promised the Lebanese boy that the husband was going to night duty. But that day the husband didn't have night duty, so they came out together. Then this boy also came into the place. And they thought they were all friends. But I think this boy wanted to make a palaver or something like that. I don't know how this thing could happen, because every time, even if the husband of the woman was there, this boy used to dance with the woman. They joked as they liked.

But I think the husband had learned something from the day when they beat him. That day they just boxed him for nothing. So he learned something. So this Lebanese boy came and danced with the woman, and then maybe they were joking on the floor, or they were saying something. And he just knocked the back of this woman's waist, and said, *"Bagatelle."*

Hey! The husband became crazy! "Why should you call my wife *'Bagatelle'?* She is my *wife!* Even maybe you do this with her when she's alone, but not in front of me."

So this was the war day in Zé Bon. *Tatatatatata!* This man said that, and the Lebanese boy also talked. You know, I said that this Lebanese boy was a very ruffian boy, so if he saw that he was talking to the friends, and then the thing came to look like trouble, he used to change, to become wild. So this boy also told the husband, "Why should tell me that?"

Then this man said, "Yes, I'm right to tell you, because she's my wife. You shouldn't say, *'bagatelle, bagatelle.'* Why did you say she is a *'bagatelle'?"*

OK? This Lebanese boy was very clever. He asked the man, "Are you a French man?"

He said, "Yes."

He said, "OK. Teach me the word *'bagatelle'* in French language. Because when I learned my French language, there were many things which
French people used to say *'bagatelle.'*"

This *bagatelle,* eh? I said it is not for one thing in French language. It's
for many things. So this boy said, yes, *bagatelle* can be something which
is bad. *Bagatelle* can be ashawo. But a real ashawo, even he thought —
he was Lebanese, but he thought that to say somebody is ashawo is not
bagatelle in the French language. So this man is a French man. He should
teach him French, because maybe he has lost his place to his French.

Then this man said, "Don't fool me."

So they were talking, and this Lebanese boy saw that the man was serious. So: what to do with this man? You know, as I said, when this woman
was with her husband, she drank whiskey, but with the other people she
knew, only champagne. Every nightclub she went: it was champagne she
drank. OK? So this Lebanese boy came and met her with the husband,
and this Lebanese boy asked for a bottle of champagne. And he served
both the woman and the husband champagne, one cup and one cup. So
they were drinking. He knew that this woman would drink champagne,
but she was with the husband, and he came and saw them with whiskey
and Coke. So he bluffed himself to serve them, you know, before he got
the woman to dance and do all this.

So they had something like a problem. The husband of the woman
was talking too much. Then this Lebanese boy just took his bottle of
champagne under his arm, and he was standing, with bottle of champagne like that, and he asked this man, "But I'm still standing, waiting
for your answer. I'm still waiting for you to answer me, because I am not
French. I am a fucking Lebanese boy. I don't speak well French. Anyway,
I think *'bagatelle'* can mean anything. But I have joked with your wife, as
a friend, you know. As I know you, you are my friend: I can joke with
your wife in any way. But you don't understand, and I also am not a
French man. I am Lebanese. Maybe I said something bad, so I want you
to show me the meaning of *'bagatelle'* in French. Or maybe it's not one
thing I think — it's many things. But I'm waiting for your answer. You
didn't give me an answer yet."

So the woman's husband said, "If it's because of your champagne,
when you served us in our glass to show us a bottle, then I can also buy
some."

Before he said that, it was too late. This Lebanese boy just shook the
champagne, and let it spray in the man's eyes, you know. Oh, *shhhh!* And
this man was dodging. And: *shit!* Then the Lebanese boy was finished.

So he got drink on this man's face, and what should this man say? This man was shouting, and people came and talked, saying that what the boy was doing was not good. And then the boy said he would leave it and go: he is not a French man; he is Lebanese. He is a fucking Lebanese, and that's why he has to listen to all this. So he went away. When he went away, this woman and the husband also went away.

About three days again, they met together. This was the time for the real blows they were going to make for their last show. This woman and the husband, I used to see them at the market, but since that day I didn't see them at Zé Bon again. They are in Ouagadougou. The nightclub they go — maybe they go to some nightclub I don't go to because it's far. But if it's not so, I have been going to many nightclubs, and I don't see them. But they are in town. Sometimes I used to see the woman in the market.

So that day, this Lebanese boy came again. And he bought his champagne. And this woman, the husband came and met her there, and they also bought champagne. They were at the counter.

Then this boy greeted the husband of the woman. He said, "Forgive me for that day. You know, anything can happen." And that and this, saying, *"Madame, il faut me pardonner; il faut me pardonner."* And that and this. "Madame, excuse me. Forgive me."

So they talked, and they understood each other, and then all three of them, they took two more bottles of champagne, and they went and sat down at a table. We put all their drinks there. So then we were sitting. Everybody had gone home, and we were feeling to sleep. And this Lebanese boy was calling, "More champagne, more champagne." They wouldn't finish. Then he was saying, oh-h, the champagne has kept long — it's open — air has gone inside. They have to change it. And this and that.

OK. So these people were there, and when he saw that *all* the people went away, then he was asking this woman, "Why? I know that you are a married woman. But before I got to know you, I didn't know that you had married. But after that, I knew that you are married. And I know your husband loves you. If your husband didn't love you, you people have two children. Eh? And you also love him. But why? Why do you want to spoil my chance? You asked me to go one day with you. And after that, if I don't have time — I know that you are a married woman. I can't fall in love on you — but every time when you see me with the girls, you want to make trouble. And when your husband comes with you, I don't make trouble, and I don't want your husband to know that you are something to me. But I thought you have told your husband something. That's why that day he was trying to tell me foolishness."

Look at this thing! This is direct speaking. The husband was there, and this man was asking this woman these questions.

So the husband said, "Ah, *bon.* Is that so? Eh? But you are my friend. You have to tell me everything, you know. I believe my wife. But you are also my friend. I can believe you too."

Then this boy said, "What kind? Did I know you before? How did we come to be friends?"

Then he said, "Yes, one day my wife introduced you to me, that she used to go to you people's store and get some things."

He said, "*Ah-hah!* Your wife introduced me to you. You are a *stupid idiot!* You are foolish! *Think!* I am Shahin. I am a small boy. I didn't marry yet. But if I marry, I know that my wife cannot introduce a man to me. If you are not so stupid, if you had your own experience — that's why every time people say that we Lebanese people are fools. *Ai!* We Lebanese — you French people say we are Africans. But that's why every time, many people used to say that the French, they are fools. Even the whole world: the countries which like you are not many countries. But there are *many* countries, where I used to hear that these French people, they are stupid. You are such stupid idiots." That day, he wanted to talk war, and nobody would hear.

Then this French man said, "The manager is my friend."

You know, at Zé Bon, we had three managers. OK? They were all white. We had two who were teachers. I told you about François: he was there, and one other teacher. The third one was also teaching, but I think he was a teacher of karate or something like that. He was a French man: Daniel. He was tall. He doesn't talk; he doesn't do anything; he's cool. But he can get people in a cool way, you know. If they are making trouble, he will come and call you like this, "Excuse me, I want to see you." When he goes outside with you, then he will say, "What is wrong?" You will talk all your matter. If it's not good, he'll tell you, "No. Stop. You see, what you say is not good. Stop. If you don't want to stop, you just tell me how much you spent in the nightclub. I will pay you. You can go off. I don't want this." He is a cool man. OK? Some people will agree that they will stop, and they will go back inside, and they will start again. Hm? So if Daniel hears your voice again, and then he comes, and he sees that you are making something like quarreling, he will just get behind you. Sometimes he used to pick the people up, you know, the men who are small like me. It's a pity. Daniel will just hook your belt here and hang you up like this! And carry you out! Shit! *Ha!* He will carry you out! And he will tell you, "From today going, it's your first and last. Go out! Don't come here again!"

So when this French man told the Lebanese boy that the manager was his friend, then this Lebanese boy just said, "Yeah, I also know that he's your friend. I don't care about him. But this fucking François, if he comes here, I will just send him out. So tell me what you want to say today. Your wife has been with me once. I don't want her again. And your wife doesn't want to see me with a woman. What is she doing?"

So—ha! *Hey!* Come and see the place that night. It was *beautiful!* Suppose you had a camera, you know, you could stand somewhere and take the picture. This French man just got up. I don't know how he got up. It was like he carried the whole table. This French man. And just—all the bottles—*ka! ka! ka! ka!* All broke—*bang!* With all the tables!

And they stood. And this Lebanese boy, all time he was talking to him, he had a glass of champagne. You see? He was holding this glass, and he went to the table and just made like a gentleman. He stood in front, and the man was sitting. And when this French man got up and knocked all these things down, then this Lebanese boy said, "What did you want to do? When I said your wife is *bagatelle,* you didn't understand. OK. The first time, I was joking with her, I think as a friendship. You didn't understand. But I want to tell you that your wife *is* bagatelle. She is a proper ashawo. I slept with her once. *Voilà.* She's here. Ask her."

This woman couldn't say a word. Then he came to the man's wife, and said, "Isn't it?" And the wife started to make a face. And the husband was coming. Then the Lebanese boy was going to touch the shoulder of the wife, and that was the place the man became *hot.* So the man came full speed. And this Lebanese boy just took this champagne glass with his left hand to strike the man so that he could wound this man somewhere. And the wife was smart: she caught the glass. And the wife's hand was cut. *"Aa-a-a!"* She was shouting! *"Aa-a-a-a-a!"*

So we all, all the servants, we had to run. That had happened two times in Zé Bon. One woman also had a wound. And this was the second time. But the way this woman shouted, we were afraid. We thought maybe she was dead. And that time, nobody was there. They were the only three people there. The husband was shouting loudly. All of us ran away. We couldn't stand it. And then, there was one boy there. He was called Bernard. Bernard came, *"Yee-eh!* The white woman! The hand is cut into two pieces!"

Then I said, "Ah?" The other woman who was wounded before was not cut like that. We girls, we took her to the toilet and helped her. But this woman, we didn't see, and then this boy came and said that the thing was cut deep. So they took something to bandage her hand, and then they put the woman in the car to hospital.

And this woman's husband, he was boiled up to beat this Lebanese boy, but then our manager, Daniel, he also got to this Lebanese boy. And you know, Daniel too, I think this woman used to go with him, and maybe this woman was good to him. So he was also a little bit jealous inside, because sometimes if this woman's husband didn't come, this woman would come alone and meet Daniel. She would go inside of the counter and she would be drinking champagne with Daniel. So we suspected that maybe she also knew Daniel. The husband and Daniel and the wife, they were also good friends. But you know these French people: you can't trust them. So I think he used to use the woman, too. So Daniel was also boiled up, and he picked this Lebanese boy out. You know, this woman's husband didn't get a chance to fight with this boy: when the wife was wounded, nobody fought with the boy. Daniel let François take these people to the hospital, and he came and caught hold of the boy and went outside with him and gave him a good slap. Then the poor boy went to his car, and he said, "OK, I will call the Patron himself." When he went outside with him, you know, we girls, we wanted to see everything, so we followed him. And he sacked us. "Any girl who comes here, she will see." So we all went back.

Then he went to his place and he got his uncle. I told you the uncle was somebody, a big man. All Voltaiques know him. Then the uncle got up. He didn't bring the boy. He came alone with one man. They were only two. He had two pistols, and he put them on. Yeah — pistols. They thought they are all right to kill all the people in Zé Bon. Two people, man. *Shit!* When he came, he said, "You people can see my card. I'm pure Voltaique. I can kill anybody here as I want. I will only go to prison. Even sometimes, if it's not my time to go to prison, if I have luck, I won't even go to prison. So: why should you people beat my nephew? You want kill my nephew? Because you people are French people. We are Lebanese people. Because we don't speak much French? What is a French man? A French man — a woman, a man — they are all bagatelle. So what do you people mean?!"

So, at that time, look: it was a wonderful thing. Daniel is a strong man, isn't it? Daniel was the first man who bent down on this fucking compound at Zé Bon. There, Daniel had to bend on his knees. He just loosened up, and he fell down. I thought he was strong; he cannot fall. But how this thing came, he just showed this Lebanese man that, yes, he was the one who beat the nephew.

You know, our country is a good country. But I think this case I'm talking, if it were Ghana, if they reported that sort of person, they would arrest him. *Huh?* For taking pistols to the nightclubs, to say that you will kill everybody. In Ghana they would arrest him. Yeah, but our place, what did they do? Nothing! Nothing! I think they reported him. I think when they gave this complaint, this man went and saw all those big people, because he knew them, and they were friends. I think so. So when they reported him, it was our manager had problems for about three days. He closed the place for three days because of this case.

Look: this Lebanese man. He speaks Fulani,[1] he speaks Mossi, he speaks Dioula,[2] he speaks Guruma.[3] *Ha!* Eh? A Lebanese man. He speaks Zambarima.[4] Look. Where are Zambarimas from? This man speaks all, a little bit. Yeah. This man speaks these languages. *Eh?* And French. When you are speaking French with him, you wouldn't believe that he's a Lebanese man. He doesn't have any different tongue like Lebanese people when they learn the language.

Many people used to talk about him. They said they had borne him in Ouagadougou and he grew up there as a Voltaique. Every time he used to travel to Lebanon and come back. I think the mother and father had some stores in Ouagadougou, and all these things, so maybe they were at home now, and he took the place of them.

He doesn't care about anything. He had a wife, a Lebanese woman. He divorced from the woman. He had two children, one boy and one girl. The girl was senior, and the boy was small. These children, if you go to his shop to buy something, then this small boy is the one who is making accounts. I don't know his age. Maybe he's a short boy, I don't know, but if I can take him as — he may be seven years or eight years old. Very *small.*

And you know what is funny? The place they were living was just near to Flamboyant. From Flamboyant to La Tringle is not far. Every night, when you don't find the father in the house, this boy will be passing from one nightclub to the other. When he goes, people will see this small boy in the bar, maybe about eleven o'clock. He doesn't mind. People are looking at him; he doesn't mind. He will go to the counter, and then he holds the counter and tries to climb up. Then he will ask, "*Tu n'as pas vu mon père ce soir?* Didn't you see my father here tonight?"

Then maybe you will say, "No."

---

1. cultural group known in French as Peul. They are spread across the West African savanna from Senegal into Cameroon, with the largest concentration in northern Nigeria and Niger. Only a few Fulani groups remain nomadic herdsfolk; nonetheless, many retain their husbandry calling and make their living tending cows for other local peoples.

2. also Jula, Djula, Dyula; cultural group in western Burkina Faso and northern Côte d'Ivoire

3. cultural group in southeastern Burkina Faso

4. or Zaberma, cultural group from western Niger

He will say, "*Merci.* Thank you."

Then he will go. He's going to the other place. He will be going around all the places which are near to them. But Zé Bon or Ricardo, he couldn't go there, because he couldn't walk on foot to there. So if he asks at these places, and he doesn't see the father, he's going to sleep. And what he does, he sleeps, but he doesn't sleep. Yeah, there are many girls who talk about this. When the man takes a woman to his place, and he comes and asks the girls again, they don't want to go with the man. When she goes there with the father, he will open the outside door and reach the door to the sitting room before going to the bedroom. And this small boy will be in the sitting room. He will say, "Yeah, I went to La Tringle. I have been to Flamboyant. I have been to Cascade. I have been to La Gaîté. I have been to La Main au Panier. Where is my Papa? They say my Papa is not there. *Yay!* So you are coming with a beautiful woman!" *Ha!*

Anyway, this man liked the boy. Every Saturday, he would take him to the nightclub, for the *whole* night. Yeah, with the daughter. The daughter is about sixteen now. She is a nice chap. But this time, I think the daughter has started to know men, so she doesn't go with the father. She used to bring a different group. And the father is with the small brother. *Ha! Hey!*

So the father will say, "Yeah? Is she beautiful?"

The boy will say, "Yes, she's beautiful. Is she from Zé Bon or Ricardo?"

You see? He knows that he has been to La Tringle, and he has been to Flamboyant, or Cascade. He didn't see the father. So he knows that the places which he can't go are these far away ones, so maybe the father must be bringing this girl from over there.

And the father will say, "How did you know that?"

He will say, "Oh, no. Because I know. Ricardo: they have some nice girls, because they have many girls. And there are some nice ones inside. If you take your time, you will get the nice one. If you doesn't take your time, you will get the bad one."

Then the father will say, "And what about this one?"

He will say, "She is nice." He will make his eyes so: "She's *nice.*" *Ha-ha!*

Not Crazy, Just Stupid

So: Zé Bon. It's only these fucking French people there. One time three Voltaiques came there, and it made me laugh. How the place was full of white people, they said they'll never come back to such a nightclub again. They said that if they come to Zé Bon, there are many whites. And these white people, you know these fucking French people, they don't bathe. So if you are near to the girls, if the place is full up, you will get different scents. So some Voltaiques used to come inside, and they say, "These people have much scent. If you go inside, they smell all white. You don't smell any scent from Africans." *Ha-ha!* So this is what they said: you could smell only the scent from the white people. *Ha-ha!*

And the way they behave there. You know, if you go to Zé Bon in the day, if you come early, or at a late hour, from two o'clock going — eh? — if you go there, you wouldn't meet any African. You will meet *all* of them white. And their women. Their women are inside. Somebody can get up from the husband and come and sit down outside with the other men. Somebody can get fed up with the wife and go and sit with another group's women. Just like that. They are just like that. I don't know how they take their lives. But maybe it's good for them. That's the way they think.

And the music they play. Every time, when you come inside Zé Bon, you won't hear music of Zaire or some place. Every time it's this soul. Soul, soul — soul music. Anyway, these French people, they are clever. They have many American records. But still, *our people* don't like *all* of it. They *like* it for some minutes, but not all the time. You know? Sometimes they used to feel like home, to hear something like Africans' music or something like that. So if they go to the nightclub and they see all these things, they will start to be annoyed. They will start talking. "Because the manager is a white man, he wants to take this place as a white country. But this country is for us, so let's fuck off.[1] We have got our place. We have our own place. Here is Ouagadougou. The land is for us. So this man can't come and *tin-tin-tin-tin*.[2] *Ça c'est quoi même? Tin-tin-tin-tin.* Every time. *Tous les fois, quand tu pars au Zé Bon? Tin-tin-tin-tin.*" It means: This is all what? Every time, when you go there, it's the same thing.

You know, I think English people, they are funny. I think English people, their own is something like funny, or what. But the French people, I think their own is something like foolishness. You know, it's something like foolishness.

Sometimes you can speak to a French man. *Hm?* You know, sometimes we used to try. Sometimes you can be with a French man. But you can't stay with them for long. You can be with them for some days. But if you try to compare their life to the others, it can't be correct. Every time,

1. in this context, leave. In other contexts, as an exclamation: "Get away!" As a verb: dismiss, snub, verbally abuse
2. the one-way beat of the American music

when you try to do this life, every time you will be lower than the French people. So, I think their life — they are just like some people, you know, in their way, they know that they know more than everybody. This is the way they think. They think that. But if you look at the truth of their life, they are like some stupid people who have no understanding. They don't have any understanding. But every time they try to say that they are the best people in the world.

So maybe you can be with a French man, you know, and maybe you will think, "OK, we are together." Sometimes he will listen to you, or sometimes you will listen to him, isn't it? Yeah, because sometimes, I think somebody can do something he thinks is good, and then the person who is watching knows that what he is doing is good or is not good. So sometimes you can try to say, "Well, this thing, you are doing it well, but it is not good anyway."

Then: "*Mais pourquoi tu me dis ça?* Why should you tell me that?" You know?

Then, "Ah, I have told you this because I think this thing which you have done — to me — maybe to your people it is nice — but maybe to me it is not nice. So you have to change this. I don't like it."

Then he will say, "My people: French! OK? They understand me."

You see? If you don't understand him, his people understand him. So his people understand him. So what are you going to say? And maybe, the time when he will say this to you, you know, you have boiled up. Maybe he has done something which is a disgrace. You want to correct him to do the correct thing, and he wouldn't want to understand you, and he is saying something like this. So what should you do with this person? You will just leave him. Yeah. You leave him. But he will be coming after you.

You know, they are very funny. The French people, they are very funny. I don't know whether it's all of them, or there are some different types. Maybe it's the Ouagadougou ones. They are so much stupid, you know. When I was in Lomé, I didn't meet many French people. I used to meet these German people more than French people. But in Ouagadougou, I met many French people. But every time I used to think that they are so stupid. It's not that they are crazy: they're just stupid! You know, if somebody is crazy, you can know that this person is crazy. But there's someone, he is stupid. He's stupid, you know.

This is why I am saying that a French man, maybe you will see that something is not good for him. And you will try to say, "Oh, you know, this thing, you shouldn't do it in this way, you know. Maybe: we are here in Africa, isn't it? You know Africa well, but I'm African. Maybe I'm with the people in town. Maybe they will start to say something about what you are doing." And that and this. Maybe I may hear something. If it's something coming bad, by all means, somebody will hear it. So if you go and tell this fellow, "Look this way you are, you shouldn't do this," and oh, and that and this. *No-o-o-o:* he wouldn't understand you.

That is the place when he is going to *ask* — in front of *all* the people, the Africans — he will want to ask at that place: "You know? In France, do you know what I'm doing? You shouldn't tell me this." He will just try to get up, and behave, inside of the people. Maybe you were sitting with him, and then maybe you thought he's a gentleman, to give him advice, and to show the people who were talking something against him, or something like that. He will just get up there, and then he will say, "Yeah, I said this, but what did you people say? You know, I'm white, but I don't care. You know, I can fight you people. Yeah, I think I have my *strength.*" Yeah! Ha! "I can fight like that. *Mais comment? Tu me prends comme*—[1] How do you think I am? How do you —?" You know? Something like that!

And then, they are causing trouble in any way, so they are not gentle too much. Sometimes we used to go and sit at Palladium. When you sit at Palladium, don't you see that there are many white people who come there? But there are many girls who come there, too, and many of them don't want to sit with the white people. They are afraid. Because a French man can just go and cause trouble. And then after all this palaver, when he sees the thing is hot, he will say, "Upon all, I am sitting with a Voltaique girl" or "I'm sitting with one African girl like you people."

You see? When he sees the thing is coming so, then all the people will start to be watching you, and then they will know who you are. So in this way, we don't go together any time. So you know, what many girls do in Upper Volta: they can get a French man as a boyfriend. You the boyfriend can go out alone. Even if you like any girl, you can take her to any place, or your place, to sex and come back. She doesn't mind. She is seeing it, and they are telling her about it, but she wouldn't mind. Yeah? She wouldn't mind because after, you will come and search for her to go home with her. She doesn't mind. She will go and sleep, and maybe you will give her something to eat tomorrow. So the girls won't be jealous of each other.

But there are some foolish girls who haven't got understanding. They used to stand at the bar and talk: "*Pa-pa-pa-pa-pa!* This man was my boyfriend. You came and met me with him in this nightclub." Have you seen this problem between girls? We the girls who work in the nightclub,

---

1. (French): But what? You take me like —

you know, we work easy. And all the girls —I think, I don't know, maybe — but I think, all of us people doing this work, I think we like it. We like the work in the nightclub, because you have not many problems. But for some people, there are many problems inside of nightclub work.

4 KƆNKƆNSA RESEARCH

: *Mr. Heh-heh-heh*
: *The Belgian Prisoner*
: *Interrogations*
: *Hope*
: *Shetu and Philippe*
: *The Trouble with Frogs*

: OUAGADOUGOU :

Mr. Heh-heh-heh

There was one French man. He was called Pierre. It's very funny. He has a big business now; he tried his best. Any time when he comes to Ouagadougou, we laugh at him. He is growing fat now. He's very short; he's not a tall man. He's a fat-short man. And what used to make me laugh, he was forcing himself to speak English. So: *"Le Ghana, c'est bon, eh?* Ghana is good! Takoradi![1] Hey, sister! I love you, *heh-heh-heh!"*

When you ask him, "What is the meaning of 'I love you'?"

"Eh, *je comprends anglais, non? Je comprends.*[2] I love you. *Heh-heh-heh. Je t'aime. Heh-heh-heh."*

Then we asked him, "What is '*Heh-heh-heh*'?"

He says, "But you have to smile, you know. So it is: '*Smile.' Heh-heh-heh.* My sister. I love you. *Heh-heh-heh."*

So he has a business. He has very big trucks. I think he is bringing some things to Ouagadougou that they use to build a house. He is bringing these things with his trucks. So now is good for him. But do you know that before he was going to do all this, he borrowed money from some

---

1. major town, former main port, in southwest Ghana
2. (French): I understand English, no? I understand.

people? He took the name of his brother's nightclub, the younger brother, and borrowed the money.

But first time — look! He came to our place, La Tringle. That time I was working at La Tringle. He bought everybody a drink. "Hey! Ghana, *c'est bon,* eh? *C'est bon!*" Then he called me, "Hey, my sister, my sister." *Ha!*

Then I said, "My brother."

"*Bois, bois!* Drink! Drink and drink!"

So I used to drink a drink which cost thousand two hundred, but I was drunk that day, so I used to take some small things and mix water, and it was looking the same color, just like a small coffee color. But it was sugar. Then I was taking my thousand two hundred! So: I had six thousand; Limata had four thousand. And this man, it was time to close when he came. So we had closed, and we had wasted all our time. And we wanted to go. Then this man started talking: *Pa-pa-pa-pa-pa, pa-pa, pa-pa.*

Then Limata said, "*Camarade.* I'm going to go first, then I will wait for you behind the place."

Then I said, "OK."

So: "Hey! My sister!"

I said, "Hey! My brother! *Heh-heh-heh.*" *Ha!*

"What are you going to drink?"

I said, "OK. Brother, I think we have to close. We will take one bottle of champagne, then we will close everything."

Then he said, "OK, OK. *OK! O-Kay! Une bouteille de champagne!*" *Ha-ha!*

They brought the champagne, and we opened it. Then he said they should play music. The boy who was playing the music had gone, so we had to get another boy to come and play the music. So that boy came in. Then I said, "The boy said he will take three thousand before he will play it, because he doesn't work here. And our man has already gone because it's time to close. If you want to enjoy yourself —"

"Oh, yeah! Hey! OK, OK. *OK! O-Kay!*" He gave me five thousand. I took three thousand to that boy, then I brought the balance to him, two thousand.

So I told him, "Oh, my brother, but I haven't got cigarettes."

He said, "Oh, go and take, go and take." So I took cigarettes for us. One packet was two hundred thirty francs, that green St. Moritz.[1] I took five packets, then he paid for it.

---

1. brand of menthol cigarettes, by Rothmans

So we danced and danced and danced and danced. Then I told him, "Heh-heh-heh — you know, my brother, my master hasn't paid me over-time, so I think we must close."

He said, "OK, let's go to someplace and have a drink."

Then I said, "OK. Before I go to someplace and have drinks, unless I go back to my place, because I don't want to go to any place with the dress I work with."

So: "OK, OK. *O-Kay!*"

When we came out, Limata was waiting for me outside, and I told her, "Let's go." So Limata followed me. We got a taxi, and the taxi took us to our place. Then I told him, "OK — heh-heh-heh — my brother, I will change my dress. I will come, and we'll go."

"*O-Kay!*"

So we went inside, then I said, "Limata, what do you think about this? What should we do with this man?"

Then Limata said, "Let's take him. Does he feel like drinking?"

"Yes."

"Let's go and drink and eat, and after we will give him a promise for another time."

Then I said, "OK."

So then I told him that Limata doesn't want to come out, because she's wasting her time.

"Oh-h, no. I know. You are my sister. Limata is my sister's girlfriend. OK. Hey, me — I make you *cadeau*. After, you sleep."

So she said, "OK."

We went to the place where he was lodging. Yatenga Hotel.[1] He woke up the watchman[2] and the boys to come and cook. By force. He said that they have to open the bar, and he will give them some *cadeau*. So, you know, these poor boys — or we girls who are working the bar — if they say they will give you *cadeau*, even if you are feeling to sleep, you have to wake up. So he woke all the boys: they started cooking, and then he was serving us.

So, you know, me and Limata: you know what's funny? In Ouagadou-gou, when we sit, every time, we don't want a man to sit between us; we used to sit close together. Even if we have many men, she must be beside me, and me beside her. Sometimes she used to take her shoe and scratch my foot — *ha!* Some funny things.

---

1. small hotel in Ouagadougou

2. a private watchman guarding a residence or business. Many bungalows in resi-dential areas have such an employee.

Then they finished cooking, and we ate and finished. We had everything. Then we said, "OK, my brother, we want to go."

So: "Oh-h, *attends, attends un peu.* You, my sister, wait, wait for me.
Small-small come." You see the English? "Small-small come": I will come
in a minute. *Ha!*

So I didn't know where he went. Maybe he went to his room, and he
was coming back. Then we heard some talking, and we came out and
saw the brother, the younger brother. About three o'clock in the morning,
the younger brother came there with one gentleman who was in up-and-
down dress, an African man. That man was a policeman. We didn't know
it. *Ha! Ha!* So he gave a paper to this man. You know, in a French country, they don't arrest people just like that: they will come and give you a
paper, that they want you at police station. That is all. So they came and
gave him the paper. *Hey!* About three or four in the morning. I think the
brother had been coming there with the police people, and he didn't meet
him. So he knew the time maybe this man will come and sleep, and he
will meet him. So he brought the people at that time, about three o'clock
in the morning, to give the paper to this man.

You see the case: the man we were with, he had a brother, and he took
the name of the nightclub of the younger brother to borrow money from
people. That nightclub was not for him, but for the younger brother. So
the people had been worrying the brother because they would go there
and ask of this man, and the brother would say, "He's my senior brother.
We have the same father, but we don't have the same mother." The man's
mother was the first wife of the father, and the father divorced before he
got the younger one's mother. So he was the younger brother, on the father's side. Then the boy was trying to tell his problem, and the people
didn't believe him, so he had to get the senior brother to pay the debt. But
when the senior brother got his small money, he didn't care about anything of the younger brother. So the younger one called the police to make
him pay. *Ha! Ha!*

Yeah! We were happy that night! Ha-ha! So this man said, "OK. Hey,
my sister, *je pense, moi cherche taxi.* I think me look for taxi.[1] You go
home? Eh, *moi,* brother, small boy, no this — *il n'a pas le sens* —" He means
that the brother hasn't got sense — "He drink — he big man — African,
comme ça, c'est quoi?"

---

1. The way Hawa is representing the man's speech, he is trying to speak English but
is lapsing and translating himself back into French, so his broken English also appears to
be broken French.

So maybe he thought that we didn't understand. And when they brought this paper, we didn't know that the man was a policeman. So when he looked at the paper, and he just made something with the paper like that, and said, "*Moi, frère*— my brother — he no —": but the time when he was talking, then we saw that the paper was from the police. So we started to fear! *Ha-ha!* The two of us.

Then Limata said, *"Camarade?"* She pressed me on the foot, then she said, *"Camarade?"*

Then I said, "What's this?" Then I looked at her.

Then she said, "Ah, if that be the case, *camarade,* then we can go."

Then I said, "Yes, we can go."

So when we asked this man, he also said his younger brother is a foolish man, and he's trying to do all this foolishness. He's bringing this big African man to show him. You know, he didn't want to say that he had a problem. So we also saw that, ah — he wants to be a man, so we have to be a woman, too. So we told him that, "OK, if that will be the case, we want to go."

So he said, OK, he hasn't got any small money, so the two of us can take ten thousand to manage, to pay our taxi fare, and then go and take the rest for chop tomorrow. So we took our ten thousand, and we shared it five-five thousand, me and Limata.

Then when we got home, Limata said, "Hey, *camarade*. No. Let's keep this money down and wait, if there's a problem on it."

And I said, "Why should we keep it?"

She said, "Didn't you see the police?"

Then I said, *"What?!* I have nothing to do with the police. *Ah!* If he went and stole it, if they catch him, they catch him. It is not my problem. They haven't seen me with him."

She said, "Oh, it is French law." [1]

I said, "OK, if it is French law, and you don't want it, give it to me."

She said, "OK, I will keep my own."

And I said, "I will chop my own."

So we didn't see the man for about two weeks' time. And the third week, he came to the nightclub again. They had got him and kept him two weeks. *Ha-ha!* We didn't know anything about it. We hadn't seen him again, but we didn't know anything about it. I thought, before, maybe he used to go to Ghana, so maybe he was in Takoradi or someplace. We just

---

1. Limata is saying that Hawa's thinking might not apply because laws in Burkina Faso may be different from Ghana.

thought maybe he had traveled. So when he came back in, too, he was dancing. Then: "Hey! My sister!"

I said, "My brother."

He said, "Will you give me a cigarette?" *Hee-hee!*

So I said, "Oh, my brother, it's bad luck for you today. I haven't got a cigarette, and I haven't got any money, too."

He said, "My sister. *En tout cas,* I want cigarette — one. You give me. Me speak you plenty, plenty." *Ha!* He was forcing to speak English.

So I said, "OK, if that will be the case, I know the cigarettes which you smoke. I will take one packet for you from the bar. Tomorrow I will pay."

Then he said, "You good, good, good, good."

So I went and got one Gitane[1] filter, with one packet of matches, and I gave it to him. Then he said, "You see? I have only six thousand today. I haven't got money. You buy me cigarette. You are good. So let's go and sit down and have a drink. We will drink with this money, eh? But I will tell you something."

So I said, "OK. What about Limata?"

Then he said, no, he wants to tell me something serious, so he doesn't want Limata to come. So we went and sat down and had our drinks and were conversing. Then he was trying to tell me what happened before he went to the prison.

The Belgian Prisoner

He said he had borrowed money from people. And the nightclub which the younger brother had made, they had made it together, the two of them. He had small money and the younger one had small money, and they made the nightclub. So he had the younger brother stay there in Ouagadougou to work in the nightclub, and the younger brother didn't do the work well, and they were coming into debt. Then the younger brother wanted to take the place from him, to say that the nightclub was for the younger brother alone. So he is not a fool: that's why he took the name of the nightclub to borrow the money from people. So these people got him. But as the younger brother was in Ouagadougou for a long time, he knew the police people, so the people tried to convince the younger brother to let him be in prison. But later, they accepted everything. This was the story he told me, eh?

1. brand of French cigarettes

So he had got a friend in prison who was a white man, but he didn't want to go there himself. He wanted to ask me seriously to go and visit this man for him. So he asked if I could go and get the papers—you know, to visit somebody in prison, you have to go to the court to get a paper. So the time the man told me this story, I didn't answer that I would do it or not. I said I would think about it.

So I went and told Limata. You know, everything we did, I used to tell Limata. Me and Limata, we are just like sisters. She knows many things of me. So I went and told Limata, *"Camarade."*

She said, *"Camarade."*

I said, "Look at what this man told me."

Then Limata said, "Suppose if I am the one, I won't go."

And I said, "Ah, if that will be the case, I won't go, too."

Then when we went home, the next morning, then I thought again, and I said, "No, Limata, I will go. I will go to this place to try to get the paper. Maybe I will see that friend in prison, and maybe he will also have a nice thing to tell me." *Ha!*

That was Friday. If you wanted to visit somebody, they gave the papers two times in a week, I think Friday and some day. So I went to get the paper, and then I passed the hotel where the man was. He was not there. So I gave a note that if he comes, he can find me at our place, that I wanted to see him. When he came, I said, "Oh, I have the paper. I came to look for you to go and visit your friend, because you told me you can't go. So I came to you because maybe you have some paper to give me to give to him. So I am ready."

So when I said I was ready, he said he liked it very much how I was trying to do that. So he gave me ten thousand to give to that white man in prison. That man was not French, and he was not English, too. I knew him. I think he was Belgian. I had been seeing him, but we didn't used to say hello to each other. He was a friend to one of our girlfriends named Hope. But he was in prison in Ouagadougou. *He-he-he-he-he-he!*

So when I went, the friend gave me five thousand for the taxi. From town to the prison is about three hundred; to come back, three hundred: it's six hundred. So I had four thousand four hundred from it, for me to keep that. Then I went to see the man.

When I called the name, they went and called the man inside. When the man came out, he didn't know me, so when he was coming, he was looking around. Then I said, "Hello."

Then he said, "Hello." Then he passed by me.

Then I said, "Oh, I came to look for you, you know."

Then he wondered. Then I gave him the letter which the man gave to me. When he read the letter, then he said, "OK, you can have a seat."

Then I said, "Yes."

So we sat down, and he said, "Ah! I have been seeing you with Hope, every time. It's a long time I have been seeing you."

So I said, "Oh, what is wrong."

He said, "You know the Voltaiques have no understanding." So what he told me, he said the Voltaiques, the people from Upper Volta, they don't have understanding, because people brought a report that he was abusing the president every time. That's why they kept him there. But that is not the case.

Then I said, "What?! But we girls, it's not difficult. I used to talk any foolish thing about this every time, but they don't keep me here."

He said, "Yeah, you know, the Voltaiques, when they want to put you in trouble, they get a small point on another part, then they get a small point there."

I said, "What is that point?"

He said they said he has been eating people's money, and that and this, and he has been abusing the president.

Then I said, "Oh, if you are not eating the money, and they say you have been eating it, even if they take you to police, if the police see that your account is correct, they won't take you to prison."

He said, "No, because they don't understand. People say you have been abusing — you don't respect the government. That's why you have been eating their money by heart, and then trying to tell them foolishness." So that's why they brought him there.

So I said, "Is that all?"

He said, "Yes."

"Then you don't go to court?"

He said he had been to court about four or five times. He said maybe they will take him to the court once in a month, or if he made trouble in the prison, maybe twice in a month. So he has been having all this problem. So he told me that, OK, when I go back, I should thank his friend very much. But he said his girlfriend Hope had traveled to her country. She was from Ghana, from a village near Kintampo.[1] Hope said that she was going to see the family, and maybe they will do something, like they will make a palaver so that they will release him. So Hope was going to

---

1. small town about halfway between Kumasi and Tamale

tell the uncle to do something so that they would leave him. So I must try
to bring him some food, because Hope is not here. I should tell his friend
that he should help me to bring him some food.

You know, in the prison, they feed you, but you wouldn't like it. You
wouldn't like it because they just make some kind of rough food. How
they do the corn, they don't mill it well.[1] They don't mill it the way to
make tuwo. The flour can't make tuwo, and it can't make banku.[2] They
just mill it halfway. If you are there in prison eating this kind of food,
you will be sick. So many people in prison — many, many, many, many,
many — they cook their own food. In a French country, you know, I think
their prison is somehow free. This is what I told you about the Togo
prison. If you have a three years' sentence, and you have spent two years,
you can be free. You can go to anywhere in town. You can go to market
alone, without any police, and then you come back. I think maybe in
Ouagadougou prison, too, they must have people like that. I don't know.
I didn't ask about it. But I think any French prison is like that. Because
I have one small brother who was in the prison, and I took him a cooking pan, and then a charcoal coal-pot, and some rice. I bought different
foods — yams and all these things, and gave to him so that he could cook
for himself. I could not go there every day, to pay three hundred or six
hundred for the taxi, and give him food. So there, if you don't want their
food from the prison, if you have people who can bring you your food
from the town, you can do that, or you can cook by yourself.

So the man was telling his story, and then he said, "Why didn't this
man come?"

I said, "Ah, the man said he's afraid, because it's not a long time he just
came from this place. So he's afraid to come to visit you. Maybe the police
will suspect him of something."

He said, "But you know, I didn't do any bad thing. I didn't steal. Only
they said I chopped money. OK. I chopped it. Then they put me here." *Ha!
Yeah?! Hee-hee!* He chopped the money but he didn't steal. *Ha! Ha!* So
then he said he's not a killer, so why doesn't this man want to come and
see him? When this man was here, he thought he was a white man like
him, so they were like two brothers here. The prison people gave them
one room. They sleep together; they talk together in the night time; sometimes they eat together; they do everything together.

1. grind it into flour
2. a pastelike food made from slightly fermented, boiled corn flour (often mixed with
cassava flour), common in southern Ghana

Then I said, "Oh, this man said that he is afraid because he is just from here. He doesn't know the Upper Volta problem, so he doesn't want to come here again."

So he said, "OK, if you go, try to tell him that he should try, that you should get some food for me tomorrow."

Then I said OK. So from the prison, I went straight to the market. That four thousand four hundred, I spent all to buy fruit and many, many things, different foods to cook. I bought it, then I took it to my place. And I went and told the other man, "Your friend said he wants to eat something tomorrow, so I should get him food. I can do it."

So the man said, "OK. You take ten thousand, and you go and buy all together with the taxi money." So: *ha-ha!* I got another ten thousand from him, you know.

Morning time, when I started making the fire, then I saw Hope, the girlfriend of the man. She had come from Ghana. The paper she used to go to the prison with, she said she lost it in Ghana. So when she came, she went to that man in the hotel and told him. And the man said that I had been there, that I was trying to cook to go to him. So the girlfriend said that she wanted to come and help me with the cooking, so that we would go together. So I said, "Oh, if that will be the case, I will cook and give you taxi money, in and out. Then you will take the food there." So I cooked and gave the food to her, and then she took it there, and I paid her taxi money. Then when she came back from the prison, she passed my place to give me my things which I put the food inside.

Interrogations

So I took her to that French man's place in the hotel. Then I was asking the girl, "I don't understand your man much, because he was telling me something, but I didn't understand him. He said he was abusing the president. That's why they are trying to give him a false charge to go to the prison, and all this."

Then the girl said, "See, my sister. I don't want us to talk in French or English so that man will hear. You know, this my man, he was stupid. Anyway, I can't say he's a stupid man, because I have eaten some of the money."

You know, this Hope was a village girl. She was living in a village, so she was not somebody who has been living in town: she was not expensive. But in her family, they have a lot of land. So this man gave her money, and she built a nice room in her village. And so because of all this, she didn't mind to be suffering for this man. Since she had been alive, she didn't see somebody who would help her like this man. This time, when she went to her village, she was a big woman. So if this man was suffering, she would like to be suffering with the man. You know? This is what she was telling me.

So every time, whatever he would do and get money for her to cook food, she would be going and giving him food. And this man told her not to tell anybody that he had hidden some of the money he chopped. So if she says this in English or in French, maybe the friend will understand, and then he will say, "Ah-h, it's true. He gave the money to the girl, so we can't help him." For a long time the man has been telling her not to tell anybody. But as I went to see the man, she knows that I like her, too. That's why I tried to see the man, for her, because she's my girlfriend.

But you know, later, when she went away, then I wondered. We were not close girlfriends. Sometimes we used to meet and talk. I think maybe the man who had sent me there didn't tell her that he was one who sent me. Maybe this girl thought that I just heard of it and went and visited this man. So she was trying to tell me all their secrets, you know, and she didn't want the other man to know.

Then, when she finished, then this man said, "Oh, what you people are talking?"

Then I said, "Oh, no. She's talking about Ghana. It's nice when you go to Ghana. They have their small problems, and that and this."

He said, "No, no, no. Ghana no problem. I have been Ghana." You know?

Then, yeah. Then I said to the man, "I saw your friend, but I don't understand. Because in Ouagadougou here, I haven't seen many white people who used to be in prison like that. But why is your friend there all this time?"

Then he said, "Oh, my friend, you know, the Voltaiques —"

Yeah? They always used to say the Voltaiques are not good, you know, when a white man is there and he has problems or something like that. You know, it's the same thing in Ghana. As an example, if a white man is in Ghana, and he tries to show the Ghanaians that he is clever, the Ghanaians also will try to challenge. So in that way, he will say, "Ghanaians are fucking," or something like that. This is what they also do in Upper Volta.

So when I was asking him about this thing, he said, "Oh, you know, these Voltaiques, they haven't got understanding. This man shouldn't be in prison serious like that, because this man doesn't do anything. This man is a free man. He is nice to anybody. He used to make friends with

anyone he doesn't know, you know, that as he has met you, you are a
friend. And he will start joking and doing all this with you. So they used
to ask him about the president. You know, we are white. We don't have
any problem. We don't have any story about the African politics, and
we don't want to take away you people's country. You people are free.
You have taken your freedom. You are free. So these people don't understand this man, this boy. He's a nice boy, a jovial boy. When he started
talking this, then they gave the complaint on him that he was abusing
the government."

Then I said, "Ah! Is that the case, and he is in the prison? How many
months?"

He said, "He is there about six months."

Then I said, "Ah, but if the Voltaiques are doing that, then it is not
good. I don't understand it. *Eh!* You know, I used to travel to some places.
But I think before somebody will get a case like this, to be in prison for
all these months, it's not from the government. A stranger doesn't know
anything about government. So what he was doing in the country, maybe
he did something bad against the country. But government alone cannot
put you in prison. We Voltaiques, every time we used to call the president's name in the bar. *Oh!* Or we will go to some place and see some
drunkard start to call, 'Lamizana!¹ Fucking that and this.' Just start mess-
ing up. You know? But nobody used to catch them. So your friend's problem, I don't understand it well. Maybe there is something inside."

He said, "Oh, no, because you know they don't like us, so they just lied
on him that he chopped some money."

So then I said, "*What?!* You lie! Why? When your friend sent you to
the prison, how did you go there?" You know, I just put an example to
him, to say that when the brother had taken him to prison, what did
he do?

"Ah, my brother took me to prison because he said I have used the
name of the nightclub to borrow money from people. That's why he
took me."

Then I said, "Why did they keep you in prison for two weeks, before
they let you go? It was two weeks. Then they left you. Why did they leave
you?"

He said, "Oh, my brother is very stupid. Because I had a big nightclub
in Paris, and you know, when I divorced from my wife in Paris, I thought
it was difficult for me. So I had to pack my things. So I told my brother

---

1. General Sangoule Lamizana, then the president of Upper Volta

that if we can find some place cool in Africa where it's nice, some place African, and make a nightclub there, we will be happy. So my brother also had been working. He has a wife, too. So we made half-and-half money to build the nightclub. So when I came back, he didn't want to mind me. He thought he had his sense. So I used my own sense, too. I gave him the money about three years now: I didn't have anything from him. So I have been borrowing with the nightclub's name."—*Ha-ha!* It's very funny!— "So when I got all my trucks. I started work. I knew that they will ask him. But I wouldn't pay that debt. My brother is going to pay that debt, because I have given him the money to work for about three years. He didn't bring anything home. So when we went to the police, they understood."

Then I said, "They understood? Why did you waste time in prison for two weeks? If they understood when you told them that at the police station, they shouldn't be keeping you long."

He said: yes, because the brother said he was broke, but even he didn't want to collect this money from him. But they have many taxes, and light, and all this. And they have rented the place to make the nightclub. And all is a big debt on him. He had also gone home and divorced his wife, so he hasn't any money. So they will take the whole place from him, and that and this.

Then I said, "But if the problem is with the family, they can't keep you in prison. Isn't it?" Yeah. You know, I thought, OK, you take your brother to police, that he's owing people, by the name of your house. As an example, eh? You tell police people, "My brother has to do that and this because I have divorced my wife, and I have many problems to settle with money." And then the police people will take your brother and go and lock him up to the prison?

Then he said, why do I want to be asking him much?

Then I said, "No, because you are not anything to me. I'm not anything to you. You don't know me. I don't know you. We say 'Girls and boys, we used to meet': we girls used to meet people like that. I can take you like, '*Heh-heh-heh,* my brother,' 'my sister.' I call you 'my brother.' You have white skin, and you are not my brother, but we can do it like that. I know you, but we haven't got anything between us. This thing you have sent me to do, you know, I had to write all my names[1] in the court, to get to visit your friend. And I don't know what problem he has. Maybe I will be here tomorrow: they can come and tell me, 'You are the one who went there.' So that's why I want to ask you. It's not about anything."

1. her full name, with her family name

So he said, "OK." He said this girl Hope has come — he said it in French; you know, that girl didn't understand French — he said this girl has many problems, and if he says anything about this man, she will go back and tell the man. So I should wait. He will come and meet me at the work place. So we said goodbye to each other. He went, and we all took taxis. He paid for my taxi; he paid for the girl's taxi. Then we went home.

Evening time, he came to our work. It was about eleven o'clock in the night. I was sitting with somebody, drinking. When I saw him, then I got up from the man, and that man was annoyed: he didn't pay the drink I took, a thousand two hundred. He left the bill there and went away. So I showed it to that man. I said, "See? Because of you, when I saw you, you know, as for me, I like good friends like that, who keep their promise. I left that man, then I came to say hello to you. And that man left my bill."

Then he said, "OK." Then he paid it. Then he said I should take one bottle of champagne. We took a bottle of champagne, and we went to sit in a corner and talk. He said, "You see, my brother in prison: he is not my brother. But we are both white. As you African people used to say, 'The white people are brothers.' You know? We are both having white skin. But he's from Belgium." And so he told me that this man is not from his country, but when he saw him in prison, he was very pitying for him. His girlfriend used to go out in the night to get people to be making love to get money before she cooks for him. So even sometimes, when they were both in the prison, this man used to talk about the girl, and he used to cry. You know? He would say, "By this time, I have to sleep. I can't sleep. Hope is somewhere. Somebody is fucking her. To get money to cook for me." *Ha! Hee-hee!* So he used to be like that in the night. Sometimes he thought the man was sleeping, and the man used to talk about these things as a dream. So the man told him his problem, and when he came out — anyway, the man was stupid. He was telling me all this.

Then I said, "Why?"

He said the reason why this man was stupid, was so stupid: he had many friends, African boys. And then he was dealing with the African girls. He said, "True, when he was in Togo, they deported him from Togo. And he got the same problem he had there. He has two babies and a wife in Europe. But he is clever; I think he is clever." So he said they deported him from Lomé. He used to work in a company in the cashier's office, or something like that. So if he got the money, he doesn't make any account of it. He will spend the money like it's his own. So they deported him for this case from Lomé. And when he got to Ouagadougou, you know, he did the same life.

So if he takes a girl, you know, he doesn't keep long. He takes you to heaven. You will think you are in heaven. But in a few days, maybe two weeks' or three weeks' time: *pam!* He will take another one. When he had money, they gave him a house from where he worked. He was living at Zone des Bois.[1] And he had one room at Hôtel Indépendance,[2] to pay everything. Because of girls. When he took a girl, he doesn't give your money in your hand. He just gives an envelope, and seals it, and if you open inside, you will be happy.

So the girls liked him. *Ha!* He will be following one girl for about one week or two weeks, going out, doing everything. But then two weeks, it's finished. So the girls used to fight because of him. "Hey! You don't see me?! This man was my boyfriend. Don't you see him with me every day? Today you are my girlfriend, and you have come to take the man!" And that and this. So they used to fight. At Hôtel Oubri, especially. He got all his girls from Oubri. I think at that place, they have many girls. And there are Togolese and Ghanaians. They have fat ones. They have slim ones. So it's the place he likes. *Ha!*

He had many friends among African boys. He used to buy them drinks. They are drinking, whiskey, everything. He used to bring the friends to Oubri. So when you are very jealous of the other girl, and the girl goes and tells him, then he will bring his group, the African boys, the proper Mossi boys, you know, to mess up. If he has left you, if you say something against him, these boys will beat you. So he was a champion like that.

Hope

So this money which this Belgian man was chopping, all was the company money. It was not for him. And then, they took him to prison, and then he came out from prison. He paid.

When he had this problem, you know, he was writing letters. The Belgians didn't have an ambassador in Ouagadougou. They had an embassy at Côte d'Ivoire. So he used to write to the embassy there. And the embassy refused, because they saw the same name from Togo, so they said, "You have many problems, and we can't help with all the problems." When the embassy refused, then this French man, he now had money, so he went and paid the debt: three hundred thousand. That was the balance.

The Belgian man also had paid some. When they got him, I think he had to make an account, and when they got his money, then he had to sell

1. residential section of Ouagadougou
2. international hotel in Ouagadougou

his property, his cars and everything from the house. And after all that, then a debt of three hundred thousand was left. So that is why they kept him in prison. Then this French man paid all this debt and got the man out. And then they stayed together in the same hotel. The French man is still going to Ghana to get these building materials. I don't know what the Belgian man is doing in Ouagadougou. And this man is with the *same* girl who told me all this: Hope. Hope is still with the man.

OK. Look at the problem. Look. When this man started in prison, for two months or three months, that time was good because he still had properties. He had many things to sell. If the girl went to see him, he would tell her, "Go and take this and sell. And what you get, you bring me this, and use this to bring me food, and you eat, too." Every day she would go with food at twelve o'clock, and she would take money, and then go and cook and return at four o'clock. She didn't go in the morning.

But after that two or three months, the girl started suffering. Their money had finished. They had sold everything to pay the debt, and the debt hadn't finished yet. And this man was in prison. So she was also try-ing every night to go out and find money. She would give him food two times a day. She would go at twelve o'clock. After, she would go again at about three or four, with food. Every day was like that. So this girl was trying all-l-l these months to get food for this man.

And then she traveled to go and see her family, if they could make juju, you know, to make the prison people leave the man. When she went, she told the man she would be back in about a week's time. Then the week was going and she couldn't come yet. That was when that French man also asked me to cook food to take to him.

So when this man got out, this girl was living with the man. She kept her own room, but every night they were together. She would go to her place and cook and bring it to the hotel. They would eat there together. *Hm?* So: do you know what this man was doing to the girl?

One night, he came and gave me a complaint. He said, "Hawa, Hawa." I said, "Yes."

He said, "I know you. I didn't know you very well, but Hope has told me about you, because Hope said that the time we were together, she al-ways used to come to you in the day time. But I didn't know you, because I haven't come to your house before. But I know Shetu."

Shetu was one of our girlfriends, too. I will tell you her story. She's a fucking girl. *Ha-ha!* I haven't seen any fucking girl like her before.

So this man said, "So that's why. But the time you came to prison and you told me that you know Hope," and that and this, and "I thought you are a friend of Hope's, too."

Then I looked at him. I said, "Yes."

He spoke nice English, that Belgian man. So: "You know, I want to beg you to go and beg Hope so that we will take her to hospital."

And I said, "For what? Take her to hospital for what?"

Then he said, "You know —" Then he started looking like somebody who was shaking or afraid of something.

Then I said, "Why should I take Hope to hospital?"

He said, "You know, it was three days ago. Hope — every time I will sleep, sleep, sleep, and maybe at three or four o'clock in the night, Hope will come and knock the door. I'm a *man,* you know, I'm a *man.* I shouldn't accept it. So today, I don't know what came to my head. It's something like a devil came to my head. I beat her. I took a bottle and knocked her head. And she fell down. She's bleeding. And I am trying to take her to hospital."

It was about four o'clock in the morning —*agh!*— when this man came and knocked my door. I was annoyed. Then I said, "Where is Hope?"

He said, "She is in my hotel."

I looked up and looked down. The way I was feeling to sleep! OK. I said, "OK, how can we get a car?"

He said, "No, I brought a taxi. It's waiting."

So I got on my dress and went to see the girl. He said he was trying to take Hope to hospital, and Hope said she wouldn't go. She said she wanted to die, so he didn't know what to do with her now, so he was try-ing to go around to see somebody she will be shy of a little bit, and Hope will feel ashamed to refuse the person to go to hospital. So when he came and got me, then I went. I said, "Hope, what are you doing?"

Then he said, "She has come now, so you must go to hospital."

Then Hope said, "No, no, Hawa. No. He's a bad man. Yeah. He can kill me. I want him to kill me today. I want to die."

Then I said, "No. If you will die, you can die another time. But I'm here. You cannot die in front of me. Please. Let's go to hospital."

So I held her, then she got up. And I tied her cloth. I put on her dress. *All this* part: *shit!* Suppose it was me — if somebody did this to me! I will cut your one ear. *Ha-ha!* I won't finish you at one time like that. But I will lie to you. You will think that I like you much, but I will get your ear be-fore I leave. *Ah!* One ear like this! One! *Ha-ha! Ah!*

You know, this Hope I'm telling you about, I have a photo of her. If you see the picture, and one day you meet her, you wouldn't know her. She is *black* like a wireless. She was a *black* one before, but she became *colored.* If you saw her, you would say that she is a half-caste.[1] You wouldn't believe

1. a light-skinned person, of mixed race, generally African and European; half black and half white

that she is a pure African. I don't know what she used. Many girls use cream,[1] but I don't know what she used to become like that. *Hey!* And you know, this cream, when it comes to spoil, you can bathe with all these soaps, you can use all these creams — *pfft!* So this girl — *ah!* If you saw the color before and you see her now! She has become *black*. I think she's blacker than how she was at first. And she can't use the cream again. That's why these Mossi people say, "Hey! This is what we used to say: any girl who likes Europeans[2] too much, after, all her life will be coming into sickness, because the white people have sickness." If they see Hope, they start talking about this. People used to see her like that, walking, and say that.

Yeah. So we took her to hospital, and the man said she is his wife. You know, when they met each other, when there was money, this man had been buying her everything. So he just went to the shop and got a gold wedding ring and put it on the girl's hand. *Ha!* She had a wedding ring — without a promise. *Ha-ha!* So he told the people that even they can see her ring. He took the ring off, and there was the name of the man inside. "She's my wife," he said to the doctor. "You know, at any time, accidents will come. We had some talks, and it was not nice. Then I think I lost my sense, to be beating her in this way."

So they gave her an injection, and we took her back to the hotel. We put some things where she hurt her forehead. After we put her back in the hotel, then the taxi took me back to my place.

Morning time, I went there to say hello to her. The man was about to go to his work. I don't know what work he was doing, but he said he was going to work. So he left us two, and this girl was telling me that — *tsk!* she will leave the man, because the man doesn't think of all that she had done for him. She said, "Since he came back, I don't know what work he is doing now. I don't ask him for money for cooking and everything. But always, I used to bring the food here and we eat. So the way he is trying to treat me now, I am going to leave him."

You know, she was still going out to find money, because the man had come out from prison broke. But she said that when they started, when he was going to work, he would say, "Hope, when you wake up, look at this place. There is money. You can take whatever you want." You see? But this time, if this man wakes up, and the girl is still sleeping, he goes away. And the girl too, if she sleeps late, she goes out and closes the door

---

1. skin-bleaching cream. The skin-bleaching cream has the reputation for causing skin to be darker after a person stops using it.
2. generic term for white people, including Americans

and gives the key to the reception. You see? But before coming back, she will bring some food and they will eat together. *Mm-hm.*

So the way the man has started to treat her, now she knows. The first time, Shetu used to tell her that white people don't do good, so she shouldn't try to do all that she was doing for the man. So she made trouble with Shetu. She didn't talk to Shetu. And now she wanted me to go and beg Shetu that Shetu should forgive her, that this time she understands. She wouldn't do that foolishness again. So I should talk to Shetu.

So I went and talked to Shetu. Then we came together. We all sat, we bought drinks, and we drank together. They were friends, good friends, tight friends, like how I was with Limata. In Ouagadougou, how Limata and I always go out together, in some places they say we are like twins: any place they see me, and they don't see Limata, they used to ask of her. So Hope and Shetu were just like that, too. Then, with this man's trouble, they had a problem. But that day, they were nice. They started to be friends again. Now they are fine. But still, Hope is with the man. She said she was going to leave the man, but she is staying with the man, following the man, still now. She doesn't know what she wants from him. Maybe she loves him. Yeah, but if you love somebody and he doesn't love you, wouldn't you change?

Shetu and Philippe

And then Shetu, huh? Shetu who I said is fucking. She is a very funny girl. She's very stupid, too. The man she met in Ouagadougou is also a young French man. That man is another fucking idiot. Philippe. He was working at a factory in Ouagadougou.

This man spent money on the girl. He bought her much. You know, we have a small motorbike like a Vespa, but it is Yamaha. It's for the women, but many men also had it. This man bought it for this girl. But he treated this girl like a *dog*. He did many things for her, but the treatment he gave her, I think I can't have that kind of treatment. She took patience to be treated like a dog, but she had everything.

Yeah. If you go when this man is beating this girl—*ah!*—you will say they have opened the floor to boxers. A girl, a woman. Sometimes I used to go to visit with some friends, because they had a swimming pool in the house. Day time, if I was feeling hot, I used to get some friends with me and we would go to the swimming pool. He had two bedrooms, a big sitting hall, a toilet in every room, and they had their kitchen and everything. So he chose one room for them to sleep inside. The other bedroom was for the friends who were coming to swim in the swimming pool, where they used to put their things.

So this girl was my girlfriend. Sometimes she used to say, "If my man has gone to work, I am alone in the house, and so I'm not feeling happy." So I used to go there with friends. Then we would be in the swimming pool.

Maybe at twelve o'clock, when her man was coming, then I would say, "I will go home."

Sometimes she will say, "Oh, no. Let's talk. Let's rest. It's nothing." The man would come. We would all joke together. Philippe would call me, "Hey, *ma petite Hawa*." They called me Little Hawa, because I'm not tall. They used to joke with me like a toy. Then sometimes, we would eat together at twelve. After we finished eating, they would sleep, and I would go to my place, around two.

And he used to invite people. He had friends, many friends, white French people. He used to go to the nightclub, and he had many friends because he had a swimming pool. Every time his house was full up with friends. Even if you didn't see the men, you would see the women, the wives of the friends, in the place, swimming. And sometimes he used to abuse this girlfriend in front of them. He would say, *"Regardez ma vieille conne, comme ça là"*:[1] Look at this—what do they say?—this old, old woman *"conne." "Conne"*: I don't know what is *"conne."* I think it's something like "stupid." So he would say, "Look at this stupid old woman," or something like that. I think so.

And this girl, Shetu, was a real Ghanaian, but she couldn't even speak "come here" in English. It's now she's learning her English from us. She speaks French better than any language. She hasn't been to school, but she learned her French like that.

So one time they fought when this man started to say that. She said, "Oh yeah, I am an old lady, you know. I don't care about my being old. I'm a fucking old lady. But how about you? What about you?"

Then this man said, "I'm not like you."

Then she said, "Do you think I'm like you? I have one son. One son. You have how many?"

The man said, "I have two!"

She said, "Two? How did you have them?"

You know, the man had told the girl his secret. He had divorced two

---

1. Look at this old cunt, like her; literally, cunt, but also, stupid asshole; *con* (m.) or *conne* (f.): asshole; *connerie*: stupidity, bullshit

white people before meeting her. The first wife had one son with him. The second one also had a son. But he divorced both of the wives. So she is the African girl who was coming to be the third girl.

Then the man said, *"Mais tu es bagatelle."* You see? He was trying to abuse the girl that she's ashawo, and he picked her up from a nightclub.

The girl said, "Yes, because I don't want to divorce many times. That's why I'm working in the nightclub. But you don't work in nightclub. I'm better than you. You have divorced two. But I haven't divorced even once. My baby, I have it from a friend. That's all. So if you are a good man, you should have been married before I met you. You shouldn't have two children with different mothers, and come and bluff yourself."

So when she said this in front of the friends, you know, maybe the man was ashamed. He had many friends with him. Maybe they didn't know this about him, and this girl was saying it in public like that. If you saw the man, he was just making as if he was relaxing or he was feeling hot. He didn't want his friends to see that he was going to box with the girl. So he stretched himself, opened his shirt, and then he got his head down. Then he said, "Hey, Ashetu!" He called her Ashetu. "Ashetu! *Mais tu me dis quoi?! Moi je suis bagatelle? C'est à cause de toi j'ai divorcé deux fois?* You too, *quand tu peux vouloir la troisième?*" You know? "What are you saying to me? You think I'm ashawo? I have divorced two times, so you think you can count to the third one? Do you think I'm going to get married with you?"

Then this girl said, *"Pfft!* Who would want a madman like you to marry?"

So he just went inside: *Dek! Dek! Tak!* And this girl was holding herself. You know, I have seen this three times between the man and the girl. But you know, the first one I saw, I think the second or the third was better than the first one. He was just blowing the girl, and the girl was holding her stomach. And the man was giving her blows: *Ta-ta-ta-ta!* And the girl fell down. She was shouting, eh? She shouted once, and then we didn't hear anything.

So at that time, everybody got up and left the party just like that. They didn't finish anything. So I was afraid. Then I looked at the man and I looked at the girl. Then I asked the man, "OK, if that will be the case, shall we take her to hospital?"

He said, "Leave her! She is a witch! She will wake up just now. You wait. My friends don't know about her. This girl will wake up now."

Then I said, "No. We have to take her to hospital. It's better."

So this man said, OK, if that will be the case, he has a motorbike. He will go and ask one of the friends for a car. So he went to take the car.

Then I went inside. I said, "Shetu, Shetu, Shetu, oh! I'm living with you now. Look what you are doing to me. You are the one who brought me here, and look at what pitiful thing you are doing. Eh? See all the white people have run away. Even your husband has run away."

Then she opened her eyes. *Ha-ha!* This is very funny, eh? Then she told me, she whispered, "All you have been talking to him, I heard. I want him to be suffering today. You just don't say anything." Then this girl stopped talking.

So the man brought the car. He said, "She didn't wake up yet?"

And I said, "No."

So the girl got to hospital. You know, she is *bad*. Shetu is a *very* bad girl. She can keep long without breathing. She can keep maybe some minutes to do this. Then if she wants to breathe, she breathes one — a deep breath — then she stops it again. So they gave her three injections! The fourth one, she said, "No, no, no, no! No! *Mɛwu, mɛwu:*[1] I'm dead." Then she said, "No. I'm not dead yet, I'm not dead yet!" *Ha-ha!*

Then the man said, "You see? I told you. Suppose you left her, she would wake up like that."

So the doctor said that we should leave her there. Then she said, "No, I cannot sleep here."

The man said, "OK, I will take her home, and I will bring her tomorrow morning."

So we got to the car. I said I was going home; they should drop me at my place. And Shetu said, No, I should go with them to their place. So we went there, and Shetu was feeling stronger, and she served us beer. So we took some drinks there.

Then, you know, she used to call me her "mother." She said her mother had a sister who was called Hawa, so she used to call me "Mama." Yeah, as for me, I have many daughters. Shetu said, "Mother, do you see? This man — *Uwanka! 'Dan duniya wa shege ne!*[2]—this man, he's a shit. I want to show him. He will beat me, but he'll get tired of me. When I was young, I haven't been to school, you know. Every time we were used to the bush at our side." I think she was from Ejura Mampong. When you are going to Kumasi, when you pass Yeji, you pass Mampong, then Ejura Mampong.[3] Yeah. She is Ashanti, but she is called Shetu. Shetu: it's *Asante Kramo*.[4]

1. (Asante Twi): I'm dead.
2. (Hausa): Your mother's cunt! Son of the world (profligate) and a bastard!
3. towns northeast of Kumasi
4. (Asante Twi): *Kramo* (plural: *Nkramo*) is a designation, occasionally used as a name, for an Ashanti who has converted to Islam.

You know the Ashantis: some people who didn't pray before, when they are coming to be Muslims, then they take a Muslim name. She was Ashanti, but the family was Muslims, so they called her Shetu.

So Shetu was with this man. Then, after one year and some months, this man went on leave. During this leave, the man was sick seriously there. They didn't think he would come back. The time had passed for the leave to end. When he was going to the leave, he had packed many things and crossed the border with the girl. And he gave her money and told her the time he was going to come back, in three months' time. After the three months' time, this girl came to Ouagadougou and waited, but this man didn't come. She was there about four or five months: she didn't see the man.

Then she went back to Ghana, because she didn't want to be waiting there and be making ashawo. You know, when she was with the man, she used to bluff a lot. So she was walking alone in Ouagadougou. She wasn't happy. So she went back home to Ghana, and then when this man came, this girl wasn't here, and she didn't know that the man had come. And the man didn't write any letter to her. Then when he came, he changed his mind again. He got another girl from Côte d'Ivoire.

This Ivory Coast girl was born there and grew up there, but she was not a real Ivoriènne because the mother was Ashanti. She took herself as an Ivoriènne because she could only speak a little bit of Ashanti. She was a very small girl, about eighteen years or nineteen. And when this man got that girl, he was happy with the girl. He didn't want Shetu to know that he had come back.

You know, this man was somebody who liked nightclubs. Every night he would go *all* around, even if there were twenty or forty nightclubs in the town, if he didn't go in all of them, he and this girl wouldn't sleep. So the friends of this Shetu were always seeing the man with this Ivoriènne girl. And one of them went and told Shetu. Then Shetu came. When Shetu came: *poo-o!* In no time: blows! With the other girl. A man who had been beating her like that, and she was being jealous because of him! They were boxing and everything.

Then the man said that, OK, they haven't made any marriage, and now he wanted that girl more than Shetu. They could become like they had divorced, so whatever Shetu wanted, she could ask him. "Well," Shetu said, "OK, you have bought me this Yamaha. When you went on leave, I left it with you. So you can give me my Yamaha. It is something like a gift you gave me. So if you are leaving me, you can't keep it."

So they went to police. The police people said, yes, it's true. He had said it was for her. If you say something is for somebody, whether you are friends or you are not friends, it's for that person. So the man understood, and he gave the motor to Shetu.

And then Shetu said, "OK, now I am going to show you African power." She told the man, eh? She said, "I will show you African power. You will cry in this Ouagadougou."

You know, this man didn't know what was happening. I don't know whether it was the show of Shetu or what, but one day this man and the girl quarreled, and this man took that small girl to lock her at the police station that she was smoking groove. But this man also was a groovier! He had smoked with the girl.

The quarrel they had: you know, this girl was just like a small baby. She used to play like a small baby. She could bring many glasses and put different things in them, and then start doing something. She was a funny girl. So one day he came back to the house, and the girl was swimming, playing in the swimming pool. Then he called her, "I have come from work. Don't you see me?"

The girl said, "Oh, wait. I'm feeling the water. So let me stay a minute."

Then this man just got his car out from the house and went to the police and told the police people that this girl had been smoking groove, so she was going crazy, so they should treat her.[1] Yeah. If they don't treat her, she is going to become crazy. So they got the girl to the police station. And that day, the same day when the girl went to the police station, this man was with Shetu in the nightclub!

Then, you know us girls here. Shetu said, "Yeah! I said I will show him. I will *show* them! *Pfft*. Do you think I will follow him today? I won't follow him. I am just doing him and he will lock his girlfriend." And you know, Shetu was first-class in doing this groove, but this man didn't know anything about it. She was living with the man. We had been coming there, smoking together, but we didn't want him to know that we were smokers. And this man was also a smoker, and he didn't want us to know. You see? But we knew already he was a smoker because he had many friends who were smoking. We knew them. So when he locked this small girl, that day he was with Shetu, and they were enjoying every place.

Then they came to our nightclub, La Tringle. Then I said, "Hey, *Diana!*" I used to call her my daughter: *"Diana!"*

"Ah! Ee mana. Har na karɓi mijina, amma ba na so shi kuma. Mother. I have got my man back, but I don't want him again."

Then I said, "Ah, what? Why don't you like him?"

She said, "You know, he locked the girlfriend."

---

1. The allegation that marijuana causes insanity is common.

I said, "For what? Locked the girlfriend?"

She said, "Yes. The girlfriend was smoking wee,[1] and he came and met her in the swimming pool, so he got police people to lock her up."

"That's so?"

And she said, "Yes."

So I didn't say anything. And they didn't stay in La Tringle up to fifteen minutes when police people came to look for the man. They came and took the man to the police station. Then I said, "Ah! He is the one who took the girl to lock her, and they have come and taken him also?"

She said, "Oh, I don't know what they said, because as for me, I don't like the man again. I just want to show him my African power. He won't keep any girl with him. It's his first and last. He can fuck all the girls, but he can't keep anyone as a friend, as the way I stayed with him."

So the next day, as I want to hear everything, I went to Shetu. I said, "Ah, didn't you go to the police yesterday?"

She said, "Ah, yeah. Me, I went there. They said the girl said the man is the one who was giving her money to search for it. So she told the man that she's very young. She can't do this kind of thing, because the first time when the man gave it to her, she was becoming like something. So she didn't want it. And every twelve o'clock, the man came from work. He thought she's sweet, a sweet darling, so he would come home to go with her. Then he would say, 'Oh, let's get this thing.' If she said she doesn't smoke, he would say, 'Oh, but take one draw. Draw on it, then you'll get it like that.' But she didn't want to smoke this thing. That's why, when the man came from work and she was in the swimming pool, she refused to come out of the water. So he was annoyed and reported her. So if it's not true, they should go to the man's house and search."

That's why they came and got the man. You see? A *bad* position: this small girl was also wicked and bad. But she had sense. When she got this groove into the man's house, the man didn't know where she kept it. She kept it in the front pocket inside his own coat! Yeah. There was an old coat he used to keep hanging. So the police people came with her to the house and searched inside their room. The girl was in the sitting room, and she said, "You people go inside and search everywhere. If you don't find groove, then I'm a smoker. But this man, he is the one who used to force me. He gets it from some African friends. He used to take me to some area[2] and leave the car, because the car cannot walk on that road. He will park the car and go between the houses and bring it. And he told

1. marijuana
2. a neighborhood or section of a town or village

me that he didn't want the African people to suspect him, so he used to dress heavy with the coat, as a big man. He used to leave me in the car and walk inside the area, so I don't know what place he walked. But I will be in the car maybe fifteen minutes or twenty minutes, then the man will come back. Then he will say, 'OK, we should go.' In the night, the man used to say that here is some groove, and that and this."

So she put *all* the problem on this man. And this man also was trying to say that he didn't know how to smoke before. And when this girl came, the way he loved the girl, the girl used to press him to smoke, "Get small and see. Get small and see." So he learned it from the girl.

But this girl put *all* the problem on him! *Ha!* The way this girl was sensible to talk this! If you saw the girl, you wouldn't say she is somebody who has sense. She did everything like a small baby who doesn't know anything. If you went and saw her at that place, alone, she had many glasses with different colors of water; and she had something like soap, she would put it in the water and then take it and blow bubbles. She liked these things. If you saw her, you would say she was a small baby.

So they had to leave the girl and get the man, because they got the thing from the front of his coat. The girl had showed the way this man used to dress up when they would go and find the thing. You see? She didn't tell them, "Go and look there." She just told them a story. Yeah. So they got this thing, and they brought it out. This man had nothing to say. He said the girl is smoking it. He doesn't want her to smoke it. He has given her warning many times not to smoke it.

Then they said, "OK, but why? If she knows that you don't want her to smoke, why should she put it in your coat? Suppose you came and took your coat. Maybe you would get it. You would say 'Ah! She didn't stop yet.' She can't hide it in your things. So this thing is for you."

The man couldn't open his mouth. He was just like that. Guilty. *Ha!* He could not say, "No, I not guilty." So they left this girl. And after that, then the factory where he was working, they also went and saw the police people about that man: he is working hard — if they don't leave him, they won't get any man like him — that and this — and they will give money. So they got the man back. Then the man was out from the police, too. But the small girl had gone.

So that was the time that this man wanted to see Shetu again. And he couldn't see Shetu. Shetu didn't have time.

Sometimes he would come to my house. One night he came: "Hey!" *Ke-ke-ki-ki-ki.*

"*C'est qui?*"

"*C'est moi.*"

"Qui?"

"C'est moi, Philippe."

"Et qu'est-ce que tu veux?"

"Ashetu n'est pas venu ici?" [1]

Then I asked him, *"Quand tu étais avec Shetu, vous viendrez ici ensemble?* The time when you and Ashetu were there, did you people used to come to me here?"

He said, "No."

"But why? A time like this, to come and ask me for Shetu?"

He said, "Eh, because I went to La Tringle. They told me that you people have closed, but Shetu was there. I thought maybe you people went together."

I said, "Don't you know her house? You know Shetu's house?"

"Yeah. But I have been there. I haven't seen her."

And I said, "Oh, that is your problem. Shetu is not here."

Then he went. Morning time, he came and passed. "Did you see what Shetu did to me yesterday?"

Then I said, "No."

"You know the time when I came from your place?"

Then I said, "Uh-huh."

"When I was coming out from your place, I saw Shetu with the Yamaha. She was in front of me, carrying a boy in back of her. It is finished! I won't talk to her again."

Then I said, "Hey, Philippe, when you people made your marriage, I was not there."

You know, first time, that boy was also a friend of Limata. That white fucking man was a boyfriend to Limata. Yeah. OK? Then Shetu came. We were at the same house. So Shetu conceived, and she went to Ghana to cause abortion. Then she kept long in Ghana, and they took her room. When she came back, she lodged with me. That was the time we were working at Zé Bon. Then I said, OK, if she wanted to work, I could take her to work at Zé Bon because there, we used to get dash, so it was good nightclub. So I took Shetu there, and then they took her to work. OK? Then she came to take this man from Limata. So Limata also was annoyed with me that I gave Shetu good advice to take her boyfriend. You see? So I was in a problem because of this. And so when they had their problem, that's when he came to me. He told me he was finished with Shetu — because he saw Shetu with a boy on the back of her Yamaha —

1. (French): "Who is it?" "It's me." "Who?" "It's me, Philippe." "And what do you want?" "Didn't Shetu come here?"

he was blowing the horn — Shetu didn't mind him — and that and this. And I said, "Ah, that is your trouble. When you people made your marriage, was I there?"

He said, "But it was at Zé Bon that Shetu told me that you are the sister. You are the one who brought her to work."

"But I have brought her to work, but I didn't bring her to you. But what? How you people met, and you told Shetu to stop work, you were staying with her. Huh! I was not there. If it's finished, it's finished between you people."

You know, but before, the first time, when he used to tell me it was finished, then I used to try to beg him, "Oh-h, now, take patience, you know. Love is like that, you know. Shetu is a small girl. She doesn't know much. But she will learn. I know her. Just keep your patience." But I know that Shetu is not a small girl. Maybe she and I are about the same age.

So when he went to the girl, he said, "Even yesterday, I have been to Hawa. Hawa told me that you are not a good girl." You see? And this girl came and told me this. So I said OK.

The next time when he came, then I said, "Look, I don't want you. You must know that if, suppose I wanted you, maybe I would have got you before the others. So I don't want you. Don't come and do all this thing. If you don't want Shetu, you don't want Shetu. I'm not the mother of Shetu, or I'm not a sister of Shetu. Go and tell Shetu that it's finished between you people. But don't tell me. Yeah, the first time, when you used to come to me first, I wouldn't say all this. I will tell you to keep patience. But if you go to her, and you people start to be talking sweet-sweet, then you will tell her, 'Even yesterday I have been to Hawa. Hawa told me that you are not a good girl.'"

"Heh, but Shetu said you are the big sister."

I said, "I am a big sister of Shetu? Does Shetu have this mouth like mine? All my family, we have this. We haven't got anybody like Shetu in my family." But I was just deceiving him to make him go away from me, you know. He was a fucking man!

Shetu too, she was fucking! *Ah!* One day he told Shetu that I said he should leave Shetu and come and take Mama Amma. But he doesn't want the girls like Mama Amma. And then the girl came and told me. So I said, "What? This man said that to you?"

She said, "Yes."

I said, "OK. I have said it. If this man says I have said it, I have said it. It's true."

And the girl believed that I said this. And I was very annoyed. So she said, "OK, I was calling you my mother. I was giving you respect, but I didn't know that you will spoil me."

Then I said, "Why should you call me your mother? You know that
I am not your mother. I know many people who have the name of my
mother. I don't call them 'Mother.' I don't say that because they have the
same name as my mother, I will call them my mother. If you don't want,
don't call me any mother."

So this girl went away. Then we didn't talk for about two or three
months. When they came to the nightclub, I wouldn't look at their face.

Then one day, the man brought himself. They came; they didn't sit
down. They came and stood in front of me at the counter. So as they
were standing in front of me, I had to serve them. So I served them, then
I went away. Then the man called me: "Hey, Hawa, I don't understand
you. About two months now, when you see us, you have been running
away from us."

Then I said, "Yes, I have to run away from you people, because I hate a
snake that has two mouths." You know, people used to say that we have a
snake in Africa that has two mouths. It doesn't have a tail. You touch here
his mouth; you touch here his head. "So I don't want people like that."

He said, "What is the meaning of what you are saying?"

"I said that because when you would come to me, I told you to take patience with your Shetu. I have seen a love which is thicker than you
people's own. But it has passed. If you come to me, I don't say anything
bad to you. So did you tell her that I told you to take Mama Amma? Do
you remember the day when you came and you said that you have left
Shetu and that I should give Mama to you? I haven't got time to go to
tell Shetu all your talk. But you have time to go and lie on me that I said
something."

He said, "No, no, no, no! Shetu, you know, Shetu, she doesn't hear
French well," and that and this.

And I said, "You lie."

So I spoke in French. I said, "Shetu, is it not Philippe who told you that
I told him to leave you and take Mama?"

She said, "Yes, it's Philippe."

Then Philippe said, "No, Shetu, *elle n'a pas compris.*" Shetu, she didn't
understand him.

That, that, and that, that. So they took that like a joke. So we joked together, then they said I should drink something. And I said, "Thank you,
I am already satisfied. I have drunk already."

So they went. Morning time, then Shetu came to me. "Hey, *Mamana.
Me ya sa ki fada ma Philippe maganana?*"[1]

"Ah! Why?"

1. (Hausa): My mother. Why did you tell Philippe what I said?

"You said the man has told you this case."

Then I said, "Yes, I have said it. Because of that, you said you won't call me your mother again. I don't want a daughter like you. I wanted to say the truth in front of you and him."

"Hey. Look, *quoi*.[1] Look what Philippe did to me because of this."

Then I said, "What did he do to you? He did you that because it is true or it is a lie?"

She said when they went home, the man said he didn't say all that. So she had disgraced him in front of me. So the man beat her. But she knows he said it, because she speaks French well, more than me.

Then I told her, "So why didn't you hear it well before you came and asked me all this foolishness?"

So we had that problem finish. Then she went to Ghana. At that time, her uncle was a big man in Ghana. She said she wanted to go to Ghana, and Philippe would follow her, and if he goes to Ghana and sees her family, he will be afraid of her. OK? She stayed in Ghana about two months.

But Philippe was in Ouagadougou. Every time, he used to come to the nightclub, "Hawa!" He used to call me to dance with him. He used to buy me drinks. If he saw some girl in my workplace, he asked me, "This girl, is this a good girl?"

I would say, "Yes. If you want the girl, you can take her."

This is not my problem. Isn't it? If Shetu was there, yes. But she was not there. She had gone, and we didn't know what she was doing in Ghana, too. So the girlfriends went and told this girl that this time, I'm the one who finds girls for the man, the husband. So when she came from Ghana —*shit!* She just put her things down. She didn't even take a bath. Then she came to me: "*Mana, na gode maka. Allah ya ƙarɓa!* My mother, I thank you very much. May God help you. What you have done to me, may God help you."

"Oh, what have I done?"

"Ah, so if — even if I am not here, even if I were you —I didn't think Philippe could come and carry some woman in front of you."

Then I said, "What do you mean?"

She said, "Eh! Every day, Philippe used to come to La Tringle. You are the one who is serving him the girls. He's the one who wrote me by himself, that Hawa is good, that any time you used to serve him a beautiful woman."

Then I said, "Philippe said that?"

She said, "Yes."

1. (French): what

"Philippe told you that?"

She said, "Yes."

Then I said, "Look, Shetu. Maybe your Philippe is making you crazy. But Philippe doesn't make me crazy. OK? I knew Philippe before he came to Zé Bon. If you ask Limata the way Limata got Philippe, Limata will tell you. I'm not going to tell you anything about it. You go and ask Limata."

"Hey, I won't ask anybody, because you are the one who took me to Zé Bon before I got Philippe. So if you take your Philippe back, it wouldn't worry me. This time, I have many things to do. I have my motor — even if Philippe doesn't do anything for me, I have a motor, I have a fridge, I have my fan, and—" You know? Look-o. *Shit!* "— so I think all this is the profit of Philippe. Even some people used to see me in town. They say I'm foolish to live with Philippe — he has been beating me, and that and this. But whatever girl you will take to give to Philippe, you won't get even half of what I got from Philippe. Even if you want, you yourself, you can test."

Then I said, "Hey, Shetu."—I told her in Ashanti—I said, "Shetu, *wonim kayakaya?*"[1]—Do you know the people who carry loads on the head? Yeah. I said that—*"Wonim wɔmo paa?"*[2] Even, if I have a load, hm? If I see somebody like Philippe — to call him to come and carry this, I don't *need* it! You see him as a white man. I see him like shit!" *Ha-ha!* "So if you have your problem with your Philippe, go and finish with him. Philippe doesn't want you again. You are forcing. *Al-l-l* this money you have from him, people will lie to you and chop it. Keep your money and buy dresses so that you will get another nice man. Don't follow Philippe. Philippe doesn't want you anymore."

"Oh, yea-yea-yea-yea-yea!"

You know, in our place, it was full up: many people came to look at this. I was quiet. And she was shouting! "If I was two — if I was twins — if we were born twins — and one has died, he is in the ground, and you take me like a girlfriend to bite me — and they say rats used to bite people and make and blow the hair — yeah, you take me like a rat friend. You bite me and blow your hair. And I think you are a rat friend — a rat girlfriend. But I didn't know that you don't need me to become somebody."

Huh? People came there and looked and heard her talking and talking like that. Then I said, "OK."

Then Limata said, "Oh, Shetu. But why? You are talking. She didn't say anything."

She said, "Yes! You people are all the same thing!"

1. (Asante Twi): Do you know what is a kayakaya?
2. (Asante Twi): Do you know them well?

Then Limata said, "Don't bring your trouble to me. Your Philippe doesn't want you."

Then I said, "What is making you hot? *Agh!* Mama, get up! Let's go to Philippe's house. Now I am going to give Mama to Philippe straight in front of you! And Philippe will *never* leave Mama!"

"*Yea-yea-yea-yea-yea!* Mama! Mama! Mama! You are Ashanti like me, no? You are Ashanti. Even if you are Fanti,[1] we are the same thing. You see? These *Pepe* people[2] want to mix us to make trouble. You know, I know that you wouldn't go with Philippe."

Then Mama said, "Oh, *phoo!* You are worrying too much. This your fucking Philippe — even if I got a man like this, I would never, never want to say his name in front of people. But why? A man who can drink and take all of his dress and put his hand on your — and take your hand on his trouser to touch his private thing — is this a man?"

She said, "*Huh! Huh!* Is it true?! So you did that?!"

So Mama said, "Ah, I did it in the nightclub. If you are dancing with him, he will just open his zip, and then you put your hand there to rub it for him. Is this a man to make a fight with me? But if — suppose I wanted to stay with this man, I would have stayed with him. But I saw him: he doesn't respect himself. The way he made me touch is the way he makes every girl touch. So I don't want to see a man like that. So if you will go to your house, then go to your house. Hawa is teasing you."

Then she said, "*Eh-heh! Eh-heh!* Now I have the truth! Now I have the truth. So this is what Philippe is doing. I'm going to meet Philippe in the house."

Ha! You know, she went and came back, and she had one eye swollen closed. *Shit!* Then she was crying, "*Mana-oo, Mana-oo.* Mama, Mama." The house was not far from our place, you know. It was just opposite us. *Ha!* It's very funny. When she came, oh! Many people had come from the house. The way she shouted: "Mama! Boo-hoo! My mother!" *Hee-hee-hee.* People came out: they saw Shetu with one eye like that.

And she had another friend called Abiba. Abiba caught hold of her: "Shetu, what is wrong?"

---

1. cultural group in the coastal area around Cape Coast and Sekondi-Takoradi. The Fanti and Ashanti languages and cultures are related.

2. (Asante Twi): Northerners. *Mpepefoɔ (singular, Pepeni)* is a name used to refer to Northerners, *people from northern Ghana, or the former colonial Northern Territories when the southern part of Ghana was the Gold Coast. The North is the savanna area north of the coastal forest, about 150–200 miles inland, that is, northern Ghana. Northerners therefore refers to people to the north of the Akan traditional area; the word is also some-times used to refer to Muslims, and sometimes applied to people from Muslim cultures in northern Togo, Burkina Faso, northern Nigeria, Mali, etc.*

"Duba abin da Philippe ya yi mini. Duba abin da Philippe ya yi mini. Naa kashe shi! I will *kill* Philippe! Look what Philippe has done to me. I swear, I will kill him! This man, he won't live — he will never live in Ouagadougou here. I will kill him! I will kill him!"

Then they took her to hospital. So from that time, she didn't go back to the man again. And now it was the man who will come to look for her. And the man also didn't meet her. Every time the man would come and look for Shetu. He could never meet Shetu, since she got that big eye.

The Trouble with Frogs

So, it used to be shit when you see things like that. You can't believe it, but if you see them, you will believe it. These French people, I don't know what kind of people they are. I don't know what — *or* maybe they only do this in Africa. Maybe they don't do this in their own town. But in Africa, they do many, many, many things that you can't believe a white man can do these things. Even in Togo, I didn't see things like that. But in Ouagadougou, I have seen. In Togo, I saw the French people, but I was thinking they were not so bad. But you know, in Ouagadougou, these people, I don't know why. I don't give them even an inch of respect. I just talk to them like that, you know. Whether I know you, I don't know you: you bring your talks. They are so, so, so, so *stupid!*

So these French people, too, they are fucking. Oh, not all. You know, in the world, a whole people cannot be fucking. Some of them may be, and some of them, too, they are not. I told you that these English people, some of them are fucking but some of them are good. But French people, I *hate* them. That's why. I don't know that they are good ones or they are bad. They take themselves — *Ha-ha!* — the French people — I think maybe I used to meet the *bad* ones. I don't know whether maybe it's the way I am, that's the way the bad ones used to come. I don't know. I used to only meet the bad ones. I don't get French good people.

They're stupid, but they think they have sense. *Yeah!* This is what they think. They think they are more than everybody in the world. You know, some of them can come from a village, but if you ask, they will say, "I'm from Paris." You know, this kind of thing, I used to say, "Yes, we know. All of you French people are Parisians. But tell me exactly the place where your father and mother are from." I used to get this thing with them, you know. *Ha-ha!*

It's because they are fucking. So sometimes I used to ask them some things, and they will be annoyed. Sometimes, you can ask someone these questions, and you will see that some of them are jovial. He will say,

"Yeah, you have sense. Who told you this?" And that and this. Then he will start to show you the real village he's from. And you will ask someone something to make him annoyed, then he will be annoyed. The fucking people, they just say, "What do you think? You think I'm fucking like you? You are just from a small village and you have come to Ouagadougou." You see? But the other ones, they have patience, you know. They are nice. *Ha-ha!* They will just tell you the truth. Oh-h. French people. They can bluff themselves. You know, we Africans, we used to like bluffing. Yeah? But the way Africans bluff, it's not the way these French people bluff. Their way is some kind of fucking way. When they bluff, they used to abuse people. Yeah, they used to talk about people. They used to talk about people, trying to show themselves[1] to be more than that.

You know, here, especially here in Africa, you used to meet African people to talk nicely. They will ask about how your people are at home, or ask how you find Africa. You know: "You have been here in Africa, and you have known a lot of Africa, so maybe you know how we are a little bit." You will be conversing. But a French man wouldn't like to say that. He always wants to say that what he is doing is the correct way. He doesn't care whether you are doing the correct way or you don't do the correct way. Everything that the Africans are doing is not nice for them. That's why, every time, we used to take them as fucking people.

You know, English people also talk about people. But maybe French people — how do they say? — French people, they are people who don't like the other tribe. Uh-*huh!* So they are just like selfish. They can talk about anybody: whites — if you are not French — other whites, American, English, they talk about anyone. It's not to say they talk about Africans only. They used to talk about English people, or sometimes American people.

Yeah. These French people, how their life is, you can't believe it. I don't know if it's only in Ouagadougou they do many thing like that. They're fucking! So it's very funny. If I see people like that, I used to talk to them. That's why, the time when this man sent me to see his friend in prison, when I told Limata and Limata said I shouldn't go, I wanted to know the story. I thought, no, I have to go and see what is inside. You know? If you don't see the fellow, you can't know the truth. So I didn't care whether it would be a trouble or something bad. I wanted to know how this thing happened. I wanted to catch his stories, you know. Yeah. I wanted to know.

So I have to do my kɔnkɔnsa research. *Ha-ha!* I just want to know

---

1. boast, bluff, act proud

about the people like that, you know. Sometimes, the way some people used to bluff, if you know somebody more, he cannot bluff. Eh? If he wants to bluff, you will just tell him one word, then you will see that he will shut up. He can't say anything again. So people like that, if you know them, you have to know their bluffing like that. People like that, I used to like them, you know. Sometimes these fucking people like that, I used to like them. I used to like — *ha-ha!* — to know how they do their ways. *Ah-h.* It's nice to see the ways.

PART THREE *Hawa Contextualizes Her Life*

5 PAPA'S SICKNESS

: OUAGADOUGOU :

Transition: Money Matters

You know, in Ghana, I didn't work. And other places, I didn't work. So I don't know much about other places. It is only Ouagadougou that I started to work in the nightclub. So how I am working, I think — maybe I think — I can say that I may be ashawo or I may not be ashawo.

OK? Why I can say that I may be ashawo, I can go with *n'importe qui:* it doesn't matter who. Yeah. It doesn't matter who. I know that maybe I don't have money, and this person can give me money. Isn't it?

But since I'm making my ashawo, I don't make a complete ashawo like that. I used to be keeping friends, to have boyfriends, you know. I go from friend to friend, friend to friend. If I have a boyfriend and it's finished, I will get another boyfriend. I don't want to be walking every time to the bar or the nightclub, to get another man and tomorrow I go to another man. As for me, I do my ashawo like private ashawo. From the friend to friend. *Ha-ha!* Then if I see that from friend to friend, they are fooling me much, and I'm getting *fed up,* then I say, "OK, if that will be the case, then I have to show myself, too. Why should I hide myself? From this man, I can get another one." And the very time when I get out, too, I can get another one. So — *Ha!* Yeah. When I got to Ouagadougou, that is the time I did my proper ashawo. As for Ouagadougou, I do my ashawo. I don't care about anyone.

So since I started to work in the nightclub, well, it's not that I don't go with people because of money. Sometimes I see somebody, and I know that this person has money. But you know, in the bar I can take my patience, because in the bar, I know that sometimes we will get money for dash. Sometimes, if you leave the bar, you haven't any money. But for all this, I used to have patience because I know that *all* my budget is coming to the ending of the month, to pay my room. This is a special thing to me, you know. So I don't used to worry much to be following people.

You know, this time, I can chop money proper. Anyway, I didn't exactly calculate and see the amount of money I eat in a month in Ouagadougou. Maybe it can reach one hundred thousand, or maybe more than that. You know, every month I get my salary. And then I get from the drinks the customers are buying. And some gifts like that. And this ashawo business, too. *Mm-hm.* But you know, this money — I think this kind of money is not heavy money. It doesn't go far.

Look, I told you that Limata and I traveled from Ouagadougou to go to Ghana. OK? Sometimes if you want to do a real shopping, maybe you are thinking, "Oh, I have to take this to Ghana. In Ghana they don't have it.[1] And here it is everywhere. I will get this to give." You can take maybe one hundred or fifty thousand to go to the market, and you will come home, and what you had prepared to go and buy, you didn't buy it yet, and the money is finished. It's not our fault. I think it is the fault of the price of things.

The last time when we were going to visit Limata's family, people said that this time in Ghana, they have everything, so I told Limata, "OK, I haven't got money. I don't want to pick any heavy shopping." OK. So Limata was going to shopping. Even the natural things she meant to take there, they seized[2] it at the border. She didn't have milk. She had soap. And for gifts, we had something like Omo[3] packets — big ones. I think it is five hundred fifty CFA, or maybe six hundred. As for provisions, she didn't have any drink. The first time, when we used to go to Ghana, we used to hold drinks. But this time, we hadn't any drinks. And some cloth:

---

1. During the 1970s in particular, when Ghanaian currency was soft and foreign exchange resources were limited, Ghana suffered serious shortages of many commodities and other goods: detergent, bath soap, tea, sugar, matches, tinned milk, etc. People coming from hard currency countries normally brought many of these items as gifts.

2. took possession of

3. a brand of laundry detergent

Limata had a half-piece of it.[1] She had that cloth, but she had cut it into two pieces. She gave them to a tailor to sew. The tailor cut all the styles,[2] but he didn't want to sew it. Every time, he would say, "Tomorrow. After tomorrow." We wasted our three days; he didn't sew it. So Limata was annoyed and took the cloth, the cut pieces, from him. So at the Ghana border, they started to ask questions. These border guards made excuse to say that, Eh-h, they are not bad people, but they have to collect this cloth because government said new cloth can't go into Ghana. But the new cloth, which they have cut into the pieces to sew, is this a new cloth again? So Limata had to pay ten cedis. And then they asked, "So, all of this thing is for you?" And that and this. And one man just came there and said that, "This soap is — anyway, I know you people. Even if you are at Tamale or Kumasi, if you send one of your friends, as you have many friends, they will send you one. But if you like, I can buy this from you."

And Limata is also stupid. She just said, "OK, take it." If I were the one, I wouldn't say, "Take it." *Ha!*

You know, how we spend in Ouagadougou is different from Ghana. When we are in the bar, you know, and we meet someone who used to go to Ghana, he will talk about Ghana. *"Ghana, c'est bon, eh? Ghana c'est bon. Il y a bonnes, bonnes, bien jolies filles."* Ghana is good: they have many nice girls — it's nice — it's got nice girls. They don't cost much and all this. And you can give, two thousand five hundred francs — um, fifty cedis[3] — *"deux milles cinq cents, quand tu donnes deux milles cinq cents, une fille Ghanaienne, elle va te marier."* In Ghana, when you take a Ghanaian girl and give her fifty cedis, she is going to tell you to see all her families tomorrow; you are going to make marriage.

And so we know the good ones and the bad ones inside this. We say we don't hear French. So he will say something in French, and maybe you will hear it. We will know that this person is maybe like that or like this. He is thinking, "When I went to Ghana, I had one girl for thirty cedis. It's one thousand five hundred, OK? And this girl has crossed the border, please. I will give her a high price, maybe two thousand, or maybe two thousand five hundred." You see? He knows that fifty cedis is plenty of

---

1. A full "piece" of cloth such as African wax-print is twelve yards. A half-piece (six yards) is used for women's traditional dresses with skirt, blouse, scarf or head-tie, and waist-wrap; two yards are used by men for shirts.

2. the patterns

3. As noted, cedi exchange rates continued to change drastically from the early 1970s. The rate Hawa is giving indicates that a current dollar would be worth 4.50 cedis or 225 CFA francs.

money in Ghana. This is the way they think of the Ghanaian girls in Ouagadougou. But where can you take a girl in Ouagadougou to give her two thousand five hundred or three thousand? Even three thousand francs, the way we buy our things in Ouaga: you can take three thousand just to cook. So this three thousand is sixty cedis. You can take a girl and give her sixty cedis in Ouagadougou. OK. And somebody who has come to Ghana, he has been with a girl for maybe one thousand, twenty cedis, or thirty cedis, thousand five hundred, or forty cedis, two thousand. And then, he will come and take you in Ouagadougou and give you that two thousand because he has already been in Ghana, and he knows all the prices of Ghana.

But thousand five hundred or two thousand is not plenty of money here. No. The way they take their money in Upper Volta — or maybe it's the way I haven't been spending it from when I was young — but when I'm spending their money, if I have money in Ouagadougou, I can spend about ten thousand in a day. Yeah, if I have money. When I went to Ouaga first, I could spend that in a day. ten thousand. And then maybe I will see a dress: ten thousand. When I was at La Tringle, I could spend this. So thousand five hundred francs, it's not a lot of money in Ouagadougou.

Look. When Mama Amma and I came to Ouaga, we bought some small-small things from a shop: two buckets, a flask to put hot water in, a big wash pan to wash our clothes inside, a small cooler to put beer inside with ice blocks. We bought these things, and we spent more than ten thousand.

When we had our room the first time, we used to take these things from a certain woman. And one day, she was talking about us. I was taking my bath, and she asked of the bucket, and they said, "Oh, your small sister took it." Then she started shouting, "I don't like this kind of life. If I — the time I need my things, I must get them. I don't need for somebody to take my things, and then the time I need them, I can't find them," and that and this. She was just talking like that. Mama was sleeping, and I was bathing. When I finished my bathing, she said, "Oh, Hawa! So you are the one who took the bucket."

Then I said, "Yes, sister, I am the one."

Then she said, "Oh, I'm very sorry. So didn't you hear what I said?"

And I said, "Oh, no. I put the water there. Then I went to get cigarettes — I am just coming now. Then I took my bath."

Then she said, "I'm very sorry. I have talked bad. But anyway, it's not my fault, because all these girls in the house don't want to buy a bucket. They think my own is cheap, so they used to take it. So I was saying something bad. But I'm very sorry. Maybe somebody will tell you."

I had already heard it, but I didn't show any face that I heard it. So I went and woke Mama, and Mama said she must bathe. I said, "No, Mama, however dirty you are, if you don't want to go out, you can stay in the house. I'm going to get everything for bathing. I don't want you to bathe with somebody's bucket today."

Then she said, "What?"

Then I told her all that this woman said. So Mama got up and dressed, and we went to the market together. I was holding fifteen thousand, and I spent ten thousand to buy a bucket, a wash pan, these small-small things. Yeah, I spent ten thousand to buy just that.

So what I'm saying, before when I didn't understand this money, the day when I got this ten thousand francs to spend, if I had known that it was two hundred cedis, even some person could abuse me: he could take a knife to cut my throat; I'm not going to spend this money! But that time, you know, I was feeling like it's shit. That woman was ashawo like me. Even she was older than me; she had been in Ouagadougou a long time. Why should I let her bluff me with all this? So I had to buy all these things. I was annoyed, too, to get everything that day. So the money I had, I just spent it like that. Uh-huh.

And one other day, I was feeling to do something like bluffing. The time when I was going out from Woman's house, when I got my room at Zongo, I was happy. I made a party in Woman's room. I didn't leave the house the same day I took that room; we were together when we made the party. I took thirty thousand francs, and I bought drinks, foods, and all these different things. We were only seven girls and two boys, and we made a party, drinking, dancing, eating. I spent thirty thousand to buy all these things, and even we didn't finish all the drink. I left it for Woman; I didn't take anything away.

So Ouagadougou, how their money is there: you can get money there, but you can spend it too. Everything is expensive. You know, in Ouagadougou, you will see somebody who has his money: he doesn't care; he will just spend it foolishly. They used to spend! Even, somebody can have his money, and I don't know why — maybe he's drunk or something — he will just lose it in one day. And the next day, he will become like someone who is crazy, or he will be thinking, or he will become like somebody who is sick. They used to do that.

But in Ghana, no. They don't do that much. Somebody who has, he wants to be rich more than the other people. And he will want all the family to enter before somebody else can come in. In Ghana they do this. But in Ouagadougou they don't do that, and they don't care about all this. They don't try to give to their family like that. But Ghanaians, or Ghana people, if they get something, they want it alone for themselves and their families. Yes, people from Ghana, what they get, they want to have it alone. They choose their families. You know: "Kwabena is working — Kofi must work." You yourself, you can see how they are working. If you are Ashanti, if you have a post[1] or you are somebody, now-now[2] you will write all your brothers and your sisters; even your grandfather, if only he can talk, you would even like to bring him in. Then the profit will enter. This is the way Ghanaians do. So: that is why their everything doesn't work. *Ha!*

But Ouaga, if you go there, you have to know that you will spend. You will get money, and you will spend it. So when I traveled, every time, I used to work in these nightclubs. First time, when I went to Ouaga, I was working in La Tringle. Then I left La Tringle to work in Zé Bon. So La Tringle and Zé Bon: Zé Bon is beautiful, more than La Tringle. And I think Zé Bon may be bigger than La Tringle. Zé Bon can take more people than La Tringle. And at Zé Bon, too, they get more foolish people, too. These French people. *Ha!* When they are at Zé Bon, it's the place for them; it's where they do their foolishness work, you know. All these people who come to Zé Bon, many of them used to come to La Tringle, but at La Tringle they don't have much chance like Zé Bon. In La Tringle, there are many Africans, you know, the young ones and the *bosuns*.[3] *Ha!* Yeah, *bosun:* like somebody who thinks that he's a tough guy. They have those people there, so the French people don't have a chance to do all their foolish things. But in Zé Bon, African people don't like there, so the French people do whatever they like. It's only Zé Bon where they have their chance to do their foolish things. Do you think they do that in every nightclub in Ouagadougou? No. So Zé Bon is a good place for them. Yes. It's good for them: that's why every time they come there. They think they are free there. When they're doing something, there is nobody to stop them, and nobody to tell them something. Yeah, Zé Bon is very, very funny.

But the first time when I was working at La Tringle, I thought that I wanted more money, and I got another work to add to that one. So I worked one bar in the afternoon, and then night time I worked in La Tringle. I went to work in the night at nine o'clock, then maybe we closed

---

1. position, job
2. just now; at this very moment
3. (Pidgin): a tough guy. The bosun (boatswain) is a warrant officer or petty officer on a boat, a rank below commissioned officers; the bosun would normally be the ranking sailor in a group of seamen hanging out in port.

at two or three o'clock. And I could not sleep well. I used to like sleeping in morning time, but I had to wake up at maybe eight or nine. To finish everything and bathe and prepare for work, it would be ten o'clock in the morning, and then I would close from that place at three o'clock, and I would come home and sleep. How many hours could I sleep up to nine o'clock? I could not sleep at that time, too. So I was not happy. But if the ending of the month came, I used to be happy, you know, because I thought my pay was heavy more than my girlfriends. In the nightclub, I had twelve thousand; in the bar, I had eight thousand seven hundred. So every month, I thought I was better, because the ones who worked in the night, they had only twelve thousand in a month, and I had more than twenty thousand. So I was happy. So it was good, yeah?

But it was hard, from sleeping. If anyone saw me, "Hey, why? You are sick?" And so it was not good, you know, and I was not happy. Then I thought it's better to work in the night and leave the day work. Then I can sleep in day time. If you work in the day, in Ouaga, they don't pay well: maybe you will get only eight thousand, or eight thousand five hundred or seven thousand five hundred francs, for a month. So it is better if you work in the night. I don't want to do double work again, but before, when I saw the way I was spending in Ouaga, then I said, "No, let me try; I must catch this money too." I have tried to find out — working two places, day and night. What? How can I work like that? I tried — I became fed up.

You know, before, when I first came to Ouagadougou, I opened a bank account. And sometimes the way I spend, you know, it used to pain me that sometimes I would take from my bank account. This was the place when I started to think that I'm so stupid. The first time I opened the bank account, I was all right small-small. But why I took the money out of the bank: we had a problem, and my father told us, all the children, to come home. I did not have much money in the bank, about one hundred thousand. And I was also holding sixty thousand. So I thought: oh, to go with sixty thousand, it's too small, because I don't know what they will tell us to buy. So I just took all of my money. I took the one hundred thousand from the bank to add to my sixty thousand to go to the village. And I spent about eighty thousand there. OK. When I brought the rest of the money back, if I had sense, I should have gone and put it back in the bank. Then I said, Oh, no. I will keep it so that it will come to one hundred thousand again, then I will take it to the bank. So I was using this money. *Ha!* Before I got to know, the money was gone. Then I said, "Wow! This is my end. This is my end."

So how I hold my money now, I told you we have a man who comes around with a card: every day, if you have some money, you give him. And the ending of the month, he will take the money of one day. I know that if I get money, I will spend it by heart. So if I get money, I keep it small-small with him. Even before I got my first bank account, I was keeping money with him to make the deposit for the bank account. I used to do it small-small like that.

Yeah, but to hold money is difficult. You know, when we first came to Ouagadougou, we had been here three months, and I was doing this card with the man. I had ninety thousand. I was doing a thousand a day for the month, so every month I had thirty thousand, isn't it? After three months I had ninety thousand. That ninety thousand, I took it when I went to my village, and then I asked for two cows. The two cows cost me about fifty-six thousand. So I have two cows in my village! *Ha-ha!* This is my bank account. I used to laugh. The last time I went there, the one cow had given birth to two. Then I said, "OK, I have four cows now."

So then I was trying to be clever to get money, you know, to be going to my village, so that I would go and buy cows, so that if I got plenty of cows, I would sell the cows to people. *Ha!* This was my mind when I got to Ouagadougou. *Ah!* When I went to our village and I saw that a cow is not costly, I thought that if a very small cow can cost about two thousand or three thousand, if you can get a small cow like that, then you will get Fulani people to look after the cow. If they are good and look after this cow well, she will come and give birth and birth and birth. If it's a woman-cow, you will get many children from the cow. You will make a big factory of the cows, you know. So when I came back to Ouagadougou, then I said, "Ah! This time I will try to work and then go and get more cows from the village."

But I have never kept the money to go and get this thing! Every time, when I get money, when I make my program to go to the village, I will get some problem, and then I have to use that money. Some time ago I always used to be thinking, "Oh, I'm going to the village. I will be staying in town for about two or three months and then going to the village. And maybe I will get about six cows, plus my four cows, then I will have ten. And next year, I will get another ten, so I will have twenty." You know? But I have been waiting, waiting, waiting to get small money to put on top of this money I have.

So I don't know. Sometimes I will get money and say, "Oh, this money: I want it to reach two hundred thousand or one hundred thousand, and then I will do something with it." And you know, when I make a budget for this money, to put it down, I will be putting it down. I wouldn't touch it. But one day, I will just see one problem which can chop this money the same day.

: KOUDOUGOU AND THE VILLAGE IN BURKINA FASO :

Country Roads at Night

Look. It was not long ago that my father was sick. I got the telegram on Saturday night. The next morning I got a car that left Ouagadougou about twelve o'clock.[1] And it was raining heavily. It was wonderful: raining from Ouagadougou up to my village. This rain was beating all the roads, over one hundred and something kilometers.

So you know, my village is not too near to the road: it's about three kilometers from the road. I got to the junction about half-past eleven in the night. From twelve noon to after eleven at night, to go this hundred and something kilometers! The road was not good and it was raining. You know, if you get a good car, you can take two or three hours to make this road. But if you don't get a good car, or if you get one of these trucks, you know, they pick up the people on the road, from one village to the next village, drop them, get their things, carry the other ones. And this car didn't go fast. The driver stopped at every village. Everywhere there were passengers. So when I dropped, it was night and it was raining. So somebody in the car asked me, "Do you know the real place where you are going?"

Then I said, "Yes. It's about three kilometers from the road."

Then he said, "Do you know the road you are going to pass? Are you not afraid in the night like this alone?"

Then I said, "No."

So they got all my things down. I couldn't carry anything. I was alone in the night. I just threw all the things in the bush. Then I started walking alone. And I had no light — good God! *Kaɛ!*[2] When I walked, I reached some place where my head got *big* like something was following me. You know, I was afraid in the night. It was dark! And I was alone there. If the

1. Transportation does not leave until the bus or car is full; travelers take a seat and wait.

2. (Asante Twi): an exclamation of objection, rejecting a situation or statement as useless

rain made the lightning, *o-o-oh:* then I'm dead. So I was just walking, going inside the water. The road was not good. There were some places where there was water I didn't see. Before I'd get to know it was water, I was inside! *Ha!*

Hey! That night, I was calling God. I was calling the name in my heart. I didn't call it in my mouth, but in my heart. I was thinking and begging God. "I'm not a witch. I am not searching for anything. I am not a thief, too. So help me, and let me get out from this bush!" You know, the place was very dark, and there was nobody, and it was raining, and these frogs were making *"kwaa-kwaa-kaa."* And I was in this water. Sometimes I would go into the water, and I didn't know, and I would hear that something jumped in the water. *Tak!* And I said, "Oh God, come down, help me! Let me out. I didn't come to do something bad." You know? *Ha-ha! Hee-hee-hee! Ah!*

You know, when I dropped at the junction, there was no house or anything. It was only the trees you could see. And under the trees, as the rain was raining for a long time, under the trees was maybe raining even more than in the rain. So you couldn't get any place to hide yourself. If there was something like in Ghana where they make bus stops, I wouldn't care. I could have slept there. But in my place, they don't have anything like that! And my torch,[1] too, I put it in my bag. I didn't think that I would be getting there late. I was sure that we would reach the place in time. I thought: as we left Ouaga by twelve o'clock, maybe I can get there in two hours' time. So I packed this torch with my things. And to stand in the rain, in the dark, to open this bag, taking the clothes out, all of that would be another problem. So I said, "Oh shit, I will try. God will take me there." You know? So — *ha-ha!*

But when I got to the water, then I said, "No. God, you are taking me there, but you have to *come down!*" Ha-ha! "*Come down!*"

I didn't know what was happening in the water, you know. Sometimes, if it is something like this, when you are walking alone like that, you used to get a bad mind. Then sometimes I used to remember some cinemas, when the animals used to come from the water. Where there was grass, and when I reached the place like that, then I would hear something touching the water: *"Tak!"* Then I shouted, *"Eee-e, God! Come down!"* Yeah! Then I started to think of crocodiles and all these things.

And the last place I passed before I got to our place, the water was up to my thighs. So when I saw the water was coming up to there, then I said I would turn back, I would wait outside this water. But by that time, I was

1. flashlight

in the middle. So I looked at the back and looked at the front. Then I said, "No. I have already known the road when it's not raining. Oh, I think this place — it will be like that." So when I started going forward a little bit, then I saw that my feet were coming out. Then I said, "Ah, suppose I went back, I would have done monkey work."[1] Then I passed that place. That was the last water which I passed.

But some places, too, you will just walk, and you don't know that there are some holes there, and there is some water there. You are just walking: *tum-tum-tum.* Then you put your feet: *dak-sss!* Then *oh! Ha-ha!* You will fall down. And that time, too, I wanted to walk quickly because it was raining. So I was falling like that up to the village. When I got to the village, all my dress was wet. Then when I reached home, when I knocked on the door, then they were asking me, "Who? Who? Who is that?"

I was annoyed: *"Open!* It's *me. Hawa!* Open the door quick! I'm feeling cold! *Why?!!"*

When they opened the door, they said, *"What?!* Where from you?"

I said, "I'm from Ouagadougou? Where is my father?"

They said, "He is at Koudougou." Then they said, "Ah, but why didn't you rest at Pouni?"[2]

You know, there is a village near us on the way I passed, just near the road. We have some people there. If it's night, if you drop at the man's place, he will give you a nice place, and the next morning, you will get a motor to take you, and the children will carry your things there. That day, I could have gone to sleep in that village, but what they told me — the telegram which I got — they didn't tell me that my father was in Koudougou Hospital. They just said my father was sick. You know, telegrams: they used to make everybody afraid because they don't give the explanations. Especially, you know, in this place, telegrams are costly, so they didn't have the way to say many things. So I had to come home. I didn't have a mind to go to Koudougou. And I didn't want to stop at that village until the morning. Maybe before the morning time, he would be dead. I wouldn't meet him. So I had to see him. If he has something to tell me before he's dead, I have to get there. This is what was in my mind when I was traveling.

Even sometimes, some people used to be working at some place, and they used to call them home that their family is sick: then you will ask the

1. useless work, work for nothing. She would have thrown away all the effort it took to get her that far.
2. As noted in Procedures to Protect Identities, the locations of these villages will not make sense because I have used names from villages scattered over a broad region.

road[1] to go and see them. So, in our African ways — I don't know your people's ways — if it's we Africans, maybe we are here: one night we will hear a telegram that, "Your father is sick, seriously." Even if you are working at some place, you must go straight and ask permission to go. They used to come to us Africans like that, from the families.

So then I said, "Where is my small brother?"

They said, "He has slept."

So I went and woke him, to go and find a motor, so that the same night we would go to Koudougou. But we didn't get the person who had the motor: he had traveled with the motor. So they said I have to sleep, and tomorrow morning, then we will go.

Then I said, "Everybody has to wake up here. Nobody can sleep. You people will sit with me up to the morning time, because I'm not feeling like sleeping."

So: my brother also was trying to do his own business, you know. He used to get beer and sell it in the village. They have no light, so no fridge. But he had many cases of beer — hot beer in the village. So I said, "OK. Hot beer: I will drink. Open it!"

Then my brothers were asking me about my things. I said I left them in the bush. So they said they would go and carry it. As they didn't have the motor, I said they should leave it. But they went and got it, I think about five o'clock in the morning. *Everything* was wet. Some of my clothes, the water went inside them. *Ha-ha!*

About seven o'clock in the morning, we went to find the motor to take us from our village to one village which is near to us. They call that place Zamo. That's where you can take a train. First we took a bicycle. You know, it was a funny thing. My brother was riding it, and he was carrying me on the back of the bicycle. *Ha!* He carried me from my village to another village about four kilometers away to take the motor from some boy there. That boy had a Mobylette.[2] We left the bicycle there, and we took that Mobylette and went to Zamo on the road. And this Mobylette also: that small thing which can spark it, that boy's one was chopped up. So if we went small, then the fire would go off. *Brrr-to-to-to, to-to-to.*

Suppose the motor was good, we wouldn't take one hour on the road before getting to the place. But it took more than three hours. It was maybe about twelve kilometers, but this motor couldn't go. Every time, if it was hot, we had to stand until it was cold. And my brother was trying to remove it and then fix it again. *A-yai-yai-yai-yai!* So when we got

1. ask for permission; ask for a way
2. a type of motorized bicycle

to Zamo, we left the motor with one of our sisters who was living there. Then we took the train straight to Koudougou. You know, from Zamo to Koudougou is not far. I don't know how many kilometers it will be, but it's not far. I think the train was about three hundred francs to that place.

When we reached the place, we walked to my father's brother's house. We met him there, and he said, "Oh, we thought maybe they would bring him out, but they haven't brought him out yet. But he's all right now." Then he was about to play me some kalabule way. Instead of taking me there, he said his car hadn't got petrol. So I was annoyed. Then I and my brother went out: if your car hasn't got petrol, then I can find a taxi. There are taxis at Koudougou. It is not a small village.

So we got to my father at hospital. It was the time when they were going to give them food, and he was refusing. He said, "Who is giving me the food?" The younger wife: she was giving him the food.

Then we said, "But you should just take something. Take something to eat."

Then he said, "No, I won't eat."

Then the younger wife said, "Do you want to kill me? That's it. You will kill me, and you will wake up from this sickness, and you won't see me. Any time when I'm giving you the food—"

He said, "No, no, no! I want my mother to give me the food."

Then he was closing his eyes. When my father is sick, he always closes the eyes. He doesn't see anybody's face. So I just touched the younger wife like this; then I took the pan. Then I said, "So you don't want to drink anything?"

Then he said, "Who is that? Who is that?"

Then I said, "Did you hear the voice? So you want to kill me?"

Then he said, "No, my Mama,[1] I can't kill you! Mother, I can't kill you!" *Ha!* Then he opened his eyes. He had been three weeks in the hos-

---

1. Hawa has the name of her grandmother, and her father addresses her as "Mother" or "Mama." This form of address is used routinely as a nickname. Among Voltaique peoples, children are sometimes named after their grandparents, and the parents would feel uncomfortable addressing them with the actual name of their father or mother; they would instead call the child "mother" or "father" or "grandfather" and so on, or sometimes, more indirectly, "the name of the mother," "the name of the father," and so on. Such children are also said to have "inherited" their grandparents, a term that sometimes refers to the personality or character or destiny of the child (or to the parents' hopes in that regard), in the sense that the ancestor has come back to the world in that child. It is also common for a diviner to help the parents know which ancestor has come back, particularly if there is a problem with a child, when it may be important to know more about such an inheritance.

pital. But he closed his eyes all the time. The day he heard my voice, he opened his eyes, and he took porridge. He drank a lot of porridge that day.

So by then, we had to leave. And that time, they had written many medicines to buy. I got all these papers, and I said, "OK, I won't sleep here. I will be trying to get back to Ouagadougou, so that tomorrow morning, maybe I can find everything."

Before I got to the train station, the train had already passed. I couldn't get any train again. And I didn't want to sleep there, too. So I got somebody; I knew the person from Ouagadougou. He said he came to see the wife, that she had delivered a child, and he came to make the naming of the child[1] in Koudougou. So he had to go back because he was working tomorrow morning. He had a Yamaha motor. So I said, "OK. I too, I don't want to sleep here, because tomorrow I'm going to look for some medicine to give to my father." He carried me with this Yamaha from Koudougou. Before we reached Ouagadougou, I was too, too, too, too: all my body was feeling pains! From Koudougou to Ouaga on motor! Yeah! And this road—*shit!* And this man too: it was night, and he didn't take his time. Just going like that. *Boom! Boom! Boom!*

Then the next day, instead of getting up about eight o'clock to go to pharmacy, I went to the pharmacy at eleven o'clock. Then I got the medicine. OK. Then I had to wait for the two o'clock train and take it back to Koudougou. And I went and gave this medicine. OK.

So I said, "I want to go back to our village to sleep there, because I don't know where to sleep."

And my mother, my father's wife, the younger wife: she was sleeping in my father's brother's house. She said, "But you can go and sleep in your father's brother's house. It is the place I am sleeping. Even, my place is there. We can sleep together." This man has a very good place. He is family, but he left this woman to sleep in his sitting room,[2] putting her cloth on the floor like that to sleep. Man, *shit!*

So when we went to the place, and she showed me where she was sleeping, then I said, "No, I can't sleep here. I know this man. Maybe we are family. But a real family, as I used to take my families, you know? Even this man: his daughter or his son can come to me at Ouagadougou, but I cannot put her in my sitting room on the floor, without any mat or any mattress to give her. Just to put her cloth on the floor and sleep? So I

---

1. a small (occasionally large) ceremony formally giving a newborn a name, usually done a week or so after the birth. Muslim boys are circumcised on their naming day.

2. In a modern house or large apartment, one enters into the sitting room (sometimes called the sitting hall), which normally leads to a corridor or directly to the bedrooms, kitchen and bath.

don't understand you people. Every time, you people say, 'This is my brother,' and that and this. I won't sleep here." So I went back to hospital and told my father, "Where my mother is sleeping, I can't sleep there. She can sleep there, but I can't sleep there, so I'm going back to our village."

So I got up from Koudougou about six o'clock in the evening. Then I got somebody to drop me at Zamo. OK. My brothers didn't know that I would be coming that night. So Zamo, we have a small bush road. These twelve kilometers: I walked it on my feet, man! *Twe-a-a!*[1] I told you we have a sister at Zamo, the one we gave the Mobylette to when we first passed there. But I didn't want to sleep with her because the house she was living in was also the house of my father's brother. My father used always to talk about this man when we were young in Ghana. He used to say that man is the only brother he had. And then my father was sick and in hospital. But my father's wife was staying with this man so that she could cook in morning time to take it to the old man,[2] but that man could not give her a good place to sleep. She was sleeping on the sitting room floor. This man had a big flat, about six to seven rooms, with his wife and his children. OK, why don't you take the children and give the bedroom to this woman, or even give this lady a mat to sleep with the children in the bedroom? I think that's better than for her to be in the sitting room. Morning time, when they wake up and she's in the sitting room, even if she's tired, she has to wake up.

So I walked by foot. I got to Pouni, that place where I said they carried me with the bicycle, and we went and took the motor. When I got there, it was night, about nine o'clock. Then I got that boy, the one we took the motor from, to drop me at our village. Then the next day I had to go back again to the same place I was from.

This was what I was doing. I didn't want to sleep in the sitting room, so I had to be going back on this road. Sometimes I got lucky. I would get a lift to drop me at the junction. Sometimes I had no luck. If I got a lift to bring me a little bit and then drop me at some place, then I would start to look for this bush road. I was asking. If I met somebody, I would say, "I am going to this village. Where is the road?"

And they would say that, "Take this road. Go straight. Don't turn left, don't turn right. Just straight ahead." I used to ask like that to pass on this road. Then some people would say, "It's far. Do you know the place?"

I said, "Yes.

1. (Asante Twi): *Tweaa* is an exclamation of disgust.
2. It is normal for the family to prepare food for a hospitalized person, partly because the typical hospital food has less meats and vegetables and is considered less appetizing.

They said, "It's far. It's too night.[1] It's late to go now."

I said, "Oh, no. It's OK. The people will come and meet me on the road. My brothers are coming to meet me." But I was lying. Nobody would come and meet me. I just didn't feel to stay any place. I knew some village which my father used to tell us, "This village is for the family. Sometimes if you pass there, if you ask the name of this person, maybe you can rest there." But I just didn't feel like resting someplace. I had to come and rest at home, because maybe the place I will go and ask, they will give me some place to rest, and maybe I won't feel to rest there. So it's better I continue my walking. I didn't stop anywhere to ask of all these people in the family.

I had a torch. The first day I came, I didn't have that torch. I told you I had packed it with my things, and I couldn't stand in the rain to open the things and take it. So I just walked on the road like that. But all this time when I was going, I used to take the torch because I didn't know whether I was going to be alone at night on the road. But sometimes, you know —

I was walking one day and I heard something. I think it was a bird or something. It was crying in the bush. It cried like, "*Ooo, ooo, ooo.*" *Hey-eh?* I don't know if it was a bird, or what. I didn't see the bird, but I was just hearing the cry. That place: *tweaa!* I thought I died finish!

You know, how the Gurunsi people used to talk about witches and all this? Then I started talking. I said, "*Ah!* As for me, I just went to see my father. I'm not one of you people." You know? *Ha-ha!* "I'm not one of the witch people. So you people shouldn't put me inside.[2] As for me, I'm from this town. I'm from this village. I'm the daughter of this man. So if you people don't know it, touch me. Fire will catch you!" I just started talking alone, you know. I was *afraid!!* So I turned the light off, because I was afraid that maybe the thing will see me, that there is somebody with a torch. I walked more than two miles without any light. I was afraid. And, you know, that time too, as it was rainy season at our place, there are these tall green grasses along the bush road. They grow big. Night time, all of them get cold, and they used to bend over the road like a cover. If you walk under, sometimes, if you don't know and you walk like this in the night time, then some grass will just brush your arm or neck, and be touching you. *Tsk!* You will shout! *Ha!* Nobody is there! That one, you keep it in your heart. *Ha-ha!*

So, I was walking. When I was hearing this bird crying, then I started talking, and I turned the light off. Then some grass on the roadside, you

---

1. (Pidgin): It's late; it's too much into the night.
2. include me among you

know: so when this thing touched me, then I said, "*Hey!* As for me, you can't eat me! I'm bitter!" *Ha-ha! Hey!* You see things in the night! *Hey!*

When my father was sick, I suffered on this road. I would come back to my village to sleep. Morning time, maybe I will take a car straight to Ouagadougou, or I will take a car back to where he was in the hospital. I was there like that until the time when they discharged him from the hospital and they brought him back to my village. Then I stayed for four days in the village with him. Then I came back to Ouagadougou. I stayed six days, then I went back again for two weeks. Then I came back to Ouagadougou again. Then I used to make one or two weeks, then I would go and see him. And from that time, if I went, maybe I slept one day. The next day I would come back to Ouagadougou. Sometimes I would come back the same day. If I got a good car to go early, then I would come back in the evening.

So my father's sickness, I think he was in hospital about one month and some weeks, before they got him out from the hospital. And I was there, going back and forth. Every time I had to go there.

: OUAGADOUGOU AND THE VILLAGE IN BURKINA FASO :

The First Useless Child

When my father was sick, I went to the village with about one hundred and fifty thousand, or one hundred and seventy thousand. I don't know. It took me three weeks. I borrowed fifteen thousand from Limata to buy medicine. I have paid her ten thousand, and it's left with five thousand. I told her I will pay later. She doesn't worry, so we are the same. She used to borrow from me; I used to borrow from her.

Look. When my father was sick, one day I went to the pharmacy. All the medicines he needed were written on paper, and I gave the paper and I said they should bring all the medicines. I had about thirty-five thousand. They brought it and gave me the bill. It was forty-two thousand! *Ah!* Then I asked the man, "Is this for all of this?"

Then he said, "Yes!"

I said, "Did you calculate well?"

Then he said, "You can see, if you can look at all the boxes, they have the names on them."

So what I had to do: I pulled the thirty thousand for them, and the five thousand, I took a taxi and went to my house and took this card and went back to see that man, the one we used to give the card. I collected another fifteen thousand to go to the pharmacy and then pay for all this medicine. And then, to go back to the village with the car, and then—*Shit!*

And when I took this medicine, in three days, they said to go and buy another different medicine again. And this old man was *sick.* I couldn't ask him for money. I know very well that he has some money. But the way he was, it was not necessary to be asking him, "You know, I haven't got money," and all this. I thought that as he was, he shouldn't hear this from his children.

And the other children, too. You see my brothers: what about my brothers? If you know African problems, you can't ask this question. This old man was always calling my name. OK? And my brothers are the ones who sent him to the hospital for about three weeks before I also got to know. OK? And they were also trying their best, and even they were fed up. They are in the village. And you are there. How can you go and ask them that they have to give some amount? All these things, you know, sometimes I feel that the way my father likes me, and—I don't know— my brothers know me, but I don't want them to know me much like, "OK, when our father was sick, she came. And when they gave her a note to buy medicine, she came home. She had to pass through the village to ask of this and this. If the old man will die, he will die."

We African people, we used to talk about each other. Even your brother from one mother, one father: if he gets you, he will talk about you in some way, so that the people will think you are a different kind of fel- low, or you are that and this. I thought about all these things, so I had to try my best by myself.

Look. Why should I take fifteen thousand from Limata? Why? OK, my younger brother is there. He sells *akpeteshie;*[1] he makes it by himself. Sometimes, when I'm going to the village, I used to get him maybe a car- ton of sugar and a carton of yeast. This is what he is using in making the akpeteshie. And I think, in the correct way, if it's something difficult like this sickness of our father, I could go and ask him, "OK, you know, I just came from Ouagadougou. The money I have is not enough. So they have written this paper and given to me. So I want to ask you if you can help me for five thousand." I can ask him. Isn't it? As for his case, even if he talks about me, I have something to say. I can say, "OK, I also was helping him, because of all these things I had been buying for him, he was selling them, and I didn't ask him for money from it." Isn't it? But I don't want it.

---

1. (Ga): Akpeteshie *(akpɛtɛshi)* in Ghana is locally distilled spirits, usually made from sugar cane or palm wine. Akpeteshie was illegal during colonial times, and the name has two applicable Ga meanings, one from "hide-out" and the other from "lean over or against."

You know, sometimes if I go to village for a visit, I used to tell this boy, "I have nothing, so give me one thousand, or five thousand, or ten thousand. If I go to Ouagadougou, then when I come back, I will pay you." He used to give me. But the problem of this old man's sickness, I didn't want anybody to lend me money from the family. I was thinking the old man was going to die, and well, if the old man is dead, I am the *first* fellow who is useless among all the children of my father. You know? Number one: at our place, I don't have a husband. OK? All my senior sisters and the younger ones who have married, they will bring their husbands to the funeral, and the husbands will start to kill their cows and sheep.[1] In our village way, my sisters' husbands are the people who are killing the sheep and cows. And I don't have somebody to do this.

So I thought I had to try my best. *Ha! Ha-ha!* I didn't want to ask any one of them for money. I just didn't want to ask anybody. So I was suffering like that, every time, and trying to ask my friends. Limata is more than my sister now. She is the one I trusted and then I borrowed her fifteen thousand. I have already given her ten thousand. It is left with five thousand. OK.

You know, in this our ashawo life, if you are following the men, there is not any kind of money that you can know that, "This is the amount I am going to take tonight." You know, there are some times, *hm?* Some times maybe you are all right.

Look. I told you that I don't force myself to be following the men, but I can tell you, the time I borrowed Limata's money —fifteen thousand, eh?—I needed to buy medicine for my father. That time, if somebody said, "OK, I will give you five thousand," I would go with him. That time I didn't have time to be patient: I would try to go with him to pay this debt, because I didn't like it. And I thought: maybe if I had been closing my eyes, to be doing this five thousand with people and keeping the money, maybe I wouldn't have had to borrow this money from her. You know, five thousand is not a heavy money. If I had five thousand, sometimes maybe I would think, "*Whew! Oh-h! Shit!* This five thousand, I will just take it to the market and finish it." This is what I used to think. But the time I had this problem, and I needed the money, even to ask Limata for this money, it took me *three days*. I didn't know what to tell Limata, you know.

Yeah. I bought the medicine. In about one week's time I used about one hundred and fifty or one hundred and sixty thousand, just like that. And

---

1. The final funeral takes place several months after the death. In the family gathering in many Voltaique cultures, sacrifices (and meat) are provided by the deceased's daughters' husbands.

I still didn't know where I was. *Wow!* I was hot. I didn't know where I was. So I used to be walking on the street, and you know, this my finger, every time I used to chew on it. In the night and day, when I would go to some place to buy something, I don't know what: I just became like somebody who was crazy.

Then I thought, "No. If I go and ask Madame Colette, she will give me." But I didn't want it. You know, I think: I'm poor, but I used to be proud on some things, and then I will be suffering. My mind was: OK, this woman, I'm working with her. And there are many girls who take advance—half of their pay. And this woman used to talk to us. She used to tell me and Limata, "This girl, ending of this month, she did not have enough money. She had take this amount of money." So I felt that if I ask this woman, she will give me, but you know, all the girls in the work place, the way she talks to me, that is the way she talks to the other ones, too. This woman will be talking of me, that my father is sick—he is in the hospital—she has lent me money to buy medicine, but I will pay her back—and this and that. This woman is going to tell all these workers. So I didn't want any money from her.

But to tell Limata, it took me three days. I thought about it for three days. Then I said I don't care. So I said, *"Camarade."*

She said, "Hey, *camarade.*"

I said, "You know, I'm in difficulty. But you know, I think maybe if I ask Mama, she will give me."

And the way Mama is in this town now, even if she has it, maybe she will give me, and maybe she won't give me. The way she is, I am not serious with Mama now, because she has many girlfriends. And you know, sometimes we used to be three—me and Mama and Limata. We can converse something like this, simply, and later you will hear it from some girl. So I don't have much interest with Mama now. I think it's the way she can drink: when she drinks, she can tell her secrets to the friends.

So I thought, "No, I will ask Limata." Even if Limata does something to me, it wouldn't hurt me much, because I have done something for her also. One time she had nothing, and she had borrowed money from me—seventy thousand. And she paid back all. She was paying me small-small, but she paid all. So even if she's going to disgrace me, if I hear it, I can give a reply. So I don't care. She had a debt with me before, so I can take a loan from her, too. Then I told her, *"Camarade,* I beg you. Can you help me? Even I need only ten thousand."

Then she said, "No. You can take the fifteen thousand, because you are going to your village with a car and all this. So I don't care. Any time, if you can get it, you can pay me."

So she gave me the fifteen thousand. I spent three days in village, then

I came back to the town for four days. Before going back to the village, I gave her ten thousand. Then it was left with five thousand. And the five thousand, I told her, "If I start work, I will pay you." So she understood. We had no problem.

So that was the time when this problem came for my father, when he was sick. When I was going there, as for the food palaver, I didn't have any problem. At my father's place, he has a wife around him: she was cooking for him. Only medicine: the doctor wrote some medicines to get from the pharmacy, and I used to be going up and down to find the medicine. I had to go to Ouagadougou for it. If I went, I didn't usually stay there for a long time. Maybe sometimes I was in the village for two or three days, then I'd come to Ouagadougou for one day; maybe sometimes I slept in Ouagadougou; maybe one day I would come to Ouaga in the morning time and go back in the evening. So I was in the village like that.

You know, my father has many children, but inside the family, there is no proper person inside. They all just don't care. Everybody is looking at himself. Everybody thinks it's best to take care of himself. No one cares about what can happen to my father. When the old man was having all his sickness, you know, he has some children who are at Côte d'Ivoire, some who are at Bobo-Dioulasso, and some who are in Ghana. They were writing to everyone, sending telegrams, but *no*body come. Nobody.

6 THE BIG FIGHT IN THE FAMILY

: *The Two Wives*
: *The Big Fight*
: *Interlude: Big Brother*
: *The Big Fight (Conclusion)*

: THE VILLAGE IN BURKINA FASO :

The Two Wives

You know, my father has two wives, and the time he was in hospital, it was only the younger one who was doing everything. He was having three wives, but my mother is dead. My own mother who gave birth to me is not in life. She died when I was three years old. And so it remains two wives.

My mother had five children, and three died. We are two who are left among my father's children. The same mother, the same father: we are only two. That one is a boy, Kofi, the one I told you about, that I brought him to Tamale when I was with Nigel: that is my brother. Kofi is one mother, one father with me. He's in Kumasi.

My brother in Ouagadougou, the one I stayed with when I got there, he is not my father's son. He's the son of my mother's big sister, the one who was in front of my mother.[1]

We are plenty, eh? Yeah, I think now we are more than thirty. We were thirty-five but two have died not long ago, so we are thirty-three now. We had two who were twins: those twins have died. Apart from my brother and me, there are two children who are from outside women.[2] All the rest are from those two women he has now. And they still didn't stop.

The younger wife is a twin. That girl, they gave birth to her as twins, one boy and one girl. The boy died. My father married that girl, and she also had twins again, two girls. They are the ones who died not long ago. And then, after those twins, she had a small one. It's now that that baby has started walking, but he doesn't walk well. I think if she has another chance, maybe she will get another one again. She is not too much old. As for the old wife, I think she may be fifty or something. But the young one, she's not even up to forty. And so my father is much older than the younger wife.

I don't know actually how old my father is, but he must be maybe seventy or eighty or something like that. He is very old. I think so, because *all* the friends who were having the same age and they grew up together in the village, all of them are dead, and he's left alone.

And so my father's wives are not the same age. You know, my father didn't marry straight. At first, when he grew up, he used to do business, traveling, buying things from Abidjan, or buying things from Ghana to take to Ouagadougou, cola[3] and different things. He used to take cola to Ouagadougou and to Abidjan, and take things from there back to Ghana. So when he grew up, I think at first he was happy in the work, so he didn't marry quickly.

---

1. As noted, only cross-cousins (your mother's brother's children and your father's sister's children) are called cousins, and sometimes they are even addressed as brother or sister. Your mother's sister's children and your father's brother's children are your brothers and sisters. In the same vein, your mother's brothers are your uncles, and your father's sisters are your aunts; your mother's sisters and your father's brothers are your mothers and fathers, sometimes called "small" or "junior" if they are younger than your mother or father, or "senior" if they are older.

2. not inside a marriage; outside the family house

3. Cola is a type of bitter seed about the size of a chestnut. In Africa it is chewed as a mild stimulant.

He got his first two children from outside, and they are senior to all of us. The second son of my father, we know the mother. But the first one, we don't know the mother. My father carried the baby from the mother at Côte d'Ivoire. He said the baby was two years old when he carried him from Abidjan. I think he just took this woman as a girlfriend. When he traveled there, he used to go and lodge with her. When they got the child, I don't know: I don't think the woman was ready to marry, or maybe she was ready to marry and then I think my father was trying to run away. So this girl just said, "OK, I don't need a baby. So if you want your baby, you can take him away. Otherwise I will dash the baby to government." And since my father took the baby from that woman, he never, never touched the woman's house to say hello to her, up to now until this boy is now old. The senior son is an old man now, this boy, the one I'm talking about. So we don't know the mother actually. Only my father knows where he brought him from. He is the oldest.

So: these two wives. The senior wife is very bad. This old man was sick, and the older wife didn't mind. She didn't even know[1] that the husband was sick. She didn't care about anything. She was in the house, cooking heavy tuwo,[2] eating, going out with people, drinking pito[3] around the village. So from there, I got annoyed with her. Even today I don't think I will be free with her again. I told my father, "What do you keep this woman for?" *Ha!*

Do you know how the young wife came as a wife? I will tell you. She is the sister of the senior wife. Yeah. You know, at our place, in the olden days, they had this thing: one man will marry sisters. Even now they still have it, but we don't mind them. But in my village, if I marry, they will give me some of my sisters to come and serve me. Young, small girls. Maybe sometimes you can get one about eight years or ten years old. Some people get their sisters with them at about four years old. You will look after the sister. Oh, some men at our village may have about four sisters.

But I don't actually know, because my father's two wives have the same father but different mothers. So I think that in this case, they also used to give the children when they are not from the same mother. If the sisters have the same father, they can be married together to one man, just like that. Your senior sister will marry, and you will come and be serving your

---

1. From her actions, it seemed as if she didn't know.
2. making big meals to eat
3. a fermented drink generally brewed over three days from malted sorghum or sometimes from millet, reddish-brown in color with a somewhat sour taste

senior sister, and your sister will look after you as her baby. After you grow up, this man has been seeing you from when you were a kid—*Agh! It's shit!*—he will look after you like that, up until you grow up to be a woman. When the first wife takes the baby sister, all the family knows already that these two children have a husband. They know that by all means, the man cannot be feeding this baby like that and then give her out. If the baby is growing up, they will just go and see the family. The senior sister will go and tell the father or the mother, "This time, I think my sister has grown up, so I think that to let my husband go and search for some woman outside, I will become jealous. Maybe—we don't know—I don't know who will die first. Maybe I will be dying first, leaving my children. Then my husband will go and bring another woman from the other country or other village to treat them badly.[1] So I want to take my younger sister to give to my husband. If something happens to me, I think that as we are sisters, we cannot be jealous." And so just like that: the man will get two wives. So my father has two sisters. *Ha!*

Yeah. They are two sisters. But they don't like each other. The senior one brought the younger sister. OK? So when the younger sister was growing up, then she also married my father like that. And from then they have had to share the days they go to the husband.[2] Then the senior one was jealous of her. Even before the younger sister started having all these children, the senior one was starting to be jealous. From that time they have not been all right with each other. OK?

The small one has her children. The senior one also has her children. Some of the boys are living in the village with my father, and some of them have traveled. And I think the younger one has more sense than the senior one. She has good sense about family as we Africans take it. If her daughter or her son comes from Abidjan with many things, she will say, "No. You go and show your big mother."[3] But the senior one, if her son brings something, she doesn't want the younger one to see it. She wants it for herself alone. You see? She used to keep her everything for herself.

1. Because children "belong" to the father, the man will have custody, and the children will be raised by her cowives, their stepmothers, who will favor their own children in the house.

2. In a polygamous household, the wives take turns sleeping with the husband. Each wife has her own room, and they go to the husband's room to sleep at their turn. In the household, the responsibility of cooking is also shared in rotation, and normally the wife who cooks is the one who will go to the husband's room in the night.

3. The older one is the "senior" or "big" mother, and the younger is the "junior" or "small" mother, regardless of who actually gave birth to the child. The distinction is not generally used in addressing the parent, and children in the house will call them both "Mother."

But the younger wife, if her children come with things, then the mother will say, "No, carry it." Then they will carry it, and the mother will give it to the senior sister, "My sister, this is what your son[1] has brought," or "This is what your daughter has brought. So I think it is better if you keep it."

Then maybe the senior one will say, "OK, if that will be the case, then you also take this." Say if it's two pieces of cloth, they will share it. But the senior one will never get something like that and share with the younger one. And if it's money they give, she will never share it.

The Big Fight

And you know, the younger wife has a very, very clever daughter who has married a rich man. He is from our village. His mother was married to someone in Abidjan, and they gave birth to him there, and he grew up there. The father had many cocoa farms, and also coffee farms. Then the father was dead. This man is the first born, so now he has a lot of money. The younger one's daughter is married to him.

But this is the funny thing, too. Our people, if the children marry rich people, every time they used to visit their children, so that maybe they will get something from the husband. But my father's younger wife, since the daughter married, it's about three or four years now, and she hasn't been there. Not even once. But the senior one made excuse that she was going to visit one of the daughters in Ghana, and from Ghana she passed to that girl's place and collected things. You know, when the senior mother came, this girl treated her nicely: "Oh! My mother!" And that and this. Everything that she wanted, this girl gave it to her.

And then: you know, we Africans have a big pot which we use to cook the tuwo inside. So this girl said that when she had visited the village, her mother had told her, "If you go back, try to buy me that cooking pot, because now the house is becoming like a family house.[2] Sometimes we used to get strangers. And this pot which we are now cooking inside, it's too small. Maybe if it's harmattan,[3] we need hot water,[4] and to put water into

---

1. In the same way that the children will call each of them "Mother," the wives will also call one another's child as "my child" or "our child."

2. the main house in the extended family, that is, a big house

3. a dry dust-laden wind that blows south from the Sahara desert during late November, December, January, and into February. The word can also refer to the season.

4. During harmattan, nights can be cold, and many people heat their bath water.

that pot and then to take and put another one, it's wasting of time. So if you can get us a big one, it will be nice." So this small girl got that type of pot and gave it to the senior mother to go and give it to her mother.

And when the senior mother came, you know, this woman didn't say any word. Maybe, at least, if you don't tell your sister, you will just tell my father, "Oh, when I came from Ghana, I passed Abidjan. I have seen your daughter." But she didn't say anything.

So you know, I told you that when my father was sick, they were writing all the family, and no one came. And after that, when my father came out from hospital, he said that we all should come and group. All the children. He had written to my sisters in Côte d'Ivoire, and Bobo, and Ghana. But no one came. That time I went to the village, so I was there, and then this girl who had sent the pot to the mother, she came from Abidjan.

Then this girl's mother was annoyed. She said, "I told you to—*Ah!* I have been asking you for this cooking pot. You didn't bring it. So thank you very much."

Then the girl said, "*Ah!* But I bought this cooking pot. I have given it to your sister, your senior sister."

"When?"

"About four months ago, your senior sister came to me at my husband's place."

Everybody wondered. This was the place when we were going to get palaver. Then my father called the senior wife. He said, "When you went to your daughter, did you tell me?"

She said, "Why should I tell you?"

And my father said, "Why shouldn't you tell me?"

"She is my daughter. I was going to say hello to her. That's all."

Then my father said, "She is not your daughter. When you came from your house, did you have any daughter there? All the children are for me. You don't have any right to go to my daughter. It's because you are a witch. Suppose, if I don't look after my children, you will go and kill her there and eat her, and then you will come here. In three days' time they will say she's dead. Isn't it?"

Then the senior wife said, why should my father say so?[1] If she's a witch, how many children of my father has she eaten?[2]

Then my father said, "All my children, they are bitter. I have boiled them[3] before I brought them out. So you can't eat one of them. But you

---

1. talk like that
2. in this context, killed
3. given them medicine or juju

can eat in your family house, because you have eaten all of your brothers and your mother."—*Ha-ha!*—"And your father!"

So it was a *big* rout[1] that day. This woman, in the night, about eleven o'clock, she put her hand on her head, and — her village is maybe roughly eight kilometers from our village — she was shouting on the road, going to her village to wake all the families — the brothers, and the mother's sisters — to come with her to our village. Come and see! My father says she is a witch!

Then when they came, my father said, "OK, you went and brought your witch group. Well, I'm here, if you people can eat me."

Then the youngest mother of this woman said to my father, "Are you drunk? Or what? What are you trying to talk?"

And you know, the woman's brother also came, "Eh-h, even if she's a witch, now she has made this big house."

Then my father's first-born, the one we don't know his mother, he got up and said, "Don't say this foolishness here. She made a house? Can she build a house for our father?"

Then the woman's brother said, "Mm-hm."

Then my brother said, "OK, the children — the children of your sister. What have they done for their father? Tell me."

So: they were having all these topics, then my father said, "OK, you people came here to come and do what? Because I have abused your sister that she is a witch?" Then you know, the senior wife, her mother too had married with her younger sister. That senior woman had died, and the younger sister was still there. So my father said, "When you were with your big sister, then you people both had children. Your big sister says she is going to see her daughter at Kumasi. From there then she passes to your daughter's place in Abidjan. So if she comes back, she can't tell you that, 'Oh, my younger sister, you know, because our husband is now an old man, he used to trouble people with too much talk. So I don't want to tell him all this. But I have passed from Kumasi to our daughter in Abidjan. So she's greeting you.' Even if she can't tell the father, it wouldn't pain him, but she can tell the younger sister all this. It's nice. But because of this cooking pot, and all the money this girl gave you, you don't say anything. But this girl said you should give the cooking pot to the mother."

Then my father's senior wife went inside and brought the pot. She threw it down. This is the property the daughter gave to her, and now they are trying to abuse her about it.

1. a fight; noise and disorder

Then my father said, "You lie. It is not only the cooking pot she gave you. This girl cannot give you only the cooking pot. All that you have brought, she has given you. Give all of it out. All that she has given you, give all of it out. If I was you, I would give *all*." You know, my father was teasing her to make her hot.

Then she said, *"Eh-heh!"* You know, the girl had given her some cloth, about four pieces of cloth, different kinds, from Holland.[1] So she was telling my father, "Eh, this cloth, I have stayed in Ghana. I know cloth. It is Holland cloth. It's not the one they are making at Koudougou here." And that and this.

Then my father said, "Yes. It is Holland cloth. Have you given her some before? When she was going to marry, you know that she's your daughter. Have you given even a head scarf?" And he went and took all these things from her.

And by that time the daughter was sitting there. We were all there. That day was family fighting. As for this girl, she is a clever girl, but she doesn't talk much. But she brought the complaint, because she told the mother that she had given the pot to the big sister. So they were talking all this, and this girl was sitting very quietly.

Then the sister of the grandmother, you know, the senior wife's mother's sister, what she had to tell this young girl was that: "*Mm,* yes, may God bless you.[2] If you can do that to divorce your father and your mother, and spoil your father's marriage, may God bless you."

Then I said, "Don't say this word. Don't say that, 'May God bless her.' She didn't do anything bad. She didn't do bad like her mother's big sister. The mother's sister came to her, and she looked after her. Maybe she stayed some days; she was eating. And I think the husband wouldn't just leave this woman. When this woman was going to join a car to our place, he would pay all the debt. And so this girl didn't do anything bad. Even, if God didn't bless her, she wouldn't have got this man to stay with."

---

1. Wax-print cloth made in local factories in West Africa is regarded as lower quality than cloth from overseas. Quality is judged by how fast the colors are and by whether the printing is done on both sides. Particular print designs from various manufacturers can become fads, but in general wax-print cloth from different countries is ranked and priced accordingly, with "Hollandais" at the top, followed by English and then specific African countries, headed by Côte d'Ivoire and Senegal; local factories also produce different "qualities" or grades. Saying different "kinds" of cloth refers to different patterns or sometimes different countries of origin.

2. A phrase like "God bless you" or "Thank you" in this situation is meant to shame another person in a quarrel, with the implication, "You are abusing me unjustly or wickedly, and I will not respond; I will give my response to God."

Then I said, "But I think, our family has many witches, but they can't eat us. Even from the same village, the same family. We Gurunsi people, we used to say that a witch — a witch eats in his house. These Ashantis also have some sense: they say before something will bite you, it is from inside of your cloth. So before a witch will kill you, it is from your house. Isn't it? But the way our father looked after us, it is very difficult for a witch to get us from our own village. And how much about the village which is some kilometers from here?"

You know, my senior mother's village is called Fara, and our place is Sibi. And to come to our village, you have to pass one village. That village is where my mother was from: Dana. My mother's village and my father's place are just close to each other. You pass my mother's village before going to this woman's village.

So then I asked her, "Do you people think, even if you people can turn to a vulture, if you pass Dana, they will just shoot you off. Your light[1] cannot work anymore. To come to Sibi and eat people: is that why you people have come in the night? To eat us? Oh, I'm very sorry for your witchcraft. But we people from Sibi, if we want to eat somebody, we eat him in day time, when everybody is seeing.[2] But not in the night. Or what did you people come here for, at this time? To come and eat us? To finish our house? Do you people think you can finish us? Look, if you eat this one, tomorrow the other one you left will bring four or five. You can't finish the family. So if you people have a case with my father, or you want to take your daughters away, this is not a case for the midnight. We don't want any witch case. If you have a case, we are waiting for you people tomorrow. So I don't want to see anybody here. So, my father, go inside." *Ha-ha!*

Then my father said, "Thank you, my daughter."

Then my big brother — the one we don't know his mother — he said he's closing his eyes for one second, and if he opens his eyes and sees everybody there, the house will be fire.

Interlude: Big Brother

This boy, even in my village, everybody is afraid of him. He's a *crazy* boy. And I don't know: sometimes I used to pity him. He doesn't know the mother. Since that time when my father took the boy, he didn't one day

1. witch light; a light given off by witches
2. that is, our witchcraft is stronger because we can do it in front of you

tell him the family of the mother, or say, "This is the country your mother is from." Never. So he was just growing up in the house like that, with us. But he is the senior of all of us. And if we get a problem with people in the village, then because of this boy, they are afraid of my father's house.

You know, these old people in the village, the old people used to meet where they are selling this pito.[1] That is where they used to be happy and get their conversing. And my father is somebody who doesn't like drink too much, but this time, since he went back to the village, he also used to meet the other old people at the pito house.

So our village people, they are funny. You know, every time when my father talks, he used to bring Ashanti small-small inside of his Gurunsi. You know, he will say something in Gurunsi and add: *"Koraa-a"* or *"Paa-a."*[2] You see? So these old people used to tell him, "You too, fuck off. We don't know where you're from, even. Whether you are a Gurunsi man or you are what. Every day *'Koraa! Paa-a!'* What is all this?" So he used to get this quarrel from the old people of his size.

And when he gets this thing, he won't do anything. *Shit!* You know, if everybody who is growing old is coming like that, it's fucking. He will just come to the house. And he will start abusing all his children. *"Pfft!* I don't know why I have wasted all my strength. I used it for nothing! A man like me, when I get many children like that, I can go to that fucking, smelling pito house, and those fucking people who don't know where they are from — even they don't — they don't know how to sleep with a woman, to get children — they will come and abuse me like that. And you people are here. For *what?!* You people —" *Ha!*

Then my big brother will say, "Hey, hey, hey, hey, hey. Come here."

So, you know, now my father is very funny. He will just go like a baby, and say, "What did you say? What did you say? Can you call me, 'Come here'?" But he has already gone! *Ha-ha!*

Then my brother said, "If I can't call you, then why did you come? What is your problem?"

He said, "Don't you see that man — that fucking man who has grown up from his youth — he hasn't — even he hasn't tried once to marry. He has no baby, he has no anything — to come and abuse me that they don't

---

1. A pito house is a place where people gather, sitting on benches, to drink pito. In front of them are smaller benches with gouged out indentations to cradle a small half-calabash that holds a person's pito.

2. These words are commonly used to add emphasis at the end of a phrase or to respond. *Koraa* (Asante Twi): at all; as in, "not at all"; *paa* (Asante Twi): good, indeed; as in, very much, very well.

know where I am from. Because every time if I'm talking, I say *'Koraa ko-raa.'* But *'koraa':* they are not people? You know? Ashantis? They are people like us."

So then the big son just said, "OK. You stop. I'm going to see that person." Then the boy walked there — *pum, pum, pum, pum.* He said, "Hey, look. You have abused my father. It is the first and last for you. Next time, if you do that, I will beat you till you're dead!" *Ha!*

So then my father said, *"Eh-heh!* You see? The time when you were young, they were telling you to marry. See? My son, come and stand. Bring your son to stand!" *Ha!* So, you know, these kinds of funny things, I used to meet them when I go to our village. So it's very funny.

The Big Fight (Conclusion)

So *ha!* So this boy, he told them that if they let him close his eyes, *once,* and he opens and sees everybody here, the house will have fire. So I don't know where all of them passed. They went back to their village.

Yeah. And then this witch-woman was sitting there crying, crying, crying, the whole night. She was sitting outside the house, crying. So everybody went to sleep. Ah, *tsk.*

Then I told my younger brother, *"Tsk,* this woman, she wants to kill somebody in this house. Why? Why should she be crying like that?

Then my younger brother — he is the boy I love in my family — he is the younger wife's first-born: this boy got up, and he opened the door. Then he said, "Mama, won't you go and sleep?"

And she was crying, and she said. *"Ooo-o, boo-hoo.* No — *sniff*— I'm not feeling like sleeping. I can sit down here — *sniff, sniff*— even if something can come and catch me, it can come and —"

Then he said, "Nothing can catch you here. It's better to go to your room. You know, all of us here, we are stone. You can't eat us. It's better you go and sleep. Or if you want to eat somebody, go back. Follow your people to your village. To be crying so the witches will come and meet you, so you people will get some meat there. But here, you are calling them for nothing. We are all stones here. We are not human beings. We are human beings, but our meat is not like human beings. It's just like a stone. You can't eat anyone. So get into your room."

Then he opened the door for the woman. Then she said, *"Ah-h-h-h,* you can do whatever you want to me."

Then he said, "You are my mother, but if you refuse what I am telling you, I will give you a dirty slap, and then you will go to sleep *just now!"*

So this woman said, *"Mm, mm,"* and that they used to talk about this in the world, that her father used to give her advice when she was young, that sometimes you can give birth to your son, and your son will come and beat you. Yeah, they have been saying that this is the ending of the world. And the son is trying to beat the mother now.

Then my brother said, "Yeah. If your mother does something, and you are trying to tell your mother the truth, and your mother doesn't listen, if you beat her, God won't do anything to you. This is not any bad thing you have done, because you have been teaching your mother to do the correct thing."

So she went inside and was talking, talking, talking, talking. Then early the next morning, I went to her *first*. I knocked on her door. I said, "Mama, good morning."

She said, "I'm not your mother. Suppose I am your mother, you cannot abuse my mother." She said I had told her junior mother — her mother's younger sister — that I told her mother that they are witchcraft people, that they can't eat us in the night, and if they want, they can come in day time to face each other. So I have abused her mother. Suppose I were her own daughter, I could not say all this. And she's not my mother who gave birth to me, and that and this.

So I said, "If you were my mother, yesterday I would have told my father, if he doesn't divorce you, I won't be his daughter again. But I thought if I do that, they will say that it is because you are not the one who gave birth to me. That's why I am giving you the respect to come and call you in the morning time. It is not that I want you for a mother. I don't want an ugly woman like you for a mother. Didn't you know my mother? You see the way I am. All my form and my everything is just like my mother. All the color, too."

You know, this woman is *tall*. Now she's growing old, so she's lean. She was a big Makola woman.[1] When she was in Kumasi, she was very *fat*. And if she opened her voice, you would think she was a man.

So I said, "You can't be my mother. Even you can *not* be half of my mother. I'm talking to you. My mother didn't talk this to you. Early in the morning like this, and you are calling the name of my mother in her grave? Don't you know that my mother has died? When you call this name early in the morning, what do you mean?"

---

1. a well-to-do market woman. Disbanded under the Rawlings regime, Makola market in Accra was formerly the main central market; its women traders had the reputation for wealth. The popular image of them, often reproduced on postcards, represents them as wealthy, shrewd, fat (from having enough to eat), and (for the postcards) jovial.

So: *Ha!* This is the time I'm going to get her. My father was inside his room. He made like he didn't hear anything. How he built his house, his room is the last room, and the second one is for the small wife, and the third one is for the big wife. And the children live on the other side.[1]

So I told her, "To call you in the morning time and say hello to you, and you are trying to talk about my mother! What do you mean? Do you think—? My mother is not—if suppose my mother was a witch, you people couldn't come here. You couldn't come. If my mother was like you, do you think you would be here? If suppose you were here before my mother, my mother wouldn't have come, because you are a witch. So my mother is not a witch. So don't talk about my mother. I'm talking to you. If you don't want my 'Good morning,' then say, 'From today going, don't say "Good morning" to me.' But don't try to call the name of my mother here."

So then I said, "It's not your fault. All the fault is from our old man. I think the time when he was growing up, they covered his face. He doesn't see anything. Or maybe he went to you people and then you just caught him, by your witch powers, so he didn't see you. If not my father, which man do you think is going to marry a woman like you? Ah!" *Ha! Hee-hee!*

Then she said, "Thank you very much. May God bless all of you people."

I said, "God will bless us? If God didn't bless us, we wouldn't be living like this. We are living free! Don't you see that? God blessed us. People have been seeing me in Ouagadougou. Did they come and tell you that they saw me taking a pan and begging for food? Have you heard that I am begging? Never. I will never beg for food. And I've been eating. I'm all right. I used to get my cloth to put on. So I think God blessed me. But it's your own: you should also try to forget about your witchcraft so that God will also bless you. Not any fucking *small* child like your own children will come and stand in front of you and say you are witch. Suppose you beg God to forgive you, God will forgive you. He will bless you too, like the way he blessed us. Nobody can come here and abuse me for nothing. But as for you, as your witchcraft is inside your heart, you don't open a white heart[2] to show the people in the house. So every day, God is giving you punishment. But as for me, God blessed me. It's not you who is going

---

1. It is a typical African style, a "compound house" with individual rooms around a central compound; the wives' rooms extend on one side of the householder's room, and the sons' rooms are on the other side.

2. clean, plain heart; happiness. She doesn't have good intentions or feelings toward others.

to say that God may bless me. God has already blessed me. So you beg your God to bless you, too, so that we shouldn't abuse you again.

"Do you see your small sister? Don't you know that God blessed her? Have you seen any one of us stand in front of her to say something? Sometimes she used to abuse us. We don't reply. Because of what? Because how we see her, she is a nice woman. She respects herself. She doesn't do the witch way. But as for you, nobody will respect you. We have all come to know now that you are a witch. So throw your witchcraft away and beg God. Then God will forgive you." *Ha-ha!*

So she didn't say anything. And that day we went to the bush. That time was the time when they had got the guinea corn.[1] They had to cut it. So that day, they were cutting my small brother's guinea corn, so we went to the place.[2] Before we came back, this old woman had packed her things and gone to her village.

Then—*ha!*—then my father said, "*All* of you people here: I don't know which one of you send to go and bring your mother. Because she has a quarrel with *all* of you people."

So my small brother who said that if the senior mother doesn't go inside, he will beat her—he is the one I said I like among the boys in my family—that boy just came out and, "Why don't you know somebody to send? As for me, if you try to send me there, I won't go. The best thing is to send her own son to go and bring his mother. That is all." *Ha-ha!*

But the son of that woman is older than this boy who was talking.[3] Then that son also came out. You see? Our family problem, when we meet in the village, it used to be just coming, just like that, like a cinema.[4] So then the woman's son also came out. He said, "Look. Yesterday, all the problem you people were having, I was in my room. Did you see me? Did I put a word inside it?"

Then my small brother said, "Yeah. What word can you say? Because it's your mother. She's taking her witchcraft to look after you, and you are growing tall, more than all of us in the house" *Ha-ha!*

This my younger brother, he's a *horrible* boy! He is a *big* troublemaker. One time he said that he is going to marry, but if the girl is not fine, he

---

1. sorghum. The sorghum had grown and was ready to harvest.

2. It is common for people to plant and maintain separate areas, and they will help each other with their plots.

3. According to traditional respect for age, the younger son should not be sending the older one.

4. like a movie story, with twists and turns, with one thing after another

wouldn't marry her, so I should see the girl first, to see if she's fine, before he will marry her. That boy is another boy. My father used to say that, if suppose we had the same mother, they would say that the same place I am from is the place this boy is from. He is a *ruffian!* So he said to his senior brother, "How can you say a word? Among *all* of us in this family, you are the tall man. Your mother has been taking her witchcraft to make you tall, to be growing you big. So you can't say a word." *Hee-hee! Ha!*

So then he said, "Eh, eh, eh, so — eh, eh — you want to abuse me as yesterday you were abusing my mother."

Then my small brother said, "Ah-h, yesterday I was abusing your mother. It is hurting you. And you didn't answer. Today your mother packed her things, and she won't give you witch food again. That's why. That's why now you have started worrying about yesterday. Yes, I have abused your mother. Your mother wants to eat us. Your mother wants to take us like those small-small fish the Togo people used to catch. Those small-small fish, they used to get them in a group.[1] Your mother just wants to make us like that and fry us. But she's not going to fry you, so that's why you didn't say anything yesterday. So what do you mean? Do you think your mother is better than our father?"

Then my senior brother said that they want to change the family. So he doesn't worry about anything. The mother can go away if she wants. So my small brother can talk these things; he should know that he the senior brother was first before him.[2]

And this boy said, "Yeah, you are first before me, but you don't have your experience. These topics we did yesterday, you are the person who should have said, 'Mama, what you are doing is not good. You have this problem with your husband, or with our father and your daughter. It's not good for you to cry and go and call your family.' But you have left all this. Or maybe, I think you led her to go there and bring the family so that they will come and eat us." *Ha!*

So that boy was also annoyed. So he said: OK, if that is the problem, my father is the one who gave the chance for the younger brother to be abusing him. So he's also going to leave the house.

Then this small boy said, "Yes, we have already known. We know that if your mother is not here, you can't stay, because as a witch's son, she used to give you some small things, to go out with her every night. So

---

1. He is referring to a type of small fish (sometimes called "Keta schoolboys") caught with a net, generally fried and eaten with pepper.
2. He was born first.

since she packed her things, I know that by all means you have to go back to your own, too. You just want the road you will pass to pack your things. That's why you been arguing this with me. So if you want, you can pack off with your things and follow your mother."

So we all got up. That day, my senior brother was inside the room. I was feeling pity for him, because he didn't talk to anybody again. So they cooked the tuwo. They used to eat together, and they called him. He said, no, he's satisfied. And me, if I am in the village, I used to eat with my father, always. So I told my father, "This boy doesn't want to eat."

My father said, "Leave him. If he doesn't want to eat, he's not a small boy. Can you force him to give him food?"

And I said, "No. I don't feel it like that."

So I went to his room. Then I called my mother to bring me my food. So she gave the food to my younger sister to give us inside the room. Then I said, "No. Even if you are annoyed with everybody, you just come and eat with me, so that—"

So the boy is a big, *tall* boy. A *big* boy. If you see him, you will be happy. He is senior to me, too, but every time, he is just like a woman. Any small thing, you will see him with tears in his eyes. So when I was talking to him, he was crying like a small baby. As he's tall, I could not hold him. So I stood up and then I took his head, "No-o, don't do that, don't do that—" *Ha!* Then I said, "Do you want me to cry, too? Do you want me to cry? You are crying. Because your mother has gone away today, you are crying. What about me? My mother died. I won't see her anymore, eh? You can go and see your mother tomorrow if you want. So what are you crying for?" So I was trying to boss him, "Stop crying and eat a little bit with me."

And my small brother — that boy, he can cause trouble in the house!— this small boy said, "Aha! You are eating with him! You will become a witch!" *Ha!* "You want to be a witch, too? You are making friends with a witch. It's night time. Eh? Go and sleep. It's better for you. This is the time they used to go out. In some minutes' time you will see him like a vulture. If you don't want to see that, go and sleep." I was afraid! *Ha!*

So I told my big brother, "Oh, don't mind him. You know he's a small boy. He doesn't have sense. You know this boy: I think he is a ruffian inside of the family. You also know. He just has some kind of character. He can't help it, but we can't throw him away. So don't mind him. He's going. He hasn't got sense so he's just saying what he doesn't know."

So: do you know that the time when we all went and slept, my big brother, this boy got up to go to the mother's village. And now he has become a mad person. He has become crazy. They took him some place to look after him. He's in some village now. I think maybe he met something in the night. You know, we African people, it used to happen. He waited till everybody was asleep, then he got up to go to the mother's village. So maybe in the road he met something, and the thing turned him to craze.[1]

We Africans, we have this belief. If you ask an old person, he will tell you about this. Sometimes if you walk in the midnight, huh? They used to tell you that there are some things that come out in the night time. Especially the village people. They like juju. They have been praying to it, so it's working for them. So maybe in some villages, if they have juju, you shouldn't go out in the night time. Every place is dark. There's no light. Maybe you can meet something like that.

So this boy went to the mother. The next day, we heard that this boy started to craze, cursing some things in the village of the mother, and that and this.

So my father asked that boy who had made him annoyed to go and see. The boy said, "Me? I am not going." *Ha!* "I am not going. He went and found his trouble."

So then my father's senior son said, no, he will go by himself. He went, and he came back with the bicycle. He said, no, where the boy is, he can't bring him home. "When I got to him, I didn't know what is wrong with him. He just took himself. And all the clothes which he was wearing, I don't know whether he tore it by himself or the dress was just torn." You know, they don't believe much in hospitals. They believe in these juju people. So they took him to some village, and the juju man said that he met something — the grand-grand-grandfather's things,[2] but they didn't want to do him bad, so that's why they turned him to be like that. If they had wanted to do him bad, he would have died. So he is living with the juju man. I don't know whether by now he has come back home.

So this thing, it was a big rout. My father and the senior wife were about to divorce. Now she has come back. But she's just living in the house. My father doesn't mind her. And she also says that because of her children, she doesn't want to leave the house. But it's a lie, because if she leaves the house, she doesn't know anywhere to go. So she's just hanging there.

1. go crazy
2. ancestral spirits

7   LIFE WITH FATHER

: THE VILLAGE IN BURKINA FASO :

Issahaku and the Fulani Thieves

You know, my father is some kind of guy like — he doesn't drink, but sometimes, if you see him, you will think he is somebody who drinks heavily. When he means to fuck people, he will just call you and fuck you. And he never fucks only one person. If I am doing something bad, and he wants to talk to me, he will talk to me up to my brother. He will say, "Your brother too, he's the same." So: my brother too, my father will tell him he did this and that and this. "And you, too! Why don't you people change your mind?" Or: "What kind of children did God give to me like that?" Then he's coming to the other one, too, and he will call and add the other one to me.

So if somebody does bad, and then he is talking like that, then I used to reply, "Hey, Papa! If somebody does bad, you must talk to him alone. But you just mix all of us like this."

He will say, "Because you used to do it, too." *Ha!*

My father can talk, oh. I can tell you. He likes me very much, but we can never stay together. If we stay a little bit, we will have a problem. Sometimes if I am annoyed, then when he sits down, I won't look at his face. And he has something, too. When he's talking to you, if you are putting on sunglasses, he will say, "Open your eyes[1] and look at me." If you don't open your eyes, then he will talk about you. Even if you are friendly and talking to him, just conversing, if you don't look at him straight, then when you go, he will say, "Oh. This is one of my children. He is a liar. If he's talking to you, he can't look at your face." *Ha-ha.* He will just take you like that. So he used to make problems for us. Yeah, my father can abuse people very well. And these children will just walk away. They don't say anything, then they will just go their ways.

1. Take off your sunglasses.

So: my father doesn't know what he has done with his life. The way he is, you know, he tried to marry to have children, but he hasn't got any good one inside. Sometimes, if I do something, he is annoyed. He will abuse me. He will abuse me, and he will abuse my big brother! *Hee-hee-heh!* Then he will call the name of our mother and my grandmother and my grandfather! *Ha-ha!*

He will say, "*Eh-heh!* I don't know self. This family: *ay!* In my family we haven't got people like that. Maybe it's from your mother's mother or something, your grandfather!" *Ha-ha!* You see? That inside of his family, he didn't have a kind of children like us. So that day, you and all your family at your mother's side, you are hot. He will make all of you hot. Then, maybe the other children from another woman will like it, but it's not one minute and he will come to someone on their side.

You know, the small wife has the boy who I said is a very strong boy in the house. He is very funny too. He and our father can't sit down five minutes without some trouble starting between them. *Ha-ha!* The boy is rough, and he doesn't care about the topics of the old man. The old man used to talk, talk, talk, talk. Then this boy will just stand up and say, "But you, self, I don't know what is wrong with you! Every day you will talk, *tey-y*:[1] 'This woman's family is no good, that woman's family is no good!' But *every* time, you don't waste your time: you will conceive them and get more bad children for yourself!"

My father will be annoyed! *Ha-ha!* So every time, they used to have problems. When that boy is coming to him, the old man will say, "It's true. Even a woman, when she is short too much, her children are also the same thing." *Ha-ha!* "Because a short woman has got an experience. And she will be giving you some different kind of children." *Ha-ha!*

Ah, old man! He's a shit! So sometimes, you know, I used to sit down and watch him. I groove heavily, and I will go behind him, and then I will sit down to watch him. Then if he talks and talks, *tey,* then he will turn to his back, and he will see that I'm watching. Then he will say, "*Eh-heh!* This is another white woman, too. She takes her dark glasses and covers her face." *Ha-ha!* "I have been watching her. *Eh-heh!* What's wrong with you? Have you something to tell me?"

My old man is a fucking man, eh? But this time, he's sick, so the sickness has made him *coo-o-ol.* This time, you won't hear his talking again. But first time —*pfft, pfft.*

Look, my younger brothers, you know, the young boys: they can go out as they like. But this old man will never sleep. If he doesn't see them come

---

1. (Pidgin): continuing on and on; the same like that

home, he will never sleep. He will go and hide himself at some corner.
And he will carry that type of stick watchmen used to carry, and then be
waiting for them. At the moment you just get into the door, he wouldn't
beat you with it; he will just make like he has missed you. He will go and
knock somewhere —*bap!* Then he will say, "You are lucky! Where from
you?"

Then you will say, maybe, "Oh Papa, I have gone out to the friends to
converse and—"

Then he will say, "Look! When I was your age, I didn't go out at this
time. Don't try to go with these townspeople and bring any witch to
this house!" What he hates in his life is a witch. He doesn't like witches.
So any baby, any boy who doesn't yet grow up, he shouldn't go out and
come back home at twelve o'clock or one o'clock in the night. *Hey-y!*
Then he will say, "You know that I used to watch my house. That's why
the thieves don't come in."

But it was very pitiful. When my father went to our country—*Ha-ha!*
Hee-hee!— he had many, many things. These grand bobos,[1] he had many!
Oh! We had a box, a big one: it was heavy wood. I think they used it to
bring a fridge from Europe or something like that. When he went back to
his village, my father packed that box with these up-and-downs, and he
carried it to our place, and he was selling these things. He used to get a
cow for one up-and-down. A cow. From these Fulani people. The big, big
dress: my father used to get a cow for it in our village.

So: these Fulani people, I think, when they would come to him to get
the thing, I don't know whether he used to open the box and let them see,
or what. I don't know. But they robbed my father! *Oh!* But when he told
me, I *laughed! Ha-ha!*

He said, "*Eh-heh!* Maybe it was you, my own people. You sent them to
come and take it, so that you people will go and share it." *Heh-hee!*

You know, this is what made me laugh, because he said he was in his
room. You know, he doesn't have a lock and key for the village door.[2] He
was sleeping. Then he saw somebody opening the door. Then he said,
"Who is that?"

Then the person told him, "Shut up!" *Ha-ha!*

Then he got up to put on his lamp. He had a kerosene lamp, but he had
reduced it when he was going to sleep. So he put on the light, and then
he saw three men, with knives. *Ha-ha!* He told me, "When I woke up, I

1. a large embroidered gown
2. The doors of village houses are often heavy woven mats that are pushed up
against the entry opening.

didn't have anything to cover myself, you know." He wasn't wearing even underpants. So he was going back to the bed to take a cloth, and they said, "Where are you going?! Stand there!"

When he told me, he said, "I was just like this. Then I made so." He was using his hand to be covering his front like that.

Then they said, "What are you covering there? Take your hands away!" *Ha-ha!*

Then he told me, "*Ah!* I am not strong. And I was sick. And all your brothers were sleeping. If I made a noise, maybe they would kill me."

So then, he just stood like that. Then they took *all.* His own suitcase was on top of the box, and they put it down and packed all these things inside. And the other one was holding him, pressing him to the wall with the knife to his throat. They finished packing the things, and then the two people carried the things and went away. And the one who was the last man, who was holding him to the wall with the knife, he looked at the bed. You know, my father had more than ten bedsheets on his bed. So the man saw that these bedsheets and blankets were many. Then he told my father, "Look you, you don't have the kind of fresh skin to sleep on a bed with all these bedsheets." *Ha-ha!* The man just wrapped all of the blankets and the bedsheets, and said, "You — it's good for you to sleep on the floor. If you sleep on the bed, I am going to come back. You will see!"

So when they went away, my father was sitting up to the morning time! *Ha-ha!* He said, "I was sitting like this." They left one black cloth for him, blue-black. It was just a white material which I dyed in Ghana and gave to him — a very big cloth. They left only that one. And he was afraid to go and take it, because the man had told him that he is coming back, and if he sees him sleeping on the bed, or if he's wearing a cloth, he will kill him. So this old man just preferred to sit down, and he didn't get anything to cover himself.

And you know what made me pity him? When he told me, why I was laughing, you see, we have some ants, black ones. They are big. They can *bite!* Do you know that one? They were in the room on this old man, and they were getting him. He said, "When they were biting me, you know, as there is not much meat, they were biting through to my bones!" *Ha!* "And then, even to take my hand to brush them away, I couldn't do it, because I was afraid the man would come back. So I just took my bones and dashed the ants." *Ha!*

And he couldn't shout, too. The man said he was going to come back, and my father was afraid that maybe they were not far, so before he would blow alarm to let these children hear his voice to wake up, maybe this man would come back to kill him. So he didn't want to say anything.

He was sitting up until something to five, and the day started breaking. Then he came out like that. He didn't take any cloth. He said he was going to see whether this man had gone, but he made up his mind that if this man was there and said, "Where are you going?" then he would say, "Oh, but I beg you. I'm going to piss." So he said that when he came out, nobody had awakened yet. Then he went to the bathroom side. He didn't see anybody. Then he came back to the compound.

When he came back, the old man was crazy. Instead of going and taking his black cloth they left for him, he said something came to his mind that maybe these people came back and the person had run into the room. So he didn't want to enter there to take the cloth. So he just started knocking these children's doors to come out. And then he was holding his prick like that.

So when—*ha-ha!*—when my younger brother opened the door, he saw our father, that he wasn't wearing anything. Then he pushed the door and closed it again. Then my father said, "Come out! Are you afraid? They have been killing me, but they didn't finish me yet. I'm still in life. Come, come!" *Ha!*

Then my brother said, "But you should take a cloth."

He said, "What is a cloth? Do you know what is a cloth? The day when they gave birth to you, were you carrying a cloth? Come out!"

So this boy opened the door and took a big towel and gave it to him to cover himself. Then the senior one came out, the one who I said is now crazy in the village; he also came out.

Then my father said, "*Eh-heh!* This is why they say a man should marry plenty of women, and give birth to many children! If somebody comes to this house in day time, he will know that I have thick-thick men in my place. To come and attack me and pack all my things, and you people were sleeping! You people were sleeping like dead bodies. So: what is the profit of you people? The profit for you to live here with me? I want to know. You people must tell me today."

Look at this. You lost your things. You have to tell your children so that they can find your things for you. But he just called them early in the morning, to start—*Ha-ha!*—to start abusing all of them. "*Eh-heh!*" He doesn't know the profit if they are here. It's better if everybody finds his way, and he will know that he's living alone. If they want somebody who has many children to give him chieftaincy, in the whole village, he can be second or third. But he slept, and the thieves came to his room.

Then he said, "I tell you people: maybe even it's your friends, because you people used to come home at one o'clock, or two o'clock. So you people came together, and you let them bring their knives to kill me and pack my things. And you just went to your rooms and locked your doors as if you are sleeping. What kind of sleeping is that? All these three tall men came and passed inside here: you people were sleeping! Why didn't they go to your rooms then?" *Ha-ha!* He just called the children, blasting them like that.

So the big one said, "Oh, Papa. Sometimes I don't understand. I think you — now you are growing old. All the topics you are talking now, it's not normal. How can we know that thief people have come to your room?"

Then my father said, "Let everybody say. You: don't say anything. As for you, I have already known you. Even maybe it's you who did it!" *Ha!* He just put it on that boy, that he should shut up his mouth, that maybe he is the one who brought the people to attack him. "They were tall like you. They were all wearing batakari,[1] white-white ones. Only that was different. But they were tall like you." *Ha!*

So I told you the small one is a ruffian. If he sees that my father wants to disgrace them, he will say: "Let's leave him."

So my father was talking, and they were walking away one by one. Then he said, "*Eh-heh!* What kind of children are like that? When the father wants to talk, even they wouldn't want to stand and listen to him. They start walking away. Yes, I know. But I didn't do that to my father. That's why God blessed me to get you people. But if you are doing that to me, God will punish you! If you are not my own children, even if you all know that I am crazy, I swear. They came and stole all my things, and you people were here. Then I'm going to tell you something, so you start walking away. Yes. Go and share it! I won't die! I didn't steal it. But God will punish you people!"

Hey! So the time these three Fulani people came and robbed him, he was talking about this thing for more than one week, that his own children are the ones who came and robbed him. *Ha-ha!*

So when I went home, he told me, "Your brother did it. But I can't blame them. It's not their fault."

Then I said, "How, Papa? How could they do that?"

He said, "*Ah!* So do you think — you, Hawa — if you are here, you can sleep in this house and people will come and pass the whole way to come and open my door, with knives, and shout on me to 'Shut up!' and you won't hear anything? You say you are sleeping! Are you dead?!" *Ha!* "In the night time, when you speak a little, it's loud, you know. You think — ? They know! I'm telling you, my daughter. You think I — ? I'm not lying. These my boys — anyway, they used to help me to farm. But they're *bad* boys like I haven't seen in my life. They are the people who did that."

---

1. a type of wide smock made from woven strips of cloth; also, fugu

So I said, "Oh, no, Papa, I don't believe that they can do that."

He said, "If you want to back them, you can back them. But I know that they are the ones who did it."

So that time passed. And the next time I went, then he told me, "Oh, you see? I was blaming your brothers for nothing. It's the Fulani people who came and robbed me."

And I said, "How did you get them?"

You know, from our house to where the Fulani people are living, it may be about one-and-a-half kilometers. So my father said a Fulani man came and told him that his cow had a baby, so he was going to see it. And you know, he had a towel he used to put around his neck when it's hot. These old, old men, you know, even in Ghana, they do it. So he saw that towel behind the road there, and he got it. So: he knows it's not his children. He was blaming his boys for nothing. It was the Fulani people who robbed him. When they passed there, maybe his towel fell down. But I shouldn't tell my brothers. They will blast him. *Ha! Ha!* This old man is funny! So he said that he knows that I'm his mother. He used to tell me his everything. Even he didn't tell his wife. He will be watching small-small. He will get some of his things before he will tell anybody. But I shouldn't let my brothers know that he knows the people who robbed him, because this time, my brothers are serious: they said that he has insulted them that they are thieves. So if they hear that he saw the towel there behind the Fulani people's house, they will be annoyed with him. Then they will say he was telling lies on them, and they will all run away and leave him.

So I said, "OK."

Then I went and told my small brother: "Papa has seen his towel." *Hee-heee!* "Papa has seen his towel near the Fulani people's house, so he told me that the Fulani people are the ones who robbed him. But he doesn't want you people to know. So don't tell the other ones. You shouldn't let anybody hear it."

So: *ha!* This boy wasn't serious. He said it. That evening time, I had brought some cloth, and I said I would give it to that boy to make a full cloth like the one the men wear. So the boy said, "Ah, well, as for me, you know, I don't need such things much. And now, I think they have robbed Papa, so we should add it to Papa's things."

So my father was sitting outside and this boy brought it. He said, "Papa, they have robbed you. Hawa has brought this cloth for me. But I think you don't have enough clothes now, so I want to give this to add to your own. I think it will be better, a little bit."

Then my father said, "As for you, you have sense. The others: they are foolish! They are stupid! *All* these children I have in this house, if not you alone, who is giving me respect?! That day when they stole my things, I was annoyed. I thought you were among, too."

Then the boy said, "Papa, I brought this thing for you. I don't want you to bring this thief palaver. The Fulani people robbed you. If you are afraid of them, don't bring your problems to me!"

Then you know, I knew I had said the thing, so I was afraid. So I said, "What Fulani people? They robbed him?"

Then my father said, "Shut up! You went and told him! I know that. You — you people I've given birth to, you my children, you are the people who are going to sell me to kill me. Hawa! You! I said you are my mother; I tell you all my secrets!" *Ha!* "So you went and told your brother? Yes? I know. You are the people who will take me out and go and sell me to my enemies, and then they will kill me. Why should you tell him? When I talked to you, I said, 'As my mother, don't tell him.' Why did you tell him?"

I was *ashamed! Ha!* I was ashamed. I said, "I swear, it's not — I didn't tell him anything." Then I asked the boy, "Who told you that? Who told you?"

Then my brother also tried. He said, "*Ah!* Who told me? Papa thinks I don't have sense. When they robbed Papa, he didn't even have a towel. It's my towel I gave to Papa. But I have seen Papa's old towel with him."

So with all this, my father got to know that I had told my brother. Then the next day when he saw me, he said, "Hawa, you see? I *like* you. You are my daughter. I *love* you more than all my children. But you did something to me. It's very serious. I told you not to tell your brother where I got the towel, and you went and told him. Do you see how you disgraced me? Don't you pity your Papa?"

He was talking like this. And you know, the way he talked about it, I was feeling pity. I regretted: *Ah!* Why should I talk to that fucking boy? You know?

: BURKINA FASO AND KUMASI :

Papa's Mouth

So my father! He can talk! At times, when the farming is finished, the old, old people used to meet someplace and sit down conversing, talking about the olden days and this and that. If you are far away, you will hear the voice of my old man *first! Ha-ha!* And then, with him, he doesn't talk one-two-three. If he's saying something, and you challenge him a little bit: *hee-ey!* Blows will come inside. He will accept, then he will start saying,

"*Tsk,* go away! You! Where are you from? You know where even your family is from? You want to make yourself like a person from this town? *Ah!* Your grandfather didn't tell you? You are from such-and-such a place. Your grandfather was from there, and your grandmother was from there. Do you know what brought you people to this town?" *Den-den-deh, den-den-deh!*

Then my father will be blasting that person, and the fellow will be getting annoyed, to fight him. And my father hasn't got strength, too. He's old, but he has a mouth. So you know, the old people, always, they won't let people fight, but they will let them be serious. Sometimes one will hold the dress of the other, then another of the old people will come: "No! Don't do that. Don't do that."

But my father, when he's finished, he's coming home to quarrel with his children. "I will show you. I will show you that this town — my name is Issahaku — I will show you I am Issahaku! You fucking man idiot! Do you have family? Come to my house and see!" *Ha!* "I will show you. You wait. One minute. I will show you something."

Then he's coming home. When he comes, he doesn't want to be right with the children, too! He will just come and blast them: "*Eh-heh!* You people heard. You heard my voice. Suppose they killed me? Is that the time you will be coming there? To cry that your father is dead? These fucking people who don't have family, trying to abuse me — to — to disgrace me like that — and you people have been hearing. What are you people for?" *Ha-ha!*

So the only person who understands him is the senior son. The rest don't care. He can be shouting like that, and they will say, "Oh, you, too, it's too much." But the senior son, will say, "Papa, sit down. Who is that person?"

Then my father will call the name. Then the senior son will ask him which area of the village he's from.

Then my father will say, "Ah! You don't know that fucking man? You don't know that man's house? That drunkard. That man who never dreams that he will talk to a woman. Even to get married. For his whole life, he only spends for drink. He's the one who came and insulted me, to tell me what and what, to disgrace me that I have stayed in Ghana — that I'm Ghana Issahaku."

In our village, they call my father Ghana Issahaku. They were calling him a Ghanaian, because every time, when he's talking with the old people, he brings Ashanti language inside. So they gave him his name.

So the story I'm telling you, when my father said that, then the senior son said, "Sit down. I will go and see that man." And this boy also takes time; he has patience, too. I think what made him to have patience with my father is maybe because he didn't know his mother. He's very quiet. He's very different from all of us. He's very, very quiet. But when he goes to you, he will open his eyes in some way on you.

So he went to that man and said, "Look, this time when you were doing something to my father, it's your first and last. I'm telling you. Do that to my father again. *Tsk!* I will show you something. Or if you have a son like me, let me meet him. My father is not a stupid old man. He is not a drunkard like you. Do you know how many we are? My father has — he is a man! He has stayed in the world long to marry and give birth to children. He's not a drunkard like you, to use all your life to drink. You don't think of marrying a woman to get a baby. And you will come and start —"

But maybe that person has children! Oh! *Ha-ha!* My brother wouldn't care because he thinks that my father has got more children than all of them. You see? He thought my father is a chief for that, so he was just blasting the man. *Ha!* Then he came back home and told our father, "Father, I went and gave him warning. Any time when he meets you on the road, if he doesn't say 'Good morning' to you, come and tell me."

Ha! This is what makes me laugh. Then I asked my brother, "If the man doesn't say 'Good morning' to Papa, Papa should come and tell you — to do what?"

He said if he comes and tells him, he will go and ask the man why he didn't say 'Good morning' to his father.

Then I said, "This is not law. If you and your father are crazy, and they get you people to some place, you will learn your sense back. You make trouble with somebody because when he passes, he doesn't say 'Good morning' to you! Is this something for your son to go and beat that fellow, to force him to be greeting the father? Huh?"

So my father, how he is, I don't know. My father is funny. As I stayed with him from the beginning, that's why I know his character. I don't know: maybe if you go to some places, you will also find many people like him. Maybe.

As for me, I love my father. *Eh?* But we used to fight! You know, when I travel, I used to think of my father a lot. But when I'm there, we won't keep long to make a fight. We cannot sit more than one hour. He will start talking and telling me something I don't want, and then from there, we will get something. We will be talking, talking, talking. Then he will come back to good conversing again. *Ha! Hee-hee!*

But when I was small, I used to be afraid of him somehow. If he was going to pick me up to beat me, I used to piss. Yes! I would start pissing. *Mm-hm.* The time when he used to pick me up like that, when I was a

small girl, you know what I used to like? My father used to have sugar.
And I liked to eat sugar, raw like that. I could eat a lot of it. My father
used to drink tea with many sugar pieces inside. So if he got a packet[1] of
sugar, you know, especially the time when they were making the Ramadan fasting,[2] they would eat before daybreak, then they wouldn't eat
again until evening time: he used to pack down[3] some packets of sugar, to
take his porridge in evening time and morning time. So when my father
went out, I would go to his room. He had a table, and he put sugar on top
of it, but he would put a big tablecloth to cover the whole table. You see?
Then I would go and carry one packet and go under the table cloth —
ha!— to be there eating it. So do you know: one time I ate this thing until
I got fed up, and I fell asleep, and took this packet to make a pillow. *Ha-
ha! Shit!*

So when my father came home, then he asked for me, "Where is my
mother?" Then they said, oh, that I was here, just around here, but they
don't know, maybe I went out to play. So my father went into his room.
Then he heard something like breathing. He didn't know. He was looking
everywhere, under the bed, everywhere. He didn't see anything. So you
know, when you sleep, you can stretch. I was going to stretch, and my feet
touched the tablecloth. Then he saw that the thing moved, so he opened
there and he saw me. *Ha-ha!* Taking the sugar packet, making a pillow
and sleeping on it! So he called his junior wife, because that woman also
liked me a lot. If I did anything bad, he used to call her. He said, "Come
and see your daughter. If I beat her, you always say, 'No, no.' Come and
see what she has done. Do you know that *all* this sugar, the ten cartons
I brought? This girl has eaten *all!* Maybe she is going to die. Look at the
way she has slept there. She is going to die."

Then the wife said, oh, she will make ginger and pump me an enema,
because I have eaten too many sweets. When they finished talking, he
bent down to pick me up. Then he said, "Is this your work?" Then my
eyes were open. I saw the sugar packet. I knew that by all means, they
would beat me. So —*ha-ha!* My heart cut![4] Some of the sugar pieces had
fallen down. And I was tired. I had already eaten a lot, and I knew that
even if God comes down, I wouldn't be free: my father would beat me. So

1. one kilogram box of sugar cubes
2. In the Muslim lunar calendar, during the month of Ramadan, Muslims fast from
dawn to dusk. People tend to eat particular preferred foods to help them get through the
day (and the month) without stomach disturbances, and some people consider porridge to
be both filling and mild.
3. store
4. My heart was broke; my heart was sick; in this context, my heart jumped.

he picked me up. *Ha!* Then I started to piss. Yeah. Then he put me down and said I should swallow the crying. "Good! Look! If you see this girl outside, you would think her eyes are strong. Look."

And you know what makes me laugh? When children are playing, or sometimes if a child of your type is going to fight you, I had the kind of strength to stand, to yab.[1] I didn't fear it. But he didn't even touch me yet: then I started pissing. This is why he said that they say that I am a strong girl: I can stand and fight; I don't fear anything. But I fear anything more than anybody, because he just picked me and I started pissing. I didn't get my stick yet,[2] and I started to cry. Mm-hm. Then he started to shout on me to shut up, to swallow up my crying.

So I had to swallow up and come and sit down. Then I was serious. I didn't look at his face. Every time I was looking down. Anyway, I was ashamed: I had stolen. So he tried to boss me. Sometimes if I am annoyed like that, he used to boss me. "You see? You are my mother. You know that I love you more than all. Why did I give you the name of my mother? Don't you see your senior sister? Do you see somebody else who is called Hawa? You see, I love you very much. That's why I gave you the name. This — all that you are doing, it's not good. Don't do that. You know, sugar, it will make you sick. You can die like that. The way you are, I'm seeing you like a human being. But if you try to eat the sugar, one day you will just fall down like that and die. And do you know, if you die, how it is?"

Then I didn't mind him.

He said, "Look, if you die, they will dig the ground and put you under. Nobody will see you again. You won't see anybody." *Ha! Ho!* I was opening my ears, you know. "So don't try to do that. If you need — if you are hungry, you should go and tell your mother that you are hungry. She will give you food. But don't eat the sugar. It's not good for you."

"So because of this you are annoyed with me?"

"If I don't tell you, it's not good. What if I don't tell you, and you eat it, and you die and leave me? I don't want you to die and leave me. You are my mother. If you die, maybe I will die, too. So don't do that the next time."

Then I said, "*Mm-m,* I didn't even take plenty. When I came, I took one, then I was feeling to sleep, so I just left it there. And then I was asleep."

Then he said, "But what did you take one for? You were going to eat it."

---

1. (Pidgin): to talk roughly (abusively or playfully), to run one's mouth, to mess with
2. I had not yet been beaten.

Then I said, "Only today I did it." *Ha! Hee-hee-hee!* So we started to converse a little, you know.

But he could abuse people! My younger brother: the mother was selling fish, dried fish. They have a *big* basket for the fish when they are bringing it. They make it with big sticks, so it is very strong. Even four or five people my size can go inside easily. She kept the fish inside this basket, and they put a sack to cover all the mouth of the basket. So this boy would hide behind the basket. I don't know what he took to dig a hole in the basket, but he was drawing the fish out one by one, then eating them.

So this boy, when they cooked food, every time he didn't eat much. When he ate small, then he would say, "I'm full up."

They would say, "Oh-h."

Then my father used to say, "*Tsk,* this my son is the only boy I have borne who eats just like me. He doesn't eat plenty."

But this boy was stealing fish! That was why he didn't want to eat plenty. When he goes behind the basket, he will eat the fish. He has finished eating. So then he's all right.

And what let them catch him: our mother was just from the market. Then when he saw his mother was coming inside, he tried to hide himself in back of the fish basket. *Ha!* When you are children, eh? It's funny. He was trying to hide himself. Look, this is the basket. And this woman has come into the room. And the boy was putting his head under the basket, and his bottom[1] was out. He was hiding his head alone. So the mother just picked him up from his pants,[2] you know, and dragged him out outside, and said, "All this is what?" It was her own son.

You know, as my father used to abuse their families when he got annoyed with them, then if a child did something, the women too would take the same way. So she said, "Eh! You people, your father gets up and says this stealing isn't there in his family. But I don't know where. My family doesn't do this kind of thing. Maybe it's from your father's family." *Ha!*

Then they got this boy out. Then my father also said, "*Mm-hm.* You too, what is your trouble? So you have been eating all this fish. Do you think that when I was a child, my mother didn't even know what is fish. I'm not a thief. I know that I am poor. But I have kept in my poverty. If it's not because of you, this fucking woman cannot abuse me! That it's my family!" Then he was turning to the wife. They will make trouble-o! "A fucking woman like this? The woman I know like my last born?" You

---

1. buttocks; underside
2. underpants

know, I think he knew these women when they were children before they grew up. So he used to tell them just like that! *Heh-hee! Ha!*

So they started to blast each other. Then she said, "It's from your family."

And he said, "Yes. In my family, I don't see any thief. When my mother was conceived, my father died. And my mother suffered. She didn't steal from anybody. She suffered and gave birth to me. And then I also suffered with my mother, before we could eat, but I haven't stolen before in my life." *Ha-ha!* "You people went and got all this thing! But you — you are telling me that it's from my blood? Did you forget? Your brother, he went to this place. Why didn't he come back? He went and stole there, and they killed him!" *Ha!* This old man! He could make false charge on people, eh? He would just ask you about one of your family.

You know, at our place, there are some people who travel. One of my aunts traveled when we were small. We didn't know her. We only heard of her, and then she came back. There are some people like that. They can go out, traveling for many years. Maybe you won't see the person again. Or maybe you will see him later. At our place, there are people like that.

So my father's wife had two brothers who were lost like that. Maybe they died. Nobody knows. And nobody heard anything about them, that they are in this town or they are in that town. So my father used to tell them that, "How did they lose themselves?" *Ha!* "They went and stole, and people killed them and threw them off like animals in the bush. You are going to tell me that the thieves are from my family? It's from *your* family!" *Ha-ha!*

So any person like that, I used to laugh. But that kind of people, too, they think they are serious. They are funny, but they don't think they are funny. You know, Africans, when they talk, they talk seriously. First time I used to think they are serious. *Ha!* They are always talking. If they feel like starting, then they start. But as for my father, *uh-uhn.* He's a somebody. He is another crazy man. You know, even the people in the village, when he's shouting on somebody like that, they just say, "Oh, this man: he went and stayed in Ghana, and then he was drinking all these Ghana palm drinks,[1] so his brain is mixed up. Don't mind him." *Heh-heh-hee-hee! Ha!*

But I think that the village people always like somebody who will make like he's a strong man. And my father is not afraid of anything, so the village people used to be afraid of him. When my father was young, he was

---

1. palm wine

in this character. When he grew up, he still had it. Every time he wants
to show that he's powerful or he's not afraid of anything. That's why he
makes his plenty talks. You know, there are some villages, when they hear
something about somebody, they will start, "Yeah, this is the person, yesterday, they were talking about him, and this and that."

But when my father hears it, he will say it in front of you. He will just
say, "Hey, yesterday, they said you have done that and that and this." He
won't go and say it to somebody behind the person's back. No. He will call
you straight and tell you. He doesn't care what you are. *Ha!* So that's why,
in this way, many people don't like him. They say he thinks he's stronger
than anybody. But he doesn't want any hidden case. If he goes out and
gets problems and comes home, he will call all the children, group them,
and tell them what happened to him.

: KUMASI :

Children Who Steal

You know, all the children of my father, we are many. OK? We have some
people who liked the meat. Some people liked dried fish. And some of
them would only wait until we eat and finish. If there was some sauce
left, maybe there was some meat inside. That time he would think, "I will
let everybody sleep and then go and eat the meat." If he is going to steal
something inside the pot: unless everybody sleeps. He is in darkness, with
no light. If he is going to open the pot, or if he has finished and he wants
to close it, sometimes you will hear *pa-kra!* They will catch him! But before they get up and put the light on, the person will go back *quickly,* and
sleep.

So how did they catch the thieves? With your experience, how are they
going to manage to catch the children doing that? You know, the children
used to sleep with the mother, beside her. So if this is happening, the
mother wouldn't say anything. She will go and start smelling the hands
of the children. You see? Maybe if they ask you, you will say you were
asleep. But even if you rub your hand with your cloth, they will still get
the scent of the soup. Then they won't say anything. They will go back to
sleep, too.

Morning time, they already know the person who stole it. They will
call him: "Yesterday, you have opened the soup. What did you want? Are
you hungry?"

"No."

And we Africans: even your own mother who borne you, if you are doing something like this, or you want to be stealing small-small things, sometimes she can talk to you, and if you don't listen, she wouldn't say anything again. She will go and give the complaint to your father.

So: your father will call you *gently*. Then: "Sit down." You sit down. He will say, "What is wrong with you? Yesterday, weren't you full up?"

And you will say, "I was full up."

If you say you didn't fill up, then he will say, "Why didn't you ask for more? Did you ask for more and they refused to give you?"

Then maybe you say, "No."

"But why? This food we keep: what are we keeping it for? I was keeping it for you people for tomorrow. Have you seen that we will keep some food here, and morning time we wake up and share it and eat, and we won't give you people?"

Then you will say, "No."

"But why?"

You see? If they ask you like this, you will become *cool*. He's asking you as if he's not going to do anything to you, isn't it? He is asking you to say the truth — what happened, what made you do this. "Are you hungry?"

"No."

"OK. You say you are not hungry. OK? But what came to your mind to do this? To come to be stealing. Or you want to be a thief? Or you want to be a burglar? Or you want to spoil the name of my family? Here you are with your family and you are doing that. Suppose maybe, as you people are many here, if one of my brothers comes and asks you to go and live with his wife, and you do this thing, don't you know that you will spoil my name?"

You see? So maybe you say, "Yes, Papa."

You know, some of us used to be afraid. Maybe you will start crying and then start to say, "Forgive me," and that and this. Then, this is the time the old man is going to *boil up!* "So you are a *big* burglar! If you see a baby who is stealing something, and you try to ask a question, and she starts to *cry*, then she is a *big burglar!*"

This is the time they are going to *beat* you! They will *beat* you! He will say, "Why? I'm talking to you! Aren't I talking to you slowly, as a man should talk to his daughter or his son. But why? What makes you cry? The day when you did it, didn't you know that you will cry? You were happy when you were putting your hands in the soup and chopping the big meat. And now you are talking to me and you are crying? So if all your sisters and brothers do that, how can I feed you people? How can you be getting grown up?" So he will start beating you.

You know, we had about three boys who were stealing the soup. When they came from school, they would go to drink water in the kitchen. And every time, my father's younger wife was a very stupid woman who was always busy with the children. If she was in kitchen, if she heard any baby make *"E-e-e,"* then even if she was making the T-Zed, she would leave it and go and see what was happening to the children.

So these boys were three. OK. They were doing this business. When they come from the school, they will go to the kitchen and drink water, and they will see maybe that this meat is just on top of the fire. And they had some kind of talk, and only these three understood the way of this talk. The first time, when this thing was going to become plain, when they started catching them, I used to keep company with them. Then they would say, *"Eetee, eetee, ata, ata, oh-oh oh-oh, tetee, tata oh."* How can you understand this? What kind of language? You see? But the three of them had this kind of language. If one said, *"Efee, efee, atee, atee, ada ada, ee ati,"* can you understand this? *"Atee atee"*: go out, go out. *"Ah-atee-akadah"*: catch a small child and beat or squeeze him, just for him to make some sound there. Then this woman will come out from the kitchen. *Heh-heh!* And when she comes out from the kitchen, one boy will just put the spoon inside the pot, and take much meat and put it in a handkerchief. Then he will go to their room. *Ha! Hee-hee!* This was their way. They would just disturb the children, and then this woman would leave the kitchen. Before she would come back, they have taken this meat.

So one day, our brother took some meat and put it in his pocket. I think he wrapped it with a handkerchief and put it inside, but this thing was very hot. So this woman, too, when she went out to see the baby, she was thinking that there was not any water on the meat, so she just took the baby and ran into the house, and they met at the door. Then she said to this boy, "Oh, won't you put water on my meat? Oh, put the water. You see your younger sister is crying."

So to go and take the water: but all this thing was burning him! *Ha-ha!* Then he took the water. The water was falling down. *Ha!* He didn't look at the water. He was scratching. This thing was burning him. Just like that, when he was going to put the water, he just poured all the water on the fire. So you know, they make the fire with firewood, and when he poured the water on the fire, the fire went off. Then my mother said, "Ah! Why? Are you sick?" Then she saw that all the pocket was oil: "Oh! Are you having trouble with your leg? What is wrong with you? What is this?"

Then he said, "Oh-h. Nothing, nothing. Nothing — it's the water."

Then she said, "No! This is oil. Look."

Then he was forcing to leave, and this woman was also forcing. She was challenging the boy, and this boy said it was water. Then he went to his room. So then this woman looked at the meat and said, "*Ah!* This meat was plenty. No! I will go and ask my son. He shouldn't do that, because I have seen that the pocket was oil."

So she called him, "But why should you do that? This meat — your father gave me money to buy for all of you people. And you want to chop all and leave the others? When your father comes, what should I tell him? If I share this meat and it doesn't reach everybody, do you want to put me in shame?"

Then he said, "Don't tell me your stupid thing! If your husband gives you money and it's not plenty, or if your husband gives you money and you go and buy your meat, and you come and chop it in kitchen, don't come and lie on me." You see?

Hey! My father's children, they are *clever!* Many of them, if they steal something, and you want to talk, they will challenge you. And the *best* thing they were doing, and why I used to laugh at them: they didn't steal something better. Just stealing food.

But you know, I also used to take food like that, but I was not stealing it like I'm stealing it. What I did: when it was something like that, I would say it the same day. Sometimes it didn't come to me to say it the same day. Then they would come and be asking questions and then they would be abusing the others. But if I saw that they started to beat the other one that he did the thing, then I would come out. I would say, "Yes, I have done it. I've taken it, because this and that."

So every time, I thought that if I come out by myself to say that I have taken it, then if you ask me many questions, I also have many answers to give you. Eh? You see? If you hide it, it is just like you are stealing it, so if they get you, you don't have power. I used to make my mind that this thing — if it's food, I will steal it and eat all of it before people will get to know that I stole it, and then I will say it by myself. This is how I used to make my aim to go and do bad.

But my brothers would just go and do the thing. You see him, you get his hand, and you want to talk to him, and he will be trying to challenge you, that he is not the one who did it. So I had four brothers: I used to call them pocket lawyers.[1] They were very good lawyers for themselves. My father used to beat *all* the boys, but before he will get one of them to beat,

---

1. A pocket lawyer is a person who acts as if he has a law degree and carries it around in his pocket in order to be ready to pull it out at any time in order to advocate, generally in his own behalf.

maybe it will take him four or five hours in questions. They will be asking questions! "OK, when you were the same age as me, this thing you say I'm doing, could you do it?" They used to ask my father this question. *Ha!* So these pocket lawyers, I liked their way, too. When the old man would get them, they would say, "Ah, upon all, what? Upon all, you are old. Can you challenge me? Do you know what we are learning outside?" Look-o. They are talking to their father. "Look. Do you think the day when you were coming up is our day? It's not the same thing." Yeah, I was having this kind of brothers and sisters.

Tales of Groove

Ha! I'll tell you a story, and it's very, very funny — about groove, eh? You know, in our house in Kumasi, my brother Kofi was a seller. He's not the one who taught me how to groove. It was my sister. My sister: she was not the same mother the same father, but we were family. Every time when we were going to market, we passed by the toilet.[1] She used to have this thing. So: "Let's go and groove."

I said, "Ah, what is that?"

I was looking, and I didn't know the thing. She used to say, "If you groove, then you know, you are feeling strong. Even somebody who has strength, you can fight him — by grooving. Groove can give you some power." I was about — almost eleven, or ten years old. When I started grooving, it's long time, eh? Yeah. We would go to the toilet; then we would get our grooving. We went there to hide the scent. So I used to be grooving with this girl.

So my brother was a seller, and I used to steal it from him. *Ha!* Yeah! I knew where he was hiding it, so when I would go to the house, if I looked and I didn't see him, then I would make quick and take one,[2] and then I would go and meet my sister with that thing. We would smoke. Every time.

---

1. Although many urban houses have an incoming water pipe, most houses do not have flush toilets; the toilet is generally in a separate place, sometimes over a deep hole with lime or sometimes simply over a bucket. People in houses without toilets use public toilets that serve urban areas.

2. take a "wrap." People rarely hold marijuana. A typical routine for a seller is that a portion of marijuana is placed into a piece of airmail paper which is cut so that it can be used to roll the cigarette; the paper is folded over and the ends tucked like a knot. People can then buy one or two or whatever number of "wraps" they need at the moment. The wraps are generally hidden outside the seller's room, perhaps in some bushes in a semi-crumpled cigarette pack, and are retrieved discreetly when a customer gives an order.

So I also had a senior sister, and she didn't know anything about groove. And I was trying to teach her, because I thought it was good, you know. "Here, cut it."[1]

She would say, "Oh, no. If I do this thing, I used to be afraid, because —"

"Because you have done it only twice. If you do it more, you will see how it is."

So every time I used to force my senior sister, you know, because I wanted her to be a guy.[2] When I was young, I liked this sister. Now we are not free like the first time. But at that time, every time I would call her to force her, then she would come and smoke. And then, you know, she also passed.[3] Even she used to send me to buy. So if she sent me with money to buy, then I would steal from my brother to give to her, and then I would keep the money. *Hee-hee-hee!* Yeah.

And my brother too, he liked me; he didn't know that I was doing something like this. He thought I was a very secret girl, and I wouldn't make any kɔnkɔnsa, so every time he was going out, he would tell me, "I put this thing here. If somebody comes, and you know that he used to come to me to have it, you can sell it to him."

Then I would say, "OK."

So I used to sell to people and give the money to him, but if I got it for my sister, I would keep the money. I would just take something for her, and then we would go together to smoke, and then the money was for me. Yeah.

When my brother would come, he would say, "Oh! This thing, somebody took some."

Then I would say, "Oh, no-o. Ah, one of your friends came and bought about one cedi, so I thought to add him one, or two. Because I thought he is — every time when he comes here, you used to give him free, you know." So my brother didn't know anything about what I was doing.

So one day, my sister and I were making trouble. And I told her, "You think you're a guy? I used to teach you to be a guy, and now you're trying to be a guy past me. Even all your two shillings, every time when you give me to buy grooving, I eat the two shillings. But I know the way to find you grooving. You are not a guy. You are not a guy, you know."

At that time, too, my sister didn't want my brother to know that she was doing this thing, and so she was hiding from my brother. He was a seller, and my father was not all right with my brother for selling this

---

1. take some, that is, smoke some
2. someone, man or woman, who is modern and hip
3. She learned how to smoke; she qualified, as if from an exam.

thing. All of us, we didn't want my brother to know. Only me, my brother knew that I'm grooving. But my sisters, he didn't know. So my senior sister was thinking that if my brother knows, if they have trouble, maybe my brother will say, "Hey, Papa says every time it's me who does it. But you too are doing it." You know? So every time she was afraid for my brother to know this.

So ah! We had trouble; now she can't get somebody to send. And you feel for grooving, what can you do? So one day she called me inside and said, "Yes, it's OK. You know, whether you buy it or you don't buy it, every time I will give you some dash when you bring it here."

So I said, "OK." Then I went and brought the groove. So then, every time she would give me two shillings. And then, it came to one shilling. Then she gave me sixpence. I didn't say anything. We would groove together, then I would be thinking, "Ah! This girl! *Tsk!* If she is doing that, it will come and be a big palaver. I won't bring her any groove again."

So evening time, the children used to go out to play games in the night, and every time we used to go there, we would pass a corner way.[1] We would groove a heavy one, and then come and play nicely. So, you know, my father had a horse, and I took small shit of this horse, and wrapped it well in the paper. *Tee-hee-tee-hee hee hee!!* So that day when we were going, she said, "Do you have some?"

Then I said, "Yes." So we passed in back of the house. Then I said, "Oh, sister. You know, today if you don't give me the money, I don't think we can do this thing, because, the last time, you gave me only sixpence. And I didn't have money to put on top to pay this man. So this one was a shilling. If you give me the other sixpence money, then we can light it."

Then she said she didn't have sixpence, but she had a two-shillings coin.

Then I said, "OK. If that will be the case, take the groove and light it. I'm going to find change before I come back."

When I came, my sister was there, *"Pppbbbt!"* Sniff, sniff.

"Ah! What is wrong?"

She said, *"Pfffpp!* Who gave you this groove?"

I said, "Ah, Kofi hasn't got some. I had to go to some place to search."

Then she said, "No-o, it's not groove."

I said, "It's what? Let me see." She didn't know what it was, but *I* knew what it was. Then I said, *"Hmmm!—Hmm!—sniff, sniff—Oh!* This is *shit! Of horse!!"*

---

1. shortcuts or indirect ways; backways, as behind or between the houses

Then she said, "So, what are you going to do? Are you going to pay him?"

Then I said, "Yes, I must pay. Because next time if he has some, he wouldn't give me."

Then she said OK. So I gave her the shilling balance. Then, three days, you know, I brought another groove again, and she gave me sixpence! So I told her, "You know, if you are giving me sixpence, then every time I will give you shit of horse. Like the last time. Yeah! Last time I gave you shit of horse! Do you know that it's because you are giving me sixpence? You will smoke shit, and it's because you don't pay."

So from that time my sister also started to be a guy, to know the people who are sellers and to buy by herself. Yeah, she thought it's better to buy for herself. Sometimes when I saw her that she was grooving heavy, I would think, "Eh! This time she doesn't groove with me; she used to go alone." Then I would also start my palaver: "Hey, sister! You grooved to-day, eh?"

Then she would say, "*Aw-w*. It's finished."

Then me: "Uh-huh? Is that so?"

"Yeah, I'm just groovy a little — not much, just small."

Then I would say, "Uh-huh. So this time, you know your way, and you go away and leave me."

Then one day she broke a plate, and I said, "So, now you can groove heavy and break everything. I will tell Mama." Yeah! She was grooving alone, and she didn't give me, and I didn't get any money from her again, you know, so I must know the way to do with her.

Then she said, "Oh-h, don't do that."

"OK, then. Give me sixpence. If you give me sixpence, I won't tell our mother again." *Ha!*

So from that time, if she grooved and came home, then I wanted to look at her eyes. And she would say, "Oh, my head. Oh, Hawa, go and buy me APC.[1] Look at my eyes. They're red, eh?"

"Yes."

"*Ah-h-h*. I'm feeling pains."

Then she was serious, you know, so I thought she was sick. I didn't know that she didn't want me to get her way. Then I said, "Oh, to take this APC, don't you think if you take grooving, it's better?"

"No, no, no, no. How my head is paining me, if I take grooving, it's not good. This time I have stopped, because I think it's worrying my head."

---

1. an analgesic tablet, no longer used, containing aspirin, phenacetin, and caffeine

Heh-heh. I thought I was clever. She's also clever now. She's getting everything, you know. So then when she would come home, every time, her head, her head, her head. Then one day she said she was sick. All her body was hot. She grooved heavy and there was much sun. You know, if it's very hot and you groove, then you used to get some kind of hot, like your body is walking fast. So she came and lay down. Then our mother came from market, and said, "Why?"

I said, "Ah-h. She says she's sick since morning time, and I gave her APC, and still she is sleeping."

Then the mother came and woke her. And I think she was dreaming, so when the mother touched her, she shouted, "Hey-hey! Hey! Hey!"

Then I said, "*Um-hm!* This girl is still in grooving. This is now free, eh? I'm going to get her again."

Then one day she said she was going to some place, and I said I would accompany her. And she said, no, I shouldn't follow her, because she is going to see somebody. So she was going, then I was following her corner-corner-corner, you know. So the house she entered, I went and sat at the door. They closed the door, and I sat in front of the door like that. Before they opened this room — *ah-h-h* — grooving was coming out. Then I ran away and passed back home. She didn't see me.

So, I was free. When she came home, then I started to laugh. Then she told me to go and buy her APC. *Hee-hee-hee-hee!* I didn't say anything. I took the money and went and bought bread and sugar. I came and put the sugar in water. Do you know that that time she was conceived? I didn't know. She was taking a shit. I started to eat. Then she was laying down and looking at me. When I finished, then she said, "Oh-h, Hawa. So you didn't bring the APC to me?"

I said, "*Ah!* I'm hungry! You, you can go and groove heavy like this, and then you want to drink APC every time. You think I am a fool? That is the money which I took to buy bread." You know, it was very funny. When she conceived, every time when you did her any small thing, she used to cry. So she started crying. *Hee-hee.* Then I went to her. I said, "O-o-oh. Don't cry. If you groove, you shouldn't feel to cry, you know. Why are you grooving and then you cry like that? Don't cry. I haven't any money, and I ate the bread, too. So I can't get this APC for you. If you have some more, I will buy it for you. Don't cry."—*Ha-ha!*—"And next time, if you groove, don't tell me you've got headache. It's not good."

So from that time, she didn't hide from me. I know she smokes. She also knows I smoke, too. She has married now, but if I go to the husband's place, she will invite me to smoke. But we are not free. She doesn't like me like the first time, and I don't like her, too.

So all this was in Kumasi, in our family house, my father's house. I was about eleven years old. But before I came to my father house, I knew all this. My other sister showed me. We used to groove and go to the market. She used to tell me if you groove, then you can fight everybody.

The first time I grooved, you know, I was feeling somewhat tired, feeling sleepy. Then the second one, it made me happy. If I smoked a small thing, then in a little time, I would become *co-o-ol*. I didn't want to hear somebody's talking. Then when I was sitting quietly, I would hear some music, light music, past my ears. I didn't know where the music was from. Every time, I wanted to be sitting quietly, and then I would start to shake my head to the music. Yeah, as for starting grooving, it's nice, you know. And sometimes, I used to look up, and then I saw something pass me; sometimes some people were coming like strangers, then I would close my eyes and shake my head. *Heh-heh-heh.*

So you know, at that time my uncle's wife said that there is some sickness that used to catch babies; the Africans say it's a big bird.[1] So if you see the bird, and you didn't see it before, you will stay and look at one place. So when I sat small, then I made so, then I would come and open my eyes, then I would sit, then I would laugh a little; I would laugh small-small. So they thought that it was that sickness, and they used to be afraid for me that, "This girl is getting some sickness, we don't know." They wanted to take me to hospital, then my uncle said, "Oh, these our African people have got medicines for that." They used to get something for me to drink, from some trees, you know, to boil it for me to drink. And I was drinking it, but this sickness could not go away. *Hee-hee-hee.*

Until I passed. When I passed and qualified for the grooving, then they didn't see it again. Then they knew that, "Ah. This thing has gone." You know! But — it was grooving! *Hee-hee!* It was not any sickness. Yeah. They told me to drink this thing morning and evening, and they put it everywhere on my things. Morning time, I will drink, and I have to bathe with this in the water, too. For about ten months, I was bathing with this medicine. *Hee-hee.* Special medicine! And it was *bitter!* So when I grooved and was drinking it, I liked the way it was bitter, and it had a scent, and I liked the scent, too, you know. So I drank much of it. *Ai-yee! Hah!*

Oh, yeah. Still now my father doesn't know that I groove. He only knows that I am smoking cigarettes, and it's not one year now when my father got to know that I am smoking. When I came from Lomé to our village, you know, I thought that this time I'm not a child, I shouldn't hide again, I will smoke it. So I gave him two packets of cigarettes. I had plenty

1. like a witch

in my things. So when I go to our village, my brother used to give me his room to sleep. I was relaxing there and my father came and met me with a cigarette. He didn't say anything; I didn't say anything. I wanted to hide it, but then I thought it's too late. So, it's OK. He just looked at me like this, at me smoking.

But you know, this story I'm telling, it's very funny, a very funny story about grooving. You know, one time my father was sick. He didn't have any appetite to eat. Then, every time, it was my brother who used to buy him tobacco. Do you know *tawa?*[1] It's what they call tobacco. This tawa, in Kumasi they have a kind of tawa, a long one, and they used to put it in a pipe. This was what my father was smoking, and every time he used to send my brother to buy it for him.

Then: my father always used to fight my brother because of grooving. I told you my brother was a seller, no? And my father would say, if my brother doesn't leave this work, he'll take him to the police. And my brother was still doing it, but he smuggled[2] it from my father. He didn't let people groove in the house. If you come to him, he will make as if he's leaving with you; then he will give you the thing.

So one day my brother came from work, and my father said, "Oh, didn't you bring me some tawa?"

And my brother said, "Oh, no, I haven't got some."

Then my father said, "Oh. But try to get me some."

Then: my brother saw that his last money was two shillings, just two shillings. He went and bought this tawa; one was one shilling. Tomorrow he must take a car and go to work: one shilling. To spend that shilling will be a problem for him. So he had one small groove rolled, and he put the grooving in the pipe, then he put the tobacco on top. Then he took the fire; he lit it for my father. And my father was smoking it.

"*Ah!*" he said. "This tawa is *good! Ah!* This tawa, it's got some scent. It's not looking like that one I smoke always. It's a *nice* one!" Then he started, *hm-mmm-mm;* then, when he finished, he said, "*Ah!* I'm hungry." *Hey!* The wife was happy.

"*Eh?!* Today you are hungry?" Since some days, he didn't eat; now, he's opening his mouth to say he's hungry. Oh, the wife was very happy! So she had to make quick-quick time and get something for the old man to eat. When they made the food for my father: *oooo!* He ate *all!* He drink a lot of water!

1. (Asante Twi): locally grown tobacco
2. hid

You know, our stepmother used to talk about my brother all the time, that my brother is bad boy, and that and this. And you know, a man used to take the words from the wife, so every time, my father was agreeing. But this time, my father said to our mother, "You see? Before, you wanted to talk!" Then he said to my brother, "Ah! Kofi, you see, before, your mother was doing something like I should sack you. Suppose I sacked you, I would be lost. Or else I would die with hunger. That's why they say, 'If you grow up, you must marry early and have a baby early, so that when you are becoming old, he will look after you.' Suppose no Kofi, to-day I will die. But Kofi made me eat today." So then he started to tell Kofi all that our mother told him about Kofi. And the wife too was there, but he didn't mind anything! Just talking: "Y-y-your mother was saying I should sack you, that you don't — you don't hear people's talks — and you are doing these things — so you will become a thief, because these plenty thieves used to come to you — but — " And *all* this, my father started to tell my brother. And the wife was getting a big head: she was ashamed be-cause she didn't know my father could say these things about her.

Then my brother said, "And now you see yourself! I be a thief? Why is it that every time I wake up four-thirty in the morning to go to work? If I know how to be a thief, I won't do this."

Then my father said, "Yeah. I know that you cannot do that, but it was just your mother who was trying to say all this. Then I thought, if I fol-low her, a wife can go today.[1] But you are a baby: even if you are not good, you will go to somewhere, you will think that you have a father."

So from this case, every time my brother used to mix small groove in-side the pipe for my father. Then one day this case came again: my father was going to cause trouble with my brother. He was smoking this thing every day, you know, and sometimes when you smoke this groove, you will like to talk some things, and sometimes when you smoke, you used to be annoyed. So my father started a palaver with my brother again. He said, "That my wife, I told you all that your mother was telling me about you, but still, you don't change your mind. You are still like that. And now I think you are going more. So if that will be the case, you can find another house to live. Because I can't live with my son, and then he's do-ing something, and I will tell him to stop it, and he doesn't stop."

Then my brother said, "What am I doing that you are telling me to stop, and I don't do it?"

---

1. A wife can leave her husband at any time.

He said, Yeah, he saw some people coming to my brother the time he used to sell this grooving, and he knows that my brother doesn't smoke in the house, but maybe they are coming to get it from my brother.

And my brother said, "So, why?"

And my father said, "You know this thing used to make people crazy! They say in Asylum Down,[1] where they have the Asylum in Accra, it's full of people who use this. And so Kofi, you must stop it."

And Kofi said, "Are you crazy? As you are there now, how you are, are you crazy?"

"If I smoke it, maybe I will be crazy."

Then my brother said, "*Ah-h!* But you have smoked it for long time! Why didn't you craze?"

"*Me??!!*"

"Yes. When you were sick, how many days didn't you eat? When you got it, didn't you eat well?"

Then: "*A-a-ah.* Is that the one you give me, then?"

"You don't know the smell? OK, wait. I will give you some to get the smell."

Then he brought some, and my father just laughed. He said, *"Phoo."* Then, *"Phm. Phm. Phm."*

Then my brother said, "You *lie!* The time when you were smoking, you told me that it's a nice scent. Why now are you making *hmm-hmm-hm?"*

So every time, my father used to like this thing. But that time, he also didn't want my brother to know. He had a Zambarima friend who used to sell sheep. And every time, this Zambarima man also used to smoke this grooving. He was an old man, too. Zambarima. And this man used to buy groove from my brother, too.

So my brother saw that this man and my father, they are now serious friends. And this Zambarima man, every time he used to buy two shillings, but now he is buying four shillings. So my brother also knew. Then one day he said, "Hawa?"

I said, "Um."

"Our father likes this Zambarima man; he used to go with him every-where. I think Papa is making a friend with Mohamadu because of smoke."

Then I said, "Oh, but Papa said he doesn't like this thing."

---

1. section of Accra

He said, "Yes. But I thought so. Because every time Mohamadu used to come and take two shillings, but now he changed. It's four-four shillings he is taking. What do you think?"

Then I said, "Papa wouldn't do that. If he wants it, he will ask you."

He said, "No, the last time, we had trouble. He won't ask me again. So we must trap him."

Then, I started to watch my father to know if he was doing this thing. Then every time he used to put on dark glasses. If it's not evening time, he won't take his dark glasses off. Then one day, he took off his glasses to wipe his face with a handkerchief.

Then I said, "*Ey-y*. Papa! Your eyes are paining you?"

Then he said, "What?"

I said, "They're red!"

Then he said, "*Ah-hah*. That's why I put on these spectacles." Then he put them back on. "If the sun is too hot like this, my eyes used to be red. I can't see well. That's why I used to put on the spectacles."

Then I went and told my brother, "Yes, I think so, because, Papa's eyes, deep down, it's like pepper."

So one day, I don't know what came to my brother. He said, "Papa, you see. This thing, I was doing it. You told me that it's not good, and I stopped. And you are still doing it!!"

"What thing?"

Then my brother said, "What thing? Do you think if some —first time you were very quiet — and this time, oh-oh, you don't give a damn. So I think you didn't stop it."

Then he said, "Because you are used to seeing me with this Zambarima man?"

Then my brother said, "*Ah?!* That Zambarima old man, too, he smokes?"

"Yes, he smokes. But I don't do it!" *Hee-hee!* So that time we got to know that our father was a smoker. So any time, if this Zambarima man came to buy, my brother used to give him about one or two rolls on top of the thing he bought, that he was giving him as a dash. Because he knew what my father was doing with him! *Ha!*

Then, from that time, I left to stay with my aunt, so I don't know what happened after. But I think that maybe my father has stopped. I think that this time he has changed. He doesn't smoke again.

You know, the time when I was in the house and he was smoking, every day, whenever he was coming and he saw me, he would go, "Hey-y, Mama-o! Mama-o!" Then he would pick me up. But before, if my father was coming from work, when we went to meet him, "Papa-o! Papa-o!" He didn't mind anything. But when he used to groove, you know, when he was coming, then he would see me and be very happy. I knew the time when he used to come. At that time in the house, every time they would send me for something, I wouldn't go. I wouldn't do anything in the house, so my stepmother didn't like me, and she used to beat me. When they did something to me and it pained me, I wouldn't say anything. I would go and stand outside. When I saw that this is the time my father will come home, I would go outside, and start to force myself to cry and get tears. If my father saw me with my tears, "Oh-h. Mama-o! Mama-o! Oh-h, what is happening? Why are you crying?"

Then I would say, "Your wife has done me that and that and this."

Then he would come to the house and shout on all of them. *Heh-heh-heh.*

But when I left to my Auntie's place, I didn't used to be going there every time. And the time I came to live with them again, by that time he was very quiet. So I think he has stopped it. Eh?

KUMASI AND BURKINA FASO :

How Papa Managed

So my old man, when he's in the house, sometimes, if he's quiet, we won't be happy. But if he wants to talk too much, we used to leave the house for him, alone. Sometimes he will start blasting everybody in the house. If you do him something, or you don't do him anything: he will get all of you people, in a group, to blast you. When it comes like that, all my brothers used to carry themselves out. Sometimes I too, I would go out. Then we would leave him alone. He will be talking, talking, talking, talking. Then sometimes, we don't go far. We will be just behind the house. When we see that he is quiet, then we will be coming back, one by one. But if you are coming: go slowly. If he knows that somebody has come inside the house, then he will start again. So we used to come slowly, slowly. Everybody would just go into his room and lock the door. Even if you aren't feeling to sleep, you will sleep; you will lay down, finish. If he hears somebody, he will say, "Eh-h, you think I sleep? You people think I sleep? I don't sleep yet. I'm going to tell you *all-l-l.*" *Ha-ha!* "Eh-heh! How can somebody give birth to a baby, and if the baby is doing something, and the father wants to talk to him, he wouldn't sit down and listen, then he will start walking out. I didn't do that. I didn't do that *at all* when I was young! Do you people know the way I suffered with my father's brother?"

You know, my father is somebody who is very pity: I feel pity for him. I think that's why, when he got a chance to give birth, then he gave birth and birth and birth and birth. He was born with the senior sister. They were two, just like me and my brother. The mother gave birth to only two. His father died when his mother was still conceived. And my father said he was about five or six years old when his mother also died and left him.

So it was the brother of his father who came and took the two children to give to his wife to look after them. And that was the place they started suffering. Because this woman, if the baby is not for you, you don't mind about the way you can treat him. My father said he was twelve years old, but he would go to the farm from morning time around five o'clock, and maybe he would come back in the evening, six o'clock, before he could eat something. And the food, they wouldn't give him the food which he would eat and be satisfied. You know, at our place, we used to make T-Zed in small balls, and they would just take one and put it on his hand and put the soup on top, without a plate.[1] Then he would just go to some corner and sit down like that, and chew it, and he would get some water and drink. This is the place he was also going to sleep. Early in the morning, they would wake him up, with his sister. He said he was doing that for a long time.

So when the sister was grown up to the size to be married, they gave the girl to a man, and the girl said she didn't want that man. So they had a problem. I don't know. My father said that the man poisoned the girl, or something like that; he said the man made her juju and killed her. So the sister was also gone. He was left alone. The only families he had were the children of the father's brothers and the mother's sisters. From the children of his father and mother, he was left alone.

So he had many children, you know. Sometimes, when the village people want to do something, he will say, "Yes. You people take witchcraft and do everything. But I have passed twenty people. I have done what God says I should do." *Ha-ha!* Anyway, he tried. Yeah, he tried.

I told you that my father was trading, but he was also a farmer: when he was in Ghana, he was a farmer there. And since he went back home to Upper Volta, too, he's still farming. But in Kumasi, he didn't used to go to farm every day. No. He was working in the cocoa farms. If it was the time

---

1. This way of feeding children was not uncommon in Voltaic cultures. The idea was to train the children to be used to hunger in case of famine.

for cocoa, he would go to live in the village where the cocoa was, to work on the cocoa. The cocoa farm was not for my father; it was an Ashanti man who had the farm. When the cocoa time had passed, then my father would collect cola. He would buy the cola nuts in the village. Then he would bring them to Kumasi. Then when it turned to the dry season, and there was no cocoa work, he would be in Kumasi selling this cola in bags.

So this is how he used to get money. Yeah. And then, sometimes he used to carry this cola to Abidjan, maybe about twenty or fifty bags. And when he would come from Abidjan, he bought some clothes and French things, and then he would sell all this in Ghana. And when cocoa work came, then he would go to the bush.

In the cocoa work, they pay once in a year. Yeah, when they sell the cocoa, that is the time they pay. My father was working like that, to get pay for the year. This man with the cocoa was having plenty of cocoa farms. Then later this man had a heavy case, and he had to sell one farm to pay for this case, and my father bought the farm from him. So now this cocoa farm is for my father. At this time, my brothers have to go to that village to work on the cocoa.

You know, these people from Upper Volta who come to work on the cocoa farms, they get their pay once in a year, so it's hard. They have to do many, many, many economics. And they have to know themselves. Somebody can buy *koobi*,[1] that dried fish with the salt, the smelly one. Eh? Some of the women can use this fish for about three, four months. They will buy one full bag, to keep it. And then they don't care: they can take this one alone to make soup and to eat fufu, without adding meat, without anything. And then also, when the husbands are in the cocoa farm too, they will go to the bush to put out traps to catch bush meat and all this. So they have not got much expenses for their eating. They get plantain free. They get cocoyam, and cassava, and all these things: they farm them for themselves on the cocoa farm. So what they need is only soup. Sometimes they will get a big animal; they can use it for about one month. They will dry it on fire and be using it.

So I think their way is good. Even, they can save more. Yeah, when we were in the village, I thought my father didn't spend much to eat, like in Kumasi. In Kumasi he used to spend much, but in our village, sometimes he could give — some time ago, maybe twenty or twenty-five cedis for a month. And the wife, maybe for a month, this wife wouldn't spend this twenty cedis. The wife was a very good woman. She was also sending fish from Kumasi to our village to sell, so sometimes she used to take her own

1. (Asante Twi): dried, salted fish

fish and make the soup. And maybe the month would come round, and then she would tell my father, "Oh, the money didn't finish yet. If it is finished, I will tell you." And so all this, how they are spending, they are making economics.

So they too, they try. They try. Yeah. They think they are coming to Ghana to search for money to go home, so every time, they know the way to manage. *Um-hm!* And then some Ghana people say that in Upper Volta there are diamonds growing in the trees! *Ha-ha!* Some Ghanaian people think there are diamonds there, and they are going to pick them from the trees. And then we, we are suffering like this in Ghana. To be farmers! Under the cocoa! You will wait one year before you get your pay!

But in the village, they don't have pay. They don't have money to buy things. It's only food they have, but to get something to spend, they don't have it. That's why we always like to take things to them when we go there. My brother in Ouagadougou, every time he used to send them some money, or if he's going there, he used to get plenty of things like sugar, because in the village there you cannot find things like that. And tea, you know: this is what they need there. They don't need corn, they don't need anything like that. Sometimes, if you like, you can take them some meat, but for the meat, too, they are funny: they don't like to eat soup with meat every time. Sometimes they have meat, and then they make soup without meat. They have different kinds of leaves to make soup. They say, "Ah, these leaves, if you cook it with meat, it isn't sweet.[1] You have to cook the leaves alone and you will get the taste." *Ha!* Oh? Yeah? Maybe a white person can understand it, but I don't understand that. Why? They wouldn't even take the meat to mix in after. They will eat the soup like that, with no meat! They say this leaf is not good with meat. *Ha! Mm-hmm?* Oh yeah.

And me like this, any time I am from Ouagadougou and I am going there, I have to buy them some soap. I think it's not possible to get soap in the village there, until the market day, and they don't got nice soap, too. They used to get soap like this skin soap, the antiseptic one.[2] So when I'm going to our village, I used to feel to buy some Cadum,[3] or some nice-scented soap to give them, then they can bathe some days with it before they will take their skin soap again. But when I give to them, they don't use it. They put it in their boxes to give their clothes a nice scent. Every time it's in the box where they keep their things. Some of them

1. tasty, delicious (not necessarily sweet); also, pleasing, good
2. Asepso, a very strong medicinal soap
3. a brand of perfumed French soap

take the paper off, and some of them can put it in with the paper. When you take the paper off and you put Cadum with your dresses, when you open the box, everything has got this Cadum scent. So it's perfume for them, and they like it. They don't bathe with it. *Ha!*

8 VILLAGE COMEDIES

: *The Sense of Villagers*
: *Introduction to Western Civilization*
: *A Strange Case at the Chief's Court*
: *How Children Get Sense*
: *Good and Bad Strangers*
: *Special Tea*
: *Pro-pro Ghana Babies*
: *Papa and the Tigernut Lady*
: *Special Agent*

: THE VILLAGE IN BURKINA FASO :

The Sense of Villagers

Yes, my people are very funny to me. When I go there, and I see them like that, I used to say, "*Ah!* Did God make these people? Or did they make themselves?" I don't understand how they were made, because anything that they do, it's something I didn't hear or I didn't see before. Anything! So it used to make me wonder. It's very funny. Some people used to think that you have to travel to see something, but this is my own village. Yeah, sometimes I used to think, of all the places I have gone, I think that our people, we are *to-o-o much* the last people who don't have understanding. Their everything is different from everyone. They are very foolish. *All!* They do things as if they have sense: if someone's doing something, you will think he's sensible. But what the person is doing, when I look at it, then I think, "This is foolish." For what should this fellow do that? But as for him, he doesn't think, "What I'm doing is foolish." He thinks, "I'm doing something good." And he doesn't know. I have met many people, and I think they are a little bit sensible more than my people.

You know, everywhere they have villages. I used to go to small-small villages, too; especially in Ghana, I used to like villages. When I am in Ku-

masi, I can't stay in Kumasi for three months without going to a small village. But I don't see such things like they have in my village. Yeah. And
Togo, too, I went to many villages of Togo. Dahomey, the same thing; I
have seen many villages of it. But I didn't find any place that is difficult
like my village. Maybe I don't understand in those places, but I can hear
the languages of all these places — Ashanti, Ewe,[1] and I understand
Mina[2] small-small. But even if you don't understand a language, and then
you stay in a village to see some things like their life and their playing and
all this, you will understand something. You know, always villages are
very small. If you stay in a village about two weeks or three weeks, if they
do something, you will hear some hint of it.

If I'm with my people, sometimes, I used to think funny things,
"Should I call all these boys and girls, the young-young ones, and give
them a lecture? Or what?" *Ha-ha!* Because I don't understand them *at
all.* Sometimes — *tsk* — I look at them. And then one time I asked my
brother, "So, how you people are here, did somebody used to give you
people advice?"

He said, "Yes!"

"What kind of advice did they used to give you people?"

He said, "Ah, sometimes if you sit with an old man, you know."

Sometimes these grown-ups used to sit outside the house to take a rest.
Many people, different kinds — old ladies, old men, some young ones —
they all mix together. So these old people used to talk some things, or they
give advice to the young ones. "The first time, they didn't do this thing:
but this time, this young one was doing that; that's why he didn't grow
old before he died." — *Ha!* — "So if they tell you that you shouldn't do
something, it's true. The first time, they used to sack people from their
family, and that's why they are poor. Even, they would be dead, but they
didn't get a way to die. But the young people don't understand; every time
they do bad things."

Then I said, "All the advice they are giving to you people is just that?"
"Yes."

Then I asked him, "Is it good advice?"

He said, "Yes! It's good advice."

And I said, *"Fool!"* Ha! "So what about a baby who was born for about
one month, and then he's dead. What did he do? He didn't grow up to do
what they told him not to do. He hasn't got a leg to go out and do something. He hasn't got a mouth to talk. How is it that the baby can die?"

1. cultural group in southeastern Ghana and southern Togo; pronounced eh-ʊ eh
2. alternate name for Gen, a cultural group in southern Togo and Benin

And he said, "Yes, this can be possible, because maybe God just said that that baby cannot live in life."

Then I said, "So it's not possible, too, if you are twenty years old and God says you won't live in life, you can die?" Then he was quiet. *Ha!* He didn't know how to give me that answer, you know. Oh! What kind of advice! This is advice to give to young ones?

Yeah. Villages. You know, in the capitals you can see funny things. If I think of some of my friends, I used to laugh. But it's a different way. I think that maybe this girl has got her sense, but sometimes, she just likes to do funny things. But my village people, they will talk one talk every time. Someone will want to direct you to the correct way, and you don't understand him. Maybe what he said you shouldn't do, you have seen that it is not so bad. Then the only talk he will say is, "*No!* What time they borne you?[1] What do you know? You just came two days into the world."[2] Then he will call some years and years and years old topics, and then he will bring them out.

Introduction to Western Civilization

You know, the first time, our people, the French Europeans used to catch them by force to get them to the army.[3] The Europeans would go to the village, and when they saw the young men, the Europeans would catch them by force. So the first time in my village, if they saw a European man stop his car, everybody would run to bush. Girls and boys: everybody had to run and hide himself in the bush. *Ha-ha!* And the Europeans caught some people to go to war, and these people didn't come back. I think they died. And the families didn't get any insurance to pay for these people. Who will even come and tell you? This European man who came and caught these guys? Who are you going to ask?

When this thing came, I think it was the time of my grandmother, and the time of my father, too, because my father used to give me that story: they used to hide themselves in the bush for maybe two or three weeks without coming home. All of them. And I asked him what did they eat. So you know, the place where you make your farm is some way from the village. If they went to the farm, every time they used to leave food in the

---

1. (Pidgin): When were you born? How old are you?
2. (Pidgin): You are young, that is, you have only been in the world for two days.
3. I also heard a similar story about the British in northern Ghana during World War II.

bush where they farmed: they would put some in the house and leave some in the bush. So war showed them that sense. If you ran away and left food in the house, then you would know where to pass in the bush and take some. Then they would go and cook there. They would have to stay in the bush for about two or three weeks, hiding themselves.

And you had to run away to the bush with all your family, because if the white people came to your home and they met the wives and they didn't meet the men, then they beat the wives to show where the husbands were. They didn't need women; they only needed men. But if they caught you, a woman, in the house, and your husband was not there, ah! You will show where your husband is. Yeah, they treated them bad. So all of you must go with your family: all of you must go to the bush. If you had a baby, and he was crying, you had to catch her, "Don't cry, don't cry," so people wouldn't know you were there. And every time you had to feed the baby. Even if you didn't have milk or food, you had to feed the baby; then you would be hungry. And people were hungry and died. My father said that some people used to be hungry in the bush, and they died. And I thought: Why don't you stay and let them catch you? If these people catch you, they are not going to kill you. They are going to take you to the army. That's what I thought. But they didn't think of that. They would go to the bush, and then all of you must stay there up to some weeks, living in the bush until these people went away.

Then I asked him, "How did you know that they went away?"

He said that they used to pass by a back way to the village to watch and see whether the Europeans were there. If they didn't see the car, they knew that these people had gone. The Europeans used to bring big trucks — about four or five — to the villages. They would catch you like a slave and put you in the truck. You are going to war. They won't train you; they won't do anything. You don't know even "A" or "B," and then you are going to the army. And our people, some of them have a heavy heart,[1] you know, so they used to do well in the war, if they caught them. But not all of our people knew guns, and the Europeans killed many of them. Not everybody knew about guns. You would see somebody coming with a gun, and you would take a cutlass to meet him on the road to cut his head. And he would kill you with the gun, you know, because he would never let you get near to him with your cutlass. So the Europeans were killing them. That's why many of our people were afraid. If these white people were coming, they had to run away to stay in bush.

---

1. They are strong; they are brave; they have a lot of heart.

So these our people, at that time they didn't have a chance to stay home. And if it was rainy season, they didn't have a chance to make their farms, because these European people walked in the bush, too. If they saw a small path, they would follow it to some village or some place. Then they would know that by all means people were there. They would catch you. So every time, these people had to hide under the grass — yeah — to leave the village, at any time, with their wife and their children, sleeping there, leaving their village free — nobody there, nobody — and sleeping in the bush. Because the time then the white people catch you, maybe you will go to this war, and maybe they will kill you. Or some people are lucky; they will go and come back.

Now they stopped. I don't know when. My father was telling me that at that time, my mother was about eight or nine years old, so it was a long time. This time they don't do that thing.

The first time when I went from Ghana to my village, when I was small, if you went to get water, sometimes you would see some white people stop their car on the road. Sometimes some Europeans wanted to ask for water to put in their car. And *all* these children, they ran; some of them dropped their pots and broke their pots, and some of them left their buckets, and then they ran. Then I stood and said, "Why are you running?"

They said, "Come! Come! Come!"

"Come for what?"

"Don't you know the white man will catch you! Come, come!" These children, I think that the mothers or the grandmothers gave them advice, so some of them were afraid of the Europeans. Still now, many of them run when they see Europeans. First time, if these children saw them coming to where they were taking the water, then *rurrr-r-r: everybody* would go and leave the place. *Ha!*

And then, you know, sometimes if this happened, I wanted to talk to the Europeans, because in Ghana I had seen many Europeans. When I was young, their hair was nice to me; especially if I saw a girl with a lot of hair, I wanted to touch it. So when these other girls ran, then I would go to them. Then they would be talking to me, and I didn't understand, so I would say, *"Mm-m,"* and then I would be talking in my language, too. So: *ha!* Sometimes the person would take my water from my bucket and put in the car. Then I would say, "OK, OK, OK." Sometimes they used to dash me something. Then when I came home, then I would tell my grandfather, "I *talked* to a white European man today! I *talked* to him!"

Then he said, "What language did you talk to him?"

"Oh, but he understood our language! The European man understood. Look, he told me to give him water. I gave him, and then after he gave me money."

Then he said, "One day they will put you in a sack and go with you." *Ha-ha!* "If you see them coming, *run.*"

Then I said, *"No.* I won't run, because if I give them water, they used to give me money." *Ha!* How I had seen many Europeans in Ghana, I didn't see any bad they were doing. But these people still thought that these people could do what they were doing. This time, the old ones don't fear them, but the young ones are still afraid of Europeans. I think they hear this story from their grandmothers.

One white man told me that he stopped at some village on the road to Diébougou, and all the people ran to the bush. Then I laughed. *Ha-ha!* I knew that it was the same area as mine. Yeah? Then I said, *"Ah?* They ran?"

"Yes!"

"Why?"

"I don't know why. I just came and I saw — I wanted to ask them for water to put in my car, but everybody ran away."

Then I said, "Oh-h-h, those people are bush people." He didn't know it was my village! *Ha!* Yeah, my people. They are suffering, you know.

Oh yeah, so village life is hard. And it's free, too. In some kind of way, to me, it's free. But it's only that the old people don't let their children be free. Every time they want to force them, "Do that, do this." You have to do what the Papa says. It's only from these things when the life of village is bad.

A Strange Case at the Chief's Court

You know, at our village in Upper Volta, I used to see many different cases. That's the place I learned how to talk. Yeah, I used to see the way the people would join their cases.[1]

How I grew up, I told you I stayed with my grandmother, no? I didn't know my real mother at all. My mother's mother: yes, I knew her. But my father's mother: I didn't meet her; she died before they gave birth to me. And when my mother died, I was about three years old, and then, I stayed with my grandmother, my mother's mother. The first time I stayed there,

---

1. to judge a case, to hear a case; also, separate a case

I didn't stay there much—I think maybe I was about four or five years old, and I went back to my father. But when I was getting some sense a little bit, at that time, all the children with my grandmother had married, so they left her alone. I went back to my grandmother until I was about eight or nine years old. Then my uncle also came from Abidjan with his children, and by then, she had many children with her. Then I made up my mind to go back to Ghana, and I went back to my father. So they always sent me back and forth. Oh, as for me, yeah! I used to go around. So my grandmother was the one who first trained me after my mother died.

And my grandmother's house, the house I stayed, it's a very funny house. It's for the chief of the village. I told you my grandfather was chief of the village. He was my mother's father. So I was staying there, and whenever they would get a case, they used to come and join the case at the chief's house. That was the house I was living in our village, with my grandmother and my grandfather. It's like if somebody does somebody bad, and he doesn't understand, then the way you summon people to court, it's like that.

And you know, there was one funny story when I was there, when they joined the case at my grandfather's house. And this story is very, very, very funny. There were two women who were married to one man. And one woman said the husband loved the other one past her, because if she is sleeping with the man, the man doesn't make love with her. But if the other one sleeps with the man, even for one month, he can make love every day.

OK. How can you know that they are making love? If you enter with this man,[1] it's you and him alone. If this other woman also enters, it's them alone. But she didn't understand this, so she gave the complaint to the chief, to call her husband.

So they called the husband, and the husband came. Then they joined this case. Then the chief asked, "Now, OK, here is your husband. Say what you told me."

This woman said, "Yes. We were two when we married together. Before, with me and my husband, when we were alone, I knew what we could do. And this time, I don't know what my husband is doing. If I go to sleep with him, he turns his back to me." *Hee-hee!* "I can't understand. So I want you, Chief, to ask him that if he doesn't want me again, he must tell me to find my way."

---

1. go to sleep in the husband's room. The husband has his own room, and the wives have theirs, so they enter the husband's room to sleep with him.

So the chief said, "OK, *Patron,* this is your case. Do you have something inside it to say?"

The man said, "Yes."

"OK. Go on."

Then the man said, "It's not my fault, because, I have been with her making love for about three or four years, and she has no children. And the one who came second, we have two children. So I think I must do my best to have more children. I don't work for free, you know. I don't work for nothing. Not to say chasing woman is good, but just to chase women without anything, I don't want it. So that's why, when this woman comes to sleep with me, I think that if I use her, then I'm wasting my water. I won't get any profit out of it. That's why every time I used to keep it for the new wife." *Hee-hee-hee!*

So I looked at this case. I said, *"Ah!"*

So my grandfather said, "OK. If that will be the case, you must let this woman go away."

He said, "No. I like her."

"Ah! Someone who you like and you can't satisfy her, how can't you leave her?[1]

He said, "Yes! If she likes another man, she can chase. But I don't want to leave the woman, because I love her. So we must live together. But not because of making love. She can get another lover, but still, everybody should know that she's my wife."

Then my grandfather looked at this, and he said, "No. You are foolish. To keep a woman in your house, and other people will be fucking her?"

Then the man said, "But that is nothing, you know." He likes the woman, but he doesn't want to make love with her. He said sometimes he used to feel to make love with her, but if he thinks of the way he has wasted all his water for three years without a child, then this thing cannot get up again.

Then my grandfather said, "Then it's best to leave her. Maybe somebody's water can work on her. Maybe your water and her water are not the same thing. So leave her to get somebody's water which can work on her."

Then the man said no. He wants the woman to find somebody whose water can conceive her, so then the baby is for him. Because he has suffered for three years, so he has to get something from this woman before she leaves. *Ha! Ha!*

1. in this context, allow her to go

So my grandfather said, "No! This is a foolish case! All of you, you must go!"

So when they left, then I asked my grandfather, "Eh, grandfather! So this is a case? They joined it? They joined this case at the chief's house?"

Then he said, "Yes. If something is troubling you, you must join it like that at the chief's house."

I said, "Ah-ha! So if somebody does you bad, you must bring the case?"

Then he said, "Yes."

How Children Get Sense

So one day, I did a funny thing. I was playing with my uncle's son, and I was knocking something, and this boy was putting his hand inside, and I knocked his hand. Then the mother beat me. Then I started crying, "*Wah-ah-ah-h!* Because you are not my mother, that's why you beat me!"

And when my grandfather came, I said, "I have a complaint to lodge, on my uncle's wife."

Then he said, "OK."

Then I said, "But you must tell many people to come and listen."

Then my grandfather called my grandmother. He called my aunt. He called one of the sons of my uncle; that boy was about twelve years old at that time. Then I said, "But when people join their case outside, you call many people."

He said, "Yes. That's an outside case. But this is a house case. So we will join it like this."

Then I said, "OK. They should ask this woman that when I came to this house, did I do her something bad?"

Then my grandfather said, "OK." Then he told my uncle's wife, "Yeah? She is asking you a question."

Then she said no, I don't do her anything bad. Why did I ask her so?

I said, "Because today she has beat me some way, I don't understand it."

Then she said, "What kind of way?"

I said, "Yes. We are two children. We are playing. By accident—I didn't make up my mind to wound the baby—I knocked his hand with this thing. Then you just came. You didn't ask any questions; you just started beating me. Do you think if you are my mother, you can do this? Or if you are the one who borne the two of us, you can do that?"

She said, yes, she can do that because I have grown past the other one; I have more experience.

Then I said, "OK. So, in this case, as you are there now, you are grown. You have experience, and I'm young. Do you think you cannot do something against me?"

She said, "If it comes, then maybe, by accident."

Then I said, "*Yes!* It is the same thing I did!"

Then my grandfather said, "Yes! You win!"

So: I'm a winner. So my uncle's wife had to beg[1] me, you know. I said I didn't want anything from her — only eggs. At that time I used to eat many eggs, because in the village you get many, many, many eggs. And very cheap. My uncle's wife had to beg me with twelve eggs.

So these eggs, do you know a funny thing? I cooked them and kept them for about two months. I didn't eat them. I was thinking I will take them to Ghana to show my father that I have won a case. *Hee, hee, hee!* And then they begged me with twelve eggs. Twelve eggs is twelve chickens! *Hee!* I was eating them small-small: when we went to Ghana, it was left with three. Then I said, "Oh, Papa. You see? I have won a *ni-ice* case from my uncle's wife. She beat me, then I took her to the chief's house, and they joined the case. Then she paid me twelve eggs. It's these three which I left for you."

Then my father said, "That's what you have seen there?"

Then I said, "Yes. She just beat me for nothing. I knocked the baby's hands with a stone by accident. Then she beat me. She said because I'm senior past him, that's why. So Papa, sometimes don't you beat me?"

Then my Papa said, "Yes, sometimes I beat you if you do something wrong."

Then I said, "Yes! But sometimes you can beat me without any understanding."

Then my father said, Yes, sometimes if he doesn't ask questions much, he can beat without understanding.

Then I said, "Yeah. That's why I won."

So my father said, "Yes, you are clever."

Yeah, in our village, they used to have palavers. Every time you see people in the chief's house. They have very funny cases. This one makes a palaver with the brother; that one makes a palaver with that and this; this one says, "My mother is a witch; she's eating all my babies." All are cases for the chief's house. Yeah. How can you know that somebody is a witch? It's wonderful. This man had a wife, and the wife had children,

---

1. apologize to, generally with a presentation

and every time the babies died, so he said the mother is a witch, and he brought the mother to the chief's house to talk about this. Then, *ah!* At the chief's house, you know, sometimes my grandfather used to say that he used to hear some cases to make him a fool. Sometimes in Ghana, I used to think of these cases when I would sit down. Then I would just start laughing.

Then my father will ask me, "Why are you laughing?" Then I will start telling him about the case. Then he will say, "So? That makes you laugh?"

Then I will say, "But yes."

Um-hum? Don't you see the case of the man with two wives? The case is funny. What kind of man is this? Yeah? He was suffering for three years with no profit from this woman. Eating free. Making love free. Buying clothes and all this. So he must get some profit before this woman leaves: if he can get somebody to conceive her, then he will take the baby; it's the profit from her. So they sacked them all from the chief's house: they can go home and do what they can do, whether this woman is going home to pack her things or whether she wants to stay and get profit for this man before she leaves. *Hmm!* As for this case, the chief cannot separate this! *Hee-hee.*

Yeah, in our village in Upper Volta, if I didn't go with my grandmother to the bush to get water or firewood, then I was with my grandfather. Sometimes I would go with my grandmother; sometimes I would be with my grandfather in the house. My grandfather used to go to bush sometimes, too, but the day when they get a case, he used to be home. Or sometimes he used to be working in the bush, and then they would come and call him that they want him in the house. Then he would go and leave us.

Yeah, our place is very funny. Our villages. They have many funny ways there. They marry family-family. If you are a man from the chief's house, you shouldn't marry to another house. You have to marry someone from another village's chief's house. This is how our village is.

So if you are in these families, they are big, poor families. The family is very poor, but it's a big one. You just have your name, that you are from the chief's house, but even the poor people are living better than you. *Ha-ha! Yes!* Some chiefs, when they show you "This is a chief," you will say, "Chief of *what?*" Sometimes I used to ask them, "Chief of what?"

"Chief of the village."

"What kind of chief? What kind of village?" Yeah! "What kind of chief is this? All his dress, you don't know what color it is. They say, 'Chief.' Chief of what?! Chief of dirt or chief of poverty?"

So when they say, "Chief of village," then I say, "Doesn't he have a wife to wash his dress?" They let themselves be dirty. You will see a chief. The harmattan has cut all the feet.[1] He's a chief! *Chief!* Even sometimes you will see him walking on the ground with no shoes. He's a chief of the village. So our village, they have some kind of people. They are very funny.

So the time I was a child, I used to get some sense from all these things. And from going back and forth, too! I lived in many places — *Ha!* — because they were sending me.

The first time, too, what made me to go around: when my mother was dead, then I think my father did rough,[2] as if maybe he hadn't got his own sense. He was always going out to travel alone. And sometimes when he wanted to travel, he liked to take me with him. And then people would say, "No, let her stay with me." The first time, when my mother was dead, there were women who were friends to my father, but my father said he wouldn't marry again. He wanted to be alone. So I think — I didn't know what was wrong. After he went round-round-round, for about two years, then he came back to the women. And you know, they were very good women, because they were waiting for him all the time. He had children with other women too, but he would just leave these women without saying where he was going. To Ghana. To Bouaké.[3] To here and there, this place and that place. Sometimes he would take me like that.

Even some of the places I lived, they were not for my family. I lived in Nandom[4] for about two months, with one Mossi man. He was a friend of my father. He used to come to my father to buy cola, and he used to joke with me; he used to call me his wife. So one time I said, "Eh, today I want to go and know your country."

When my father and this man finished with the cola, I told my father. Then my father said, "Eh! This girl will kill me. This man, I don't know him well."

I said, "Oh-h. I want to go with him."

So I was crying, and my father said, "OK, go with him."

I stayed for two months with him and the wives. He had three wives. And the small wife liked me. Everywhere she went, she would go with me. Yeah. You know, when he was talking to the wives, I didn't under-

---

1. During the dry harmattan season, the skin or callouses on the feet sometimes crack.
2. took his life in a rough way, lived carelessly
3. town in northern Côte d'Ivoire
4. town in northwest corner of Ghana

stand their language, but I think he said, "Yes, my friend in Kumasi who I used to take the cola from, this is his daughter, and she was crying that she wanted to follow me, so I have brought her for some days and then I will return her back." My father used to give him credit on the cola, and if he finished selling, he would come and pay. So maybe that is what he said.

So I was living with them and I was — free. Everywhere the small wife goes, she will take me. We will go round round round round round. We go to shopping, we come and cook, and all this. And if this man comes from work, he will say, "Hey! My darling, my darling, my darling." And I also will call him, "My darling." And when he goes out in the morning, he will give me two shillings. At that time, two shillings was a lot for me, and I didn't know how to spend money, so I used to hide my money. When I went back to my father, I had about one pound and two shillings. Eh?

Then after, when I was sixteen, I went there for two days. The man owed my father some money, so my father sent me there to go and take the money from him. It was because I already knew there. The very day I went, he said he hadn't got the money, so I must wait until the next day. The next day he got me the money, then they put me in the car back to Kumasi. I slept one day on the road, and the next day I was in Kumasi.

So all this is how small children move around and get sense. There are some children, every time when they are with the old people, and the old people are talking, these children don't say anything. They are always quiet. If you see them, you will say, "Ah, this baby is very quiet. She's a very quiet girl. She's very nice. She understands, when people are talking, she should listen."

But she's listening for herself, too. It's very funny too. Maybe sometimes she will be telling her friends, "Ye-ah, yeah. I was at that place when they were saying these things." When children go out to play together, then they will say, "In my house today, this thing happened. In your house, too, what happened?" And then we children will also start discussing *all* these things. *Ha-ha.*

: KUMASI :

Good and Bad Strangers

You know, we Africans, if a stranger comes to us from my father's family or my mother's family in Upper Volta, maybe my father will try to buy a lot of meat, or he will kill about three chickens, to make food for him. And when you are a child, it's something funny. That day, all of us children will want to eat the food they give the stranger, so when a stranger comes, all of us children will refuse to eat the food they give us. Yeah. We want the food the stranger is going to eat because they will give him plenty of meat.

And the good strangers, they won't eat all the meat. They leave some meat for the babies who carry the plates. If the stranger eats and finishes, the small children must take the plates and clean the place where he ate. And there are some strangers, they don't eat the food like the fufu or the tuwo; they just eat the meat and leave the food. And that one makes us *hot*. When it's something like this, then we will start to speak Hausa or Ashanti about him. Maybe he cannot hear Ashanti or hear Hausa. You know, we were not too much small, and we could understand all of these languages like that.

When I started to speak and learn the languages, the first was my own language, Gurunsi. I spoke Gurunsi when I was young. Even now I still have it a little bit. I don't speak it much. But when I was young, I was very clever in it. It was the language I started with when I learned to talk. But when I got to about four or five years, I could speak Ashanti, I could speak Hausa, and Gurunsi. The Hausa and Ashanti, when you go out to play together with the children, you must understand it. If I speak only Gurunsi, none of them can hear, so I must learn what they are speaking. And by then it was very cheap[1] for me to hear it. So in Kumasi, all of us, we spoke Gurunsi when we were in the house. But sometimes, if a stranger came from Upper Volta and he could hear Gurunsi, if we wanted to talk something bad of him, we would talk Ashanti or Hausa. *Hee-hee.*

So when the stranger eats all the meat, then we will start: "Yeah. This stranger is not a nice stranger. What kind of stranger like this? He eats all the meat."

If we go and we don't see any meat on top of the food, we won't remove the plate. Everybody will say, *"Pfm!"* and go back. Then our mother will shout, "Won't you people remove the plate?"

"We are eating." *Ha!* That's the time when we are going to eat our own with the little meat they gave us. We wanted more meat to eat, but when we don't get it, what can we do? And our mother could not tell us to get up, because in my father's house, if the children are eating, you don't send them to do something; if my father is there, he will be annoyed. So in this case, we wouldn't eat quickly. You must finish eating before they will send you. So we will be sitting there, and some of us will be making palaver. "Hey! You took a big piece of meat! You left me small meat!" And then

1. easy to learn

we will start fighting. So my mother will go and remove all the things of the stranger's food to clean, because there is no meat.

But the day the stranger leaves the meat, nobody will tell us. We will all force to clean up after the stranger. Sometimes my mother will ask, "Where is the plate from the stranger?"

And we will say, "Oh-h. We ate it. There was soup inside." And then the day when nothing is there, we won't take it out; we will leave it there. Then we start to talk about the stranger in Ashanti language, or in Hausa, I with my sisters and brothers.

: KUMASI AND BURKINA FASO :

Special Tea

So one day, one old man came to us, and this thing makes me laugh. Every time when I remember it, I used to laugh. Morning time, they made tea. Then he put plenty of sugar. I thought he never drank tea before in his life. He came from my father's village. So morning time, my father said they should make everything quick, and the wife made tea with bread. They put margarine on the bread, and this man liked it! The way he was eating the bread, it was a thick one, but I think he just cut it[1] about four or five times, then it was finished, you know, *Nyum, nyum, nyum, yum, nyum-nyum.*

Then he started with the tea. So: he was shaking a little bit, and the cup was full, so when he was going to pick it up, some of it fell on his dress, and he drank and then put the cup back quickly. And then — *nyum, nyum, nyum* — he was drinking where the tea had fallen, sucking it, because of the sugar on his dress. Then I started laughing. Then my father took a stick and said, "Go out!!" Then I went out.

So I went and called all the children in the house to come and see this thing, a wonderful thing I never saw in my life. So! *Ha-ha!* We all came; we couldn't go inside, so then we started putting our eyes in the hole of the door. If you look a little, then this one will push, "Let me see, too! Let me see, too!" And you know, it's very funny: when we were doing that, then we knocked the door — *bong!* Then my father said, "Who is there?"

"Oh, not anybody! Not anybody! Nobody's here!" *Ha! Hee-hee!*

Then we were looking at this old man. When he finished the tea and came out, then all the children in the house started to laugh at him.

1. bit it

So one day I was fighting with one Kotokoli[1] girl. She was in the house with us. And every time I used to beat her, because I was strong past her. You know, when you get somebody cheap, then every time you want to do with him. So anything she did, even if she didn't do any mistake, if I felt like beating her, then I would start. So one day I was beating her, and she said, "Heh! That's why the people from your father's country, they never drink tea. Even if it falls down on their dress, they drink it. They like to chew the dress on top of drinking the tea." *Ha ha!*

Then my father was there. "*Hey!* Come here! What did you say?"

Then she said, "No. Not you. I'm talking to Hawa. The people from her father's country." She repeated it! It's funny when you are a baby. She thought she was abusing me; she didn't know it was rather my father she was abusing, that the people from my father's village, they never drank tea before, when it falls on their dress, they want to eat the dress.

So my father said, "Yes. It's Hawa you are talking to. Or you are talking to me?"

"No, Papa.[2] It's Hawa who beat me. You didn't beat me. I'm talking to her. I'm abusing Hawa."

Then my father looked at this child, then he started to laugh. He told me, "Yes, Mama, when I sacked you, suppose you didn't call them to see, they wouldn't know what was happening in the room. It's you who told them. And now they are abusing you. It's good for you!"

Yeah, it's good for me. I alone saw this thing, then I called everybody to come and see, so they have to abuse me with that. Suppose I hid my secret, nobody will know this.

So the time I left Lomé and went to Ouagadougou, when I went to my village, I saw this old man, the one who drank the tea from his dress. I brought a lot of tea and things to the village, with sugar and milk[3] and all these things. The tea in the packet, I brought it from Lomé, about three boxes. So when I was giving some to them, they were many, so I was giving them one-one packets. And they hadn't seen the tea in the packet before, and they could make this one packet of tea about twenty times. Yeah, I told them that it's the way to use it. I said, "Oh, even you can use it for one year! It's a special tea which white people make." You know. So this man, I gave him one packet. How he was using it, when he puts it in water to make small tea, then he will put it in the sun, and dry it. Every

---

1. cultural group in northern Togo
2. It is not uncommon for a child to address any grown person as "Father" or "Mother."
3. in small cans

time he thinks it's something. He will just put it in the water, then he will take it out, then he will put sugar, put milk, and — it's tea! White water, with sugar and milk, and then: *mm-mm-m-m, ah-h!* When I left there, and when I went to Abidjan and I came back and passed there, this old man still showed me that tea. Then I laughed. He said, "I still have my tea, but the sugar and milk have finished."

And I said, "Oh, I have milk, but it's not plenty, so come and get two cans of milk with one packet of sugar." So he still had this! It was about one year! *Ha ha ha ha!* So these people still have one-year tea with them now.

Pro-pro Ghana Babies

But as for my father, he knows things like this, you know, so sometimes if I bring some things for him, to boss him like this, then he will say, "Oh, these *pro-pro* Ghana babies, and their *kone-kone* ways,[1] I know all. I know these things. They didn't even borne you before I knew this thing."

My father is a very funny man. Yeah. If you are talking to him, then he will say, "*Hmm?* Yeah? You, this time, you these girls, small-small girls like you, you think you know *too-o-o* much. This kind of *kone-kone* way, me too, I know it." Do you know *kone-kone?* It's something like how we children used to lie to the old people. You can tell them something like lies to take something from them, like, "Papa, they said that and this and so you must bring this and that."

Then he would look at me and say, "Do you think that what you are saying is true?"

Then I would say, "Oh, yes, Papa. I have told the truth."

He would say, "No! These *kone-kone, pro-pro* Ghana babies, I don't believe them!"

Pro-pro Ghana! Then I asked him, "Papa, what? Every time when you talk, you say, 'Pro-pro Ghana!'"

He said, "Pro-pro Ghana is the children who they borne in Ghana-town. They grow quickly, and every time, they think they know past their father." *Pro-pro.* It's *proper* Ghana! He's very funny. Yeah, my father is very funny.

You see? I was born in Ghana. I am pro-pro Ghana. This is the meaning of pro-pro Ghana. OK? So the old people used to tell us "pro-pro-Ghana." My father used to say it, too: "Pro-pro Ghana babies." You know?

---

1. (Pidgin): clever, lying; from the word "cunning," as in, "He is a kone-man."

That is: real Ghana children. All the old people used to say it. It's just
something like the children who are wild. Pro-pro Ghana: when you
know this thing is a lie, but then you say it's this thing. Yeah. You think
someone is old: you go out, and you see something white, and then you
are coming to tell him it's red. *Ha-ha!* This is why they used to call us like
that. Pro-pro Ghana. We are proper Ghana people! The liars! *Ha-ha!*

You know, one time I went and gave my father coffee. Then I said,
"This time they have changed the coffee. So: how every time you used to
feel lazy and then you used to be weak, if you are taking this coffee every
day, two times a day, morning and evening, it will be good for you."

Then he looked at this thing. *"Oh-o-o?"* Then he said, "You know, this
writing on the tin, I don't know anything about it. But I know that this is
coffee. I was making a coffee farm when your mother didn't even conceive
you. So this is not medicine. You can just tell me if I don't want to sleep,
I can drink it. I will understand. If I want to do some hard work, I can
drink it: I understand this. But don't tell me that if I'm weak, or if I'm
sick—"

If you are telling him something, every time he used to look at your
eyes. He will sit down, and then he makes his head like this. He won't
say anything. When you finish, then he will say, *"Tsk. Ah-h. Um-m.* This
thing, I will try it and see, but, ah, the way I know it is not the way you
are telling me." *Ha ha ha!* My father is very funny.

So when I was young, maybe I was also funny, but I have one sister
now who is very funny more than me. *Ye-e-eh!* She is eight years old, but
if she is talking to you, you will say that somebody told her to tell you
what she is saying. She is very, very, very funny.

Look. When I went to our village, she came to me and said, "Sister, did
you see what Papa did?"

I said, "What did Papa do?"

Then she whispered, *"Sh-h.* I'll tell you later."

Then my father said, *"Hey!* I know you! Kɔnkɔnsa! *Tell her! I want to
hear."*

Then she ran from the room. Then later, she came to me and said,
"Sister, if I tell you, will you tell Papa?"

Then I said, "Oh, I won't tell him."

"OK. When you are going to sleep, you should call me. I will tell you
something."

Then when I was going to sleep, I said, "Zinabu?"

"Yes?"

"Let's go and sleep."

Then she came, and she said, "Now, I'm going to sleep with you?"

Then I said, "Yes."

Then she said, "I will show you what Papa did to me. I was sick, and
every time in the night, if I was asleep, I saw some people standing on top
of me, like I was dreaming. Then I was shouting. So every time, Papa
used to put me on his bed. Then I would sleep. Then one day Mama came
to sleep there. And they pushed me off of the bed! Then I was going to fall
down, and I was holding Papa, and then Papa took my hand off, and
threw me away!" *Ha ha ha.*

So I said, "Didn't Papa sleep by that time?!"

She said, "No! They didn't sleep. They didn't sleep. Then Mama was
saying, *'Uh-h-heh, uh-heh, uh-heh, uh-heh!'* And Papa was saying, *'Um, um,
um, um.'*"

Then I said, "Then what was that? Then Papa was sick?!!"

"No, they were not sick! They were doing something. I saw them."

Hee-hee-hee. You know, she's eight years old, but look at the way she's
talking. She saw these things in the night. But no light, eh? When they
sleep, they put off the light. So she wanted to say this thing, but she can't
just say it. Maybe they didn't push her. She saw it and she wants to say
she saw them, so she has to get something like an excuse, to talk about it
in some funny way, that it was because of that. Yes. This sister, she's very,
very funny.

So children are very funny. Any time I remember this girl, I used to
laugh. So when I was growing up, I was also funny a little bit, I think.
Yeah. Me and my father, we are funny, eh? My father is very, very funny,
because every time, he does funny things. When I was a baby, he liked
me a lot!

You know, at that time, I was a very big kɔnkɔnsa in the house. If I had
something to tell about someone, I would run. Full speed, even! A heli-
copter wouldn't fly like that. I was flying good! I have a good big story! So
I had to run quickly to the house. "Hey, hey, hey! I have a *good* story, but
I won't say it."

Then my father knew that I am very funny, and I'm very kɔnkɔnsa,
too. So he will say, "What did you see?"

I will say, "No, I was not talking to you." Then I will say, "Who likes
me?!" You know? *Ha!*

Then all the children will come. "I like you! I like you!"

I will say, "No, I'm not talking to the children. I mean *all* the people,
the old people in this house: who likes me?"

So my father knows that I have a story. Then he will say, "Yes! I like
my mother *first!*"

Then maybe one of my mothers will answer. Maybe the other mother
will answer. Maybe the other senior brothers. They will all answer that

they like me, but I will say, "No! My father is the first person who answered. So it's only my father who loves me. Not anyone loves me. Because my father said it before you people. So if I have a story, I won't tell
anybody. Papa, nobody will hear it."

Then he will say, "Come here. Can you come with me?" *Ha-ha!*

You know, sometimes my father used to say that if some man — the
men who used to make love to their daughters, it's not their fault. It's the
fault of their children. You know? *Ha-ha!* So: "OK, let's go."

So my father will say, "OK, OK. It's between me and my mother."

So that day, he will put me his bed. He had an iron bed. Even he still
has it in the village. If you put a small mattress with cotton on top of it, it
is always singing. So if I had a story like that, he used to put me on that
bed. He had *nice* bedsheets, white. Then I would be *jumping. Ha!* That
time I was a kid, you know. Then he will say, "Yes? Nobody is here."

Then I will say, "They will hear! They will hear! Close the door!" *Ha!*

And you know, my father is very funny, too. And he is a *bad* man. He
used to keep biscuits or a cake to take with coffee, or tea. But if he was
taking it, and you asked him, he would say, "Hey! This is medicine. Children don't eat it. You know, that way, as I am old, I want to keep long to
look after you people. That's why I used to eat this thing. It's medicine
from the doctor." So: *ha!* But the day you have a *good* story to tell him,
maybe he will give you a piece of this thing. Then he will say, "You see?
What I have given you is not food. But if it's somebody who has a *good* intelligence, like you, if you eat it, it make all your experience come clear.
So all your brothers and sisters, it is *only you* I am giving. Don't tell the
others."

You see? *Al-l-l* the story you have in your stomach, you will vomit it all
out. *Ha! Hee-ha!* Yeah. My father and I are funny, eh?

: KUMASI :

Papa and the Tigernut Lady

OK. My mother used to go to market. Then some woman used to come
around. She was selling tigernuts.[1] Do you know this woman was a friend

---

1. a kind of dried, small tuber, slightly sweet. One chews it for the juices and then
spits out the roughage. Its juice (tigernut milk) is also extracted and made into a kind of pudding. Tigernuts have the reputation of being an aphrodisiac, and sometimes people refer to
them as "charge-your-battery," as in "I want to buy some charge-your-battery."

to my father? I didn't know, but every time, when this woman came to the house, then my father would send me: "What do you want?"

That time they used to have some chewing gum that looked like a two-shillings coin. It was round, and it had some gold paper on it. I used to *like* this chewing gum. So if this woman came, my father would give me money to go and find this chewing gum. Where I will go and get it, before I will come back, maybe they will finish everything, no?

So one day, he gave me the money to go, and I was outside, talking to the other children. He thought that I went. It was in the day time. There was nobody in the house; all the women were in the market. Then I heard my father's door close, *kpong!* Then I said, "Ah, what is that?" Then I went back. I saw that my father's room was closed. He had a table on the veranda, and this woman put the pan of tigernuts on top of the table. So I didn't say anything. I just climbed onto the table and sat on it, eating the tigernuts. *Hee-hee-hee!* I ate *well!* Eh? I was eating these things, and when I ate them, the dry part that you will spit out, instead of spitting it out, I put it inside the pan together with the tigernuts, then I mixed it, then I took another one. I was eating them like that. Then I heard a noise from inside the room, and I ran from there. Then this woman came out. "Issahaku!"

Then my father said, "Yes?"

"Come and see. Look at what your children did."

Then my father came out. "No. My daughter is not here. You were here when I sent her to go and buy chewing gum. I don't know whether she has come." Then he called me, "Mama! Mama!" Then I ran and came. So my father said, "Who did this?"

I said, "What?"

"This!"

I said, "A-a-h, I came. Then your — the door was closed. I didn't see you. I didn't see this woman. I thought maybe she gave you this thing, and you were going outside and closed your door. So I thought it's for you. So, I am the one who ate it."

Then he said, "When you ate it, why didn't you put the — this thing — out."

Then I said, "If I put it out, you wouldn't know that I ate some. You will think maybe I stole some. So, it's better." *Hee, hee, hee!* "That's why I ate it and put it inside. But *where* have you been, Papa? I have come here two times, and I didn't meet you."

"Yeah. I was discussing with that woman. She wanted that room at the back, so I took her around the house."

I said, "But I passed all there."

He said, "No, you are lying."

"But I was *there.*"

Then I laughed. I didn't say anything. But when the wife came, you know, I wanted to challenge this. I was not finished. I wanted tell the wife. Then I said, "*Eh-heh!* As for you somebody, every time when you send me, I don't go, so you used to beat me. I have a good story but I won't tell you." *Heh-heh.* I didn't call her name.

Then she said, "Who is that somebody?"

I just making something like singing. "*Eh-heh.* Somebody who does-n't like me — I have a good story a-bout her — but I wo-on't tell her."

Then my sister said, "Oh! But you know I like you much."

"It's not your story; it's for Mama, Mama's story."

Then our mother said, "Come, come, come, come. What kind of story?"

I said, "Ah! You don't like me, but as for me I like you very much. But the way you don't like me, if I hear of your story, I don't want to tell you."

Then she said, "What kind of story is that?"

Then I said, "I don't know."

So then my father called me. My father knew that I was going to make kɔnkɔnsa, so he called and said, "What do you want?"

I said, "I want Ovaltine. Ovaltine with sugar in a cup, with bread."

So he said, "I think your mother won't finish cooking quickly. If you are hungry, you can eat that."

I said, "Yes."

Then he sent my big brother to go and buy it. And he said, "Sit down. I want to talk to you." So they brought all these things, and then he put it in water to make a nice Ovaltine, a cold one for me with my bread. Then he said, "What kind of something — what kind of secret do you have to tell your mother? Then you said she doesn't like you, so you don't want to tell her?"

Then I said, "No. But, *um,* I thought that this woman, when she was going away, she squeezed her face [1] and looked at me and made '*pfm-m!*'"

"Which woman?"

Then I said, "That woman who is selling tigernuts."

Then he said, "So you want to tell your mother?"

Then I said, "Yes. Because this woman has abused me. So if tell her, if I tell my mother, the next time she sees her, then they will make trouble. I didn't say anything to her. I thought this woman gave the tigernuts to you, or you bought all. That's why I ate them. If I wanted to steal, I would take

1. frowned

them in back of the house and eat them and hide the things. But I put the things inside — to let you know that I am the one who ate them. But she made me '*pfm-m!*' So I want to tell Mama." *Ha!*

Then he said, "You see, if you tell your mother, you already know that she doesn't like you. You know that she's not your own mother?"

Then I said, "Yes."

"And you know that she doesn't like you. Every time when I go to town, she used to beat you."

Then I said, "Yes."

"Even if you tell her this, she will still beat you. She wouldn't leave you because you have told her a good story. So it's better you don't tell her anything."

Then I said, "Is that so?"

Then he said, "Yes."

So, I didn't say anything. My mother was forcing me to say it, that day, but I didn't say it. I said, "Oh, I was playing." So it was finished.

After about three days, this woman, I don't know what: she had her idea, too. She bought a lot of fish to come and make a stew. Then she said, "Oh-h-h, Hawa, come and help me cook." She didn't send me to do anything. I just sat down. Then she said, "Come and look at the way to make the fish." I was just sitting down. And when she was frying the fish, she fried about two, then she put one on a plate and said, "Eat this. You have to watch well, eh?"

Then I said, "OK." Then I started eating this fish.

Then she said, "*Ey-y,* Mama. You are good, you know? Sometimes Papa used to do some things when we go to market." She didn't ask me anything, whether the fish was sweet, whether I was enjoying the fish. But I wanted to tell her everything, for her to like me from that day; then every time she will give me this big fish, you know. *Hee-hee-hee.*

Then I said, "Yes. Papa used to do some thing which — which is not good. One day when you go to market, come home around eleven o'clock. You will see them."

Then she said, "What? Who?"

I said, "You know what? Papa used to bring some tigernut woman here. One day I ate the tigernuts, then I put all the this thing back inside. Then this woman looked at me '*pf-fft.*'" So I wanted to — that was the day I wanted to tell you — then Papa give me some bread and some — Ovaltine — and he told me don't tell you. Don't let Papa hear it, eh? Papa told me that if you hear it, you will beat me. If you let Papa hear that I told you, then if I see something, I won't tell you again."

Then she said, "OK." She didn't say anything. So one day she went to market and then she came back home about eleven. This tigernut woman had come, and my father gave me money to go and buy chewing gum. I met my mother on the road, "Come. Come! They are inside! This woman is there."

When my mother came, they had closed the door. My mother just sat on the veranda. When my father opened the door, my mother took the tigernuts from the table and threw the tigernuts and the plate, all of it, into this woman's face. *Bim!* Then this woman fell down. Then my mother caught her. You know, when I saw that my mother was coming home, I didn't go to buy my chewing gum again. I was standing. I saw all this trouble: *tat-tat-tu-tu.* And then my father said, "What are you doing?!! What are you doing?! Don't do that!!" *Ta-ta-ta-ta-ta-ta! Hee-hee.*

Then the woman left her plate and everything, and went away. So then my mother started to abuse my father, "You haven't got sense! You are a foolish man! An old man like you! Do you cook for yourself? You have money to take a girlfriend!"

Then I was standing there, and my father couldn't say anything, so I had pity for my father. Then I said, "O-oh, Mama. Won't you stop? It's OK, if he understands you." *Shit! Ha-haa!* Then my father was about to suspect me, because when I was saying these things, I was looking at my father. Then my father looked at me. Then I said, quietly, "Mama, won't you stop?"

So my mother started shouting again. You know, some women, when they are doing something and you tell them to stop, then they start shouting: *Tat-tat-tat-tat.*

Then I started crying, "Leave me. Leave me —*sniff! sniff!*— leave me. What you are doing to Papa, I said 'Stop'; but you don't stop. *Sniff-sniff.* Leave me. I won't tell you something again." *Hah!*

So: my father got to know that I was the one who told my mother! I didn't know how to hide a secret! Sometimes I used to think I'm hiding something well, then I will want to say something and — it will be out. So my father didn't say anything. He pretended that he didn't hear. About three days later, he came home, then he called me, "Mama. Come." Then I came. He said, "Mama. You know, of all these children, you are the one I like. You are my mother." Then: "Why are you doing me so?"

Then I said, "What did I do, Papa?" And I started smiling. That time I was very funny: when you say you are serious, you will make me laugh.

Then he said, "*Hey! I'm serious!*"

Eh? Serious? How can I meet this serious? So — I started laughing.

Then he said, "*Sh-h-h!*" He took a stick, so I stopped. Then, if I wanted to look at my father, I wanted to smile. So I had to put my head down; I didn't look at his face. Then he said, "What did you tell your mama about this tigernut woman?"

Then I said, "Ah, I'm not the one who told her. I told her that some tigernut woman has abused me. She came to you; she has abused me; that's what I told her. But I didn't go to the market to tell her that this woman is in the house. I don't know the time when Mama came. So I don't know anything about it."

Then he said, "But why did you — you were telling her that if she doesn't stop, you — you won't tell her —"

I said, "Yes. I told her that this tigernut woman has abused me. But I didn't tell her that she did something with you. I said you bought me tigernuts from this woman, then I ate it, then I put it back on the plate because I didn't see you people. But you were discussing with her to get some room at the back of the house. That's the way you told me, no?" *Hee-hee.*

So my father said, "From today going, I won't give you anything. I won't buy you a dress. I won't buy any shoes. All your dresses will tear and leave you like that."

Then I went to my mother. I said, "Mama, you see. Because of you, Papa won't buy me any new dress. He told me he won't buy me anything."

Then my Mama said, "Leave him. I will buy everything for you." *Ha-ha-ha.* "Watch him. If he does anything, come and tell me."

So from then, if my father had someone, he wouldn't bring her to our house. He would take her to a friend's house. Then, the baby of that friend was also my girlfriend. We used to play together. So one day this girl came and said, "*Ey-y!* As for you, your father, every time he brings a woman to my Papa's room!"

"For what?"

"Your father is not tired?"

Then I said, "Eh?"

"He is not being tired of this thing: every time he used to bring a woman to my father's room."

Then I said, "Eh? What did you say?"

She said, "I have said that, your father, every time he used to bring a woman to our house. Even just now, I met him in the road with some woman. He asked me whether my father was in the house. I told him that my father is not in the house, because I don't like a man like that."

Then I said, "So what do you mean? You want to say that my father is a bad man?"

So I got a palaver with this girl, me and her. We started fighting —*Bim bim bim*. Then they came and caught us. "Why? Why?"

I said, "But why should she come and tell me foolishness that my father is not a good man, that he used to bring women to her father's house?"

Then there was one Kotokoli woman, and she asked this girl, "What did you say to her?"

She said, "I told her that her father is not a good man. Every time he used to bring women to my Papa's house. Then she started to tell me foolish things. That's why we are fighting."

So when my father came, this Kotokoli woman said, "Hey, my brother Issahaku. Come here, I want to tell you something." So my father went, and she said, "You see, the children are not good. If you are going to do something, you have to do it seriously. This girl came and told your daughter that you used to bring women to her father's house, so they fought today. If your wife hears this, it will be another problem for you, eh?"

Then my father called me. You know, I got some small-small scratches. So he took my hand, where it was scratched, and he said, "What made here for you?"

Then I said, "I have fought with somebody."

He said, "With whom?"

Then I said, "That girl from Alhassan's house who is called Jimama."

Then he said, "What did she do before you fought her. Didn't I tell you not to fight people?"

I said, "Yes. Because this girl told me you are not a good man. You used to bring women to her father's house. So how can she tell me this? Then she started abusing me. That's why we fought."

Then he said, "Don't let your mother hear it, eh?"

Then I said, "Will you buy me a dress?"

He said, "Yes! Tomorrow I will buy you a new dress, with shoes!" *Haha! Hee!*

Yeah, the next day, in the morning time when he was going to work, he said, "Oh, Mama. Can we go together?"

I said, "Yes!" Then we went to the market. He got me shoes with socks, and a dress. Ah-h! That day, I was happy. When I came home, I said, "Yeah, I'm a big girl."

Then my mother was also thinking, "No." Maybe my father did something bad, that's why he bought me this. He said that he won't buy me anything, and it's a long time and he didn't buy me anything. So my mother asked me, "Who bought you these things?"

Then I said, "Papa."

"Did he do that? So you got something nice. Did you tell him something nice?"

Then I said, "What thing nice?"

"But he bought you a dress."

Then I said, "Yes. Because I told him if he doesn't buy me a dress, I'm going to live with my grandmother. That's why." I didn't want to tell my father's secret to my mother again, because the day when she abused my father, it pained me! I didn't want her to disgrace him again. So I hid this one. I didn't tell her anything. *Hee-hee.*

Then from there, my father liked me. If he did something bad, he would say, "Eh, Mama. Between me and you, eh?"

Then I would say, "OK, Papa." *Heh-heh.*

So from then, every time, I used to eat with my father. I would get plenty of meat: he would give me all the meat, the soft one, and say, "Take this one and suck.[1] Take this one and suck." *Tee-hee.*

Yeah, so when I was young, me and my father, we were funny. We were very funny together. It's now when I am grown up, when he used to do a funny thing, he makes me laugh. But before, when he was doing things like that, I used to be serious. I thought we were serious. It's now when I have got my sense, if I think of the time I was young, I think it was funny — a little bit funny, you know. But when I was a child, and I was doing all these funny things, I didn't think it was funny. I thought it was all serious. Kumasi! I used to laugh if I remember it.

Special Agent

You know something funny? You know what I used to do? If somebody stole or took something in the house? You know, how children are, if they are in a group, at any time, somebody can go and take something from the mother. She won't even know. But the child will come and tell you, "I have got this in this way from our mother. She has this thing plenty, so she can't know. And we are many. Maybe she will think it's the other brothers."

So then you will say, "Aha! Is that so?"

Then somebody would say, "Ah, you know, yesterday, I had something like that from my mother. But you shouldn't say that I am the one. Maybe

---

1. consume thoroughly

she will catch the third or the fourth one in back of me,[1] and then she will say he is the one."

And I will say, "Yes, as for me, at our house, anybody who has a chance will take, because if one person takes, they beat everybody. So anyone who has a chance used to take."

Then somebody will bring his matter, "*Uh,* as for me, as for my mother, if you take something, that day you take the thing, she wouldn't be worried. She wouldn't look at it that you are the one. But the day when you don't take the thing, and maybe somebody took it, that is the day when she is going to beat you and say that you are the one who took it. So because of that, I have been doing it every time."

You see? Everybody will bring his problem about how they used to get these things from the parents. So: you can know all of them like that.

Yeah. So if somebody was taking things in the house, I used to tell. If I think about it now, I laugh, but I was serious at that time. It was not a joke. *Ha-ha!* They were beating them. But it was very funny because if they stole something, I would share with them. You know? Maybe if they got something, or some money, they would go and buy something: you will eat it together fifty-fifty, and you won't tell anybody. I will say, "Yes, I won't tell anybody." But later I will say it. So it was very bad—*ha!* I have taken my pay in two places.

And the old people liked me. They thought I was a good girl because I watched everything. If I saw something, I would come and tell them. And the children also thought I was good, because I used to say, "Hey, nobody should say it. If I hear it, I will know that you are the one who said it." You know? I used to give the other people warning, so the children also knew that for my part, I'm good.[2] So: *ha-ha!* And the old ones, too, they knew that I was good: I will tell them everything. And I will get my share, too.

So if anybody had any small thing, it was, "Oh, as for Hawa, she is a good girl. Hawa, come and have small." You see? And the children's side too: whenever they say something, they will say, "Ah-hah. If Hawa is there, she is good."

Sometimes I can tell something, and then I will put it on somebody. If I feel I can beat you, if I see that I'm stronger than you, then I will say, "He is the person who said it." You will say I lied. I will say, "It's true. You said it. I know you. You used to do things like that." Then we will start fight-

---

1. the younger children
2. They thought or were sure that I was not the one telling.

ing. And the others will believe me and tell you, "So you are the one!" They will beat you, too.

Only my brother knew my lie. Kofi. He used to *beat* me! He used to box me like I was his type.[1] When there was something in the house, if they called him and asked him, he knew that by all means it was me. He wouldn't say anything. He would wait until the day when my father would travel — you know that my father used to travel much — then he would call me, "Come here. That day, this matter I heard, I know that not anybody can say this. It was you. You told Papa this."

Then I would say, "What? What? What? You want Papa to know that you are trying to lie about me? Why don't you ask me in front of him?"

He would say, "Shut up."

Then he would just catch me, boxing me: *tak tak tak, kuk pip pip!* Then I would start to cry and then he would throw me away and go away. So only he knew I lied. But all the others, they didn't know.

So there are some people who have many children, and maybe one child will take something. The time you will ask them, maybe the one child doesn't know how to talk well, and he's afraid much, and you will think he's the one. You will catch that one and beat him, because the way he will talk and the way he will shake, you will think he's the thief. But the thief is *clever.* The thief will never have a slow mouth. Every time the thief is too much: he knows how to speak nicely, and he knows how to be doing everything for himself. So he will be saved, and they will beat the other one who didn't steal.

OK. You know, they are teaching him to steal, too. The other one will say, "They been beating me every day, that I'm the one who took this thing. And I didn't take it. And I know the one who is taking it. And they never touch him. So maybe I will become like him, and they won't beat me, too." You see? This is the way the children used to do. If they have been beating you every time, then one time you will think, "Ah, if I get a chance now, I can do it. Because even if I didn't do it, they have been beating me. They say I'm doing it. So it's better I do it than they just beat me, you know, so today I will get a profit on that all right."

The time when we used to do all this, my brothers and sisters in my father's house, you know, we were *plenty.* And we had many *bad* sisters and *bad* brothers. We had the ones who can steal money. We had the ones who were stealing sugar — like me! *Ha-ha! Hee-hee!* I used to steal sugar when I was young. When I was a small kid, I liked sugar like something. And they had some kids who were stealing fish, the dried fish. Some of my fa-

---

1. his size; someone like him

ther's wives were selling dried fish. I told you about my brother: he hid himself—*ha!*—behind the big basket of fish.

So you know, in our family, every time, they will catch two or three children who are stealing. In our house, every time it was like that. They will go and find somebody. And—*ha-ha!*

So you know, the people who used to bring this fish, many of them were friends to my father. When they came, the wife would buy them in cases like that from them. So there was one small boy, he got some iron and cut a hole four-square, so that he could put his hand inside the fish basket. This boy was different from the other one I told you about, but he was also a son of my father. Any time we were sitting outside, maybe conversing or playing, he would go inside the house: he's going to sleep. He would say, "I'm feeling to sleep."

So one day they caught him. And from the first day when they caught him too, they were catching him many times, but he didn't stop. Huh? Until he grew up. So now, they used to make rough with him. If he's doing something, if they say "Stop," and he doesn't, then they say, "*Pfft*, fuck off. He is stealing fish."

And when they would catch him, you know, every time, too, he used to challenge. He will be chewing the thing in his mouth. Then you will say, "What are you chewing?"

He will say, "I'm chewing nothing." *Ha!*

They will say, "What were you doing there?"

He will say, "Why? I shouldn't sit down there when I'm not feeling to sleep?"

Hee-hee-hee-hee! He was a clever thief, that boy! He used to challenge the mother every time. So if they caught him, my father would come. And if he was going to sleep, as they had been catching him on this case, they would go to the room. If he had gone to sleep a little bit, they would say, "Go and see." If you go, you won't go into the room. You would just be looking behind the door. Everybody had his mat, in a line. If he was not on his mat, you will look everywhere: there wasn't anybody in that place. Then: *Ah!* The cat has gone again! He is not on the mat! So my father would just get up, with his stick. Then if he went inside, you would hear *chp! chp! chp!* "What are you doing there?! What are you doing there?!"

Then he would say, "But I'm doing nothing! I'm sitting down! Why? Can't I sit down?"

Then my father would say, "How can you sit down in this corner there?"

He would say, "But yes! I don't feel to sleep. I feel like—" *Ha!* He wouldn't cry too. *Hey!* This boy! When he was young, they beat him proper for fish. He didn't steal anything else. Many women's children used to steal money and all these things. But he didn't steal money. Only the fish.

Sometimes, when he was going to school, he had his knickers[1] on. He packed fish here and here, in his pockets and inside the front of his knickers. The front would wake up like he had conceived. *Ha! Ha!* Then he would carry the fish. They would call him, "Come here! What? Come and take this."

Then he would answer that he was going. He would say, "Oh, don't you see that I'm late?" He had stolen. Sometimes we used to run behind him and catch him on the road and take the fish from his pocket. *Ha-ha!*

That boy, I didn't used to make kɔnkɔnsa on him. No. This boy used to get fish, and as for fish, I didn't want it. The ones I used to make kɔnkɔnsa on, the sisters and brothers, were the ones who used to steal money. You know, when they stole money, they would go and buy some things. So they were the people I used to make kɔnkɔnsa on. But this boy was just a fish boy.

And those children, how I used to get them: when they were going to do it, you know maybe sometimes I was in the house. OK. All the women and some of my sisters were selling things, and they used to go to market, and every time they used to leave me with the small children in the house. So if anybody came to the house, in the day, I would know who came first and who came second. Then if something was lost, this is the way they would ask me.

So: somebody is coming; he is coming to do something. So anyone who comes, if you have come first or you have come second, I will just follow you in the way that I like you: conversing—where you have been, how is it, is it nice, and all this. You are going to all the rooms, and I am following you, just talking. You know? Then I will see that maybe you want to do something. But maybe you are afraid of me. You know, sometimes, the way I knew them—my brothers and my sisters who used to like to steal—was if they would go into the room. When the families are not there, they showed me where the key is. I didn't used to open the room; I didn't have time for that. We had only one room key they would keep outside, and all the other rooms' keys were in that room. My first mother and second mother, and my father's room, and my brother's room—the ones who were grown up—they put all the room keys in a line, like hotel keys. So if anyone comes home, he knows his key. So the one who comes

1. wide-legged shorts; also, women's culottes

and takes the key and goes inside that room, maybe he will open three or four rooms.

And every time, when you are opening all these rooms, I will be following you, talking to you. Maybe you will go and open one of the rooms, and I know that place. So when you open there, then I have a mouth, so if it is our brother's room, I will say, "Eh-h, the last time, when I come here, it was this place which brother opened, and he has given me some money."

I wouldn't tell you straight that this is the place the person used to keep his money. But I wanted to tell you that I also know where they used to keep money. So in this case, when I see him doing that, and then when I talk this, somebody will leave all the doors open and come with me outside, then we will be outside talking, talking, talking. Then he will say, "Oh I forgot. Let me lock the rooms." You see? Maybe I too will forget, getting some mind to be playing with the children. Then he will go and lock the rooms. And then maybe he has taken something inside.

So OK. If they come home, then they will ask me who was the first person who came, and maybe I know this fellow was the first person, and the way he did to lock the door, I will know that he is the one who could steal this thing, because of the way he got into the room alone.

So this case, I would tell my father that when he went to work, I was also in the house, but I went out a little bit. Then maybe I will take the second or the third fellow who came to the house, to say that he came to the house, but he didn't keep long, and this fellow also came. So I don't know. When I tell my father like that, my father will say, OK, he will find the person by himself. So he will just shout-shout. He couldn't get the fellow, so he can't beat anybody, so he will just shout on anybody, and then he will stop it. He will say, "The fellow who has stolen this thing—"

You know, sometimes, when we were very young, when we were afraid of things, he used to call all of us and give us some story. He used to get some charcoal and give it to us, that you should swear everything, then you should touch the charcoal with your tongue. If you are not the one who stole it, there's nothing that can happen to you. But if you are the one who stole it, then your stomach will become big, and you will die. Sometimes he would say that your tongue will be coming out and hanging down, so that when you are grown up, you will be walking and your tongue will be following you. So all these things, if you are the one who stole, you will be afraid, and you will say the truth. But the seniors who were grown up, they knew that this was a lie. They trained them with this, and they know it well, and they don't have belief in it, so they don't care. He is the one who took it, but he can take this charcoal, and swear everything, and put it in his mouth, and even be chewing it. So my father couldn't know them much.

But he used to be pulling us young ones. We all used to get a problem, because we were the ones who were staying at home. Maybe our father would think that we were the one who stole. So we had to get a special C.I.D.[1] for these things, and you know, I was the head of this work.

So every time, when they were all going to town, my father used to leave the house early. The second wife was the one who was leaving last. So my father used to tell her that I am clever: if she's going to put the key anywhere, she should call me and show me. Every time, if she was going to the market, when we were playing outside, she would call me. Then she would say, "See where I have put the key? Watch it. Anyone who comes and take it, you have to watch the fellow."

But we were the *same* people! You know? There was not any outside person who would come and take the key. All of us with the same father, and all different mothers, we were inside. But she would say that any one of us who would come and take the key, I should watch him well. So I was the watchman, and I had to do this, because every time they used to think that we people who were in the house when they all went to work, we were the ones who used to steal. And at that time, you know, I was not tall. I couldn't go to where they used to hide things. So it used to be wonderful. I had to be a good C.I.D. at that time.

I had one sister who used to steal. When she stole from our brother's room, then I went to talk to her the next day. When my father asked me, you know, I told you that I would tell my father that I didn't know the person who went into the room. I just said that the third person was the first one who was coming to the house, and then he didn't take a minute, and then some other people came, but I didn't see anyone open this room or that room. But then I would go back to the first fellow who came to the house, if I was sure that he was the one, and I would talk to him alone. I would say, "You see how I like you? You know, suppose I didn't like you, I could say that you were the first fellow. Even if you are not the one who took this thing, they would say that you are the one. But the way I like you, you know, that's why I didn't say this thing. So you should know that I also like you. So the next time, if you are going to go and do something like that, you should wait until somebody comes to the room before going out. If you do that, I can even say that it is that fellow. Because if it's not you, you know that I don't like anybody like you."

1. detective. The detectives on a British police force are the C.I.D., or Criminal Investigation Department.

So I was doing this with all my sisters and brothers, the seniors. Yeah. If I get you, I will get you alone. I won't get you when you are two. No. If I say I like you, the other one will get to know that this is also the way I am doing with him. So anyone who does something, I will just get him. And I used to watch them. The time when they think they are alone, they have been sitting, or they start doing something: then I will go and stand there. I will say, "*Heh!* You are busy!" You know? I will start laughing. "*Hee-hee!* Are you busy?"

Maybe you will say, "Yeah."

Then I will say, "What are you doing? Can I look? Can I come and have a look?"

Then, you know, as I am the younger sister, maybe the senior one will think, "Ah, this my younger sister, maybe she has some good mind on her today. She has come to see me like that." So he will say, "Yes, you can come and see what I'm doing. Yes."

So when we are sitting, then we are looking, and what he's doing is serious. Then I will say, "You see that day? That day, what happened? Don't you think the way I talked for you is good?" *Ha!* I was smiling all the time. You know, when I would be saying this thing, I used to have a *big* smile. *Ha!* "Yeah, don't you think I have been good to you on that day?"

And maybe, you know, I had some bad sisters and bad big brothers. So then he will say, "What—What—What did you do? What did you do for me?"

Then I will say, "Oh? So is this nothing I have done for you? You know, the time when Papa came and asked me who has come to the house, is this not a big talk I talked for you?"

Then maybe that fellow, he will be doing something, so he wouldn't mind me. He will say, "Mm-hm. Mm-hm." You know? Yeah. "So what is that?"

Then I will say, "Yeah, because I like you, you know. I like you. I don't want— the way Papa used to hate the others, I don't want Papa to be hating you like that. That's why I said that. You don't believe me?" Maybe the fellow will believe me nicely, and then I will say, "Oh, I'm going."

Then maybe he will say, "Good night" or "Bye-bye." Then I won't go. I will be sitting down again, talking a different thing. I will bring different talks, you know, that one day, sister had taken a cedi or two cedis from Papa's pocket. She gave me a shilling, and she told me not to tell Papa. I didn't tell Papa, because she had given me a shilling. But one time I told sister that I was going, and she didn't give me anything. So I will be talking these things. And—you are—*ha!* I will be talking different things like that, so maybe, if you have sense, you will think that, "Yeah, this my younger sister, because she got something from that one, she didn't say anything. So maybe she needs something from me, too."

But the ones who didn't have experience, they wouldn't mind me at all. I would be telling them I'm going, I'm going — about four or five times. If I say all these things, and you don't mind me, then I will be fed up and I will say, "Won't you give me a sixpence?" See? I wouldn't leave it free. Kaɛ![1] You will let me talk a long time like that, and you want to leave me like that? So some of them would say, OK. They were just fed up with me, you know, because I used to do this thing with them every time. So they would say, "OK, I don't have sixpence, but I have threepence."

I would say, "Never mind. I can buy porridge with it tomorrow morning."

And you know how very funny I am? When I was going, I used to collect money. I had a box from the carpenters. I used to keep money, *plenty* of money, inside it. Nobody knew how I got it. The time when it was Christmas, and I brought it out, then I told my father to go and buy me some guarantee shoes. Everybody wondered. It was under my father's bed, where he used to pray.

Yeah. I used to keep this box seriously. All this money, I used to collect some from my sisters and my brothers. And there were some people outside who used to see me as a small baby. They used to say, "Smile!" You know, when I was a baby, I think I was very funny. I used to have a name: they said I had small, *small* teeth. I think when my teeth changed when they became big. But my father told me that when I was young, I had *small* teeth like a rat. But they were very *white*. You know, a baby doesn't know how to chew a chewing stick,[2] but my teeth were very white. So some people used to call me, "Hawawu!" Then I would run to the person.

Then he would say, "Laugh!"

Then I would say, "I won't laugh. I won't laugh."

Then he would say, "Oh, don't you like me?"

Then I would say, "No, I don't like you."

Then: "You don't like me?"

Then I'd say, "No."

Then, "Suppose you liked me: you would laugh?"

Then I'd say, "Yes. But I don't like you. I won't laugh."

Then he would say, "OK, laugh for money."

1. In this context, the word is an affirmation of the position she is taking, as in, "What?! You lie!"

2. the indigenous toothbrush, a small piece of hardwood used to polish the teeth. One chews it for a while, and then the fibers become like a brush.

Then I would make my hand like this. And among all the money, what I liked, the heavy money of all the moneys, was the *kobo* which had a hole.[1] If you gave me the white one, then it was *big* money. I didn't want the red one: only the white ones. So if you gave me that money, then I would laugh. Then I would go. You see?

So *all* these funny things which I used to do when I was growing up, many people used to dash me money. Then a time came when I didn't feel like doing these foolish things. Then if somebody saw me, he would say, "Ah, this girl, when she was young, she was very nice." And some people would see me doing something by heart, and they would say, "No, no, no, no, no! The world has changed. This girl, when she was young, you would like her!" And some people would say, "My wife, come and take two shillings."

So I used to keep this money from these people and add it to the amount I was collecting from my brothers, too. I kept all of the money together.

So I was between all of them. Only my brother, the one from one mother, one father: he knew my secret, because I was so stupid, I said that we are brother and sister, and I thought that as we are from the same mother, the same father, we are the real, proper family. So I had to tell him my secret one day. And he got me in this way. So he used to beat me, everywhere, for anything that happened to him in the house because maybe I was the one who had said it. But I had my box for that. *Ha!*

So what I was doing with my brothers and sisters, if I got this money, if you gave me this bribe, then I knew that: yes, if you didn't do it, you wouldn't have given me the bribe. Isn't it? You have done it.

Then I will go to my father, and I will tell my father, "Look, do you know this thing which is lost, the one which you have been asking about? This fellow has been saying this and that to me, and he made me swear

1. British West African currency, used in Gambia, Sierra Leone, Nigeria, and Gold Coast from 1907 through 1958, had different coinage with holes: penny, half-penny, and one-tenth penny. Hawa's classification of "white" and "red" reflects the fact that tenth-pennies, half-pennies, and pennies were coined at different times in bronze and in copper-nickel. Kobo is now the name for 1/100 of a contemporary Nigerian naira. The word is borrowed from the English "copper" in Hausa as well as Krio (the creole language of Sierra Leone) and was also widely used throughout West Africa in Pidgin. My Dagbamba teachers in northern Ghana told me that when coins initially replaced cowrie shells, they used the word kobo as a name for the penny, which was one hundred cowries. In Asante Twi, similarly, a penny is kaprɛ. When the Ghanaian pesewa replaced the penny, some people used the various terms interchangeably. Holed half-pennies and pennies were common souvenirs people gave me when I first went to Ghana in 1970.

many things — you know — and as my mother has died, I have sworn on all these things and — so that's why I don't want to say it — but I want to say it to you because I'm in the house — maybe you think that I'm the one who is doing it — or the others — maybe I have an arrangement with the others who are doing it — but I know nothing about it. But that day, that fellow came. He opened all the doors. When he went to this place, he opened the place, and I told him that this is the place where maybe Papa or Mama or my brother used to get money from that place to give to me. And then he opened it, and when I was talking to him, he came out, and then I was following him. So he went to outside and then when we started to converse, he said that he was going to lock the room. So before he locked it finish, then he put the key there. When he came, he didn't take time, and then he told me that he was going to the market again. So I think that he is the one who took it. But that day, why I didn't want to tell you straight, it was because he was there, and he let me swear a lot of things. So I think that you are my father, too, so if I tell you, even if I swear on my mother, if I tell you, I don't think anything will happen to me. This is not some kɔnkɔnsa that I am going to make, but you shouldn't let that fellow know that I am the one who told you."

Yeah. You see? The fellow: maybe he didn't give me any warning or make me swear anything, but I just used to say this to my father, that because of that, he shouldn't tell the fellow. If the fellow gets to know that I am the one who told him, it is bad. So I just lied. The person wouldn't say, "Don't say it to Papa." *Eh?* They wouldn't be warning me or something like that. No. But I am going to tell my father that the person warned me, "Don't say it." So my father will believe in this, you know.

Then maybe my father will say, "OK, if that will be the case, you try to watch the house well. I won't ask the fellow today. I know the day I will ask the fellow."

So the day I would tell my father this, my father wouldn't ask that fellow. He wouldn't ask you about that. He would forget about it, because that thing has passed. But when something or some money was lost from the house again, another day, then he would call you, the same fellow I said was the first fellow who came. Maybe you are not the one who was stealing that day. But I have told about you so they know you. So that day, you will get your share. You are the one they are going to beat. The real one who stole the money that day, he will have his body cool, and then he will sleep nicely. He ate a lot of chicken or something outside. You know? But the next day, I am going to see that fellow, too, to collect something. And then I will collect it, and your own will come maybe a week later, or after three or four days. *Ha!* So they were all getting their beatings.

And what made them not to know that I was the one who was doing it: you know, the day they will ask about this thing, the way I would talk in front of everybody, they would believe in me, that I was not the one who was going back to say anything to Papa or something like that. And maybe the day Papa will get you and put this problem on you and beat you, you are not the one who did this thing. So not anybody had any bad idea on me that I was the one who was doing this thing.

9 YOUNG LOVE IN THE VILLAGE

: *The Sister Who Refused Marriage*
: *Marrying Sisters*
: *Escape to Bobo*
: *Further Varieties of Village Seduction*
: *A Village Courtship*
: *Catching Chickens*
: *The Sweetness of Villages*

: THE VILLAGE IN BURKINA FASO :

The Sister Who Refused Marriage

So you know, the time we were growing up, we were funny. Yeah. This is why I said that village life is free. As children, too, we were free. Everybody will do his own. It is only that sometimes the old people will force the children, and that one, sometimes it is very, very bad.

You know, there was one of my sisters. When I knew her, I was maybe about seven years old at that time, or something like that. This girl grew up in Kumasi, but then they sent her to our village in Upper Volta. So she was there, and then they were going to give her to a man to marry, and she didn't agree. Every day my father was beating her. And my fathers[1] used to tie this girl with a rope! They put her on a tall table, then they tied her hands, and they drew the table out. They just hung her up like that, from morning to afternoon for three days—*oh!* She was just hanging there. Her foot was not on the ground. At times she would look like she was dead. And then they would put her down, and they would put

---

1. her father and his brothers, or senior men of her father's generation in the area

water on her and lock the room. She would be sleeping. Morning time, she was there. She didn't die. She was strong, so she couldn't die.

When she was in the room, if my father was going out, he would lock the door and take the key. That room had that type of door; it wasn't this village door, the woven one. This girl couldn't get water; she couldn't get anything. We children used to pass in the window. There was no screen, only some wire, so if she wanted something, we could give it to her in that window.

She had chosen the boy she wanted to marry, and our father didn't agree. They took the two of them, the boy and the girl, to the chief's house. They beat these two people very well. Then they put them in the sun. Oh, that thing was very hard, you know. After about three days, before they left them free, this boy said he didn't want the girl again, and the girl too said she didn't want the boy again. Then they said this girl should go to the old man. This girl didn't say anything. She went to the old man. After about two or three weeks' time, she got up early in the morning, and then she and this boy ran away.

From that time, when I was seven years old, for many years my father didn't have any letter from her. It's not long ago that we had her news, but for many years, he didn't hear anything of her. And she didn't come back home, too. I thought maybe she was somewhere enjoying, or I thought maybe, too, the way they beat her, maybe she had died. I used to think she was dead, because if it was me, I would let people know where I am. I would come home and show you people that you tried to kill me, and I didn't die yet. You will die and leave me! *Ha-ha!* Yeah? Yeah. It was very bad. But if she's in the world and she doesn't come home, it's not good. Even she could write a letter: "I'm still living in life. But I don't want to see you people because you treated me bad." That one would also be good. I wouldn't give my address: you will see the letter; you won't get any address to write me or to think that one day, "Oh, now I must go and find this girl!" No! You will just see the letter. If I like, I can give you a copy of my picture, to give all my families, to know that they didn't kill me. So I thought that maybe she's dead. She was a nice girl. Of all of my father's children, she was a nice, beautiful girl. Even still they have her picture, because sometimes my father used to think of it.

So from that time, if my father gives you to some man, and you say you don't want it, he won't force you too much, or be beating you. He will say, "OK, it's finished. You can go your way. You are not my daughter." *Ha!* Yeah, that's what he used to say to us. He said it to many of us, that we should go away. Eh? We came back. But as for her, she went away, and she didn't come back. The way he treated her was very bad.

Even my father used to say that he treated the girl so badly that even if she's in the world, she doesn't write him. And so he is begging God to give her a good place to rest. When he said that, I would say, "*Ah-hah!* Now when you don't see her, you are saying that. Suppose if you see her, every day you will abuse her." *Ha!*

So our sister was lost. It was very, very bad. Stupid! People are stupid. If it was me, I would kill somebody there. *Ha! Ah!* If I don't kill you, then I will know that I don't have power to kill you. I'll poison you. Even if you are my father, and you treat me like that, I won't say anything; I'll live in the house with you, and I will poison you. *Ha-ha!* When you die, will you come back and do me bad? *Shit!*

So sometimes when he's talking of this case, he will make like we should pity him. Then I will say, "You pity! *Pfft!*"

Yeah. I have many sisters: this girl passed all of us. She was a nice copper color. This rope they used to catch her wrists made a mark—black, black—like the thing some people make with needle to put writing or something in their hands.[1] And then, these our people, they are very bad. You know that kind of rope with the rough thread: when they tied her and finished, then they would take the hand and put it in water so that the rope would tighten very well. So this girl's hand: here was big—swollen up—and then here was making some black marks. When they left her, she could not carry heavy things.

My father hung her like that for three days. If he hung her from morning time, then at twelve o'clock, this girl would be like she was dead. He would put her down on the table. Then they would loosen the rope. They would put water on her. They didn't give her food. We children used to steal food for her, when my father went out. And sometimes when we stole this food for her, she started crying. She couldn't eat it. And when we saw her like that, we also used to cry.

Then my other elder sister said to her, "Look, you should just agree for the old man. It's nothing. Even, this old man won't keep long. He is going to die. So it's better to live in your life. It's better." Then my sister would say no, that she wished to die, rather than to go back to this world. They must kill her. It's better for her. And then they would start crying again. So if the two of them were crying, then we too, all the young ones, we also cried like that. It was a pity, you know.

Then if our father was coming, everybody would go and wash his face and make his face nice. We would sit down. If they saw that you are doing that, you would also be among the ones for them to beat. They would say

1. tattoo designs on the hands

you are spoiling her. Once my father came home, and my other sister didn't
know he was coming, and she was talking to my sister at the window, and
he came and caught her and beat her. He said, "Why are you talking to
her in the window? That's why she's a bad girl. She doesn't want to listen
to my talk." And then this girl's mother just became slim. It was very pitiful. The mother had nothing to say. She also couldn't eat, too.

Our people are very bad. He kept her for about three days, hanging.
Every day, he hung her from eight-thirty in the morning to twelve o'clock
in the day time. Then after the third day, he asked her, did she change her
mind or she didn't change her mind? Then she said she cannot change
her mind. Whatever he likes, he can do with her. Then they took her and
that boy to the chief's house and beat them well. And then this boy said
he didn't want her again. And she also said she didn't want this boy
again. So they said she had to go to the old man.

You know, when they were treating her like that, the old, old people,
some of them came and begged for her. These old people, if they are in
the same area, if they see the other is giving the child some treatment like
that, sometimes they come and beg the person to leave the girl. So then:
that was the time they took her and the boy to the chief's house. Then
from there, they left her. They didn't tie her any more. She went to the
old man's house. She used to go to the pipe and bring water, and she was
doing all this work in the house. Nobody knew she would go away. She
did that for about two or three weeks' time, then she just went off. She
ran away from the house. And I think maybe, when she and the boy were
at the chief's house, that was the time they made their plan, and later
they went off. I think so. When they left, the boy's family didn't hear of
him, and the girl's family didn't hear anything about her either. We cried.

For many, many years, they didn't see her. When she came back home,
she had two children. She is now in Kumasi with the husband. Even she
talks to my father. But I don't talk to her. At that time, I thought she was
good, but when she came back, she used to show some kind of way that I
didn't like. She used to talk about me in some kind of indirect way, like
she is giving me advice but she is saying something against me. I don't like
it. You know our people, sometimes they advise people: they are just abusing you. I don't want that kind of advice. So I don't agree with her.

Yeah, the time they tied this girl, when she said she wanted to go to toilet, they would put rope on her hands, and either my father would go
with her or my big brother. They would loosen the rope to let her enter
the toilet. And people were looking at her. If this girl had something to
poison herself, she would have poisoned herself, because she was seeing
many, many, many disgracing things. They wanted to give her to a man in

our village, but this girl was born in Ghana, and she grew up in Ghana. How can you go to this fucking village and give her to some man to live in that village? She cannot live there. And she was also a bad girl, you know, because she refused. Our place is like that: when they give you to some-body to marry and you refuse, then everybody is annoyed. You know? They will say, "You don't listen to your father's talk": it's a heavy abuse. So if a father tells a daughter to do something, whether you like it or you don't like it, at our place, they say you have to do it.

So every time, oh, when this girl had to go to the toilet, they would tie her. Then they were outside with this rope, and then she would enter the toilet. And the children would come out to look when she was passing, and then everybody would say, "They are bringing her, they are bringing her." Then everybody would come out to see her. You know, because they tied her with rope, it was wonderful for everybody. So they used to come and watch it and say, "They are bringing that bad girl." Many people came and watched.

Now, not many people will do all this. But before, they had these things, and nobody will complain. Some boys, they grow up, and the father will marry for them. They will find a woman for you: you don't know the woman. The day you will know the woman is the day when they are going to bring the woman to the house, when they have made all the marriage.[1] And you a woman, too: they can find you a man: you will never know the man until the day they make your wedding to take you to his place. It's very funny. Maybe they will take you to the place, and you won't like it. Then if you try to refuse —*ehh?*— it's war. Yeah, all the village people, the whole country: they are against you. Even if they are killing you with knives, nobody will come and say, "Oh-h, don't do that. Oh-h, leave her." And when you are passing, you look like somebody who is a bad person, to them. And everybody will say, "Yeah, it's that one. It's that one." Then everyone will try to come out and look at you, you know, and all this is disgrace.

Yeah. When they brought her, we were about four sisters who fol-lowed her. At our place, we are supposed to stay with her to cook for her. Every time, when Muslim people make marriage, the younger sister and some friends have to stay with the girl for about one week, or two weeks. Then everyone can find his way, and these girls will leave you with your husband.

---

1. In this type of ceremony, the marriage prayers are said at the woman's father's house; the husband waits in his house while some of his family and friends attend the cere-mony and then walk with the bride to the husband's house.

Marrying Sisters

I told you that at our place, when you marry and you have many sisters, then if you like, you can bring a younger sister to stay with you to be washing your plates or anything. And the two sisters can marry one man. I have told you about it already. *Ha-ha!* My father's wives, they are family. But as for them, they are not the same father, the same mother. They have the same father but different mothers. But they are the same family, from the same house, as "your daughter and your brother's daughter." My father has those two wives now in the farm.[1]

In our village, I saw it with sisters from one father and one mother. *Ha!* When the senior one married, they gave her the small one. That's what they do. The young one will be with her senior sister until she also grows up. If she grows up, if you are the senior and you like your younger sister, and you know that you cannot feel jealous on her, you can give your sister to your husband. When I saw this, then I said, "*God!* One father, one mother — it's *wonderful!*" She's not different; even, if she was a different friend, it would be better, you know. *Ha-ha!* Yeah. One father, one mother. I saw this in our village. If you ask a real Voltaique,[2] he will tell you this.

So our place: they are very funny there. You see this thing? If you marry, you will take your younger sister. You cannot take your older sister with you; you will take a small girl, about six years old or something like that. Yeah? So this girl I was talking about, my sister: when she was going to get married, they brought her to our village. We were four sisters who followed her to come. The three sisters will leave, and the one she chooses, that one can stay with her and serve her. So if you grow up and then your sister likes you a lot, and she doesn't want you to go away from her, then she will give you to her husband. Then you start to have babies with your sister's husband, sleeping with the one man. Yeah. He is your husband, too. *Ha!*

You know, I have a younger sister called Ayisha, and the first time, I used to have fun with her. She was always with me. Then one time my father told me that Ayisha is growing up, and he said that if somebody asks Ayisha who she is going to marry, she says she won't marry unless I also come home to marry. Then I called Ayisha and said, "No. This time they don't choose for you. Anyone you see, if you like him, then you can marry him."

1. in the village
2. a person from Upper Volta who knows the customs there

Then my father said I didn't say it well.

Then I said, "Why didn't I say it well? So I must tell her what? To wait for me? If I get a husband, then I will come and carry her with me?"

Then my father said, "Why are you pressing like this?"

Then I said, "No, because I don't want — you know, I like her, but I don't want to marry one man with her. So I must tell her — if she can find a good one and she knows that she can stay with him, if the man is a correct man." *Ha!* Yeah, I gave my father that reply, because my father was saying that thing: he was telling me that people were seeing that this girl was growing up, and this was what she was saying.

OK? Our village is like that: when they see a girl who is growing up, and she is starting to get small-small breasts, then somebody will come and say, "I want your daughter to marry." Yeah? She hasn't grown. Maybe it will be after three years or after four years before that person will marry the girl. But when the girl starts to grow, then at that time some people can come and ask the father.

And the father will also say, "Oh, she has a sister or she has a stepmother, or you people should go to see that fellow before seeing me. As for me, I'm the one who borne her, but I'm not the one who is looking after her." You see their ways?

So that fellow who wants the girl, he will come and find that person, the one they told him about, maybe the senior sister, or maybe the stepmother, or the grandmother. Then you will go to that person, that you are asking that you want this girl to marry, and that and this. Then maybe that person will say, "OK. I accept," or "I don't accept," or "I will ask the girl." This time, they used to ask the girl, because many girls refuse men. So they used to ask them.

If they ask the girl, the answers she is also going to give: maybe the girl will say, "Ah well, in this case, my senior sister is not here. She is the one who is helping me at any time." Or: "My mother is the one who is helping me." Or: "This person, so if you see her, if she agrees, then I also agree." It means that the girl maybe likes that fellow. So the person she shows, if that person agrees, then she will also agree to be married to that man. By that time, the girl is your wife. But she won't go to your house yet. If the girl is still little, she can stay with the family, maybe for three or four years. But if it is someone who is getting breasts, then maybe after one or two years, they will marry this girl to that person and take her to his house. That's the way they do.

So my father said that somebody came to marry my sister, and she said, no, she cannot marry somebody now because she's waiting for me, "If Hawa comes, I will say yes."

Then I said, "Ah, yes. But she cannot wait for me, because I'm not getting married, and I don't know the time I'm going to do it. So it's better if she can find somebody she likes. Even if I marry, I cannot take her with me. I like her, but —"

You know, that girl was saying that maybe she will marry somebody I don't like. So she wanted to see my mind. So I told her that anyone she sees that she likes, I will like the fellow, too. So she can marry him. The way I like her, even if she marries some bad fellow, I will like the person too, because she is a nice girl. Yeah. We cut it short.

So at our place, some sisters marry the same man. And some sisters fight later, too. Look: my father's wives, sometimes they can fight for about two weeks. They won't come together to talk or eat or anything. But they are sisters. Sometimes the big one used to say my father loves the small one past her. And sometimes she used to beat the younger sister.

In our country, too, even if you are strong and your senior sister is small like me, she can even beat you. If I am senior, then if I challenge you or if I slap you, you can't reply. At our place, you won't do anything. Some of my younger sisters are tall and fat, but I can slap them free. One time when I got grooving, I said, "Is this thing true?" I didn't believe I could just slap them, so I said I will test this girl and see if it is true. I brought some topics to one of my younger sisters, and then she said something. Then I just said, *"Shut up!!"* Then she didn't reply. Then I thought, "Oh. Pity!" *Ha-ha!* I know that as for me, if my senior sister slaps me, I won't forgive her like that. *Ha!* So if I tell one of my younger sisters like that, and she becomes quiet quickly, then I feel sorry.

Escape to Bobo

So this time, now people are choosing more and more. Sometimes, some girls choose the husband, but they don't like to refuse the parents. And I think that before, some people also used to refuse. But they say that the people who refuse to marry, such children become bad: they don't want to marry; they are just going around. So if somebody sees that with one of his children, then when something comes like that, he won't allow them to refuse. He will think that if I allow her to refuse, she will be like that other one, and all my children will be bad. So she must leave. That girl cannot refuse and stay here again.

And so this time, some girls, if a girl likes a fellow, then when she sees that the family wants to force her, then she will make an arrangement with that fellow she likes. Then the two of them will run in the night time: in the morning time, you won't find them. Maybe they will go and live at Ouagadougou. They can hide themselves. Especially, the woman can hide herself in a room for about six or seven months. And some women, if they do that, they can conceive. They will give birth to their child. After, they will go home to greet the family: "We have come back." Then at that time, you cannot take her from the man again, because she has already got a child with him. So you will accept.

So that's the way some of them make their marriage at our village. Yeah. Some people go with the men to Abidjan, or Bobo. Before she is coming, she has two or one children on her arm. Then when they come to the family, the family has to accept. They cannot say no, because these people have already got a family. So how can they say "no" again? And that man they were forcing you to marry, maybe because you have already got a child, he wouldn't like you again. Some of them used to do that.

And then some of them wait until they make the marriage with the man she doesn't like. The girl also has a boyfriend, and after maybe one month, then she will make arrangements with the boy. One night the boy will come and pick the girl from the husband's place —*pffft!*— they are away. Before they come back, maybe they will have two or three children. Then the boy will say to the husband, "Ah! Why? Can you take my wife with the children? You can't. If you like, you can take your wife. I'll take my children." And the husband won't like the girl again, so he will just say, "She's for you." So these boys and girls in the village, they have an easy way to marry. You know? *Ha!* Yeah. But it's a problem, too.

One baby from my mother's big sister, she did that. She went to Bobo, and now she is in Abidjan. She had two babies, and later she came home to stay with the mother a little bit, then she went back again. She came with the husband, and then the husband was also working, so he stayed two weeks. Then after about two months, this girl followed him. The family cannot do anything about it, so they must accept their marriage.

So in our place, there are many people who are marrying like that. And sometimes the family will report them to police, so if they reach somewhere and somebody sees them, the police will catch them. And maybe they will take a car to catch them. So these two who are running, if they reach any place where there is a border or a police barrier[1] on the road, they don't pass there. They drop from the car, and then they leave the road and walk across the border, or they pass into the bush behind the barrier, you know, to cross, and then they will come and join another car again. So they have problems.

---

1. Border guard and police checkpoints are common on major roads.

That girl of my mother's sister, the girl who came home, I asked her: when they were going, didn't she fear. She said they woke up from our village at three o'clock in the morning. *Ha!* They started to walk; they didn't get a car. They walked past about two villages before they got a car. When they got to the border of our area — on the Bobo road, there are some police people on the road there — when they got to that place, they had to drop from the car and go through the bush. There was a very small path, so they asked one small boy, and the boy directed them, and they had to dash the boy something. Then they passed from that place and joined the road again, behind the police, and then they joined another car again. If they were dropping, they just said that they will drop there, and they took all their bags. They didn't leave their bags that they were coming to join the car after. No. They carried all their things on their heads and then passed. Then they had to stand there for another car again, until they got to Bobo.

Then when they got to Bobo, she was seven months in a room. She didn't go out, because there are many people from our village in Bobo. They were afraid that if these people saw them, they would come and give the complaint, and then maybe the family would come to take the girl. The boy could go out; he could do anything. He was working. If anybody saw him, "Oh, you are here?" "Oh yes, I came here, because our place is terrible. I liked some girl, and because of that girl, they hate me. So if I didn't leave the village, they would say it's because of me the girl doesn't want to marry." But the girl was with him! The boy used to do shopping for about one week, and put it down. They had a kerosene stove, so before the boy would come, she would finish cooking.

And then she told me a funny thing. She used to piss in a pisspot, and this boy had to carry it and throw it. Then I said, "Oh, but just outside the house, nobody can see you."

She said, "No, we were afraid that maybe one time, somebody will come there to visit somebody — maybe he doesn't know I am there — and then he will see me. So every time, we did everything in the room. We were afraid."

"And shit, too?"

She said, "Yes! I used to shit in the night." She didn't shit in day time. There was no toilet in the house, so the people in the house had to go to the public toilet. So she would go to the bathroom with a pisspot in the night and shit in it, and then the boy would carry it to outside. She would bathe early in the morning — about four o'clock or three-thirty. Then there was nobody awake in the house. And the night, after about ten o'clock, when people entered the rooms to sleep, then she would come out and bathe, and then she would go to shit. *Ha!* And that is how she lived. Seven months — those seven months — oh! She had about four months and she conceived, so then when she reached eight months, she could go everywhere she liked. Everybody saw her with the big stomach. They had nothing to say again. Whether they tell the man or they don't tell him, all is off. It's too late. Yeah. That is what she did.

And some people used to run, and they don't get a good place to hide themselves, and then the families will go and bring the girl again. If you don't have luck, they will bring you back. That's why they used to hide themselves very well. If they get you back, it will be hard to find a way to go away again. So these things, we still have them in our village. Yeah. Still people run away with the girls, or they take somebody's wife and run away.

Some of the boys, this time, they are something like psychedelic, you know. Somebody can come and steal somebody's wife. These boys come and change the woman. I don't know why the women used to agree, to leave your babies and your husband, and you will follow the other one. Maybe because your husband is old, and he never traveled before, and you are not old, or you are very young. If she sees the boys who used to be from the village and they are now staying at some place like Abidjan, when they come with these big guarantee shoes and these dungarees, then they will boss you to take you from your husband and leave your children. *Ha!* And you will go with that fellow. *Ha!* Oh, yeah, it's very, very funny.

My father's small brother — he's not from the same mother, but they are the same family — he brought his wife from Ghana. He had two children with her. Some boy just came and stood up and — *pffft!* — with this girl. They don't know where they are. When I went there, my father was telling me it was about one year when this girl went away.

Yeah, they will come back, too. They will stay until they get children, and then they will come back. And then the family will make the marriage for them, too. Uh-huh. And then the first husband cannot take the girl again. You are the first husband, and you have your first children. But how are you going to take her back again, when she went and had about one or two children with another man? Will you like that girl again? Before she will come back, maybe you have got a good wife again.

So it's finished. She will pay nothing, because she has children with you. Even if she hasn't got any child, she has nothing to pay. All the things that you bought to make the marriage,[1] she will leave them with you. These women, when they are going like that, they don't carry things.

---

1. In Muslim marriage, the man will buy many cloths and cooking and household items before the marriage will be performed.

Maybe they will carry about two or three cloths and then tie them in some scarf. She won't hold any bag. And all these other things you bought to marry her, she will leave all of them. If you want, you can keep your things. Some of the nice people used to take the things back to the family. He will say, "Oh, it's not you people's fault. If the girl doesn't like me, then I have nothing to do with those things. I'm not a woman. I will marry someone else, but if I want to marry again, I won't give this one to that woman I'm going to marry. So you people can have it." Yeah. And some bad men used to say, "I will keep it with my things. I bought it, so you can't take my anything. I'm lucky. I can be married to another woman and give to her." And some men who have children, they used to think, "OK. I'll keep it for the children, when they grow up." Yeah. So some of these girls leave their old husbands like that. And then even some people can be married when they are young together, you know, and the girl will run away from the young husband like that with a new boyfriend.

Further Varieties of Village Seduction

You know, some of the young boys stay in the village. They were born there and grew up there, so they don't know *any* other life. You will see a young man about twenty-four years old: if you see him, you will say that, "Ah, maybe he is about forty or forty-eight years old." This sun: every day they are in it, doing hard work, digging to make a farm to get something to eat. You will see them so, and then, too, I think they don't have enough water, so every time you will see their feet, and this place in the back is cut.[1] Yeah. If you see the face, he is a nice boy, but if you see the body, you will think that he is somebody who has caught about forty years.

And the young ones who run to Abidjan, Ouagadougou and these big, big towns to work, to get pay at the ending of the month and buy many things, and they bathe there and they become clean, maybe when he was going away, maybe some girl was a friend or something to him before. Maybe he has gone away for about two years. He doesn't come. Then this girl cannot wait: she has to get married. When the man comes back, if this girl still loves the man, or if this man still loves this girl, then he knows why he's going back: he's going to take this girl from the husband. Whether you have one baby or two babies, if you like the boy, you will leave all these babies and follow him and go away. And some of them, too, they don't know each other. She will just meet him and like the way the

---

1. The callouses on the heels are cracked.

boy is. Then she can make up her mind to leave the husband and follow that fellow. *Ha-ha!* Oh yeah. So every place, they have their things.

Sometimes when I go to my village, I will stay there about one or two weeks. When I came to Ouagadougou with Mama, I stayed one week only, and then I came back to Ouaga. When I was going to Banfora, I passed there and stayed for two weeks. When I came back from Banfora, Mama was not in Ouaga. I went back for three weeks. Those three weeks, I was enjoying more! I didn't even want to leave, but I was short of money. That's why I said no, I can't live here. But any time I go there, I stay until my money is finished.

But even if I have been in Ouaga and I go there, I hear everything that happened in the village. All the time, these people used to talk to me. Someone would come and say, "You see that house: this family is that and this. Their daughter has run away, and that and this."

Then I asked, "How? The girl doesn't like the man? How can she stay and born two babies with him?" Then they said that maybe she liked him the first time, but when she saw the other one, maybe she didn't like him again. Then she left these two babies. So I said, "She doesn't think of the babies?"

"Oh, maybe if the baby grows, he will know the mother."

Then I thought, "*Ah!* Like if my mother married my father and ran away and left me when I was a child, I would suffer before I grow. Will I say, 'I know you. You are my mother'? *Shit!*"

Ha! Yeah. But when I'm there, you know, I won't put my mouth inside their talks. No. I will just watch. I will just watch what they are doing. Because maybe I don't know about these things much, so I must understand before I can get something to say. If I just hear it and I want to say something better, then I will think maybe it's not the way they talk, and then they will all turn their eyes on me, because these village people don't understand. So you must understand them well before you can give them some answer or some talks. If they are talking some things, if some palaver comes and then they are talking, then they ask everybody to say his mind. When they ask me, I will say, "Ah! *Tsk!* This one, I don't — I don't know much. Because the way we talk here, if it's a case, it's different. So here is French, and I don't know anything about French land, even how to walk and sit down." Before, when I was young, I used to put my mouth into any talk. When they talked something, even if it did not concern me and they didn't ask me, sometimes I had to put my mouth into the talk. Then my grandmother would say, "Go away from here!" *Ha-ha!* But when I grew up, I thought, "No, these people are like this. You must understand them."

And these young boys who are growing up in the village, too, they don't have money for marriage.[1] Even, you can see a big boy of about sixteen years, and he is staying with the father, and the father used to buy him trousers or a shirt to put on. This boy hasn't anything to do to get money. All that he's doing, every time, he farms guinea corn and all these things, and they eat that for a year. So in the village, these boys haven't got money to buy anything. The ones who have money for marriage are men. And the girls who are reaching fourteen, fifteen, and sixteen are ready for marriage. Yeah.

So these boys and girls only play together. As for that one, in the night, it's everywhere. You know, everywhere they do this. In the night, the young girls and young boys, they can go and play, or they can make some dancing. They can make some tam-tam,[2] and some girls can play their hands like this, clapping, and then throw each other up. And they have some dance mixed up with the boys' dancing,— oh, it's nice. They dance, they turn, they turn, with this tam-tam. At my place, they have tam-tam. They will play, play, play, then dance. The boy stands, then he shakes his waist, then he does something with the girls, you know. *Ha!* So there: they have this some nights. But the time they used to like playing like this is if it's moonlight. But if the moon goes in and it's black, they don't play.

And the small children, and some of these boys and girls too, they also used to play their games. They will tie one person's eyes, and then the other ones, everybody will run and hide himself. Then after, you will go and find them. When they all go and hide, then you will take the cloth off your eyes to try to find where they went. And the one you catch with your hand is the one they are going to tie his eyes next. So in this case, maybe some people will go to some corner. The others will play about two or three times, and these people won't come out yet: maybe they are doing something. *Ha!* You can't know, yeah?

Last time, my sister was telling me. She said my younger brother went with another girl. And I said, "Where?"

She said, "In back of your room, for a long time. We went there three times, and they didn't come out yet."

Then I called my brother. Then he ran *fast,* and he came, saying, "I am here."

Then I said, "What are you doing there?"

Then he said, "Oh, no, I'm doing nothing. This girl tied her eyes, so I wanted to hide myself."

1. money to buy the things for the new wife
2. play some drumming

So I said, "So? But they did this three times, or four times."

"Oh, sister, I was pissing." *Ha!* You will go for pissing and then: *phoing! phem! phoing!* So I didn't say anything. Then that girl didn't pass the same way. She went and passed a back way, then she came and sat *quietly* behind me. Then she started looking at me. I didn't ask her any questions. *Ha!* I just asked my brother questions, but as for her, I didn't ask her any question. *Hm?* Yeah.

A Village Courtship

They are funny, eh? The boys and girls are funny. One time I gave some dungarees to my younger brother, and my other brother said, "Why didn't you give that dungaree to me?"

And I said, "Oh, but I think I gave you some trousers."

Then he said, "Yes, but if you like, we will make exchange. The one you gave to me, give that one to my brother, and give me the dungaree."

And I said, "Why do you want it?"

"Sometimes one of my friends used to tell me to accompany him to his girlfriend's place." They opened a school near my village, so some of them were going to this school. So his friend's brother brought him the same dungaree, and the girl used to ask the boy where did he buy it. So if I give that dungaree to him, he will like it past the one I gave him.

So I said, "OK." I took the dungarees, and I put it on top of what I gave him. Then I gave the other brother different trousers.

Then he said, "*Aha!* Now I have *two* trousers! All these girls in this village are for me." *Ha-ha!*

Then I said, "Yeah? You've got a girlfriend?"

He said, "Oh, no-o-o."

Then, one time my father was talking to my brother about one of the village girls, and my father said that the girl is nice. Then my brother refused; he said he didn't want that girl. So then my brother said he wanted to tell me something, but I shouldn't tell anybody. So I said, OK. He said he had a girl about ten kilometers from our village, and he liked the girl because the girl was *bluffing*. Every time when he went to this girl, this girl just talked to him foolishly. So if I can help him, then one day he will take me with bicycle to that village, and I'll talk to that girl for him. Then I said, "Ah, is that the case?"

He said, "Yes."

I said, "OK. I'll think about it. Tomorrow I'll give you a reply."

He said, "OK."

So we didn't talk. The next day, early in the morning, he came and woke me. "Sister, I have put your water in the bathroom. Won't you have your bath?" Then I went and had my bath. Then he made tea. "Sister, I made tea for you, too. The way you used to make it, I made it in the same way."

I said, "OK." Then I said, "Let's drink tea together." Then he come and sat and we drank.

Then he said, "Sister, how did you think about it? Can we go today?"

I knew he was pressing me to go now-now, so I said, "No. We cannot go today, because this girl—Do you know the family?"

He said, "But I can show you her house; after, you can know the family. Every time, when they are doing some playing, even when you come, you don't meet her. Where we last went, this girl was there, and I was trying to talk to her. And the brothers wanted to beat me, and this girl also was bluffing." *Ha!*

So I said, "OK. We will go tomorrow." You know, it was a secret between me and him. I didn't tell my father. I just told my father that my younger brother is at the other village, where the school is. So I said, "OK. Papa, I'm going to see that boy, so I want my brother to take me with the bicycle." He said OK.

Hey! That bicycle too was another thing—*ha!*—sitting on the back of the bicycle, and my brother was tired, sweating, going, *"Eh-eh, ungh-unh, eh-eh, ungh-unh."* When we got to the village, he said, "This is where the girl is living." Then I asked him the name of the girl, and he told me. So I went to the house of the girl and greeted them—the mother and the families. They were sitting outside, about five o'clock. Then I asked the girl's name.

Then the mother wondered, because she didn't know me. And then, in my village I always used to wear trousers. So she looked at me, "What kind of—? What is your name?" Then I called my name. She said, "Oh, so you are a girl?" *Ha!* She was touching me; she was thinking I was a boy. So when I called my name, then she shouted and called the girl. This girl was inside the room, and she came out.

Then I said to this girl, "Oh-h. I was coming to see you. Do you know me?"

Then she said, "No."

I said, "Yes. I saw you one day when we went to the village where they were playing tam-tam. I told my brother to tell you that I want to be a friend with you, but my brother is foolish, so he didn't give me a reply, and I didn't see you. So I came to see my younger brother, then I asked of

you. Then they said here is your house. That's why I have come to see
you. Do you want to be a friend with me?"

She said, "Yes."

I said, "OK. Let's go out." Then I gave the mother excuse. So when we
went, my brother was there, and then she said, *"Pfft."*

Then I said, "Oh, why? This is my small brother."

"Oh, he is your brother?"

I said, "Yes."

She said, "Your brother is *bluffing* too much. Every time he's — tell
him to don't bluff like that." *Ha-ha!* So my brother has said this girl was
bluffing, and this girl also thought my brother was bluffing! So I thought
this thing: maybe these two people, they like each other. You know? It's
funny: the children, when they like one another, always they are like
that. So I thought of this, and I thought, *"Eh-heh!* Yeah. Now I get the
point." So I said to her, "Tomorrow, will you come to our village?"

Then she said, "What is the name of your village?"

Then I told her, and I said, "When you come to the village, you should
ask for our father Issahaku, and they will bring you to the house."

And she said, "OK."

So the next day, I was in the house. She also let her brother bring her
with a bicycle. Then we sat down and we drank pito together. And then
I had brought some blouses from Togo, woven ones. I gave her two, different kinds, and then I gave her one pair of trousers. Then she said,
"Thank you, sister! Thank you!"

Then my brother said, "Do you think she is going to wear the
trousers? A village girl like this? She can't wear it."

Then she said, "Did you hear what your brother said?" *Ha-ha!*

So the next time when I went back there, then I asked my brother, "Is
this girl still bluffing?"

He said, "No. Every time, she used to come here and ask of you, with
her brother."

Then I said, "Now has she agreed with you?"

"Yeah, now I even told my father I'm going to marry her." So the father
also accepted. He said she is a nice girl, and the mother also liked the girl.

Then I said, "Uh-huh."

So every time he used to go to the girl's village. Sometimes the girl used
to come to our village. But then I asked him, "She used to sleep here?"

He say, "Yeah, she sleeps with my Mama. Sometimes she comes here
for two or three days." Our father had gone to see the family of the girl in
their village, so every time, this girl can come to our village. But she sleeps

with the sister and the mother. She doesn't sleep in the boy's room. So this is the girl he is going to marry.

So village people, they are very funny. Yeah. The last time, when I went, I gave my sister a skirt — midi. Then my brother said, why didn't I give it to the girl, why did I give it to my sister? And I said, "But she also has got to be nice for somebody to find her."

He said, "Yeah, but that fellow too, his sister can't do for him? Try to help me. But you are giving to this foolish girl. She doesn't respect you. Don't you know that?" Now he wants everything from me, for the girl. So the last time I gave her some shoes, like guarantee. They weren't a full guarantee, but they were a bit high. I had bought them in Togo. So he told me that if this girl is walking on the road, she takes the shoes off, but if she is coming to the village, then before she enters, she puts her feet inside the shoes. So I shouldn't bring such shoes for her. I should bring her slippers. Slippers are good for her. She doesn't know how to walk in this kind of shoe, so I shouldn't waste all my money to buy it. He thought it was brand new, you know, because I washed it and polished it nicely. But I had used it more than one year. Mmm? Then I told him I bought the midi-skirt for five thousand five hundred in Togo. So he was happy. Then he said, "Every time, when you come, we must try to go and see her. Every time she asks of you."

Then I said, "OK. Next time, if I come, we will go and see her."

He said, "OK." Yeah. So they started. They first started to make a friendship, and now they are going to be married, too. So I'm watching them — to see how, if they marry, how will they live. They are funny, you know, the way they used to talk to each other. Then I thought it was because they didn't grow up yet, to get their sense. The girl is about fifteen, but my brother is about sixteen years. So we are going to see their lives when they get married, whether they will say all this when they get married, too. It will be funny for me every time. When I meet them, I will say, "Ah, don't you see my brother is bluffing me?" *Ha!* I will always say this to remind them, because if I see that they are married and they are always serious, then I will think of when they were first starting and how their starting was funny.

Catching Chickens

Eh-heh! This village marriage! Our place has some funny things. These young boys and young girls, they don't have money to make a marriage

like Amariya.[1] Their marriage is different. Somebody like my brother, if
he sees a girl like that girl and he wants to marry her, they won't make
Amariya. He will wait one day, if this girl comes to our village, then when
she's going away, then all that boy's crew — about twelve boys — all his
friends — he will call them. They will go in the bush behind the road. You
are going to be married like that, oh-oh. *Ha-ha!* Yeah, it's the young ones,
the young boys: their marriage at our place is like that. They don't make a
day to come and make you Amariya. No. Sometimes, if they see in the village that you are growing up, then maybe the boy's mother will say, "But
now your girl, your wife, is growing up, eh? It is good if she comes home
to sit here with you. It's the age for her." Then the boys: every day they
will go to your village to watch you — where you get your water, where
you go to the farm, where you do that and that, where you used to go
alone. They will be timing you for about one week. If they know the exact
place you used to go, then they will go and hide themselves there. When
you are coming to pass, whether you are with people or you are alone —
Oo-o! You are with your mother, with your father: these boys will come
out and carry you. They will be holding you: you are crying, and you are
beating them. *Ha-ha!* Scratching them! *Ha!* And they are running with
you. So if the person you were with is strong to run and catch them, then
sometimes they will fight. Then one boy will steal the girl away and other
ones will stand and fight that fellow. *Ha!*

Then they get you home. They put you in a room and close the door.
You know, the Northerners make some kind of door with grass; it's a
thick woven one. It's like a door, but they haven't got a key, and it's
funny — *ha!* — they used to put you inside the room with this grass door,
and then they will put one stick to go up and then they will put another
stick across. If you push, you can't open it. They will leave you inside
there. *Ah!* If it was me, I would just find something to cut this place, and
run and go away.

Then, for maybe two or three days, the boy who took you like that to
his house, his mother, or if he has a nice sister, she will start to come to sit
with you and boss you. Every day, you are feeling pity for yourself: they
have locked you in the room; you left your family; they just forced you,

---

1. a full Muslim marriage. After the man buys all the things, there will be Muslim
prayers and a ceremony for the new wife to be brought to the husband's house. The Amariya
also is the most recently married, or newest, wife in a polygamous household. The word can
also refer to a woman without cowives who was married in a Muslim ceremony, since she
is still the new wife.

fought you. Every time, they have to boss you before you will eat: you are crying. *Ha-ha!* Yeah. The girl is always crying; always she will be crying, crying, crying. Then maybe the sister of the husband will come, or the mother, and say, "Don't cry, don't do that. You know, my son likes you. Oh, the way we are — you know, we are not going to kill you. We are not going to do anything." And that and this and that. For you to eat, they must boss you like that. "You don't eat — if you don't eat, it's not good. We will take you back to your people to see them before we bring you back here." All this. And you know, as village people, always they are young, so they are fools. Then this girl will start to eat. So then they will see that in about two or three days, when you stop crying, then you will start to talk to them. And laugh. And then they will leave you free.

And you know, the day when they caught you, they sent somebody to go and tell your mother and your father, "Your daughter is with us. We have caught her." *Ha-ha!*

So some people's fathers used to be annoyed: "No! It's not possible! I'm going to take my daughter!" And he will take up his cutlass to put on his neck, saying, "I'm going to that fucking village."

Then the people will say, "No — don't do that, don't do that — you know, the young ones, the way they marry, if your girl doesn't like them, then they would not — ah — be planning this thing — to catch her, you know. So the girl likes them. How the girl is there quietly, it's good." Then he will come back home. He was just making it for show, so that people can beg him! He won't go anywhere. *Ha! Ha!* So it's very funny.

Then: this girl will be staying there, maybe for about one month, then the boy who has married her like that, and the family of the boy, they will take her back to the father's house and greet the family, then they will get what they can get, to give some things to make it like a correct Amariya. They can't buy everything for a full Amariya, but they will try to get some small-small things. Then maybe you the girl can stay at your father's house for one week, and then they will make you Amariya and bring you to your husband.

So why I thought of this: my younger sister, my brother also took this sister to one village. My father sent them with bicycle. So when they were coming, some boys came and picked our sister from the back of his bicycle. Then he *threw* the bicycle away; he took a cutlass; he said, "If you don't leave this girl, anyone I get, I will cut his throat!" So they ran away and left the sister for him. *Ha!* Then he brought her home. So from that time, he doesn't want the sister to be on the back of his bicycle, because if they come and catch her, our father will say that he made arrangements with these boys. So he doesn't want trouble. If my father asks him to take this girl to some village, he will say, "No, I won't go. If you like, let her learn how to ride a bicycle." *Ha!*

Then I asked him, "OK. When you refused, and you took a cutlass, the day when you will want to catch your own, what if they take a cutlass, too?"

Then he said, "No." Because the girl's family knows him. But he hasn't known these people at our house. He didn't see them even one day to come and ask my sister for marriage. And so people used to do that foolishness. They don't ask; they don't do anything. They just see a young girl passing, in their village: that day, they can force to catch her, and she will become the wife. You haven't seen him before; he hasn't seen you before. None of your family knows him. Yeah, they catch women by heart. They can catch you and put you in a room, and lock you inside.

Our place is a very nice place to stay, yeah? If you stay there about two months, or some weeks, you will see that something will happen like that in front of you. It's their habit. They are doing it every time. If you don't hear that somebody stole somebody's wife, you will hear that they caught some girl. *Ha!* Yeah, this is their life there. They see the girl passing, and then they say, "Ah, this girl is nice." Then this one will say, "Let's go and catch her." Then another one will say, "But we don't know her." The other will say, "No-o-o. No. Let's go and catch her. When we catch her, she will say where she's from. Then we can go and see the family, and then it's finished." And then it will be so, too.

One day when I went to greet my uncle, my uncle told me something. He said when he was coming from the bush, some boys at the other side of the village were talking that some girl came to some man's house. So they must wait here. If she's going, they will catch her. So he thought maybe it was one of his nieces. Then when he came and saw me, he said, "Ah! You are the one who came?"

Then I said, "Yeah."

"Ah! I was hearing these people saying that some girl has come to my house. So if girl is going, they will catch her."

Then I said, "*Eh!* For me, I am not a chicken.[1] Nobody can catch me. Uncle! This village? Who?! Where are the boys?"

---

1. a young woman or girl. The expression alludes to chicken as a preferred or special meat for soups or stews, as well as to the way that a chicken will just be walking around for anyone to catch easily. In this context, Hawa is saying that she is not someone who can be caught, that is, she is a grown person or a big person.

"There is the one."

So I started to fuck them, you know. I said, "To catch? Do you know what is to catch? Or you people haven't caught something before? For me, if you catch me, I will turn to a snake, eh? I will bite everyone. I will poison all of you people! What the hell! Do you think I am a small girl? I'm short: but I'm grown. I'm not a girl, eh? So if you ask my uncle my age, I'm not the one you people can pick on the road. I'm not some chicken."

So they said, oh, if they knew that I was the one, they wouldn't say it, because they *know* me well. *Ha!* So even if my uncle went to the bush and didn't tell me, if they went to the road and they saw that I was the one, they would never touch me. They themselves, they know they cannot touch me. But why should he go and tell me, and then I will come and be talking these things, and everybody is hearing?

Then I said, "Yes." *Ha!* They are funny, to catch a woman like a chicken. Even I think a chicken, you cannot catch it if you don't know the owner. But then, they can catch you without knowing the owner. Ah! When they catch the girl, then they will ask her, "Where are you from? Where is your family? I will take you back to your place." Then they are bossing her, and she is also a fool, you know, and she will tell them. They will send one person to go and tell the family that, "Your daughter is with us. She isn't lost. We will bring her later." After that, it will be one month before they will bring her, and then she becomes the wife. And you know, I wonder. I think some girls like it, too. If you don't like it — in this case, I won't stay if I don't like the man. *Ha!* You just see the girl that, yeah, she's a nice girl, so you want her, so you go and catch her and put her in your room and lock the door. Yeah. Oh, our people used to marry like that. *Eh?*

The Sweetness of Villages

Yeah, so village life, you see funny things. That's why I think that village life is free. They have some ways they will do what they want. It's only that the old people used to force the children, like the way my father forced my sister. But apart from that, you are free in the village. You are living a good life. You have not many problems. When you live in town, you have more problems than in the village. *Hmm?* Many people who have married in the village, when they come to town, they don't enjoy. I think that in a town, like if you are in Accra, every night you will think to go here, think to go there. But when you are in a village, there's no-

where to go. In the night, what can you do? You just go and take one
beer or something, and then you come back home, then you will sleep
nicely so you can get up early in the morning. But when you go out in
Accra to these nightclubs, and you come back home, maybe it's two or
three o'clock. When you sleep, what time do you think you can get up?
Six o'clock? It's a problem.

So when you are in the village, you don't see anything nice pass. And
then, especially women, if you are a woman, when you are in town and
you see a nice girl, and she puts on some nice clothes, you will think,
"Yeah. Suppose I get money, I'll buy these clothes." Then you will start to
think of it. In the village, you see everybody with the one color — brown.
Ha! So you wouldn't think of *anything,* you know. Yeah, if you can find
something to sell and get small-small-small money to keep you in your
life, you won't think of nice things. You won't think of nice shoes. You
won't see anyone with guarantee shoes come and pass — *klup klum klup
klum.* And you won't see anyone with a nice wig, eh? So: you are free.
You don't see these things in the village. When I go to the village, if I put
on trousers, they ask me, "Are you a boy?" Or they say, "A girl can put
on trousers?"

I say, "Yes."

"But when I saw you, I thought you were a boy."

And I say, "Yeah, I am a boy. I'm a boy-girl." *Ha-ha!* Yeah, they didn't
see that before! And so what we are doing in the town, all this, it is not
their life. They don't think of it. So the village life is not bad. They don't
see all these things. If I go there, I enjoy.

The first time when I arrived in my village, about four-thirty in the
afternoon, the small-small babies were in the house playing, together
with my younger brother. Then they ran. "Hey! Hey! Hey! *Kwasi bra ha!
Kwasi bra ha!* — Kwasi come here! Kwasi come here! Come and see a
white woman coming! And she put on wig!"

So then my brother came and said, "No! It's my sister!" *Ha!*

Then they said, "*Hey!* As for you, you are lucky! You have a white
sister! Oh? You've got a white-woman sister."

Then he said, "Yes! My sister has all her hair like a white woman.
Don't you see it?" *Ha-ha!*

Then I stood looking at them. Then I asked him, "Where's Papa?"

They said, "Papa has gone to farm." Then I said they should go and
call him, because his farm is not far from the house. So one of the small
ones ran to go and call my father, and then my father came, and then my
mother also came with my sister. But my other sister had gone to some

village, with my two brothers. They were making some tam-tam there.
Some chief was dead a long time, and they were making a funeral,[1] so
they all went there to look at the different, different dances. So the whole
night I could not sleep because when I didn't see that girl, my sister who
went with the two brothers, I wasn't happy.

The next morning, I got some boy and gave him my father's bicycle to
go and bring my other sister. This sister, I like her! She is called Fushena.
When he went, he told her I had come, and then she was also *happy!* She
came with the bicycle, and then she gave me pito. They put it in a cal-
abash bottle. My brothers were carrying it and following her. My sister
came before them, and then she said, "Oh, I have got you some nice pito."

I said, "Yeah?"

She said, "Yes! When they came and told me that you have come, I
didn't know what to bring for you. So I think I have got you some *nice*
pito. They are bringing it. It's not strong. It's sweet like sugar."

Then I said, "OK. Then we have to wait for it."

She said, "Yes."

So we started talking. Then my father made a face, and I was watching
him. So I said, "Oh, Papa, but why do you do that to us?" *Ha!*

Then he said, "No, I'm just doing that because you people are funny."

So I said, "Hey, Fushena. Let's go out and talk." Then we went out; we
sat down. We were talking when they brought this pito.

Then my brothers: "Oh-h-h! Hawa!" They were all happy! We were
shouting. So I had a small wireless — even I left it for them — and we
opened it.[2] That day was Sunday, and we were listening to some *nyama-
nyama* music, and they were happy. We drank this pito. Everybody got
drunk! *Ha-ha!* We were dancing. Yeah. Then you know, it was funny. My
brothers went to town and said, "Hey, our sister has come! Our sister has
come!" And *all* these young boys from the village filled up our house.
They were asking me: if they go to Ghana, can they find work? Or can
they get a good living? What do you do to go to Ghana?

I said, "Oh, this time, I didn't come from Ghana. Now, I came from
Lomé."

They said, "Hey! That's the place I want to go!" *Ha-ha!* "I heard of
that town. Is it a nice town?"

I said, "Yes."

---

1. a final funeral, performed months after burial, with dancing and drumming continuing all night

2. turned it on

Then you know, I had some old-old trousers which I didn't want again. And my one brother is very tall and fat, so he cannot get my trousers. But I bought him a shirt and some materials to make some trousers. But the other ones who are short like me, the young ones, they all got trousers. I took all my old-old trousers for them. They were putting them on. Some of them got these round-neck shirts; some of them got shirts. They were happy! "Hey! So you are the one who brought these trousers for your brother?"

I said, "Yeah."

"Hey-y-y. The foot is big![1] Look!" You know these trousers with big legs? "Can you give me one?"

Then I said, "Oh, but it's finished. So if I go, then I will let them sew one for you. But can you show me your measurements?"

"Oh, anything that's good for you; I am like your brother." *Ha-ha!* "I am the same size like him. I can put on these trousers. Even the last time, I came and borrowed some trousers from him to put on. Ask your brother."

Then I said, "Ah-h. OK. Then I will bring you some."

So the next time, when I was going there, I took three trousers, my dungarees. I had sewn them in Lomé, and I went and gave to three of them. Then the other one said, "Oh-h, as for us, you didn't give us because you don't like us; that's why you didn't bring us some."

Then I said, "No, I cannot bring all in one day. So I must bring them small-small. So the next time, if I am coming, I will bring you your own."

"OK! Sister! Try, eh?!"

And then I had plenty of pictures — photos. They shared the pictures. So do you know what was funny? One brother and one sister: I gave one photo to the sister. Then this boy went and took the photo and cut it into two. And he gave my legs to the sister, and he took the head. *Ha! Ha!* Then the sister brought the half of the picture; she was crying, "Do you see what brother did? You see what—"

Then I said, "What did he do?"

She said, "Look at the photo. I don't see the head." *Ha!*

Then he said, "Yes! But we shared it! I gave you the legs, and I took the head." *Ha! Ha-ha!* So, they are very funny. Oh! These children, I used to be happy with them when I go there.

---

1. The lower part of the leg, the cuff, is wide; that is, bell-bottoms.

PART FOUR *African Independence*

10 PROBLEMS OF MULTICULTURALISM

: GHANA, TOGO, BURKINA FASO :

Stuck in the Village

You know, when I am in the village and I see all these things, then I used to tell some of them, "Ah, you are nice, but what are you living for?"

"Because I don't—I don't know anybody. I would like to go to Ouagadougou, but I don't know anybody in Ouagadougou.

Then I said, "When I went to Togo, I didn't know anybody."

"But sister, as for you, you can speak every language. But as for me, I cannot speak any language apart from our language." So that's why some of them used to fear to travel, because they just speak this language from the village, and this language doesn't go anywhere. You see? In Ouagadougou, you can find our people, but unless you hear them speaking before you will know that they are from our area. We have mixed up too much—with these Bobo people[1] and all this. We have the same marks,[2] so if you see somebody with this mark, it can prove that either he's Gurunsi or he's Dioula or Kaalo.[3] All these people, they look like the same

---

1. people from Bobo-Dioulasso and its environs
2. facial marks; cicatrization
3. cultural group in western Burkina Faso

people. The languages are not the same, but they all have this kind of mark. So you cannot choose. Maybe you will see somebody. If I am walking in Ouagadougou, I can see someone who is Dioula, and he's calling me with the language, and maybe I won't understand. And he will come and tell me, "Oh, I am talking to you." Then he will start his language, and I will say, "Oh, I don't understand." Then I'll show where I'm from. "Oh, I thought you are one of our people." Then I will say, "No."

So even to leave the village and go to Ouagadougou, you cannot find it easy. Unless you hear that people are talking the same language before you will know that they are our people. And some of them from the village, when they go away like that, they don't want the people from the same village to see them. They know they will suffer before they become a bit all right. Before these people from the village will see him, maybe he is working or he has changed a little bit, you know, and his life is better. So if they don't hear another language, it's hard for them to go out. And they don't get any money to think that they will have enough money even to get transport. When someone goes, he won't find a place where he can lodge. As for hotels, they don't know all that. They are just in the village, farming for their fathers and mothers to eat. They haven't got anything. And they don't know the way they will pass and go to the towns. At least, if you want to go to the town, you have to know somebody there, so that you can be staying with that person for some time. And then you will be learning the language of that town. They would like to come to the towns, but they don't know the way.

Yes, you must hear languages when you go to any place. When I'm in Ouagadougou, I speak Mossi and I speak Dioula, and there are some places where I think it's important. If you don't hear it, to ask for something is hard. It's good to hear the people's language when you are living with them. That's why I want it. I want to learn all the languages because it's good. If I can learn all, I will like it.

Ten and a Half Languages

The languages I can speak are many. The first language is my language, isn't it? Gurunsi. When I was young, I was speaking Gurunsi. That was the language I started to hear first. OK, the second language: from Gurunsi to Asante.[1] From Ashanti to Hausa. Hausa language, as for that

---

1. Ashanti is the English form; the language is Asante Twi

one, when we were young, in Kumasi, we used to go and play together
with some children from Hausa people. That's why I hear the Hausa.

And from there: Dioula. I speak Dioula. It's now since I have come to
Ouagadougou that I am better at Dioula, but you know, first time, when I
was young I used to speak Dioula a little. I learned Dioula from my
uncle's wife, that bad woman I talked about. When I was young, I told
you I stayed with her. She was from Côte d'Ivoire. Every time she would
shout on me in Dioula. So I got to know Dioula there, small-small.

And before, at my father's house, my father used to get these people
from Bobo-Dioulasso. They used to come from Bobo to come and buy
things from Ghana to take to Bobo. They were businessmen. So if they
came there, they didn't hear any Ashanti language. When they wanted
water, they would say, "Go and bring me water." All my brothers didn't
hear anything. I was clever among them. I used to get money as dash from
them, so anything they said, "Go and bring," then I would go and bring
the thing. But my brothers, when they told them, "Go and bring this,"
they started going, and turning themselves around. Then I would just
leave them and go quick-quick, and get the thing for the person, so that
the next day, when he was going out, maybe he would give me dash, two
shillings or a cedi or two cedis. So I was getting money from them well.

Sometimes, they would send the children to go and buy them porridge
in the morning. And they didn't know the name of the porridge. The children would be asking the man in Gurunsi language, and they would be
asking each other, "What did he say? What did he say?" And they would
be standing there.

So I would go to the fellow: "What did you want?"

Then he would say maybe, "I want porridge."

Then I would say, "OK. He says you people should stop. Don't go
again. He said I should bring the money back to him." I would take his
money from my brothers, because if I said that the man said I should buy
the thing for him, my brothers would ask me what he wanted. And this
would make confusion, you know, because if they go to buy the thing,
they will get the dash. So I used to just come and cut it in short way: "The
man said he's going to the town. The time has passed, so you people stop
what you have been sent for. He doesn't need it again because the time
has passed. So he said I should collect the money and bring it."

So if they gave me the money, then I would take a pan.[1] You know,
every time, when I was small, if I saw something they would give me dash

1. a round metal plate

inside, then I used to take a pan to be my steering wheel. I used to be driving a car —*brm! brm!*— with the pan, then *dt-dt-dt-dt-dt-dt! R-r-r-r!* Running. Then: *brm! brm!* Then: *dr-r-r-r!* So I would go quickly and come back quickly. Then I would get my dash.

So this Dioula, I heard it in Ghana. I didn't hear it in Ouagadougou. But the Dioula I was speaking in Ghana, it was not too much. If they spoke some words, I used to understand. Yeah! Many of them used to come to my father, to buy things and take to French countries. They were selling cola, cloths, and some things. They didn't speak any Ghana language, and they didn't speak Gurunsi either. It was only Dioula. So: they would ask me, "Give me water," or "Do that," or "Do this for me," or "Help me," or "Lead me to this place." Then I started to learn Dioula, too, so before I got to Upper Volta, I spoke Dioula a little bit. So when I was learning it, it was not hard again. Anything they said, maybe I had already heard it before. But only the tongue, to speak it like them, is hard. But I can speak some.

So the time I was young, I knew Gurunsi, Twi, some Dioula, and Hausa. Then from Hausa to English. As for English, I think it was when I was fifteen or fourteen. To get somebody to teach you English is not hard, you know, because maybe you can have some friends, and they also want to speak English. So if you go in that group, you will all speak English. When I was learning it, we used to go to groove at some places, and everybody was trying. We used to make rough with it: you can get some way to talk about the one who doesn't understand English, just some kind of joking. *Ha-ha!* So to learn English was not hard. It didn't take long; maybe it was about six months when I could understand English. Then I started to speak. And after that, I was controlling all of it, I thought. After English, you know, I was about to speak many languages, but I didn't speak them really. I could understand some things, and I could not understand some. When I spoke English, I had already spoken three languages: I could speak Ashanti and Hausa; these were necessary for Ghana, to speak in Ghana. And my language: Gurunsi. Then I learned English.

Then after that, you know, I was trying to speak Dagbani, the language of Dagbamba.[1] When I was with Nigel in Tamale, then I learned Dagbani, too. When I went to Bagabaga,[2] there was a girl and her mother's sister who were living with me, and they didn't speak any language apart from Dagbani. The girl used to speak English some times, but she was shy. Later she spoke Hausa and she spoke Ashanti, but the first time, she didn't hear anything but Dagbani. So every time, I had to force to speak

1. cultural group in northern Ghana, around Tamale and Yendi
2. suburb of Tamale

to them. That was when I started learning Dagbani. And at that time I was speaking it well. I spoke nice Dagbani, but I cannot speak it like their tongue, you know.

And the Ga[1] language is also like that. I can speak, but I cannot speak it fast. As for Ga, I don't speak it much. And if I'm speaking, my tongue is not correct. I never learned any language that is hard like Ga. I think their tongue is a heavy tongue. So I cannot speak it. I understand it small-small, but if I speak it, I speak it like Ewe. *Ha!* So every time they used to laugh at me when I speak Ga. But any kind of thing they say in Ga, I hear it and I understand. The time I was in Accra, I understood it.

So from that language, then I learned the Togo language: Ewe. Even when I was in Accra, I also started learning Ewe a bit. And Ewe: I don't know why, but I thought Ewe was an easy language to learn. The time I learned it, that woman from my house in Accra was Anlo,[2] and the Ewes in Ghana and Togo are all having the same language. She used to speak this language to me, so if she spoke, then her daughter would show me, "This is that, and this is that." And the time when I went to Togo, then they also spoke the same thing, only a little different. So I got to know Ewe quickly. I learned Ewe fast, even faster than I learned French.

Yeah, I can speak Ewe very well. Eh! Especially when we got that case and we went to that prison, our prison in Kpalimé.[3] Every time we had our church. *Hey!* It wasn't praying. *Ha-ha!* Oh, it was funny. We were three girls who were Muslim — Ladi, Tani — no! we were four — no, five! — and Nana, Susannah — Susannah was also a Hausa girl, so she was praying too. Every time we used pray in Muslim way. We said we were praying for God to forgive us, to let them take us out from that place, because we didn't do anything. Then at night time, we would also make church with this Ewe music, the Christian one. *Ha!* And we were singing and clapping our hands. Then these police people who were guarding us would say, "You people know God?" *Ha-ha!* "You know God? Suppose you know God, won't you go and marry? You don't marry, and then when they catch you, you say you are praying to God. Which God knows you?" *Ha!* Then we would start fucking them off.

But every night we had to make church, in the Ewe language — singing — and then praying, "God forgive me," and "Let these people take me out because we are — we haven't done anything bad." And the people, too, who they took their pictures, they also prayed, "Oh, God

1. cultural group in the Accra area. The pronunciation is nasalized as "Gã."
2. southern branch of the Ewe people
3. See *Hustling Is Not Stealing*, chapter 14.

forgive me. Anyway, I have made a mistake. I was drunk — I didn't know what I did that time. So let them — let them think to let me to go away."

And sometimes we used to make trouble with the girls who made the pictures. We would say, "Bad-luck girls like you people to go and make these bad-luck pictures. And they came and arrested all of us." We were living in the same place. *Ha!* Yeah. And all these girls, they spoke Ewe. Only Tani could speak Hausa, and one other girl could speak Ashanti. But the rest, only Ewe. If you didn't understand it, you could not hear the language they were speaking together.

And so when I went back to Lomé, that was the time I really spoke Ewe. Everybody wondered, "Ah-h — so this time you hear Ewe?"

Then I said, "Yes. Do you think I will go for prison for nothing?"

Ha-ha! I didn't do anything bad, eh? I didn't have this bad picture. OK? Then I went to prison, seven months. *Ah!* I must get some profit there! So the language, the one I learned from Togo, that was the profit. *Ha!* When I first went to Lomé, I didn't speak Ewe much like the time when I came back from prison.

So to learn a language is not hard. If I go to some place and I need to learn the language, I used to be a friend with the people who are from that place. I will be talking to them, and maybe sometimes I go to visit them. They will say some words, and then I will ask them. Then always I get somebody who can understand one of the languages I understand. If I say, "What does that mean in your language?" he will know what to say, and then maybe he can tell me, "It's this." Then the next time, if somebody says it to me, I have understood it the last time they said it. So this is the way I learn the languages from people.

Yeah, and then sometimes, I used to learn from the children. If I live in a house, if there are nice babies there, I used to talk to them. Every time I used to call them, "Come and take tea with me," and that and this, and I start bossing them. If you want to hear a language quickly, the children are the best teachers. When a small child is saying the words, the way he is saying it, to me, I used to understand from the children quickly. Some children, the way they play and the way they talk, if you don't listen well, you won't hear what they are saying. But if you understand a child, and you start on that way, then people who know this language will start to laugh at you. They will say, "Are you a child?" What you said, you learned it from children. So then the person will say, "Ah, how did they say that?" Then he will also say it, and as you are already on it a little bit, you will get to know it. Yeah, the children speak slowly, very slowly: "And that — and — and." *Ha!* You know? Then they say, "And this too — and — and — and." And so what they talk, it's plenty, but it's only one word at a time.

When the child gives you one word, you will have some time to think, to get that word. They are very good teachers for the language. You see Ashanti: maybe you will go to ask of somebody and you will meet a child. The child will say, *"O-nni-hɔ. ɔ-kɔ-baa-bi"*—very slowly—"He's not there. He went somewhere." But if some senior person comes, he will say, *"Onni hɔ. ɔkɔ baabi,"* and he will say it quickly. That one, it will just pass in your ear, you know—*fmmm!* But the child's one, the way she will talk it, even if you don't understand the language, you will see the way she shakes her head, you know. Many children used to shake their head when they are talking. I like that kind of children. *Ha!* Yeah.

I learned all the languages by myself, and it is only Ewe I learned from the children. My first landlord had about six children—small-small ones. I don't know their ages, but if you saw them, you would say they gave birth to all of them on one day! They were the same height. You know, the father didn't take care of them, and the mother, *hm-m*—so early in the morning, when they would wake up, they would wash their face, they would take their bath, and then they had to go to school. The father would maybe give them about twenty-five francs to go to the school. So when I saw them in this way, I used to call them to my place. I wanted to hear their language. I would say, "Every morning, when you people finish bathing and you dress up, you should pass here to take your tea before going to school."

Then I will be ready with the tea. I will boil the water and put everything on a table. When the children come, then I will serve them. Then when they came back, twelve o'clock, I would give them *fufu.* I would give it to them one by one. I had everyone's plate with me. There were six plates. I just wasted some money to buy small-small plates for them. I didn't let them eat together, because I wanted everybody to be calling the names of things.

Yeah, so this is how I used to learn Ewe. When I went to Togo, the first language I was trying to learn was Ewe. I was not much serious about the French language. Only the Togo language. I said that is the natural language I have to hear first before French. So when I started to hear the Ewe small-small, then I said, "Ah, this time I think I can speak a little bit of this language. So I should try for the French, too."

As for French, I started it from Togo, you know, and then after, in Upper Volta. Now it's not bad, because now I can talk to them. If I need something, I can ask them. If they talk something, too, I can understand them. As for the French, I had some girlfriends, these Togolese girls, and they used to speak French. And I had one *nice* funny girl: Marie Zazu. If you knew her, you would like her. She was very *fat.* She could smoke groove about two or three cups a day![1] *Yeah!* She was *nice!* This girl was a very jovial girl. So she always wanted to hear English, and she also learned English from me. She can now speak English a little bit.

So this girl would tell me things in French, and she understood English a little bit, but she didn't know pronouncing well, you know, so if she told me the name of something in French, then she would say it in broken English. The way she would say it, you would know what she meant. And sometimes she would bring it in Ewe language. So from there, if she couldn't say something in the English language, she would ask me, "This thing, they call it this name in French, so in English language, how do they call it?" She would ask me this in Ewe. Then I also would tell her the name of the thing. So she was telling me the French and then I was telling her the English.

So that time, she was a good girlfriend to me. *Every* time, you would find this girl in my house. Every time. Sometimes, when she came, she would say, "Let's go to Hôtel le Benin, to the swimming pool."[2] And I used to be afraid of water. I don't swim. So I would just go and sit with her. She would be swimming and coming to me, and we would talk, and she would be going to swim. Then we would just be in front of the swimming pool, drinking and talking. She was a good girl, Marie Zazu.

Then: German. It's not that I can hear it, but if they are speaking something, you know, one-one[3] of it can go inside of my ears. When I was with this German man, he didn't speak English well. And I didn't speak French well then. And he couldn't speak French well, too. He spoke small-small French: "Moi, do-you-speak-this?" And English, no.

So I didn't hear their German language first. Then sometimes he would bring German language inside his talk. Sometimes, if he called something's name in German language, maybe I didn't know the thing. So maybe if he had the thing, then he would bring it, and he would say that in German, they call this thing like that. Then, I would say the name to him in French, in my broken French. Even I was better than him in French language. So he also used to be happy that he could learn the French language from me. But he heard the English more quickly than French. You know, English and German are somehow close.

Then: Mossi. Moore, the language from Ouagadougou, if the Mossis are speaking, I understand it. When I went to Ouagadougou, I tried to add

---

1. While many marijuana smokers buy individual "wraps," others buy it by the measuring cup; the amount seems large, but such smokers are rolling very large quantities and can easily smoke that amount (especially with a little help).

2. Some hotels open their pools to the public for a fee.

3. a little bit, a few words

Mossi. Do you know why I could hear Mossi quickly? Because I hear the Dagbamba language. If you can understand Dagbani, it's not far from Mossi. It's just like when I say that English and German people are not far from each other in their speaking. Sometimes, there is something they will call the name in German, and when you get it, you will see that in English language, there is just a small difference, but it's the same thing. So Mossi language and Dagbamba language, you can also take it as just something like Fanti and Ashanti. You know, it's the same language, but it's only that the tongue is different. So if the Mossi people are speaking, if I want to reply, then the Dagbamba tongue is coming out, so they start to laugh. They say, "You are a Dagbana."[1] They know the tongue of Dagbamba too, and Dagbamba know Mossi.

So these languages, and some small German, these are the languages I hear. But there are many people who can speak more than that number of languages. In Africa, we have many languages, so if you go around, you will hear all these languages. But you people don't need it. You don't mix up with other people. You don't know what to do with the other languages. There's nobody there speaking it. That's why.

OK: suppose, the way I want to learn the languages, this time I understand the Togo language. OK? I can go to Togo, but even in Benin, I can get somebody to talk to, because in Benin, some part of the language is just like Togo. And some part, too, they speak like Yoruba. These Beninois, they are different kinds. There are two people there at Cotonou.[2] Sometimes when I would go to Cotonou, to make a shopping in the market, it was not difficult for me, because there are many of them who can hear this Togo language. And I will find it easy, because they think that maybe I'm from Togo, you know, that we are the same family, so they cannot get me in a cheap way like if they know you are from Ghana or Upper Volta. Maybe this thing is costing one-and-six;[3] they will tell you that it's two shillings. But if you are speaking the language, you get the thing more like the country people. That's why I used to like to learn the language when I go to someplace.

So we Africans used to mix with each other. As for Africans, we used to be together like that. But in Africa, too, we have a kind of people who don't mix like that. You can meet somebody, and he doesn't understand the language you speak, so maybe he won't trust you, or he won't want to take you as a friend. But he can't show you directly that the way you hear

1. singular of Dagbamba
2. major town of Benin
3. one shilling and sixpence. Hawa is only giving an example; the currency in Benin is CFA.

this or that language, that, "I don't like you." He will be going with you, but he will not be free: he won't give you a free heart to walk with you. He thinks that maybe if he's some place with you, you will change the language, and then he will be inside. In Africa, we used to have this kind of people.

But there are some kind of people, too, you can just see them that they just agree-agree; they are *free-e:* up, out. Anything: even if you don't hear the language, if they are conversing, they will tell you. As we are here, we are conversing in English: if I have a friend here and he doesn't hear English, then when I finish talking with you, I will tell him what we have been saying. So if you get that kind of free people, that's the way you can hear their language, too. You know? It can be easy to get their language.

And some people, when you want to hear their language, people will be beating you before you will hear their language. You will start, and they will also start to tell you the bad words. You know? And you will go to town, and you will be talking, talking to people, and they will be abusing you all around. *Ha-ha!*

You know, all the languages I hear, when I'm in the country of the people who are speaking that language, I like to speak with them so that I will hear more. But if I coming from that country and I meet the people who are speaking that language, I don't show them that I understand that language, because sometimes, we Africans are funny. Even I think it's everywhere. Someone can see you like that, as if she likes you as a friend. And then if you move with her a little bit, she can get you in some language that you don't speak, and then she will start to talk something about you to the others. So when I saw this case, first time, from then, if I meet somebody someplace, I wouldn't let the person know that I hear that language. I just pretend as if I don't hear. Then one day, if she's somebody who likes me, I will know. Maybe we will be together for a long time, and she wouldn't speak something bad about me. But some people don't have their own experience. Maybe you will just go out with her, and she will meet the friends who are from the same country, and they will start to ask her about me, "Who is this fellow?"

And maybe she will say, "Oh, she is my friend. She's just like that. She doesn't hear anything. She saw me, then she said she liked me, that she wanted to make a friendship." But maybe you are not the one who said you wanted to make a friendship with her: she is the one who told you. And then now she's telling her friend that you just saw her and you wanted her as a friend.

So if this case comes, then I will say, "I didn't see you to like you as a friend. You saw me that you wanted me as a friend. This your language, don't try it on me. You should know that some people know the language, but they don't want to speak it. So as for me, I wouldn't say anything. But if you don't take care of yourself, you will meet some bad fellow and he will do you bad. I been following you as a friend. I like you as the way you say you like me. But you shouldn't turn your language [1] and talk this thing."

Some people, when they talk about me, I wouldn't mind. They will talk maybe three or four times like this, and I wouldn't mind. One day I will come to you in your house, and then I will say, "You know, at first I liked you as a friend, but I think this time, the way we walk, you can't be my friend. Because that day you were saying this about me, and saying that and that and this. You know, this language, I have stayed in your country, maybe a year or some months. So I think that even I don't like you people, but I thought you would be different from them, as you have traveled. That's why I wanted to be a friend with you. But if this will be the case, it's finished. You are no more my friend."

Then she will wonder, "Hey! How did you hear it?" And some of these friends used to make trouble with each other, you know. The way I have come and asked you in your house, you will be thinking that the person you were talking to went back and told me, so you will go and ask her. You see?

: OUAGADOUGOU :

Undercover Research

You know, when you hear many languages, it's very nice. Yeah, one time Mama Amma and I were in one bar in Ouagadougou, called Dessambissé. There were some boys there, and they saw us. They thought we were strangers and we didn't speak Dioula. They just thought they would take us like some foolish girls, to make trouble with us. Yeah, some boys used to do that to Ghanaian girls. So we were drinking. We were buying our drinks. So we were drinking our drinks, and then the one boy served Mama Amma with his own bottle, the one he had bought. Then they were playing. And you know, Mama Amma used to like to laugh, so Mama Amma was laughing. And these boys were speaking Dioula, and then this boy told the friend that, "Ah! This girl doesn't know that she is drinking fire. Suppose she knew, she wouldn't drink this drink."

1. change to another language

Then I thought, "*Ahaa!* These people!" I had heard that at that place they are ruffians, so I thought, "*Aha!* These are some of those people." But I didn't say anything. I was very quiet. Yeah, he was telling the other one in Dioula. Then, at first, I wanted to tell Mama, then I thought, "No. If I tell Mama, it will become hot quickly. I won't tell Mama anything." So we were getting to finish that beer, too, and then this boy served Mama again. Then I called another beer again. So we were drinking. Then I said, "Mama, let's finish this one and go."

Then we continued our drinks. When we finished, then we excused ourselves, and Mama said, "OK. We want to go."

Then this boy repeated the same Dioula, "*Hey!* I said this girl doesn't know; suppose she knows. Suppose she knows that when she drinks this, she's going with me or she's going away." He said this to the other boy.

So when we were coming out, this boy also come out. Then he said, "*Ah!*"

Then I said, "Mama, let's find taxi."

Then he said, "But Mama is not going."

"For what?"

"But Mama told me that she is going with me."

Then I said, "Mama, did you tell this man that you are going with him?"

She said, "No."

And I said, "For what do you say she is going with you? She didn't say anything to you."

Then he said, "Yeah, then she has to pay for two bottles of beer. I gave her two bottles of beer."

And then I started to speak Dioula with him. I said, "What time? Because I was there when you gave her the glass, the first glass. When you gave her, you said she is drinking fire. Then, I'm here: I want my sister to drink fire to burn all her stomach. Then the second glass, you gave it to her. If I was afraid of you, you know, I wouldn't allow that. I would have told her not to take the second one. But I wanted her to drink the fire. Is that the meaning of fire? That if she drinks this beer — these two glasses of beer — if she doesn't go with you, she has to pay the two bottles of beer for you? Is that the fire? Maybe you don't have any money to chop tomorrow, so it's your last money. Yeah? But why? We: we are all one. We are all Voltaique. Why are you talking this? Why are you people doing things like this? You must know, even if you saw me — not that somebody will tell you — you must know that I am also Voltaique like you. But if you are doing things like this to other people, you must know the people to do it to. You shouldn't do this to me. If you like, your two bottles of beer are how much? It's hundred francs each — two hundred. OK, you can take this five thousand and find balance for me."

Then he said, "But why were you quiet?"

"Why shouldn't I be quiet? I want to see the way you people are, because they have been telling me about you people here. I didn't believe it. I said 'No. We Voltaiques, we don't do bad.' But I wanted to see how bad you people are. That's why I didn't tell you that I hear Dioula."

"Oh, sister, don't do that. You know, we are one."

Then I said, "You see this girl? She's my younger sister. Only her mother is Ashanti, but we are one father. That's why she cannot speak Dioula. But don't teach her. Even if you see Mama, if you watch her well, you must know that she is Voltaique, no?"[1] *Ha-ha-ha-ha!*

So then this boy started to beg me, you know, "Don't do that and this."

And then the other one was putting fire that he should take the money, saying, "I'm hot! Take it!"

Then I thought, OK, now they are forcing, so I didn't give him the money: we have to go to police, then will I pay this money. Even I had the two hundred in coins, but I didn't want to say it. I wanted to bluff them a little. I wanted to show them that I wasn't afraid of police station. If they want, we can go. Then I said, "Yeah! You come and take it, because you are a hungry dog. Here is the five thousand. I am giving you nothing. If you like, let's go to the police station, and then you will give me a receipt in police station. I'm not going to give you *any*thing. If you like, we can go to police station."

Then some people came around. You know what they say: "Small trouble, people come." And many people wondered, you know, because they didn't hear me talking Dioula before. They said, "Hey, you know this girl used to hear Dioula? And we used to talk about her, and she didn't say anything." Sometimes people used to abuse me, you know. I didn't care. I would pass. If you abuse me alone, it's not anything to me. But to come and hold one of my friends, you will hear that I speak Dioula, you know. *Ha!* But to abuse me when I'm passing, oh — it's shit for me: I wouldn't mind you. So, that day, everybody came and said, "Oh! You speak Dioula! So you speak Dioula?"

Then I said, "No, I'm just trying. I don't speak, but I am just trying."

So from there, many people learned that I speak Dioula. So I wasn't happy in that area again, because if I was passing, anywhere, "Oh, Oh!

1. Of course, Mama is Ashanti.

N dɔgɔnin!"[1] They would start to greet me in Dioula, and I didn't get a chance there again. *Ha-ha!*

Yeah! I don't like that kind of game: I like where I will go, and nobody knows me there. If they think I don't hear their language, then I can hear something from them. Yeah, it's nice when you hear a language, and you don't say anything.

So we didn't go to police. I just took my taxi with Mama and we left. And you know something funny? That Voltaique boy became my friend! Yeah. Even now-now-now, he is my friend. If I go to Dessambissé, he's calling me his younger sister, *"Ee! N dɔgɔnin! N dɔgɔnin! I ka kɛnɛ?"*

"Kɔrɔ!"

"N dɔgɔnin! N dɔgɔnin, i bɛ mun min?"[2] He used to buy me beer free. When he sees me, "Oh, small sister, what are you taking?"

"Beer." I will get my beer. Now I used to get full bottles; before it was just half glasses. *Hee-hee!* He's owing us, so now he gives me a full bottle for free. He was ashamed.

Even the last time, some boys were trying to make trouble with me. And then he came and said he wouldn't allow. There was a girl who stayed with Limata; she was working at Hôtel Oubri. One day, we went to Dessambissé, and we bought drinks. Then one boy came to talk to us, and this girl went to the toilet, and the boy knocked her drink down. When she came back, I told her, "Ah, this boy pulled your drink down."

Then he said, "Why do you say '*this boy*'? I am not a boy." He just wanted to cause trouble with me like that. Why should I call him a boy? Do I think he is boy? He's not a boy, so I shouldn't call him a boy. I should say, "This man" or *"Mister."*

And I said, *"Ah!* What a bloody hell! To call you Mister?! Don't you think I know who is Mister? A boy like you?" Then he was hot, because he didn't want to me to tell him "boy." And I repeated again, "A boy like you?"

Then he started: *Ta-ta-ta-ta-ta.* And people said to him, "No, you don't make any palaver inside here. If you want a palaver, wait for the fellow at the gate." So they threw him out. Then he was at the gate, talking-talking. I didn't mind him.

So then this boy, the one I said became my friend, he came and said, "What's wrong with you and then that boy went outside?"

1. (Dioula): My little sister!
2. (Dioula): "Hey! My little sister! My little sister! Are you well?" "Senior! (Big brother!)" "My little sister! My little sister, what will you drink?"

"He came and said that he wanted to talk to me, and then he pulled somebody's drink down. So when the girl came and I told her that this boy pulled her drink, he said he's not a boy — he said I should call him 'Mister,' or 'This man.' So I don't have the time. I thought he's a boy — to me, he's a boy. He's not a man. And he's not a mister too."

Then he said, "Yes, you are all right, my sister. That's why he's outside. He says he's waiting for you. Wait. If you finish, I am here. Just call on me. We will go out together."

Then I said, "OK."

So the time I finished, he was at the counter, and then I told this girl to tell him that we are going. So he said he will lead us out. That boy said he is waiting for me, so if that boy beats him and finishes, then that boy can get me to beat me after, you know. So we went out. And that boy, when he saw this man was walking with us and talking to us, then he said, "Oh-h, *grand frère*— my big brother."

Then he said, "Yes?"

"You know these girls?"

"Yes. They are my sisters."

"Oh-h. They are lucky. I was going to beat them today."

Then he said, "From today going, if you see this girl and say something bad of her, you know that on that day it's finished between me and you." So from that time, I got another friend again! *Ha!* That second boy. *Ha!* Yeah.

That boy had stayed in Kumasi before. They call him Kumasi. I think he was a very *bad* boy in Kumasi. He had an accident, but I don't know from what. He used to walk limping on his leg. He's every time in Dessambissé. He is a very bad, wicked boy. In all of Dessambissé, he is the one who is always causing trouble — but now he is my friend, too. Any time, if I am annoyed with somebody and I'm talking loud, then he comes, "What is wrong? Who is troubling you?"

Then maybe I will say, "No, it's finished. There is nobody who can trouble me."

Then he will say, "No. When we are here, nobody can trouble you."

Then I say, "OK. I have soul brothers."

Sometimes they buy me a drink. And sometimes when I go to there and I see them, and they aren't drinking and they don't ask me what I will drink, I know that they have no money. So I also try to ask them, "What are you taking?" And they say beer; some of them say whiskey. And I say, "OK. Go and take and bring the *facture*¹ to me." And then I pay. Some-

1. (French): chit, bill

times they pay for me; sometimes I pay for them. So we are good friends. They are no trouble for me there, and nobody can make me trouble there, too.

And so when you hear a language, you shouldn't try to say it at any time. When you are in the country with the people, to know their goodness and their badness: you must keep quiet as if you don't speak their language. They will bring themselves. Some of them are good. Some of them are bad.

You know, when Limata and I were with Woman in Ouagadougou, Limata had two Togolese girlfriends, and every time they used to come to Woman. So these Togolese girls used to say, "Oh, Woman is a good girl," and that when they need grooving, they can come to Woman and take it. Every time they were friends. And if Woman had groove, she didn't give it to Limata; she would rather give to these girls.

But you know, these girls used to talk in Ewe about Woman in some bad way. If they were there, they would cook together, and then they would start to play and laugh, and they would speak their language. And then Woman would say, "The thing you said, what did it mean?"

Then the one would say, "Ohh-h, I meant that as for you, you are my darling friend," and that and this. But I also heard it. Do you know the one was telling the other one that she had been to Bolgatanga before? Woman was from Bolgatanga, and you know, at some of the small villages near Bolgatanga, the girls just wear a towel or some small thing to cover their vaginas. And the one Togolese girl didn't know Ghana, so the other one was telling her, "Hey! The world is spoiled. This girl, if she goes to her country now, her ass and this thing, too, she is meeting guys like that!" She used to tell the other friend that! When these two Togolese girls were grooving and happy with Woman, then they were playing, and then the one used turn the language to Mina — that Togo language — and then she would say to the friend that she knew the country of Woman and she knew many villages of Bolga. So the world now is hard, because this Frafra girl is coming here and boasting, and she knows how to dress, but if you go to the village she's from, you will see *nice* girls, but they don't wear dresses. You see all their asses and this thing.

So she said that to the friend, and the friend said, "Yeah, I want to go there and see." Then she told Woman in Hausa, "Woman, I wonder, one day, if you are going to Bolga, I would like to follow you. My sister was telling me that Bolga is a beautiful town." *Ha!*

And at that time I was a stranger to them. I was also a stranger to Woman a little bit. I used to lie down on the bed when they cooked things, and I didn't say anything.

So one day I called Limata, "Limata, these girls are friendly to Woman for a long time?"

Then she said, "What?"

"Ah-h, I am asking you, because I thought they are good friends, because every time, if Woman gets groove, she calls them. So I want to know."

Then Limata said, "Why? Did you hear something?"

"Oh, no. I didn't hear anything. But I just want to know, because these Togolese, I don't used to like them."

Then she said, "Why?"

Then I said, "As for me, I've been to Togo, so I know them. I don't used to like them."

Then she asked me, "Do you hear the language?"

Then I said, "No, I don't hear it." So even Limata didn't know that I could hear this Togo language.

Then one day they came to groove. Then we were making tuwon zafi, and we made some sauce with some vegetables. So we called these girls to come and eat. Then the other one said: Hmm — as for her, she doesn't want to eat food from us because sometimes she used to see us cooking with dawadawa.[1] Do you know dawadawa, that black thing they sell in the market? You know, it's very smelly, and many of these Southerners don't like it. So this girl said she used to see that every time Woman goes to market, she used to buy this thing, so she doesn't want to eat. Then other one said, "Oh, but this one, there is no dawadawa inside."

Then she said, "Oh, *tsk,* but it is the same cooking pan which she was cooking with. So I don't feel it."

Then other one said, "If you don't eat a little, our friend will think something against us. So let's go and eat small."

So then I said, "No. If somebody doesn't like something, don't force her to eat. She doesn't like it." I replied her in Ewe, you know.

Then she said, "*Dada vi, ese Ev egbe a?* Small mother, do you speak Ewe?"

And I said, "No. *Nye me sioɖe.* No, I don't speak. Only this is what I hear. I thought you people are good friends to Woman. But sometimes I thought, the kind of friends you are, if I am Woman, one day I will lock the room, and then we will start fighting. If you people will beat me, you can beat me. Because I hate friends who are talking with a friend when we are together, then after you will change your language. I thought you

---

1. (Hausa): a pungent seasoning prepared from the pods of the tree *Parkia clapertiniana*

people liked this girl. But it's just to call her foolish. She will groove with you people nicely; then after, you will call her foolish. It's not nice. If somebody is good with you, you must be good with her, too."

And these girls said, "Oh-h, but what thing did we say? With this food which we are talking about?"

Then we were trying to make an argument, so Woman was asking, "What did you say, and now you are talking?"

Then the one said the other doesn't want to eat the food because maybe we put dawadawa inside.

Then I said, "No, she didn't say that. Even we told her there is no dawadawa. Then she said we used to put dawadawa in the cooking pan, so even she doesn't feel to eat food from that kind of pan."

Then she said, "Oh, yeah-yeah-yeah-yeah. It's so. I forgot."

I was talking the Ewe language to her, you know: "Every time you come here, you used to give complaint about the food. Why don't you stay in your place and make your country food and eat that? Every time you come here and eat, and you hide your money. But don't complain about it! If you want to complain, if you go out, you can talk about it. But you should know that by all means, if God makes friends to meet, maybe one of them will hear a language, and one will hear another language. If I don't hear your language, maybe one of my friends may hear it. So why every time do you want to make a complaint like that?"

"Oh! Oh! *Dada, meɖe kuku sia.*" She was calling me a big sister.[1]

Then I said, "No, you shouldn't call me your big sister."

Then she said, "I beg you. You know, we are all one: Voltaiques and To-golese. We are all one; we are all in French country," and that and that.

And I said, "No! We are not one, because when I was in Togo, I saw how you people used to deal with each other. I used to see how you people used to test each other with your poisonings. *Mnɔ Nagokpɔme kpɔ sia. Me ganɔ Royal Hotel. Banigla. Menɔ afime.*"[2]—I was calling the names of the areas I stayed—"Look, we Voltaiques, we are not like you people. *Mi me wuna ame o.* We don't kill people. We Voltaiques, we like everybody. Only we are poor, but we *like* everybody. What you are doing here, in Togo you couldn't get a free chance to do it. In your country they never keep up to six months without arresting the girls. As you have come here Ouagadougou, have you heard that they have arrested the girls before?"

---

1. "Dada" can be used for either one's elder sister or one's mother, as above.
2. (Ewe): I lived in Lagos Town (in Lomé). I lived at Royal Hotel. Burial ground, I lived there.

She couldn't say anything. Then she said: oh, she was joking with the sister — she didn't know this would come to be problem for her — so the sister should beg me.

Then I said to the other girl, "Hey you, eat. Don't say anything. She has been saying this every time. And you can't tell to her to stop, that maybe these people, one day they will hear this language. So you can't beg for her."

Then I said, "Then the other day, too, the same girl told you that in the village of Woman, they don't know how to put on cloth, but now Woman is heavy here in Ouaga. She didn't tell you that too?"

And they said, "What day was that?"

And I said, "Hey! You know this language? I speak it! I stayed in Togo. And I was staying at Kpalimé." Then I started to call the names of these Togolese girls — Marie Brizzard, Marie Zazu, and all these girls.

Then she said, "Oh-h, no. But you know, it's not so, because I don't know Bolga."

Then the other girl said, "Oh yeah, I know Bolga, but it's long time ago. It's not this time."

Then I said, "Yeah, but it's not good for you people to say that. Even in Togo there are some places where they put on leaves. I have been there. I know there, too. Do I lie? When you are going to Dapongo,[1] after Eyadema's village,[2] there is a small-small village. There are no people there like the ones you saw in Bolga?" Then she was quiet.

Then I said, "Woman, here are your friends. Every time, you want to be friends. But they don't know how to be good friends. If you don't hear somebody's language, don't try to be a friend with her, because every time, she will teach you. So that's why for me, every time I used to be a friends with Ghanaians. Me, I am Voltaique: I am supposed to be a friend with Voltaiques, but I don't make much friends with them, because I don't speak all the languages here. They can do something bad to me. Even they can go and kill me, or make an argument to kill me. I don't know. This girl, too, you think she likes you, but she is the same." *Ha!*

Then this Togolese girl said, "Oh-h, you know, if somebody grooves, she can say anything." So it's grooving that was bringing these talks! Grooving used to let her say things on people! She said she didn't think she could say something like that to Woman.

1. town in the far north of Togo
2. General Gnassingbe Eyadema, the Togolese head of state, who is from northern Togo

Then I said, "Yeah, but if you weren't doing it every time, you would never change your mind, because every time you used to do that to people. That's why." *Ha!*

Yeah, so then they were ashamed. They didn't come to Woman again. Woman didn't tell them not to come to her, but they were ashamed. They didn't know that I could hear this language and tell Woman about them.

So if you hear the language from some people, sometimes they will do you something which is hard. Don't mind them. You just keep quiet. Let them do it over and over. Then the day when you are going to ask them, you will say, "This day you said that and that." That person, even if he's strong, you will see him losing hope. He will have nothing to say. And he will be in big shame. If he sees you, he will be shy of you. Yeah.

These girls, if they saw me in the market, they would dodge[1] as if they didn't see me. Sometimes I used to shout and call them. Then they would say, "Oh-h-h, how are you? We didn't see you."

"Yeah. I was seeing you people coming from over there. That's why I am standing here." *Ha!* They didn't feel like seeing me again. So just like that: I used to get these Togolese when I came to Ouagadougou.

So to travel, it's hard, because when you go to some place and you don't speak the language, you cannot even know your friends. You will be suffering to get something to spend or to better yourself, but sometimes even your friends will be talking or doing against you.

: TAMALE :

I Could Sell Her in Accra

Yeah, when I went to Tamale with Limata, there was a girl from Takoradi. One day she started to tell me, "Oh, you are good," and that and this. So maybe if I can come to Takoradi once, I will like it. Then she asked me if I had gone to the South[2] before?

Then I said, "No, I haven't been to the South." I said that I used to come to Ghana with Limata, but I used to stay in Tamale every time. Because of Limata I used to come to Ghana, but I haven't gone far. I only used to stay at Tamale and Bolgatanga.

1. avoid me; also, elude
2. the south of Ghana. From northern Ghana, the former Northern Territories, the South is the former Gold Coast colony.

So she said, "OK, if you come to Takoradi, you can come and see me,"
and that and this.

And I said, "OK. I don't know Takoradi, I don't know there."

So she and the sister became like my friends. And when she went, the
big sister was also asking me, "You said that sometime you will come to
Takoradi."

Then I said, "Yes. Maybe by next year, after Christmas, I would like to
come to Takoradi. Oh, even I have to pass Accra first, because Limata's
husband is there. She has three children with the man. He is a warder,
looking at prisoners at Accra. So Limata said we will go to Accra. So we
will go together and from there, then we will pass to Takoradi."

Then this girl was also trying to show me her house in Adabraka:[1] if
I go to the cinema in Adabraka, even if I see a small child, if I ask about
Auntie's house, they will bring me. So she asked me, "Do you know
Accra?"

Then I said, "No, I haven't been to Accra before." So I was asking her,
"Is Accra a small town, or is it bigger than Tamale here?" Yeah. I asked
her. Then I said, "In Accra, do you people have nightclubs?"

And she said, "Many."

Then I said, "Ah, then it's a big town then. Bigger than Tamale here."

Then she said, "Yeah, about ten times bigger than Tamale. So if you
come to Accra —"

Then I said, "You know, in some nightclubs in Ouagadougou, you have
to pay before you go inside. But there are some nightclubs you can go inside like that. And at our place, they don't force the girls to be buying
drinks and all this."

Then she said, "In Accra they have some nightclubs you have to pay
for the gate fee before you go inside. When you go inside, you have to buy
your drink."

Then I said, "Oh, but in Ouagadougou we have many nightclubs, but a
girl hasn't got a problem. If you are a man, you go to the nightclub, they
will come and ask you what you will drink. But if you are a girl, even the
place where they take the gate fee, the girl doesn't pay. A woman doesn't
pay in Ouagadougou. And Accra?"

"No, Accra is not so. You have to pay, and then —"

"Why should they pay? A woman should pay for the gate?"

She said, "Because there are many girls, you know; they go to the
nightclubs and find the people."

1. section of Accra

Then I said, "Yeah, in Ouagadougou, too, they used to do that, but they don't take gate fee from the girls."

Then she said, "Ah, then Ouagadougou is good. I wish to be coming to Ouagadougou one day."

So I said, "OK, if you come to Ouagadougou, you come to La Tringle. You ask of Hawa."

Then she was asking me. Then she said, "But this Tamale is very hot."

Then I said, "Ah, even this is comedies[1] you are seeing here. If you go to Ouagadougou, wow!"

Then she said, "Ah, I know. Every time Ouagadougou is hot."

Then I said, "It's not every time. You have rainy season. If you come to Ouagadougou in rainy season, you will like Ouagadougou. But this time, if you come to Ouagadougou, it's very hot."

So she said, OK, maybe she will wait until the rainy season time, and then she will be coming to Ouagadougou.

Then I said, "OK, if you come to Ouagadougou, you come to La Tringle and ask of Hawa. You will see me."

Ha! Do you know what I was thinking? I could sell her in Accra. Yeah! I was thinking this, you know. I didn't tell her. I just thought in my heart that this girl doesn't know. If I got her in Accra, I could sell her any time, because I know the town more than her. I think I could know Accra more than her because maybe she was staying with the Auntie. But I didn't stay with any Auntie, and I was going around. So I know the town more than her. But I pretended as if I don't know the place.

So that is the same way. If I know some language, I won't let the person know that I hear her language. Look. Even Ashanti: I was born in Kumasi, but sometimes I can pretend as if I don't hear Ashanti. Yeah. When I speak Ashanti, if I want a knife, in the right way, I can say, *"Mepɛ sikan:* I want the knife. But I don't say that. One time I was with some Ashanti people, and I said, *"Mepɛ wei no nea wɔdetwa adeɛ no.* I want this thing that you take to cut something."

Then the one said, "Ah, what does she mean?"

Then I stood and I looked up. Then I said, *"Eh-heh, eh-heh, eh-heh, dadeɛ, deɛ wɔyɛ sei no, wɔdetwa nam no:* yes, yes, the thing that is used this way to cut meat."

Then the other one said, "Aha!" Then they went and brought it for me. So that is the way.

---

1. previews and short subjects before a movie, that is, something small but not the main show

11 BABES IN THE WOODS

: OUAGADOUGOU :

The Smell of a Place

Yeah? So that's what I'm saying. To travel — or to go someplace like Ouagadougou or Lomé — how you will find the life there, it's difficult. Some of
the girls who run to these towns are suffering. But still they are coming.
Babies. They don't know anything. They don't hear any language. They
have no experience, too. Do you think — the time I went to Ouaga, I had
some experience, eh? And still, I saw all these problems. From my
friends! And this our work, too, our ashawo work: *e be trouble-o!*[1]

Do you see these Ghanaians, especially these Tamale girls, running to
Ouagadougou? Huh? *Ha! No!* You can see Ouagadougou to be quiet, or
somehow quiet, and Tamale is also quiet. Tamale is not a village, but
Tamale cannot be the same. *Hey,* Ouagadougou is a capital. *Ha!* It's the
capital of the Voltaiques. So you cannot take it to compare to someplace
like Tamale. *Eh?* Tamale cannot be Ouagadougou. Maybe some time will
come and Tamale too will be like Ouagadougou. *Ha-ha!* But even Ouaga,
if it is quiet, even if we don't have anything at all, it won't be quiet like
Tamale. Yeah, some Tamale babies used to think it will be sweet if they
come to Ouaga, and they will come. What they will see, they cannot say
it. They cannot say the truth, that when I went to Ouaga, I have suffered
this and that and that. Some of them don't say it when they go back, but
I think that in Ouaga, some of the girls are suffering. I used to see them
myself. I feel that they are suffering in Ouaga. When a girl goes back to
Ghana from Ouaga now, with her new clothes, with her grand bobo and
her big guarantee shoes, she is OK. She will be bluffing. She won't say the
truth, how she suffered there.

---

1. (Pidgin): It's very hard; it's difficult.

Like me, the time I went to Lomé with my small bag, *um-hmm?* When I went to Lomé, I was crazy. I didn't know what to do, so I just picked my small bag with one dress and went off. OK, when I came from Lomé, I brought that big iron box. If they see it, these girls will think that Lomé is sweet. But the way I told you all I have suffered in Lomé, do you think I will tell them? No, I won't tell them the way I was sick and the way I passed and all this. I will just say, "Lomé is good." *Hee! Ha!* To the friends, yeah?

"Oh-h, Hawa! Hawa! When did you come? Oh, you kept long in Lomé!"

I will say, "Yes."

"Oh, how is Lomé?"

"Oh, it's beautiful. Even I am not keeping long here. I am going back there."

When you also go to Lomé, too, you will smell it. If you want the way I have forced you, then you must smell it. If you come back, the friend you will meet, too, you will never tell her the truth. You will also want her to go and smell it, so she will know that "Yeah, *um-hmm!* So, this way, it's going like that."

Passage by Contract

Do you know how some of these Ghana girls come to Ouaga here? Some are students who are in school in Ghana. There are some big women who come from Accra or they are from Ouagadougou, and they go to their towns with plenty of dresses and cloths, and they will be changing their dresses every day. These small girls used to follow them.

These women are a size like your mother's size. Maybe she is a friend to your mother, and she comes to greet your mother. This girl will be following this woman till the time the woman wants to come back to Ouagadougou. Then maybe the girl will just run and follow her, you know, without telling the parents, and come to Ouagadougou. So when these women bring the girls like that, the fucking work they put them to do is to be sitting in the door for people to be using them for one hundred francs. You know, this is what is in Ouagadougou now. Somebody can be in Ouagadougou for a *long* time. These women who are sitting in the doorway for a hundred francs, they are *old*. And still they don't want to leave the country, because they can get small-small any time.

But if they go back to Ghana, they try to get the young students and take them here. She will pay your transport and everything. If she takes you maybe from Ghana to Ouagadougou, she will charge you and tell you, "I will take you there, and I will get you this and that. All your transport. Even if you don't have a carte d'identité, I will get it for you. I will pay all this money on the road." Maybe they can charge somebody about fifty thousand francs to take her to Ouagadougou. Some of them charge one hundred thousand. You see? If they see you are beautiful, and maybe you will get plenty of people, then they will charge you heavily.

When they bring you, they will get you a small rubber bucket and they will get a cooking pot for cooking hot water. And they will get a chair for you. And then a coal-pot.[1] Every day you put your hot water to be cooking on the coal-pot, or every evening time. Evening time, I think they start from about seven, or half-past six, or five. Some of them sit outside in the day time, too. Somebody will come; you go inside; you come out; you take hot water; you go and wash; you come and sit down again; you wait for another man. One hundred francs. *Agh!*

And many of these people who are doing this are Krobo[2] and Ashanti. *Many* Ashanti and Krobo. This is their business in Ouagadougou. And now many of them are rich. They have big houses in Ghana, in their villages. They don't care. If they bring you like this, you have to be doing this one-one hundred work until the time you finish your debt, about one hundred thousand or fifty thousand or seventy thousand. If you finish this debt, then you can work for yourself. So the time when you come, you are just like a prisoner. When you close, you will make account for your master. And she will take her part, maybe, "OK, I will keep this, and you take this for your chop and to buy your soap." Then the old woman will be keeping some of the money up to the money for the debt. Then you can be free, and you can do your business for yourself.

OK, a girl who doesn't know much: maybe she has been doing this thing and she becomes conceived. Maybe she will try to cause abortion, because maybe she doesn't feel to go home and stay in Ghana and give birth. Maybe she was thinking that she will just come to Ouagadougou and get money quick-quick and go back. But when she comes, even if it's difficult, she shouldn't conceive. So they will try to get some kind of abortion, and it has been killing them in Ouagadougou.

Some time ago, even the Ghana embassy said that it will let them sack all these old ladies who are doing this hundred-hundred francs. They said these old ladies are the ones who are spoiling the children, because every time, when you see a small girl die, she is with an old woman. If the girl

1. a small charcoal-burning stove
2. cultural group from southeastern Ghana

dies, then they will see that the family has come to look for their daughter. So they want to sack them. But you know Ghana: they want bribes. So I think these women went and gave the embassy people a bribe, so they didn't say anything again.

So they say Ouagadougou is sweet, and then all these girls are running there, up and down, and all this. But if you meet them, if you stay in Ouagadougou for some time, when you see them, you will pity. Somebody who has a mother and father, even if they don't have anything at all to give you, but still you will have and eat. But you will come and suffer like this in Ouagadougou. There are many girls like that.

Even they said the Ghana ambassador had a party like a meeting, and they made this party to find the girls who are eighteen years old, or who are not twenty or twenty-two or twenty-one, that they shouldn't live in Ouagadougou, that the Ghana ambassador will help them and send them home. So they said they would have a party, and that day, all the Ghanaians who are in Ouagadougou, girls and boys, they should come there to the ambassador's house. So the ones who know that they don't have the right age, or that they don't have any papers or identity card: they know that if they go there, it will be trouble for them, so they won't go. You cannot come and catch somebody at his house by force, you know. You will come and catch him on the road[1] that you are a Ghanaian to go to the party. But the boys and girls won't go near there, and these people too can't find them. *Ha!*

They started this thing when I first went to Ouagadougou. They started it, and they didn't catch anyone inside. Every time, they will talk, talk, talk. And every time, if you go to the party, you will see only the old, old, old grandmamas, the grandmothers who are sitting in Ouagadougou for this quick-quick business, they are *all* the only ones who are at this meeting. You will not go and see any young girl inside of them. They can't find the girls. They are just making this way to catch them. And someone will say that it is the old ladies who are spoiling the name of Ghanaians, and the old ladies also go there and say that the young girls who come are the ones who are spoiling Ghana. Who knows? They don't know the one who is doing it. Because maybe I will say, "You are spoiling me," and you will say, "I am spoiling you? Ha! Who is spoiling somebody?" No? So they are every time like that. They will not see the girls. But there are many girls from Ghana in Ouagadougou. You will see a nice Ghanaian girl. The way she lives, and the way the Mossis are treating her, you will pity her.

---

1. get him through the way; in this manner

Ghana Girls in Ouaga

I am a Mossi, no? Yeah. Even if I am not Mossi, I am from the same country: Ghanaians are Ghanaians, Voltaiques are Voltaiques. But I used to feel that my brothers are doing bad to the girls. I can't help it. It's the girls who brought themselves. It's not the old ladies who brought them. They are many, and they are too rough.

And what I see with Ghanaians: every time they think they are the best. They are the best people in Africa. Some of them, that's the way they think. They will say that they are better than all Africans. You can see a Ghanaian girl talking, *"Wopɛ koraa. Wokɔ London, wokɔ Amerika, wobɛtɛ yɛn dini, yɛn Ghanaians deɛ, yɛn na yɛ'ani abue first."*[1] She is saying that even if you go to London or America, you will hear of Ghanaians, that everybody knows that Ghanaians are clever, that they are in front of the others. Ghanaians will be talking like this, but maybe somebody can hear that language, and maybe it's his place. You know, in Ouagadougou, there are many Mossis where these girls are, or people like my father, and they hear Ashanti. My brothers and my sisters in Ouagadougou, they all hear Ashanti. Maybe they are there, and then these Ghanaian girls will talk this. Maybe you think that somebody doesn't hear the language, and you want to say something against him: you will meet somebody who is more that you. He is going to turn on you, *cha-cha*, with a slap: *"Wo na w'ani abue, sane kɔɛ!"*[2] Maybe you have fooled one of the people from there. You will try to say some things like this in a bar or in public, and somebody will be there who understands it. "You are disgracing my brother! You are disgracing us because you are better than us! So?"

So these Mossi people, they don't understand that way. When the girl says this, they say, *"Ma yedga biiga! Tampiirā!"*[3] *"Ma yedga biiga"* is like when Ashantis say, *"Woni 'twɛ ase re!"*[4] Do you understand that? *Woni 'twɛ ase re* is like if you say to somebody, "Your mother's vagina!" You know, in Africa we have that abuse: "Your mother's vagina." In Mossi, it's *ma yedga biiga.*[5] So when a Mossi man says that, *Ko-o,*[5] you will see that he is hot. If a Mossi says that to a man or a woman, then you people must bathe before you will be all right again. That place will be *hot.* And he will start to beat the girl, too, and people will think that she is dead.

1. (Asante Twi): If you want, at all. You go to London, you go to America, you will hear our names, we Ghanaians, as for us, our eyes are open first (before others).
2. (Asante Twi): You and your eyes-open (your enlightenment), go back!
3. (Moore): Child (son or daughter) of your mother's ass! You bastard!
4. (Asante Twi): your mother's cunt (vagina under)
5. in this context, "Man!" or "Brother!"

There was a girl in Ouagadougou. She was a very strong girl. She was called Vida. She was a Fanti. She was a boxer, a good boxer. A girl could not stand her. Even a boy — some boys who say that they are strong and they can do, this girl could stand them, with bottles and everything. Then she came to Ouagadougou: they made her *small*. You would pity her. She slept in hospital for two weeks. When they took her to the house, she was four days in Ouagadougou, and she went away. She said, "No, I cannot live here. If I live here, my life will be nothing. And even now, I don't think I can be strong again." They broke the bone here, and the doctors had to join it. They broke it with blows — blows! They gave her heavy blows. This girl didn't speak French, but she started: *"Ta-ta-ta-ta,"* and she started abusing people — how the Mossi people are, and how the Voltaiques are fools, and all this, that Ghanaians come to find money and go and build their houses and live with their husbands. She just said all that to the people, when she was drunk. She was abusing them, "Yeah, you people are fools. You people's women are not nice. They don't know how to bathe; they don't know how to do this and that. That's why you people are following us Ghanaians, because we are fooling you people to go and have nice places in our country." — And that and this — "I'm not a fool. I have four children. I left all of them at home with my mother. And I have a husband."

So are you disgracing yourself, or you are disgracing Mossis? How can you fool them? You leave your husband and come to us and you are fucking many men. It's one hundred or two hundred francs, or maybe you take five hundred. OK, it's ten cedis in Ghana. Then who a fool? You don't know that it is a disgrace to say that you have a husband, and you have children, and you gave your children to your mother? She didn't know that she was disgracing herself. She wanted to say that she is a bosun, that she is a somebody who is heavy. What respect does she have? You know, some people used to like Ghanaians. But even if a Mossi person likes you and he hears of this, then tomorrow you will go back to Ghana.

Even many Mossi people have married many of the Ghanaian girls, and they have children with them. But every time, they keep their children here. The woman can come to Ghana alone, or he can come with the woman, to see the family, but they will not bring their children. Yes, there are many ashawos in Ouagadougou like that: they have children with the men, but the men keep the children. They say that if they have a baby with a Ghanaian girl, if she takes it home, it is for the family. They think that all Ghanaians take this Ashanti kind of life.[1] If you conceive with a

---

1. Ashanti children inherit from the mother's family; however, apart from Ashanti, in most Ghanaian cultures, a child belongs to the father.

Mossi, and you have gone to stay with him in his house, then he won't let the child go to Ghana. You can come and see your family, your mother or your father. They can come to visit you and him. But he won't want to take the baby there and maybe your people will take the baby away, because they say that they heard that in Ghana, if you have a baby with a girl, then the baby is for the girl. And so they will keep the baby with them.

There is a nice woman in Ouagadougou. She is from Kumasi. She has about two babies with one Mossi man, and the two babies don't know Ghana. But the man used to bring the mother to Ghana every day. He opened a nice place for her — a bar, selling drinks. The one boy, if you see him, you will say that he is an Ashanti boy. A nice boy! But the children don't come to Ghana with the mother. The father won't allow it. The father can come with the mother, but he won't bring the children. So Ghanaians: Ouaga is good for them, but it's not good for them.

Yeah, and then, you know, Ghanaians used to *bluff*. And they like to bluff *heavy* bluffing. They bluff, and people know them after, and then they are really nothing; they are not anyone. The Mossi people themselves, they used to say that the first Ghanaian girls who were coming to Ouagadougou used to profit. The one who hadn't got sense, maybe she lost; but the one who had sense, she got some properties, without any troubles. She could save some money and then take some property to her village. But this time, no. This time, you can get, but the way you will suffer before you get, it's better you don't come. If you stay in your country, maybe even if you stay in a village, and you suffer like that, maybe by that time you will also have it from there, too. The girls suffer this time; they are not free like first time.

I think of myself as a Ghanaian, too, but as for me, I think I am not suffering much like them. When I see them here, I think they suffer more than me. You know, I am suffering at every place I go, but I think that, here, I'm better than them. Not because I have sense more than them, but I think the place where you are a stranger, you know, you must take time to know the people a little bit. Yeah? But they don't — they just come, like how they are. Maybe somebody told them how she is living here: but maybe it was before, not today. Even what you can see in Ghana today, you will go to Ouagadougou and say it, and maybe you will come back after tomorrow, and it's changed. Everywhere is changing now, so you shouldn't take any place like it's every time. Everywhere you go, you must take your time.

I am from Ouagadougou. I am Voltaique, no? But when I came here, I was very quiet. Many people don't know that I am Voltaique, but some of them who are clever, if they saw my marks, they would say, "No! This girl is Voltaique." And they would challenge me. Sometimes we used to sit, me and Mama, and somebody would come and say, "Oh, sister, don't be annoyed. Where are you from?"

And I would say, "I am Ghanaian."

"From where?"

"From Bolgatanga."

Then he would say to the friend, "*A-ha!* I told you! She is a Bolga girl."

Then the other one would say, "No, she is lying. She's not from Bolga. Look at her well."

I would hear all this in their language, in Dioula. I would hear it, but I would pretend as if I didn't understand them. Then I would tell Mama, "Look, they are talking about me." But I wouldn't tell them anything. Some of them can make me out, but still even now some people are sure that I am Ghanaian.

Yeah, they can challenge: they can be sitting, and then one will say, "OK, if she is from here, I will pay for this drink." I will hear all of it. When he comes and asks if I am from Ghana, I will say, "Yes." But the one who says I am Voltaique, I will say, "No, I am not Voltaique. I am Ghanaian." I hear all the talks they make on this case. You know, I have to know them. Maybe they will talk something about me. And if they know that maybe I from here, if they know that I am Voltaique, then they will think that maybe I might hear some of their language, so they won't say it. So I must know how they are. *Ha!* You see, I'm not clever, but I'm trying.

You know, if there are many girls, people will be saying this or that. *Eh?* Maybe some people like the Ghanaians because they are Ghanaians, and they are all the same people. And sometimes some people like the strangers, the girls who are from other towns. If they come and ask you, if you say, "I'm from Ghana," then maybe someone will say, "What Ghanaians are doing is this and that." Or somebody will say, "Ah! This one looks like our people. She is *nice*." As for men, when they meet, they always do this. I know. They will talk about the girls. I will hear what this one says and what that one says, and then I will get your point. They will not ask you where you are from for nothing, you know. Maybe some of them will make their plan: "We are going to see. This girl is from our people — the same Voltaique — so she's a nice girl. Voltaiques, they are easy to get along with," or something like that. Or someone too will say, "Oh, this girl is not a cheap one: maybe she will be a Ghanaian."

Yeah. Do you see? *Ha-ha!* Even if you go to Togo, it's the same. Every place you go. If Voltaique girls come to Ghana, they will be expensive. Voltaique girls are there, in Ouagadougou: suppose they used to travel like how the Ghanaians travel, their price would be more than Ghanaians. It's everywhere this thing used to happen in Africa. When I went to Togo, I saw that Togo girls are cheap in Togo — for the Togolese, for everyone in Togo. They are very cheap. If you go to Upper Volta, it's the same: the Voltaique girls are very cheap more than Ghanaians. If you go to Abidjan, there are many girls in Abidjan. Now they are also strong, but still, you can get Ivoriènne girls cheap. But I think if those people were also traveling the way Ghanaian girls travel, they would be the same.

Do you know why they are cheap? *Hmm?* When I was in Ghana first, when I used to visit my family, I used to go round, round, round. But not much. And I was afraid of money. If I had plenty of money at home, people were asking me many questions. So I didn't want all this. When I was with my family, if I went out, I would have one cedi, two cedis — that time it was sufficient for me. This is the way to go — the cheap way. So: *ha!* In Ouagadougou, when someone sees that you are a Voltaique, he will know that maybe he will give you five hundred, and you won't mind. Five hundred: you are not cooking, you are not doing anything. You follow him and in the morning, you go home: your mother cooks, and you eat. And if you want a nice dress, you will ask the person to buy one for you, "I want one dress like this." Yeah. You don't want to keep the money and your family will see you with money, and they will start asking you: "Where did you get that? Where did you get this? You are not married yet. You are a young girl. Who is giving you this money, and we don't know the person?" All this is a problem. So this is the reason the girls from that place are cheap.

But in Ouaga, you cannot go with a Ghanaian girl and give her five hundred. If you give her one thousand, she will know that it's twenty cedis in Ghana money. If you don't give her that one thousand, she will put fire on you. All the people in your house will hear of you.[1] So some people who like cheap ways, they used to go with the girls who are from the same town. Then, the people who think they are high, they go with the girls from outside. And the people who like to boast, to bluff themselves, that "I have a nice girlfriend; she is from this place" — and that and this — "Even you can see the way she dresses, she is not Voltaique." So every time, when they see girls, they used to ask, "This one is from here? That one is from where?" Especially if they see my marks, you know, these Voltaique marks, they can come to me and ask, and I will close my eyes and say, "No, I am a Ghanaian."

"Ghanaian? The other one sitting with me says no."

---

1. from the noise, from the shouting or loud talking

Then I say, "Yes. Why? You are my father? I know where I am from. I'm telling you. Can you force me to be Voltaique?"

"No."

"Then why?" At that time I used to be serious, you know; it's not like the way you will see me when we are friends. *Aha!* If you don't know me, if you see me serious like that, you will say, "Ah, ah, ah, ah! This girl is not good *at all!*" Yeah. You can be talking to me like this, and try to fix me,[1] and then I am looking somewhere. I won't look at you. Before I will turn my eyes to you, maybe you will go away. You won't like the way I look at you, so you will go away.

Togo Girls in Ouaga

Yeah, I told you about those Ewe girls who were abusing Woman in Ewe, and how I fucked them. So that time, we were carrying on and carrying on about my country people, then she said: E-eh, some time ago they arrested all the Togolese girls, and put them in police station — in Ouagadougou. Yeah, they did that. They arrested all the Togolese girls, and some other ones ran away to Abidjan, and some other ones ran away to hide themselves in villages. Because these our country people, they have one life: it's Voltaique, you know.

They saw some striptease pictures from one white man in Hôtel Indépendance. This man also was so stupid. He was a stranger. He came one time and took one girl and took her picture. He told the girl that when he comes back, he would give her the photo. So this man came back to Ouagadougou, and the girl didn't know. Then this man showed the photo of the girl to the steward, the boy who was making the room, to ask him, "Do you know this girl?"

And the boy said, "Yeah, I used to see her here."

So when the boy looked at the photo, the girl didn't wear anything. You see? Then this boy went and gave the complaint to the reception. And the reception also didn't have anything to do: he just rang up to the police straight. Then they brought one C.I.D. You know, in Ouagadougou they also have something like C.I.D. So this C.I.D. went to the man's room and asked him for the photo he had showed to the steward.

Then this man said, "Why?"

The C.I.D. said, "Oh, that girl, she's staying with me. This boy came and told me about the photo, but the girl has traveled to Togo. She will be

---

1. to know my place; to identify me

taking three weeks before coming back." Then he said, "Anyway, if you know that you are going to stay here about three weeks' time, you can keep the photo. When she comes, I will tell her. But if you won't stay, then I can give it to her."

And this man was from Abidjan, and he had come to do some work for three days. So he couldn't wait. He put the photo in an envelope and sealed it and gave to the man. Then the man put the photo in his pocket. He didn't say anything.

That *very* night, this girl came to the hotel. They were four, with the one girl who had the striptease picture. So this C.I.D. man was in the bar, watching the girls who were coming to Indépendance. So when he saw the four of them, he went and sat down with them, and he was conversing with them, asking them what they were drinking. Some wanted beers. Some of them wanted whiskey. He let them serve all of them correctly. And they drank and finished, and he asked that very girl that he wanted to go home with her. So the girl didn't want. You know? She had come to look for whites; she didn't come to look for Voltaiques. So she didn't want to go with the man. And then the other girl was trying to say, "Oh, but the man is a good man, you know, the way he bought us a drink. You know, some of the Voltaiques, they are good, too."

So the girl said, "Why don't you go with the man, then?"

So then the man said, "OK, even if you don't want to go with me, lead me to outside. I want to tell you something."

So the girl left her bag on the chair at the table with the friends. When they went out, then he said, "Here is your photo. OK? You know, here in Ouagadougou, we don't do this business. I have heard that in Togo, you people used to do that.[1] You people are free to do that, but here, in Ouagadougou here, we don't allow it. So I'm taking you to police."

Then she was trying to beg to get her bag. And he said, "No, you can't get your bag."

She said, "I'm going to tell my sister."

He said, "No. When he took the picture, your sisters were not among. You can't go and tell anybody."

He just took the girl like that and left the purse. Then the three girls were waiting. They got tired. Then they said, "Ah, where did she go?" They came outside; they didn't see her. They were asking the watchman, "Didn't you see our sister with one man here?"

Then the watchman said, "Oh, they went inside the taxi."

So they went. They took the purse and went home. The next morning,

---

1. See *Hustling Is Not Stealing,* chapter 14.

the police people were going around. If you are Togolese and you don't
have a husband, they will take you. They just were getting them like that
and locking them at police station. They made a telegram to Eyadema
that he should come and take his children, because they are spoiling the
country. In this country, they are not allowed to do so. So many of the
Togolese girls were running at that time! They were lost from Ouagadougou. That time we didn't see them because of the way they were hiding
themselves.

A Greenhorn

So when you travel, some small-small things can become a case. Unless
you know the way before you will see yourself all right. Yeah. Traveling.
You know, these children in the village I was telling you about, many of
them want to come to the towns. Many of the young girls and boys are
running from the villages. How they suffer, I used to pity them.

Look. The fourth baby of my uncle is a girl. She came to Ouagadougou.
I'm fed up with her. Every time I have to talk, talk, talk. I don't know
how to say this — she doesn't have a husband, and she is not a real girl
who can take herself out, as the others. OK? She is just like a greenhorn.
Every time she gets a man in the vagina, she conceives. That is her problem. She has two children.

When I asked, "Where is the father of the first one?" they said he's
a Senegalese. "Where is the man?" They said he has gone. The second
baby is a boy. The father is from Bobo-Dioulasso. So I asked, "Where is
the man?"

When she came to Ouagadougou, you know, she had two senior sisters
here, so she said she just came for some things. We didn't know any problem. So when she came to me, if she saw any cloth: "Sister, you wouldn't
give me this?"

Then I said, "Ah? To give you? I didn't have anybody to buy it for me.
I bought it by myself. Your own is better: you have children. Maybe even
if somebody doesn't want you, the father of the children will pity for you
now."

Then she said, "Because of that I have come."

I said, "Because of what?"

"I have come to see my son's father."

She said father of the son is from Bobo, but she knew the man in Kumasi. She just saw him for about two or three months' time, and the man
came back to Ouagadougou, and she was conceived. The man gave his ad-

dress. When she had the baby, they wrote to the man. The man came and made the naming. He did all that they have to do, and then he left her there and went back to Bobo. And she said he hasn't written for more than one year now.

"And now you are trying to find where he is?"

She said she was looking for the man.

Then I said, "But if you see him, what are you going to tell him?"

She said, "If I see him, I will know what to tell him."

So I said, "OK. When are you going there?"

She said the big sister, the senior of all of them, is in Ouagadougou. So the big sister said this girl should wait till the ending of the month, when they pay her, and then she will give her money to go there.

Then I said, "From here to Bobo is not very costly. I can help you to go. If you like, I can give you five thousand tomorrow. Will you go?"

She said, "Yes."

I gave her five thousand because I knew that she would go there and come back, and then I would hear something. You know? So she took the five thousand and went to Bobo. She stayed two months in Bobo. Two months. When she came back, she was very, very, very lean. But the baby had grown *fat*. And she was lean. *Ey!*

You know, it was one of my brothers who told me she came back. So I knew she would come to me. So I told Limata, "Look, I'm going to sleep. If this girl comes, you people should tell her that I have slept. So she should come in evening time."

I was going to the toilet, and I saw her coming. So I just got inside the room quickly. Then when she came, Limata told her that I had slept. Then Limata said, "Hey! It's a long time since we saw you."

So she was trying to give Limata the story. She said, "Oh, but I have been to Bobo. I am just from Bobo now. But I want to see my big sister, you know, to tell her how this man has treated me. Look how I am. The time when I came from Kumasi, was I looking like that?"

Then Limata said, "I think you are sick."

Then she said, "No, I am not sick. You know, I went to this man. This man has married another woman. So when I got there, this woman also was conceived."

When she went there, in about three days' time, the woman had delivered a child. So she was the one to cook, to wash the things, to do everything for the woman. She just became like a slave. And the way this boy was with her in Kumasi, he didn't have that time with her in that place. She said, "Every time he was sending me, and sometimes he gave me three hundred francs to cook, and three hundred francs to cook is very difficult. And then, getting to three or four weeks' time, he changed to give me one hundred for cooking, because that time they had corn flour." So she just would go and buy some fish and some dawadawa, some okra, or something like that, which she would use for in the soup. She would make the soup: she already had the flour to cook. So she couldn't eat, because she had been eating good sauce, but when she went there, she couldn't eat more.

And you know, this girl's son was still taking the breast. So when she went there, the man was getting a sense to stop the child from taking the breast, so he would get the child away from the girl, then he would sack the girl.[1] You see? So he didn't let the baby take the breast. Before, when she passed to Ouagadougou, this baby didn't know how to eat. But coming back from Bobo, this boy was eating anything. You know, if you are hungry, and they don't give you the breast, you must eat. So then, one day, the man told her that he would like to take his son to show the mother. And the girl said, "Ah, if that will be the case, I can see the mother, too. Then the mother will know that I am the mother of the son."

So this man saw that there was no way. So they went together. Then he left them there, about one week, with the mother in the village. And he said that after, she could come back to him. So she went back to Bobo.

And as this man was trying to do all this, she also tried to change her life. One day, she was going to the market, and she saw an *old* boyfriend, from when she hadn't got a child at all, from when she was young. She said she used to have a boyfriend in Kumasi. This boy was also from Bobo. Now he had left Ghana, and he was staying at Bobo. He was doing his own work. He had a shop in the market, selling things. So once she was going to the market, and she saw this boy on a motor. So she shouted on him, "Hey! Hey!"

The boy also started shouting, "Hey! Hey!"

So, you know, they saw each other. "Hey! What are you doing here?"

Then she said, "Ah, you see, after you left, I had a man who was from here like you, and we had this son in back of me.[2] So I came here. When I was in the house, every time my brothers used to tell me that I have my children, but they don't have a father, and they used to abuse me. So because of that, I came to find my son's father."

So the boy said, "Mm-m. It's nice."

Then she asked the boy, "Have you married?"

The boy said, "No, I'm not yet married."

1. because he would not take custody of a nursing baby
2. She was carrying the baby on her back.

She was telling this story to Limata, you know. Then I was also in the room, but I didn't sleep. *Ha!* Because as for me, she wouldn't tell me a story like this. She used to tell me the opposite one.

So then the boy said, if that will be the case, he will show her where his shop is. So the boy took her on the motor, showed her the shop, and he gave her five hundred francs. *Hey!* Somebody they give one hundred francs for chop, and then somebody gives you five hundred francs like this? It's millions! She was happy. So from there, every time, when the husband [1] went to work and gave her money to go to the market, she would pass at this boy's shop. The boy would send for beer to give her and drink. *Ay-ay-ay!* They would drink, and then when she was going, the boy would give her five hundred.

So this five hundred: do you know what she was doing? She was not spending the money. She was hiding it. She hid it till she had enough. She bought the baby clothes, about three dresses for the son. Then she bought three half-pieces of cloth for herself, complete ones to make a dress. So the husband asked where did she get money to buy that? Then she said, "Ah! When I came, did you want me to open my box and show you what I have brought? Or what? If I see something that is nice, I know that I am not going to stay here. I have only come to visit you. I know that I am going back. So if I have my small money, if I see something is good, I must buy it. In my place, I won't get some."

So the husband didn't say anything again. Going, going, going, going. And there was one girl who stayed in the house; she wasn't married. My sister also became a friend to this girl. And when she was cooking, as this food wasn't good, she cooked but she didn't eat what she was cooking. The day when this girl cooked, she would give to my sister. And this girl also used to talk Hausa to her. Then the husband said, No, he doesn't want her to talk Hausa in this house, because when they talk Hausa, they will start to talk about people.

Yeah, he didn't want her to talk Hausa because the wife didn't hear Hausa. If he goes to work, my sister and the other girl, by all means, they will talk about the wife. So the wife knew this. She gave the warning to the husband, "Maybe if you go to work, they used to abuse me with Hausa." You see? So the man was trying to stop this girl from talking Hausa, or even don't talk to that girl.

And she too, she said, "No, I can't live in a house with people without talking."

---

1. the father of the child. Hawa is using the term as a euphemism; such figurative use is common.

Then he said, "OK, you can speak Dioula. That girl also speaks Dioula."

She said, "Yes, but sometimes we don't feel like talking Dioula. Sometimes we feel like speaking Hausa." Then this was the place where the girl got trouble. He *beat* her. Then *both* her eyes were swollen. So she was telling Limata, "When I was packing, ah! Do you see these marks? Look at me. He tried to kill me."

I was about to laugh, but I didn't laugh. She finished all her talk and then went away. Then I came out. I told Limata, "Ah, *camarade,* this is *good!* The way they treated her is good, huh? She will go home. When she goes now, she will find a way. You wouldn't meet her with any man, and then '*huh-huh-huh-huh,*' like a dog, getting children like that. Who will look after them? Who will send them to school? Your brothers? They will also find [1] their own children. When they get married, they will get their children. They will like them, too. They wouldn't want to waste their money on your children for school and all that."

So the next day she came, but she changed the talks she had talked for Limata. She didn't say the same thing for me. She just said that when she went, this man just wanted to treat her like a child. And she had no life, so she couldn't help it. So when she was coming, she ran away from the man. That boy was the one who paid her transport.

Then I asked her, "Are you going back to that boy?"

She said, "No, because of my son. My father wants to see me. He has written to my big sister that I should come home. Maybe I will come later to see that boy."

Then I said, "You are going to that boy? He will do you more than what your husband did you."

Then she said, "Oh no, but he didn't treat me bad. What he was giving me every day, even I didn't want it."

Then I said, "Hey, hey. But you were telling my girlfriend that they were giving you a hundred francs for chop money. Why don't you tell me the truth? I am your sister. You shouldn't hide it from me, you know? I mean, even what you tell my friends, it is better you tell me myself."

So then she asked Limata whether what they converse, Limata used to tell me.

And I told her, "It's not Limata who told me. The time when you were talking, I was inside. They told you that I had slept."

She said, "Yes, but I saw you sleeping."

I said, "I didn't sleep. I heard all. But you should tell me the truth as

---

1. look to get

you told them. It's better, because you went and suffered. You suffered, and you came back. I can't tell you anything. I can't beat you. Even when you were young, I didn't beat you. How much about this time?" She is very funny.

So when she came, you know, our landlord he saw her, and he *liked* the girl. "Hey! Is this your small sister?"

I said, "Yes."

"Oh, she's nice, huh? But, why should she speak Dioula better than you?"

Then I said, "The mother is Dioula. This girl's mother is from Ivory Coast, so when they were small, they were speaking Dioula. So I am not like them. They speak pure Dioula in Côte d'Ivoire."

Then one day, this man came to our place about seven o'clock. He said, "Where is your sister?"

I said, "She has gone."

He said, "Where is she living?"

Then I said, "She is not living here. She is living with the other sister."

"Can you show me the place?"

Then I told him, "Somebody can show you, but not me. In my country, when you search for a small girl, you are looking for her. I am her big sister. Somebody will send you, but I cannot do that. But I am telling you: don't try it, because she has a small baby. If there is some problem there, we will share your properties."[1] *Ha-ha!*

So he said, "You, you are bad." *Ha-ha!*

It was because I know this girl. He wouldn't go with her much, just two or three times, and she will conceive. *Huh!* Seriously. I don't know how she used to get her babies. So I was afraid that if this man took her that one day they would say: Aha! When she came to me, I was giving her to my landlord without paying. Africans — they will *say* it. I know them. They will say I just took her to the man to go and fuck, so that I wouldn't pay my room rent. But I am paying. So I had to tell him something to be afraid to touch her. *Ha-ha!*

1. his things. That is, he will be dead.

12 THE ASHAWO ALTERNATIVE

: OUAGADOUGOU AND OTHER PLACES :

Women for Themselves

Anyway, you know, to be ashawo is not good, but I think I'm one of them, so—*Ha! Hee-hee!*—so I can't say that what they are doing is not good. It's not good anyway, but I think it's good also. Why do I say it is not good? Because we didn't come to do this. We didn't come to the world to be sexing for money. OK. We understand this. We know that it's bad things which we are doing.

OK. You don't have a good husband, OK? You don't have a good husband, so you go out.

Then: somebody has a husband, and she has a bad husband, and when she got out from the husband, she was *hot*. Maybe somebody can divorce from her husband, and she has only one or two cloths. Then she thinks, "Ah, if I'm going to marry now with these two cloths, they will finish. So I have to go and find more cloth before I marry."[1] When this kind of person is coming to do this work, what do you think? She has to sex for money, OK?

And some of us are from a poor family, you know? Maybe your father says you should marry, and you don't want the person, and that can bring a problem. Maybe the father has given his daughter to marry, and the daughter doesn't want it, so she is no more his daughter. But maybe this girl will also try her best to be somebody, so that even the father will come back to her. Or some girls try to hide their sexing at some place, to become somebody, and then they will come straight to the house and beg the family, "What I have done is bad." And the way the family will see her, they can't refuse her.

1. She is thinking that in another marriage, she might not even get any cloth, so she has to get her own.

And then: maybe the family doesn't need you, and you don't care too much about the family. So you think, "OK, I'm a woman. I'm going to make my way. If I gain, it's that place where the family men will come and find me." We have this. Yeah. We have the kind of people who go out from their family, and their family doesn't care about them.

You know, we African people, we are funny. Africans just want to see you looking nice, and they think that maybe you have something in your hands. That is all. Then if you do something, they don't look at your talk, whether you talk nicely, or you don't talk nicely. No. I know many girls who have been in a way like that, you know, from the family.

We have one girl now: she just went away from the husband like she had traveled. Then this girl went back. She met the same man again. Now they have three children. First, when she left the man, they had one baby. She just went out like that. And then, when she went to the parents, the father also said, "If you can't stay with this man, don't stay in my house." So this girl just got lost. About two years. Then she went and begged the father, "What I have done is not good."

I knew the girl before in Kumasi, when she was with the husband. And when we went to Ouagadougou, I met her. One afternoon we were in the house when they brought a telegram for her that fire had chopped her son. He was in hospital. He suffered wounds in many places. So this girl had to go away. She didn't even pay her rent. She didn't have money to pay, so she gave all her dresses to the landlord. She told him he can keep it, and then if she comes back, she will pay, because they brought this telegram and they said that her son is sick in fire. So the money she had, she couldn't use it to pay the room. She had to pay her transport to go. Until today, the man has her things. She didn't come back again. And now she has two more children with the husband. The same husband.

You know, in Africa, many girls, when they see somebody with money, they think they can become rich by *themselves*. This is what many girls think: "If I marry a rich man, he will be giving me, even for me to have my servant. But it will come to some time and he will say, 'Yeah, I did this and this for you.'" OK? There are many girls now who wouldn't want to hear that kind of talk. So many of them are trying for themselves. They want to have their money before they marry, and they try — they think they can make it by themselves before. Yeah, there are many girls who are thinking of this.

And then some of the girls think, "OK, if I don't make money before I marry, maybe I will be suffering with my husband. I don't want to do this work, but I have just come to find a lot of dresses and cloths. Then I will go and marry. Even if the man is a poor man, he can get money for me to eat. Then I will have my clothes. I will be all right with him." There are some girls like that, too.

And some of them think also, if she's rich and she's married to a rich man: if you are a big man, then she thinks she is also a big woman and you are afraid of her. This is also different. So all: everyone and their way of thinking, you know.

And some people think that the family is poor. She has come out of the family. She wants to make the good name of the family. Maybe she has come to do some different things for the family.

For example, my mother had one sister. I think our mother's house was poor, isn't it? But this girl — the sister — built a house in the village, so that everybody was calling the name of the house. There are some people who do that. But she didn't make ashawo. She made it by her own experience. She married one man and made him spend a little bit, and then she divorced, and she married another man, and she came and completed the place. *Ha-ha!* It's very funny. She didn't make ashawo. When she started, she was a student. Then the time she was at the college, she conceived with the first husband. She said that how she showed much love to the first husband, he came and did a small thing for her. OK. After the baby, she divorced and married another man. And with that man, she said, "Because of you, I have left this other man. I have left that place. I have a baby with him." Then this man came and completed the house. And now she has a baby with that person, too.

So yeah. You know, as for me, if I get a good husband, maybe I will marry. I want a person who is someone that we can understand each other. Someone like: "I can't say that what you say is a lie." And he too can't say something about what I'm saying. I want something like that, so that we understand each other.

You know, there are all these confusions. OK. We are together. Eh? I think this is a problem for many people. Somebody will see you today. He likes you. OK, you are together. Then, maybe, I know — every man, every kind of man, it's not white or black, it's any kind of man: they are just like a dog. He can go out and do whatever he likes. And what makes me have a big heart: I don't agree with my people. He will say, "Yes, yes, yes," and later, after a little time, then he will start bringing other talks from outside. You know, we have this kind of our men. Although some of them are intelligent, some of them are not. When he starts seeing something outside, then every time, if he comes to the house, he will make a problem with the woman. You know: *ta-ta-ta-ta-ta.* You don't do something wrong, but he will say, "This is wrong." I have seen this kind of life, too.

So this is why I think, maybe, if I can get somebody who has understanding. But, you know, I used to start with people, then I will study if it could be all right. But the way I will see coming: no. I didn't want it. And then you know, I don't want to chop my heart. *Ha!* You know? I can't chop it. So I have to stop.

And so as for marriage: maybe. I think maybe-maybe. Maybe I will get some, or maybe I won't get some. So I don't think of it. *Ha!* Ah, yeah, it's true. I don't think of it.

You know, when I started my life, I didn't start it in an easy way, to go there and go there. I used to like friends. OK, what is a friend? I think, if you are with somebody, you will know the person, and the person will know you, isn't it? If it's something like marriage, I think, you people can see. But, you know, I was trying all this way, and every time, I think, I used to be quickly annoyed and go away and leave the fellow. But as for me, you know, I am not someone who gets annoyed. You can see my character: I don't used to be annoyed. Even I can be talking to somebody as how we are talking today, and laughing and doing everything, but I know what I am going to do tomorrow morning: I'm going to pack my things, and you wouldn't know. I used to do these things. Because if something is hurting me, you know, to *say* it — to say to the fellow, "This thing hurt me" — it used to be difficult. And sometimes my heart used to give me some advice that, "Oh, this fellow, maybe he doesn't need you anymore. That's why he is doing this to you. First time, he didn't do this kind of thing to you. So he doesn't need you. He wants to do what you hate. So better than to tell him anything, just go away."

Then I follow my heart. What my heart tells me, I will follow it. I won't say anything to the person. Then, morning time, maybe he will go to work, and then later when he comes, maybe he will see a note: "Thank you very much. I'm leaving. No problem."

Yeah, so my heart used to teach me. So I can't say that I can marry or I cannot marry. I don't know. Maybe my heart will be changing, to say, "No, don't pack. Wait for him and tell him." But every time, when I am annoyed with somebody, my heart used to tell me, "Why should you wait for all this nonsense? This man hasn't married you. You are just sitting with him as a friendship, and he's trying to treat you this way. Maybe he's fed up with you. He just doesn't know the way to piss you off.[1] So in this case, show him that you too, you have taken notice about that, so you are leaving. So don't say anything to him."

---

1. to make you leave; to make you piss off

You see? I think that—to me—for a man and woman to be living together, I think you the woman—*first*—you have to accept yourself, to
know all that your mind wants. Isn't it? To *me*—I don't know—not for
every woman, eh? Because I don't have everybody's heart. As for my
heart, it used to tell me that if you are with somebody, you have to know
all that this person wants before you will start to know the person. If you
don't know all this, and maybe you are quick to know,[1] then you have to
think, "Oh-h, I should have patience. Maybe I like this fellow, or I love
this man, so I'll be patient with him to know who he is, or to know what
he wants, not to disturb him, or get some place to be annoyed."

So I think that it's the best thing for a woman. They used to say—oh,
anyway, some people say that women are bad, but I think some place they
also used to say that it's the woman who has patience. She has to be patient to see what the man wants, if he's all right with her. So sometimes,
I used to watch like that. And then, going to the ending, I will see maybe
how this man is in his life, and he wants that and that, but my life, I can't
compare my life to his life. So we can't live together. It's better that I
leave. This is what I think.

The Patience of a Mossi Mistress

Sometimes you will see some men, if they make a friendship with a girl
and the girl wants to leave the man, he will start making trouble with the
girl. And some men, too, if he wants to leave the girl, and he can't find
a way, he will give something heavy to the girl so that she will not be
annoyed. Yeah, this way, you can get it from the white people. But not
Africans. There are some white men, if you are packing your things to
go, he can say, "OK, I didn't sack you. You are fed up with me. But you
can take this to enjoy yourself for some weeks." But not Africans. He
wants something from you, or you want something from him. *Shit!*

You know, the *real* Voltaiques, I haven't been with one of them. I
haven't got time for them even to be a friend. I know many of them.
Somebody will be trying to follow you, for some days, some weeks, two
or three weeks, and if he doesn't get you, then he will go off. I get people
like that, trying to follow me: "Tonight I will wait for you."

Then I say, "OK, tonight I have a rendezvous," or "I have some
troubles," or "I'm not well." I will be teasing you for about two weeks;
then you will get fed up and go your way.

---

1. You make up your mind easily or quickly; you can jump to conclusions.

But I have seen the Voltaiques. They have been with many girls in Ouagadougou. The way they treat them, if you have that patience, you can't be poor, and maybe you can't be rich, but you can't be poor, too. If you are Ghanaian, maybe you can become rich. Many Ghanaian girls are rich, because you know that our money, if you change it to cedis, you will get plenty of money for Ghana. I know about three girls in Upper Volta who are Ghanaian, and they have houses in Ghana, with upstairs.[1] It is Voltaique money they built it with. And they stayed with the men. They are still with them. But the treatment the men give them: no. I can't help it. I can't do it. I like money, but—

Look. That treatment is: a man who knows a girl or a woman, he doesn't know the parents. Number one, huh? He doesn't know where you are from: he doesn't know the name of your village. But you are living with him as your husband, for some years — maybe two or three years. Your family doesn't know anything about it. Any time you are coming to visit, you have plenty of money. The people like it. But the kind of man you are living with: he also has a wife, and children, and his home. Maybe he has rented a room for you at some place. And any time, he has many people to be watching you to see if somebody is coming to you, or you are doing something. Anything they will come and tell that man, he will believe them. When he gets you, there are not any questions. He will start *pa-pa-pa-pa!* "Do you think I am a fool? To do this yesterday?" But he was not there yesterday.

"OK, what did I do?"

Maybe that fellow they saw coming to me, maybe he could be my brother. This Voltaique man doesn't know my family, isn't it? The one they saw could be someone coming to visit me from Ghana.

There's one girl, she had good living in Ouagadougou. Anyway, she is not a girl; she is a woman. She had an *old* Voltaique man. He opened a bar for the girl. Her brother — the same father, different mothers — came from Kumasi to see this woman. This boy had to sleep in a hotel. The Mossi man didn't agree. He said Ghanaian women are bad. They can take their boyfriend and make him their brother. The wife said that this boy is her brother; then the Mossi man said she should pack up and go with the boy. So this boy had to sleep in hotel. And the next day, the sister had to steal herself to go to the hotel and give him money to go home, because if somebody sees that she's coming to give this boy money, this man will sack her. And now I think they said she is rich in Kumasi. This kind of

---

1. a second story or upper stories

patience, I can't have it. I can't have it. I can't have a kind of patience like that.

So that's why I don't follow them. Yeah. As for me: if I want to stay with somebody, I will stay with the person; if I don't want, then I don't want. OK? I think a woman who hasn't got a husband, you know, she's going, going around before she can meet a man to stay with. She has seen many people before she preferred to stay with that fellow, isn't it? It's not that maybe the fellow will be thinking, "This girl, I don't trust her. Maybe if I go out, I have to put people to be watching her. And maybe if I go to work or if I go to my house, people used to come to her." If you take this way for me, it cannot work. I can't make even three days with the fellow. I have seen them with this kind of life — many of them.

So if I get them, I don't say I don't want to follow them. I used to answer, and then I bring my way. I say, "I'm Voltaique. I'm not a Ghanaian. I'm not a Togolese, to come here and search for money. I'm from this country. Before I will go with somebody, I have to know the fellow, who he is and what he is and his character, because I don't want to shame my family."

These Voltaique girls used to talk like this to their men, and the men understand. So when I say this to them, they also used to understand me. We will be like that for some few days, or maybe one week or two weeks' time, and every time when he's following me, it's the same topics I am saying. Then the person will get fed up and leave me alone. So the Africans, as for me, I have many friends among them for joking. *Ha!* They are foolish.

Who Wants to Live in an Institution?

So as for marriage, well, I don't know. Why? You know — how do I say this? — I don't want any humbug. Yeah. It's humbug. Because look: our men here. You can't know the good ones, and you can't know the bad ones. Maybe you will think a man is a good one, then he will come to be a bad one.

Our men here: maybe the first time you meet with the man, you will be happy with him, and you can be together, but some time in the future, maybe you won't feel like that. You see? Maybe the life he will start to show you, you will get fed up. So to be going here and there, to marry here, and from there, to divorce, and go and marry again: I think of all these things. I think the best thing: if I can get something to do on my *own*. You know, something that is profitable. To me, I think that is better.

You know, sometimes our men chase women outside. But I think even for a man who has wife, this is not important. But my problem is: maybe you will meet the fellow and marry, and you are staying together — OK?— it won't take a year, and maybe he will tell you he's going to marry another woman. And that woman will come. He wouldn't take even a year again. And you know, as much he is marrying, as much he is changing. Because, maybe before, when you were alone, sometimes you could get time to sit down to talk together, to do some nice things. The time he marries again, you wouldn't get all this time. You are not alone. He has to be there and be there and be there. And so you can't really know what he wants.

Do you see? Some of the men, when they are going to start, they will start it on this way. As you have been there, maybe you know that, "Oh, I used to do this thing when we were alone. My man liked it." But when he wants to start these things, maybe you will do something for him, and he will say, "Oh no, this thing, you shouldn't do it like that." But you have been doing it! When you people were together, you have been doing it, and he accepted it. And this time he's trying to tell you, "No, you shouldn't do that and do that."

All this is trouble. These things: maybe because of the new ones, he's just getting tired with you, and he cannot tell you to go, so he will pass on top of some things. Anything, when it's not wrong, to him it's wrong. And then he will be starting it. Then you will be there. He doesn't say he doesn't like you. And maybe you can't say, "Let us divorce," because it's not many African women who are strong to divorce their husbands. Always, the men divorce their wives.

You see my big brother: he has two wives, OK? He has divorced the first wife, but the woman is still living in the same house with him. She doesn't want to leave her children. So some of the men don't get really divorced, but the man doesn't take care of the woman, and the woman also can't go her way. She will be there suffering. She can't get any nice dress to wear, because he won't buy her a dress, and she hasn't got money. And she hasn't got money to do any training or any work. So she will just be there like that.

So I think of all this, in my life. If I get things like that, it may be a problem for me. So I used to think of myself, if I can do something by myself. So, maybe I can stay by myself: I think that may be better than to get all this kind of problems.

You know, if you can find a man who understands, maybe you will be all right, eh? But this time, how I used to see the people: I don't think they understand. In the olden days, I think in my father's time, the man could have two wives or three wives, and they will understand themselves. Maybe you can have the first wife and then you add the second wife. You will have understanding with your first wife. The two wives will be like sisters: nobody will hear about them. Even if they have a quarrel between themselves, nobody — even inside of the house — nobody will know. They will hold themselves seriously, that they understand themselves.

But this time, it's not many people who have it like that. But if it's not this understanding, then maybe the one wife will want to be jealous, to be taking action against the other one. Any time this man goes to the other one, she will say something. And he will go to other one, and she too will say something. Maybe the man will start getting fed up with the other one, because maybe she is the older and now he has got a young one. Even if the older one is right, he wouldn't give her the right. He will give the right to the young one, because he's getting that one now. Or maybe the man trusts his first wife, and this woman will be talking to him and spoiling his mind about the new one.

So all this is the case. This is why I don't have a feeling to marry. You know, sometimes I'll be thinking, "How can I ever marry?" Sometimes if I'm thinking of all these things, if I'm in bed, I used to say, "Shit." I will think, all this, there is no need of *any* of it. I think somebody can be married, and somebody will not be married. It is not any problem. It depends on what you think.

You know, even you can get somebody and you have understanding with him, and he will be free with you and doing everything with you, but still — you know, we Africans, we have much believing. OK? If the man has two wives, maybe the one will go to a maalam to make juju, maybe to make her husband quarrel with the other one and sack her, because she wants to live alone with the man.

All this juju, Africans believe in it. And they have been doing it. You know, I think maybe if you have belief on the thing, if you do it, it used to work. Or something like that. This thing is happening all the time. I can see that there are some women who make it. As Africans say — you know, they used to say that maybe the one wife made the other wife some juju and she became a crazy woman, taking off all her clothes, walking in the street. These things used to happen. In villages. Even in town, it can happen, too. I think many people in the village, they are the people who are living in town now. Isn't it? So if this can happen in the village, it can happen in town, too.

You know, there are some women who are nice women. You can see this. Some women are good to the husbands. Maybe when they are together, if the husband goes to get another wife, or he sees a woman he likes, this first woman will try her best to be going to this other woman, to be free with her, or to treat her like a sister. She is going to visit or greet all the families of that woman, so they will say, "Oh, your husband has a nice wife. She is not a jealous woman. This woman is nice." You know?

But maybe this girl will come to marry and in a short time, that first wife will start getting fed up. Or the second one who is coming now, she will get fed up with the first one. What will happen? Before, they understood each other, but when they meet for some time, then they will get fed up from each other. Why do they do that? Just because there are many problems for the husbands and wives. Those who used to take many wives, maybe he takes another woman, and it's not that he doesn't love the other. He loves them also. But maybe he loves one more than the other. You know, even for children, some people can give birth to many children, but they have one child they like more than the others. So to marry a man who can marry many women, it's the same thing. There's one he loves more. And the one he loves, every time, maybe he will be giving her things, or be giving her some money as help for herself. And he will leave the other ones.

And maybe that woman also will try her best. She is trying for herself. I can see that some women who are married, they are suffering for themselves. They buy their own cloth, and they sit outside and tell the other wife of the husband, "It's my husband who bought it for me today." But she bought it with her own money. If you are jealous, you will think your husband is giving her money more than you. You will start to be heartsick when you are going to your husband.

And maybe some men can be keeping other women and treating them well, doing everything, and the other ones are there suffering. Then maybe the other one will think, "This man, when I was with him first, he wasn't like that. What is this kind of life?" She will start thinking. But as she has started getting all these problems, she cannot say, "I don't like you again. I'm going." Maybe she has some children. Some women used to think of their children: "Well, if I leave this man, my children will be here. This fucking woman will teach my babies bad ways." So she wouldn't want to leave. Yeah. You know, here in Upper Volta, the children are for the man. If you get a divorce, your children are not for you. You don't want your husband anymore: even a one-year-old baby, even one month, if the man wants, he can take the baby away.

This time, they used to have this case in court, and the government doesn't give the babies to the men. They don't allow them to keep the small babies, because some man will divorce the wife and keep the baby, from one month old, and maybe the baby will grow, and maybe sometimes these babies die. He doesn't care. Yeah. So this time they will give the baby to the woman if the baby is very small, up to the time he has grown, and every month, the man will send money to the baby. In court, they will tell him how much he can send for the month so that she can feed the baby with that. But when the baby grows a bit, the man will take the baby.

So to marry: I used to see the women become jealous. As for me myself, I don't know it much. I don't know how to make a jealous way, I think, maybe because I didn't marry. Sometimes I can be annoyed. This is not jealousy. If I'm with somebody, and I'm seeing him with another woman, I can be annoyed with the fellow. The next time he will come, I will say, "No, I'm sorry, but maybe I think you have another one who will be better than me," or something like that. He can go home. I used to get annoyed quickly and just piss off by myself. *Ha!* It's not jealousy. What do you think? Is this jealousy? I get annoyed quickly, that's all. I just don't like the way. I will tell you, "OK, go out with her. It's finished between us." If it were jealousy, maybe I would be trying to force, to say, "Don't follow that girl again." This is what I think is jealousy. *Ha!* I don't think my way is jealousy. Really. If I give you a free chance, it's finished. If I were jealous, then I would try to fight with the other woman, or I would try to say, "OK, today, if you are going to this place, we will go together, and that and this." But I don't do that.

Just, you know — I want to be free any time. I think, when I was young, I had many problems, so this time I want to be free. If I see something that will come and trouble me a little bit, then I will get myself out. Then you can continue with the others. So to me, it's not jealousy.

If we are two of us with one man, I wouldn't mind. Well, if the man says I should love the other girl, then as for me, I can love her. If the girl can also love me the way I will love her, we will be together: I wouldn't mind. But maybe I will answer, yes, I would like to meet this girl as your girlfriend. And maybe the girl wouldn't like to meet me as your girlfriend. So in this case, I wouldn't like to sit and see all this.

So the best thing, if I see you with her, I am not asking you a question: "Do you love her or don't you love her?" I'm not asking this girl, "Do you love this man?" or "When did you know this man?" *No-o-o!* I will just tell you, "OK. This is the case. This is what I saw. I think if we are going to be two girlfriends for you, then you are giving me a problem. I don't know what she's thinking. She doesn't know what I'm thinking, too. Maybe I think I'm doing something good for her, but to her, maybe it's not good. So the best thing: I want you to be with this girl. She is a nice girl anyway.

Any place I see her, I would like to be a friend of her. So I think it's better that you continue with her, then I am out. Any time, if I see the two of you people, I can come and greet you people. We can sit together, or we can have some nice conversation. I won't care about that."

Ha-ha! Yeah. Maybe he wants to have me and the other girl, and maybe the other girl wouldn't like it. There are some girls who can show their face that they like it, but they don't like it. Even I can be showing myself to the other girl like I like her, but maybe a time will come and I wouldn't like her. She can decide so. You can decide so. But this is what I'm telling you. *We* know that when we are coming out, we will like each other, but it wouldn't take us a long time and you will see that we will start to be fed up with each other.

You know, if I see maybe two or three women with one husband, if their living is nice, you know, if they understand each other, then I used to like them. It's nice. But this is what I hate, because — look — here, in Africa, if you stay in a house with women like that, the first time you meet them, you will think that they are nice. Maybe you are a stranger, you don't know well. You will stay in the house. If you study them, you can know their character.

This is the problem I saw from my landlord in Lomé. He had four wives. Every time, two will come for about two or three months. Then they will go away, and the other ones will come. He was bringing them two by two. You see? He didn't keep all four of them together in the compound. When two of them come, they are nice. They are cooking together. They eat together. They can converse together. They do everything together. The work. Anything. But by all means, one will come and tell me, "You see my husband's other wife, she has done that, she has done that." OK? The other one also will come: "You see that woman. You have to take care with her. She is that and this and that." But if you see them outside, or if you don't know them, or the way they live, you will think that they like each other. Yeah? So why did this one want to come and tell you that the other one was doing that and this? This is your problem? It's not your problem: you are not her husband. Why should they come and tell you this kind of thing?

To me, if I'm living with a husband who has another wife, and I like this woman, maybe she will do something I don't like: I wouldn't fear her. To me, I wouldn't go and tell somebody. I would call her and say it in front of her, "Look. This is what you have done, but I don't like it. Anyway, I don't say to don't do it, but don't do it to me. I don't like it." You see?

Then, if this woman is continuing to do that, I will call the man: "This

is what this woman is doing to me, and I have told her I don't want it."
So if the woman understands, or the man understands, maybe they will
talk about this, or we will go to people to talk about this, and then it will
be finished. Isn't it? I will accept it. If she's finished, I will know. If she
doesn't finish, I will see too. *Mm-hm.*

And sometimes, too, here in Africa, you will see this problem in our
Muslim custom. I don't know the Christians. But in the Muslims' custom,
the day you are cooking in the house, you are the one who is going to
sleep with your husband. OK? And the other wife is there. Sometimes,
maybe the wives eat together. But sometimes there are some women who
are very clever: they make two kinds of soup. These soups: she puts all
the meat inside the man's soup, and the soup for the house, or for the
families, maybe she will put some small meat, or she will just find some
fish and put it inside. And then when she comes to eat with the others,
she won't eat much: "Oh, I—I have cooked today. I am tired. I can't eat
anything." And she will leave. And after, she will go and eat the other
soup with the husband. OK?

You see? They want to take the husband from the others. She's doing
that so that every time, when it's her time to cook, this man will like her.
And when it's the other one's time, maybe she doesn't have this experience. She just buys food for everybody. And the man wouldn't like to eat
that food. And he also doesn't know the experience that the other one is
using to cook for him. And so some men can refuse their wife, or they can
like the other wives because of the way they cook.

Especially here in Upper Volta, there are many Mossi people who used
to tell me that they are married with Voltaique wives, but they don't like
their food. But they get a Ghanaian or Togolese girl; they cook good. So
they don't understand why the Voltaique women don't know how to
cook. OK? If this kind of man has a girlfriend, then all his property is for
the girlfriend. He will give her more and more. You are in the house, and
you will start suffering. And maybe it's not your fault, because maybe the
money he is giving you to cook can't reach what to buy to cook better. But
when he starts with this girlfriend, maybe one day he will give her three
thousand, four thousand or maybe five thousand. This girl will be happy.
That day, maybe she will say, "Today I want you to come and eat with
me." And she will use the money to make some nice food. She will get this
man from you. And he doesn't think. He can spend more on the girlfriend
than the wife, because he's getting all the good food from there. The wife
will be in the house, dirty. And he doesn't think that because of the
money he gives to the girl, that's why the girl can cook a good cooking.

Suppose he gives that money to the wife, even if the wife doesn't know cooking, maybe she will try to do something better than what he has been eating every day.

There is one man. He has a shop. I think he has about two or three wives. When you see him, you will like him. If you saw the man outside, you would say, Oh, this is a nice man. But the children: go and see the children in morning time when they are going to school. It is their mothers who will take one piece of their cloth to tie around the neck of the children to go to the school. And go and see where the girlfriend lives. She has a fridge. She has a big changer:[1] it can play records; it has a tape, together with a wireless, a big one. She is living at a good house: twenty-five thousand for the month. And the wives are with the children, and they have to put old cloth around the children's necks to go to school. If you have this kind of life, what are you going to think? Or if you see somebody like the girlfriend, what are you going to think of your life? Yeah. He just feels that the way he likes the girlfriend, that is all.

And even there are some men who can tell the other wife, "Be careful with my senior wife," or "Be careful with my younger wife." If he says that, what will you think about it? You will think: "OK, he married both of us two. And he's telling me to be careful with the other. Or, he is telling the other to be careful with me." How will you think of it? Some of the African men, if you go inside of them, the men themselves, this is what they do: they can go between the women. The women will be coming good friends, and the men can separate them as they like. Any time they want to separate them, they can separate them. If he tells you different things and goes and tells the other one different things, maybe tomorrow you won't want to see the other one's face. She doesn't want to see your face also. You see? What is it going to start? You are going to start to scratch each other. This is the way. Some of the African men do it.

In this our African way, you know, you the wives and this man can be together, having nice conversation. But the day when you and he are two together, he knows what to talk to you. He won't tell the truth. Maybe what he will tell you, you will think, "Ah-h-h." And when the other one also comes to him, it's different talks again. So this is *all* problems he's causing. This is what many of them do. *Shit!* It's *shit!*

So some girls look at all these things, and they don't want to marry. They say they don't need to marry. Even, if they want a baby, then they just have the baby by themselves because they don't want to marry.

1. sound system with record changer

The Issue of an Issue

But to me, anyway, I don't think it is good to have a baby, and you don't want to marry, to say, "OK, I have two babies, so I don't think of marrying again." Because of a baby, you want to marry, but then if you have the baby, you don't need marriage again.

To me, if you haven't got a husband, what do you want children for? This is what I think. When my mother died, I suffered. If I thought I was going to have a baby, maybe if I know that this is the father of the baby, and he is all right, then maybe. But as for the other girls who want to get a baby, and they don't know who is the father, or they don't bother about the father, I'm not thinking of it.

You know, I like children. Yes. But even if I might feel to have children, the way I am, I don't feel it. I don't have a way to look after a child. What I don't want: to have a child, and this child is just living with the mother all the time, growing up.

You know, if I have a child, I can keep her in my village. They will look after her. My father will be training her in this bush way. Maybe she will be all right, or maybe she wouldn't be all right.

But I just feel something like — OK, you can get a child. Maybe you just make a sometimes friend with a fellow. Isn't it? And you have a kind of child. And maybe the fellow goes away. You don't hear anything about him again. And this child is with you. Sometimes, there may be some problems, some talk and something like that. Maybe the child will bring something like he is clever, and they will just say, "Oh, get out of here. You can be clever. Do you know your father, even, to be clever?" In Africa, we have this kind of talks.

I told you my father has one son and we don't know the mother. Isn't it? And sometimes in our family — the same family — somebody used to get annoyed with him and say, "Oh, shit. I won't mind you. You don't know your mother." It's abuse. And how much if they say "You don't know your mother and you don't know your father." It's more abuse than that. And you know, if you are a woman and you are there, maybe at that time you will be an old, old woman, and maybe they will insult your child like this, and you will think about this talk. You know, it is not the baby they have insulted. It's *you*. Suppose this baby had a father: you are the one who knows, isn't it? So this case, when I think about it, I don't want to have cheap babies like that. I would like a baby. Not to say I don't want to have a baby. Yes, I would like to have a baby. But in this kind of way: no.

Sometimes too, I used to think about the way I grew up. My life when I was young, before I grew up, I think that is enough for me to take some mind like that, not to bring somebody in the world to be suffering. I know: maybe my mother didn't know that she was bringing me to be suffering, but she died and left me. OK? But in my own way, the way I am, I wouldn't want things like that. I don't feel it. I don't feel to be getting a child without a husband.

OK. I have a friend, and I have a baby, and I'm happy with the baby. It's my baby, my own baby. Maybe I will get a time[1] for him to stay with me, to be growing up. OK? Maybe I wouldn't get a time too. But I think, this kind of baby, what does he do? He goes there and there and there. And he wouldn't get good treatment, eh? Before he grows up, he wouldn't be good. I don't want this way. I don't feel it. The children for a woman alone: I don't feel it.

You know, I have conceived before. But this time I know much, so I won't conceive. Before, when I didn't know anything, yes. I conceived about three times. The first one, I caused abortion, but it was not the real abortion in a hospital. At that time I was at my parents' place. I told you that there are some friends who used to show the medicine. There was one of my girlfriends who showed me. This is what I said: some people have luck. Some people don't have luck: they die. You know this blue powder which they put on dresses?[2] I drank it but I didn't die. But somebody can drink it and die. Yeah, to cause abortion, some girls die with it. But some girls also cause abortion with it and get up.

Then other times, you know, I was afraid, because the first one, how I suffered, I thought I was going to die. So the second time, I had to go and see a doctor. So they did me with the instrument, you know, D&C,[3] to cause the abortion. So that one passed.

And the third one, oh, he was not old. He was about two months. I got these African women who are selling these trees. You know, there are some African women who are selling many, many, many medicines. Even men used to sell: many, many kinds of medicine. All are from trees. You have the one you can pump; you have the one to chew it; they have the one you put in drink. They have many, many things.

So I got one woman, and then I told her that I wanted this medicine. You know, it was very funny. She asked me, "Have you got a baby?"

1. have a chance; have a way
2. a laundry whitening agent
3. dilation and curettage

I said, "Oh, Mama, I have a baby only three months old. So I'm very ashamed for people to see this."[1] You know, she didn't want to give me the medicine, so I talked to her like that.

Then she said, "OK. So — and your man has agreed?"

I said, "Oh-h, even it's my man who told me that if people see, it will be a shame for us."

This woman didn't know I'm ashawo. I don't have a husband. *Ha!* I was bossing her, because there are some kind of old ladies. Some old ladies like that, when you tell them you didn't have a baby before, she will say, OK, that she will give you medicine. But she can give you some kind of medicine, and you will take *any* kind of medicines to cause abortion, they can't. If you play with it, you will die with it. There are some old ladies, bad ones like that. So I was talking a sweet talk to her. So she said, "OK, I will give you this thing. In three days' time I will come and see how it is."

Then I said, "OK."

"I won't charge you for anything. You should bring forty pesewas."[2]

Then I said, "OK." Then I gave her the forty pesewas.

So she just went away. I wanted quick. I went and ground this thing, put water on it, and took it out of the water, and heated it in the fire, the way she showed to do it, and I went and pumped it. You pump where you go to the toilet. So when you pump, you go to the toilet.[3] OK? Then you go and rest. Then fifteen or twenty minutes: good God! You feel some *pains!* Yeah. When you pump this, you will shit all this water, with shit or anything. And you are free. But in fifteen or twenty minutes, you start to turn up, your waist, your stomach, everywhere. Then sometimes the medicine will leave you for a *small* time like you are sleeping. You don't have a good sleeping; you are just like you are dreaming. Then maybe you will feel like, "Ah-h, I have some blood."

So it's very difficult to cause abortions. I have done this three times. And God should forgive me: I wouldn't try it again. So I have to take care

1. The shame would be that she has had sex while caring for an infant. Among many Voltaique peoples it is felt that a woman should not become pregnant and give birth when she is still nursing another baby, a situation thought to be detrimental to the children's health. In some societies, it is customary for a woman who has just given birth to stay with her family until the baby walks before returning to her husband's house. Hawa is bossing the woman to save her from the disgrace of having had sex too soon after giving birth.

2. unit of Ghanaian currency like a penny: one hundred pesewas to a cedi, ten pesewas to a shilling

3. as an enema

of myself. I don't have any way to do. I don't take anything, but I know the day I have my menstruation, OK? If you are serious with the day, and the day doesn't pass much, it is not serious. This is not abortion. If you know the correct day when you used to get your menstruation, and you have counted on it, you know, you won't let it pass two weeks, or one week. That one is not hard. It's not like abortion. You can do anything and then you will be all right. There are many, many small things that used to take care of it. Look, you know that maybe you will pass menstruation on the twenty-second or twenty-third, then you don't get it, up to the thirtieth. It's one week, eh? You don't get it. OK? Even APC, if you take about four, if you don't have strong blood, the next day you will see you will pass menstruation completely. I think some people's blood is different. Some small tablets like that, if they are serious tablets, sometimes they can bring your menstruation.

So if you know that you don't want this thing, then don't keep it. If you keep it to a week or two weeks' time, then you are giving yourself suffering. But if it's two or three days' time, like that, it won't give you a lot of problems. But if you keep this thing and say, "OK, maybe my time has changed," then maybe you will see problems.

You know, there is a saying, that sometimes some months can change. Yeah, we know that some months can change. But I wouldn't know whether it's the month that is changing or what. So that time, if I delay my menstruation, I have to take something. Sometimes I can take APC. Or sometimes I have a tablet, and if I take that one, it will go; it comes by itself. That tablet, at first I got it from a clinic. I went to a clinic, and they wrote all these things for me. They wrote down many tablets and many things for me to buy. I kept the paper, so any time I used to go and buy the medicine by myself.[1]

So to me, if I don't get a child, it's OK. If I haven't married and I don't get a child, I'm OK. Some people used to say that a child will take care of you when you are old. But anything can happen. *Mm-hm.* Look at the way I grew up, huh? Isn't it? To get a baby, a child to come and grow up in my way, you know? Shit.

But, you know, many girls are coming to be in trouble at this point, on the part of babies. They don't know much about all these things, or maybe they don't want to know. Some of them know, but they just want the baby. Their way is that if they want, they have their baby. You see? They are happy to get their baby. This kind of people in Africa, they are plenty.

1. Many pharmacists in West Africa dispense medicine directly like that.

But at our side, if my mother is going to divorce from my father when I'm young, then my father is taking me with him. At our place, all the children will follow the father. They won't follow the mother. You see these Ashantis: if they go to divorce, the children follow their mother. I know this about Ashantis. That kind of woman, if she has a child and she doesn't have a husband, she likes it, because already, when she is married, all the children are for her. But many people also follow the father, like at our side. Ewe people, I don't know much about them, but I used to see many of them who have the name of the father, so I think they follow the name of the fathers. And even there are also some Ashantis who don't care to follow the name of the mother.

So the girls who don't want to conceive, some take pills. And then somebody doesn't take pills. Any time, she feels like, "I will let it come, and then I'll go and cause abortion." Well, I think there are not many of them who take pills — to go to a doctor and all these things — not many girls.

And you know, some of the girls used to go to the doctor and cause abortion. And maybe someone doesn't get the real doctor, and then she can be dead. Some of the girls, when they conceive, they don't want to be telling many people. They don't even want the doctor to know about it. So they tell only some of the friends, and the girlfriends tell them, "Ah, the last time, I took these things, and then I have caused abortion with this and that." You will get the same thing. But maybe you are not the same as her, so it can chop you off. Then you are going to die.

You know, in the house where we are in Ouagadougou, there was a Ghanaian girl who was there before we came. We heard this case when we were in town. This girl was conceived four or five months. There was another Ghanaian girl: she used to cause abortion herself. She doesn't go to a doctor. She has her own African medicine. There is a flower; it has a big, big leaf. When you cut it, the water comes like milk: white. It's a *poison*. There are many girls who cause abortion with this. But that flower is poison. Yeah. They take it and peel all the skin, and then put it inside their vagina — yeah — and leave it there, from morning to evening, then change it again, like that, so that this thing can cause an abortion. So this girl showed the conceived girl this thing, and she brought her the thing. Then maybe it was not good for her. When she was doing it three days, blood didn't come, but she was feeling some kind of bad pains. They took her to hospital. And she was dead. Before she was going to die, and she said who was the girl who gave her the medicine to cause abortion. Then that girl went off from Ouagadougou. People said she is in Abidjan. And this other girl just died like that.

So the abortion: some girls used to feel like they can do it by themselves, you know. They die. And some people too used to meet the wrong doctors. They won't meet the good doctors. And they also die.

This thing, in Accra, I think I saw it about four or five times. And Ouagadougou: oh, as for Ouagadougou, *whew!* I have seen it more than ten times. I heard and I saw. I've heard and I have seen, more than ten times.

So the girls who conceive, some are happy, and some do not want it. Some are happy because they think they can give the baby to their mother or grandmother to take care of it. Yeah. But you can give the baby to somebody, and then maybe you don't have enough to give that fellow to care for the baby: all is suffering. And if you don't have any good thing to put this baby in school, maybe this baby is just coming to be like you yourself. Or maybe your own is even better than hers. So this case, I think some people are happy with their baby, but I think that it is not correct.

These babies, in future, when you can't look after them, how do they become when they grow up? If they don't get a good education, how do you think they are going to come? They're going to be worse than you. If it is a boy, he is going to be a burglar, a thief—first-class—trying to put his hand in pockets. Burglar number one. Don't you see that? If it's a girl, too, she wouldn't reach twelve years when she will start to be following everyone. You know? This is the business you did and gave birth to her. She hasn't seen her father, and you didn't send her to any good school, and she can't continue to live with you.

But there are some children, when they see the father, sometimes they will be better. You know, many children don't fear the mother as much as the father. And sometimes, too, maybe if the girl doesn't marry to that fellow she has the baby with, then later if she is married, her husband won't look after that child well.

So if you have a child, without a husband: how do you see it? You know, we are talking about the girls who have children as they like. Some people want their children because, "I have my two children; I wouldn't need to marry." Some people think they are all right just to show that she also can have a child. To them, maybe it's good, but to me, it's not good. Maybe they can't care for the child, isn't it? This child is going to grow bad. If the child doesn't have a father to take care of him, he will start doing all these things. Even, I think that the girls who have children like that, they're the people who should search to marry quickly. It's better for them. But they don't know. To have children and not to search for marriage, to me, in any case, I don't think it is good.

So our village girls: if it's somebody who is in a village when she has a child like that, she will try to find a man to marry quickly. The village girl. What she doesn't want: maybe this child doesn't have a father, and maybe she will be going around again; the second time, she will get the same kind of child. So she has to find a man to marry quickly.

Serial Monogamy

You know, to me, I think it is good to stay with one person. But the reason why you have to change boyfriends is not from anything: it's only the men. Maybe you can see somebody. Maybe you like the person. You don't know who he is. You will think he's that and this. But unless you go some time with him before you will know his character. So: unless you see, before you can know. This is what I say. Maybe he's not the kind of person you think. So what should you do? You should leave. You can't help it. For me, this is my way. When I walk with somebody and his way is not a good way for me, then I leave him.

So if I get a nice person, I'll follow him and just see how far it's going to go. You know, there are some people, hm? They cannot say something direct to you. Maybe you will be all right, but in future, maybe he will become fed up and he cannot tell you that he's fed up with you. OK? He will start to find some ways, you know, just to kick himself or something like that. When I see this way is coming, I wouldn't like to wait until you kick yourself. I think it's better to say, "OK, if that will be the ending of the show, then OK. It's the end. I don't need it anymore."

Usually if I have someone, I am not fed up. You know, this is what I told you, because I don't want to be there and there and there. OK? I think it's better if you are in one place. Then you are not so much like the other friends, whereby you will get a bad name. Maybe it's not like that, but maybe people will think that you want to be in one place. Every time you used to be some place; you are not just doing this ashawo for that and this.

And so I used to be happy to be living with people. I don't used to be happy every time to go to nightclub, and from there to another club, tomorrow with this person, and now tomorrow it is not good, and I'm going to change for another person. I don't like this much, you know. Even now, I'm trying to do it, but I don't like it. Sometimes I force to do it. I force to do it for what? I think, OK, maybe tomorrow I will have to do something but I won't have the money. So maybe if I try to go with somebody, I can get this money to do what I want, to do it tomorrow. And that and this.

But if you are with somebody, the way you can be with somebody from the starting, it's *nice*. You will think that if this thing can go like that, you people can stay together forever. But you will be starting like that, and then after, you will see that this thing is moving roughly. It will start making rough. Any small thing, maybe you will think of that thing as joking, something to laugh about, and it's not something for this person to be annoyed, but he may become annoyed at that place. Or he will bring some excuse, this is that and that is this. So this is what I told you. When I see this thing start coming, I think that the person is fed up, but he hasn't got any excuse to say, because maybe you didn't do the fellow bad. So he just finds the place now to make some excuse.

So this case is not a case to join and argue, to say, "Before when I was with you, this thing didn't happen," or "I don't know what you are bringing now. If you are fed up with me, you have to tell me." I haven't got time to ask all these things. If I see that the sea is changing to red — the sea is blue, but if it's changing to the color red — then I kick myself before the sea will become red.

I think that between a man and a woman — even we all know this — if you have a girlfriend, and this girl is starting to become fed up with you, there's some kind of way you will know. But there are some people who think, "Oh, this thing, it can come like that. He can be going off like that, and we'll be together again." But she doesn't know. She thinks he will be going away and coming back, and you people will stay together again. And that is the time when the boy will be getting power. He didn't marry you. He doesn't know your family. You people have just met as a friendship. So to me, if I see that somebody is playing this way, I will just stop it like that. It is not a problem.

So my way, on the part of friendship, or my way, how I'm living with people: sometimes, you will meet some fellow, and you will think that maybe this fellow is a nice fellow. He is not rough; he is not doing this way or that way. Maybe if you are living with him, you are not having any problems. Maybe on your side, you will be all right. You wouldn't be rich — not to say you will become rich when you are living with this fellow — but you wouldn't become poor, too. What we Africans say is: you don't come rich and poor. But if the fellow can feel for you all right, and then you people are nice together, without any quarreling, to me, this is what I used to think.

You know, if I try, and today I go out, I will get one man. Tomorrow, that man doesn't want me, or I don't want that man. I will take other one. OK? Maybe the other one I have taken yesterday is good, and the one I'm taking today is somebody I don't know. Maybe he's going to show me something. But I don't know this. This is what I use to make up in my mind, if I get somebody and he is nice, and he's a very cool guy, and any time, when you are together, it is: "What should we eat?" and he will say, "OK, you can take this and go and provide." And sometimes this person will know that, "Oh, this girl is with me. I should buy her a cloth." If it is in this way, then I think — to me — I think that it is better than to go out.

Private Ashawo

Today you go with someone; tomorrow you go with someone. This is the problem in Ouagadougou: there are many girls, huh? They used to go out. OK? They don't want to work in any nightclub.

And this man with the bankcard, the one I told you who is taking one thousand or five hundred a day: any money you give him, he keeps it for the ending of the month. Some people pay five thousand. These girls who are walking round like that, they do this: five thousand a day. Ending of the month, how much does she have? She has plenty money.

But sometimes you will see her in the hospital, or you will see her somewhere, and you will have pity. Somebody will just carry her to the bush side and do what he wants, and then leave her in the bush. Or if she's not lucky, they have wounded her, and she will go to the doctor. So when I think of all these things, it's better if somebody understands, and you are living with him, and you are doing everything correctly.

All these troubles, I don't know which people are doing these things to the girls, because the girls can't say. Some people say it's white people; some people say they are black. I was not with them. They used to come and give their complaints. So some white people do them, and some black people do them. And the white people, you cannot know if they are French, or they are what kind.

This ashawo: every girl has the way she is inside The Life. And I think we are all the same, but as for me, on my way, the difference is because maybe the others don't want to be keeping friends. They are thinking that keeping friends with you is a waste of time before they will get your money. And they can be also hustling every time to get their money every day as they want. There are some girls who think of that. There are some girls who are sharp: they used to get them quickly. Every time they used to talk this, but I think that it's their luck. Maybe it's your luck which God gave you. Today you will get this from this fellow. This is your luck. But I don't believe what they say, actually.

As for me, since I had my problem in Accra, when I kicked off from Accra, I didn't have a boyfriend. I don't keep a boyfriend because I think of what I have seen inside it many times — it's not once, you know. I think that maybe it may become the same thing. When I went to Oua-

gadougou, it was only one German man I have kept friends with, because
he was trying well. That's why I stayed with him. But from there, I didn't
have a boyfriend.

When I got to Ouagadougou, then you know, the *first* day we went to
the nightclub, we had one white man to be drinking with him. A French
man — some fucking boy — he was only twenty-six years old. He's a fucking boy. He was spending money and taking us to the other places, and enjoying with us. He was at Hôtel Indépendance. He was just coming from
France to work in Ouagadougou. This kind of people, you meet them first.
And the way they show you —first, second, third, fourth one — you will
see things. This man showed me a lot of experience when I started with
their people. This is why I started charging them. You have to start rough
with them.

You see me today, and you say, "OK, I want to go with you."

And then I say, "What way do you want to go with me? I'm not like
that, 'to go with me.' If you want to go with me, you have to be serious."

He will say, "Oh, but I can wait for you to finish your work."

Then I will say, "OK, if you can wait for me." I wouldn't say any price.
OK, you have been buying me drink, you've been dancing, and then the
drink you bought me, maybe I have some commission for it. So after fin-
ishing the work, this is time I start to make rough a little bit. I will say,
"OK, we are finished. What do you say?"

He will say, "OK, we will go to my house?"

I will say, "No, but we don't go like that. You have to tell me what you
are going to give me, you know."

He will say, "OK, you are the woman. You have to say what you want."

Then I say, "OK. I want fifteen thousand." Maybe I will say I want ten
thousand or fifteen thousand.

Somebody will say, "Ah! Fifteen thousand! For what?!"

And I will say, "Oh? For what? For me. Why do you ask? In France,
you can't take a girl for fifteen thousand."

He say, "*Oui, mais là c'est en France.* Yes, but there it's France."

Then I say, "A-ha. *Ici, c'est Ouagadougou. C'est Haute-Volta.* This is
Ouagadougou. It's Upper Volta."

And some people used to get annoyed like that, and they will fuck off,
and I don't care. I know that he has already spent some money to buy me
a drink, and I have something inside of the drink, so it wouldn't hurt me.

You have to make this kind of life with them, because if you say that
you wouldn't do it, they will always be teaching you. Do you know what
is teaching? It is cheating. You know, he will talk to you, and you will
agree with him, and then you will go with him, and the morning time,
maybe you wouldn't find him.

Some people who are bad, and they know the countrymen, maybe they can take you to one of the friends — an African boy's house — or take you to somewhere and just use you, and then when he sees that you are falling sleep, he will leave you at the place. Morning time, maybe you will wake up someplace and you won't see anybody. You don't see a cook; you don't see anybody. You open the door and go out, you don't know where to go to the street. You know? All these things, they used to happen to the girls. Some girls meet things like that many times. Some place which you haven't been before, and it's difficult to come back to your place. Tomorrow if you meet the others, you wouldn't believe anybody! You must be doing your own believing.

Sometimes we used to refuse. There are many girls who refuse to follow a man to his house. They have been seeing things in town many times. She will say, "I have my own room. If you like, we can go there. If you don't want, you can fuck off." When you go to her place, and she has slept heavily, and you wake up and get your chance to open her door and go away, even you can rob her: she prefers that than to go to someplace she doesn't know, or to be suffering.

So this time, many girls in Ouagadougou don't want to go with men to their houses. Even the whites: there are many girls who won't go to their houses. If you want her, you will take her to her house. You won't sleep. You will give her money and go.

Sometimes you will see some heavy girls. They are the people who are rich in Ouagadougou. But sometimes, if they tell the story to you, you will pity for them. How the men used to take them with a motorcycle or a car and go and drop them in the bush. Somebody will just pick you with the car — pr-r-r — and go to the bush side and tell you to drop down. He wouldn't use you. He wouldn't do you anything. He will say, "Drop down." When you don't want to drop, then he will hold something and say, "If you don't drop, I'll knock you." Then she will get dropped in that bush. He will spark his car and go and leave you there. How are you going to come back to the town? If you are not lucky, you can die.

There is a story which we heard about two weeks ago. There was a boy, an African boy, who carried one girl to the bush. He put the girl on the ground. And where he used the girl, they said it was on top of a snake. It is people who said it; I was not there. Yeah, the snake bit the girl. When this boy used the girl and finished, he wanted to call the girl to go. Then the girl was saying, "Mm-mm-mm." You know? The boy didn't know the snake bit the girl. And the girl, too, it was night! She didn't know what bit her. Or she thought it was a thorn, or what, I don't know. I think the boy was making love to her when she got this bite from the snake. So the time the boy finished, this girl could not get up. "Mm-

mm. Mm-mm-mm." Maybe the girl didn't agree with the boy, the way he used her, and boy was thinking the girl was trying to bluff herself. Then the boy just threw the girl away there and came to the town. After he went away, I think some watchmen or some people who used to wake up about two or three o'clock to walk to the town to go to work, maybe they were from the village, and walking, and they heard this *"Mm-mm."* So they went there and found this girl. They took her to hospital. The girl had two days in hospital and she was dead.

But they said that in the hospital, when the girl was going to die, she said she went to the forest with some boy, and when the boy made love with her and finished, then she couldn't get up. She was feeling heavy in her body, and she was feeling pain everywhere in her body. So she asked the boy to help her, to take her home, and the boy didn't want to carry her. She said the boy left her there. I was not in the hospital; it's the girls who said this. They said when the girl said this, then she died.

And that boy also died. I don't know the boy. But that time, about two or three weeks, there was a boy too who became crazy, calling the name of the girl and taking his clothes off and shouting and jumping and that and this, and then after, he fell down like he was sick. They thought he was a crazy man. They took him to hospital, and he also died. All the Ghanaian girls said he was the boy who killed the girl, you know, because he was calling the girl's name. So many people said he was the one who killed the girl. So he was also dead.

So all these things, you will hear of them. Then to be going out, to be searching for men on the road? Or you don't work: you go to this bar, and from this bar to that bar. It's not good.

And even there are many men who think they respect themselves. They don't want to be picking girls from the roadside, or from the bars. Some French men: their life is different. Sometimes a French man will get one girl from the road today, then tomorrow he will get a different person. But every time, when he takes you to his house, the first thing to ask you is, "Where are you working?" If you are working in a bar, he likes it.

But "I'm not working": *Ah-a-ah!*

"But what are you doing?"

Then you say, "I'm doing nothing."

"So does this mean that every night, you just take your bath and go to the road, to be going with every one?"

You see? So if you think of all this, it's not very good. You can gain one day and you can lose one day. Or sometimes, in these problems, you can get some sickness.

Oh, there is a *nice* woman. Auntie Mawu. I knew her in Accra, and she came to Ouagadougou. One black beauty woman! Now, if you see her in

Ouagadougou: *agh!* She is not even in Ouagadougou; she is in a *small* village, with about two or three houses there, taking care of herself. She has just become like that. But she was one of the women who were the *first* women who had big money from Ouagadougou, when Ouagadougou was Ouagadougou. But now if you see her, you will pity.

So why am I forcing to make my ashawo more than first time? Yeah, because I have to try to make it. Because I think people were teaching me. I wanted to be a good friend; I wanted to have a good understanding; I don't want problems. But I think of the way the people are teaching me. *Hm?* When I am living with people, maybe they used to think I like dresses. They used to buy a lot of dresses, or food, and anything. But you know, sometimes if I need money to do something, if I ask them, they will be trying to tell me their story: tomorrow, the day after tomorrow, tomorrow after, tomorrow. So I have to be hard on this way.

So I have had to change my life, to make ashawo, so I will know that if you are going with me, I will take my money. OK? Tomorrow if you come, and you do as if you don't know me, I wouldn't mind you, too. This is OK. *Eh-heh!* I won't have a problem that I was suffering from this person, or that and this, and I have been asking him for this, and he doesn't want to give me, and all that. No. We don't have this problem.

So this time, I'm making my proper ashawo.

13 SEX STORIES FROM THE LIFE

: *Not a Captain of Sexing*
: *The Dilemma of Big Pricks*
: *Limata's Boyfriend*
: *Ginger for Sex Workers*
: *The Italian Man with a Prick Problem*

: OUAGADOUGOU, LOMÉ :

Not a Captain of Sexing

The girls who are making ashawo, this is the way they find to make money. Yes. Some of them think it is good. This is their chance.[1] And

---

1. their luck, their destiny

some of them can get heavy money, and then they give it to the boy-friends. You see? There are some girls like that, and they are not serious. There is one girl, Solace. When she was with one Lebanese man, the money Solace took from this man, she could build a house in Ghana. Maybe three or four houses. She gave it to one African boy — a Sene-galese — to chop. You see? There are some girls like that. They can get the people and get the money from them. This Lebanese man has a night-club. When this man is not there, they are making the account for the girl. Sometimes, maybe this man can travel, and if the man comes, she will say, "Ah, when I got the money, I was drunk, and people went and at-tacked me, and that and this, so the money is lost." *Ha-ha!* You see? Yeah, some girls, they have this heavy money at one time. They don't have it small-small and then try to hold it.

But I myself, I think, my money: I used to spend it by myself. I can spend it in a foolish way. But I don't used to have a boyfriend and give him money. Limata was trying to do that in Ouagadougou. I'm the one who took her out from that.

As for me, you know, I don't like a boyfriend because of good sexing or something like that. I used to like somebody for his way; it's not the way he makes his sexing. Even if I like how he can make sexing with me, but it's not because of the way he makes his sexing that I like him. I used to like people just for the way they are. Somebody who I think, "Ah, this man is not like the others. He respects himself. He is not like this or that": I think that maybe if he doesn't know sexing, then if I don't say it, nobody will hear it. Isn't it? So the way he respects, or the way he moves, you know, I used to like people from this way. For me to like somebody or to love somebody, I can say it's not from the sexing.

As for sexing, to me, I don't always need it. I don't know about some-body else. You can have your feeling, but in anything, not all people have the same feelings as you. Maybe there is someone who needs sexing all the time. She just likes it. There are some people who feel they need this sexing for themselves: they think it's food for them, every night. OK? But I don't know. Sometimes, I can be in Ouagadougou, and if I start thinking some things, I can make about two or three weeks and I don't need some-thing like sexing. For me, actually, I don't like much sex, every time, every day. I don't like to have it plenty. I don't need it plenty, just sometimes. Sometimes yes, sometimes no.

So if I get somebody who wants to sex me a lot, I wouldn't like it. Maybe you need to make sexing. OK? I think once you have discharged, from that part, you have to sleep. You have nothing to do again. And sometimes there may be some days you don't feel like sexing. OK? Sometimes you can be with a man, but you just don't feel like doing something like sexing. Yeah. You see him, he's a man, but you don't have any feeling. Doesn't this happen? Yeah, so in this way, if you don't feel it, you shouldn't force to do it. I think so.

But sometimes you can be with somebody, and you don't feel for any sexing. But maybe the fellow is not forcing you, but the way he will be doing with you, he will start playing with you, you know. Then you get to change your mind, and you will be following. But if it's not so, sometimes when you go to the bed straight, you just don't feel it. But if you are with someone, somebody can make you to have feelings.

You see? You can be with somebody, but you don't have any feelings. You just feel like you have to sleep, or he is disturbing you. Sometimes somebody can be playing with you in the bed, and you will get feelings, and somebody can be doing you so, and you haven't got feeling. Maybe that day, you just put up your mind like that. So in this kind of case, if you know that you are on this way, you shouldn't go with someone. You should sleep in your house, and think about yourself better.

So to me, I think it is good if you don't need sexing too much for yourself, but when you get it, it's all right for you. *Ha-ha!* But you know, I'm not a captain of the sexing.

I don't know how others are. I think some girls like the boys because they can do the sexing. And some boys like the girls for that. But I don't like people from that. Even if I meet a somebody who says, "I know sexing," then I don't feel it. There are some people who used to bluff themselves that they know sexing. Some people feel themselves that they know sexing, and they used to say it. If I see this kind of people, I look at them. I think — for me, I think sexing is nothing for me, so if you say you know sexing, then I just look at you.

But you know, there are some girls, too, they want a boyfriend who knows sexing. I used to get some friends who used to tell me, "You know, that boy I went with yesterday, I didn't believe he could do this. Ah-h, he has done a nice thing."

Things like that: to me, they are funny. I used to get friends for that, for their funny things. So when they talk this, then I say, "Did you get it?"

She'll say, "Yes."

I'll say, "Ah! So you *feel* it!" You know? I don't tell her that I'm not like that. I let them think that, yes, I'm also like that. But if they are telling me, I used to wonder too. Because I don't know how they are feeling.

But sexing, I think that you can sex with a man. OK? Sometimes, without a man, maybe you can sex yourself. So I think of all this, and I think that if you see that somebody knows how to sex, then it doesn't mean that you will be following him. Maybe a time will come and he will be throwing you off, and then you will be going away, crying all over the place. Look at this. *Ha-ha!* You see? If maybe you like to be sexing alone, without a man, you can be sexing. OK? So why are you wasting your time to go with someone because you think he sexes you well? Maybe you know really that he's not going to marry you. OK? And you know that the way you will follow him every time, you won't get anything from him. There are some girls like that. So what is the use? To go with good sexing, without anything. Why don't you make your sexing for yourself?

Yeah, this is what I say. I think somebody can be sexing with you, and you don't need his sex. OK? This kind of sexing which you get, maybe you wouldn't discharge. Maybe the man can discharge, but you the woman wouldn't discharge because you don't feel the way he is. You don't feel anything from him. You go with such a fellow because of money. OK?

So in this our ashawo life, sometimes somebody can be sexing you, and you don't like it, but you will close your eyes. And the way you will do the fellow, too, if he is a man who has been following women, he will know. He will just say, "Oh-h, wake up."

"I'm tired."

"What? You — what?"

Maybe it's not a minute, and you will start shouting on him. He himself will be making quick-quick to get up. He knows that this is only for money. *Ha!* It's not anything. Even if you don't give him a good sexing, and he is annoyed with you, he will pay. He can't say anything. As for that one, if someone says that I didn't give him good sex, then we will fight. If I didn't give you good sex, could you discharge? When you discharge, there's not any good or bad. *Uh-huh.* He will say he didn't get good sexing. I will say, "Aha! So you pissed in your bed."

You know, but this is what I'm saying: some of the girls *like* it, many of them: "Ah, this boy is a sexing boy; he knows how to sex." [1] To me, it's foolishness. But to be sexing without any feelings, too, it's a problem. Yeah, it's a problem, but you have nothing to do about it. Isn't it? You will like it, or you won't like it.

You know, all my girlfriends, when they come in morning time, they will just say how they were with their friend, with good sexing or not good sexing. Sometimes, a girl can go with somebody, and when she comes back she will say, "Ah, shit."

So good sexing. You know, this is what I say. You can go with somebody, but you don't feel to be with that kind of fellow. OK? Maybe you

1. The adjective "sexy" would refer to someone who likes sex a lot.

think that because of money you will go with him. And then, everything which he is doing to you, you won't see anything nice in it. You will see everything he is doing as just like you are seeing something bad. You don't have that feeling.

We girls, too, we are very funny. It's funny. When I was staying with Limata, when we went out to the work, maybe we have met someone we didn't know before, and she followed that person. The next morning, when she would come home, we would talk about it, "Hey, *camarade!* How do you feel? Yesterday, how was the fellow?" You know? Then: "OK, the fellow is this or that," or "Anyway, it's nice in this way, but you know, in that way, it's like it is bad, or this is —"

So this is the way the girls used to talk to each other. The first time, when I was with Mama Amma at Dapoya, at that house there were *plenty* of girls. And that house in Togo where Mama and I stayed, too, that house had many ashawo girls. So sometimes you will sleep in the morning time, and the time when you get up from sleeping, some girls have just finished their everything, and they are outside. They will start conversing.

: LOMÉ :

The Dilemma of Big Pricks

So when the girls are sitting outside, they will be talking. And then everybody is talking her own. Especially when we were in Togo, in that house with many girls, somebody will say, "Hey! I was very lucky that today I didn't die."

"Why were you lucky?"

"*Ah! Tsk!* The person who — that fellow who took me — *tsk,* if you see his prick —!"

Some girls run away and leave their dresses. You know, it's very funny. You can go with somebody, and he takes off of his dress, when you see what he has, maybe you will forget the money and your purse and everything there, and you will just excuse yourself to go out the door to piss. You will leave everything, because if you are carrying your things, the person will know that you are going. So you just ask God to let you *out* of the room! Even without a dress! This thing used to happen to us girls like that.

You know, there are some kind of people who have big pricks, eh? So if you see this kind of prick, then you will think, "Eh! This thing, I can't — I can't take — if I take this thing, maybe I will be sick, or I will be cut in some places." And the time you will see this thing, maybe you have al-

ready taken your dress off. OK? And this man also has taken his dress off.
So how can you make excuse? You can't. You can't tell the fellow, "This
your prick is big, so I can't." Ah, if you tell him that, the fellow wouldn't
agree. If it's his house, maybe he will make trouble with you. So sometimes, you will ask him for the toilet, to get outside. And there are some
clever people who have a toilet inside, and when you start pissing inside
there, then you will start to think of another thing. When you finish the
piss, where should you say you are going again? OK. When you come
back from the toilet, you will just say, "Oh!" All your dress, you will start
searching inside.

Then he will say, "What?"

You will say, "Oh, maybe my key has fallen!"

Then maybe if he has a car, he will say, "Go and look at the car, the inside of the car."

Or if you came with taxi, you will say, "Oh, when I was in taxi, it was
in my shoe."

Maybe if the fellow has a torchlight, he will say, "OK, take the torch
and go and look where we dropped. Maybe it has fallen down."

When you go out like that, you are not coming back again. You will
leave all that you have inside. You will try to find your life. Because you
know this thing is big, and maybe it will wound you. And if you are going
to wound, you don't know how you are going to suffer to look after yourself. You don't know how much medicine you are going to buy before you
will save yourself in this life.

And some woman think, "Ah! This fellow: maybe I can take this
thing." You know, there are some women who like a *big* prick. I have
many girlfriends who say that. When we are sitting, if the other ones
come and talk about this, then the other ones will say, "Oh, you are a fool.
You don't know what is sweet." You know? It's very wonderful. Some
people like a big one, and some people are afraid of it, and some people
like the small one. And the ones who like the big one say the small one is
just like a needle, chooking[1] you. *Ha-ha!* You know? It's a hot one. So
they say that the big one used to go *slowly,* and it's full up every place, so
there's no chance. *Ha! Shit! Ha-ha!* And maybe you can meet a man with
a very *sma-a-a-l-l-l* prick. But it is very *long.* OK? Some women say that
one is poison sea. Yeah. You will think you wouldn't want it, and when
you are getting it, it doesn't have a feeling, but it is poison. You see? They
don't give you poison, but they throw you in the middle of the sea. You
can't come out. *Ha! Ha! Ha!*

OK. Sometimes, you can meet a man who has a small, short prick, but

1. (Pidgin): sticking, pricking, stabbing

it is like iron. It is very strong. That one too — is a *shit! Ha-ha!* Why it is shit: it is very strong. So what he wants, he is just forcing. Even if this is not the place, he is forcing, because he is very strong. He doesn't feel anything. *Ha-ha!* Yeah. Shit. So that one too, maybe he will be forcing to get in, and by then you have already got a wound. You are feeling pain everywhere. He's like some iron that sees the wood, and he's going to chop inside. So — *ha!* So it just goes inside like that — *wang-wang-wang-wang-wang-wang.* But a vagina is not wood. So iron with wood: it used to chop it, so that it's painful. And you wouldn't feel it. Maybe you will see a man and say OK, this is a normal one of a man. But when you get to the bed with the person, you will see that this one is not the size you can fit, because it's just like iron. And then you will be feeling pains. So there are sometimes, we girls used to see this.

And the kind of sexing I think is good, if he's understanding, to go slowly — *ha! Hee-hee-hee!* When you see that kind of sexing, then maybe it will be better. He must know that his prick is not inside wood, you know. *Ha!*

So if you see the girls are sitting, especially ashawo girls, if they go out at the night, some people will come and sleep in the house, and some people will sleep outside. But when they come to meet, early in the morning, you used to see them. They used to talk *loudly* and be laughing much. It's all about what they saw in the night. They will just be sitting down. They don't have any talk to talk. They just say, *"Hey!"* You know: starting. So you take your ashawo way, and you come back to the house: you can tell the friend, "Oh, this man doesn't know sexing" or "This man, he has a big prick," or "This man has a small prick." *Ha-ha!* You know? You will see the first person who is going to open the floor. Maybe you are talking about some different thing. She will say, "Hey, hey, hey. Stop your topic. I have a story for you. Hey, yesterday, you know what happened to me?"

Then the others: "No." "Hey!" "Yesterday did something happen to you?" You know, we all want to listen. So we say, "What happened?"

She will say, "Yesterday I went with somebody. I swear, since my mother has borne me and I started to know what they say is a 'man,' I haven't seen something like this. Just like this big black snake!" You know, that snake which very tall? You know? Some girls are just saying shit like that. They say, "Hey!"

In Togo I had a girlfriend: Vanessa. She came home with only pants and a *small* towel, tied around her. She was knocking the door: "*Aff!* Open for me! Open for me! Open!" The way she was breathing, we thought something was happening to her. So we wouldn't open the door.

We opened the window first and looked to see whether some thieves were holding her to come and kill all of us. Then we saw she was alone, and she was with a small towel and her drawers. Oh! She has two babies: both the breasts were hanging. She came home like that.

Then we said, "Hey, what is wrong with you?"

She said, "Eh, give me a cigarette. Give me a cigarette." She was just like that. She said that when she lay down with this man, you know, the first time with somebody she doesn't know, maybe she will try to play romance and touch that place and see how it is. Isn't it? So she said, "When I touched it, I just touched the thing like this. Just like my *leg!* So I said, 'Ah, I don't believe.' So I was trying to find the head: I didn't. Just to find the toes: I didn't! So 'Hey!' I said, 'What is this?' And this man said, 'What is that?' Then I said, 'Oh, I want to piss.' So the man didn't have a toilet inside. He said, 'Open the door and go behind the house.' Then I wanted to take one cloth, and he said, 'Oh, there is nobody. You can take this towel.'" This girl got up with the towel. *Pip!* Then she came home.

So it was six days or one week's time, we saw this man. When we saw the man, Vanessa said, "It is the man! That's the man!" Then everybody was looking. Yeah! She didn't want the man to see her, so she was hiding behind us, and pushing us. So we all stayed there.

And then, you know, there was one girl called Akosua. But you know what was funny with Akosua? Do you know, when Vanessa was talking about that man, Akosua had said, "Hey! As for me, because of money, I can't do that." *Ha!* Akosua just went nicely to the man, and then very slo-owly, she said, *"Bonzwoir, mezzieur."*

Then the man said, *"Bonsoir, mademoiselle."*

"Si vous voulez aller danser un peu? Can we have a small dance?"

They were dancing slowly. When they finished dancing, then she said, "Oh, can you buy me a tot?"

So this man said, "You can drink whatever you want." Akosua used to like cognac. So he bought her a cognac. Akosua drank with this man. Then they left.

Morning time, Akosua brought him in the house to know her room. And Vanessa was in Akosua's bed, because they are friends, and they were in the same room. So when the man came and saw Vanessa, then he said, *"Celle-là, c'est bandit."*[1]

Then Akosua said, *"Tu la connais?* Do you know her?"

Then he said, "Ah, when you went to my place, didn't you see her

---

1. (French): That girl, she is a scamp (or ruffian, bandit).

dress there? She came to me, and I don't know what happened. She said she was going to piss. I was waiting—I didn't see her. I went out. I looked for her everywhere. I didn't see her. Since that day I didn't see her. Only today I saw her. She is your sister?"

Then Akosua said, "Yes."

He said, "Anyway, I didn't have any sexing with her. As she is your sister, tomorrow if you come to my place, you can bring her clothes to her."

So when this thing happened to Vanessa, when we were talking about this thing and Akosua had said she can't have it, so we asked Akosua, "And you have it now?"

So Akosua said, "Yes. As for me, a man like this, I used to *screw* him! Because every place is full up." She said she used to have feelings for men like that. This one can let you discharge, and that and this. OK. So that one passed. This man became a boyfriend of Akosua. Every day he was coming to our house. Everybody was happy. He bought everybody drink. He bought biscuits, sweets, many cakes. He was a rich man, and he gave this girl her money.

Some of the girls have been saying that somebody can get a wound from a big prick, but I haven't seen it from them. I think maybe many girls can wound, but they won't tell you. Look. A girl can go with somebody, and the next day, she will come home. She can make maybe one week without going out with a man. She has been wounded. Yeah. And then, in our African way, you know, sometimes, when they get this wound, they don't go to a doctor to take any injection or something like that. She treats herself with hot water. And then she will get medicine. There is one medicine you put in hot water, in this piss pot, and you sit on it. All the heat is getting inside. It's painful too. It's getting inside of you. Or sometimes, if you don't get medicine, you can take camphor. You know camphor? Yeah, you boil hot water, boiling it well, and you put the camphor inside and put it in a small pot and sit on it. Maybe it can take you one week without going to sex. *Ha!* And you will be resting. This is your holidays.[1]

So, you know, this thing with the pricks, I think this thing is from family-family. You know, first I will say Togo, and Dahomey. OK? And Côte d'Ivoire. And Voltaique. If you follow the Africans, you will meet this thing, the *big* prick which you have never seen in your life. I think it's the French country where this thing is from. I don't know. But you know, in Ghana, I didn't hear much talk about these things. But if you are in Togo, or you are in Ouagadougou, or you are in Ivory Coast, you will hear many girls who are giving complaint about these big pricks.

1. vacation

This man for Akosua was a Togolese. A very *short,* small man, eh? *Very* short, but he didn't have any flesh. His bottom was dry, completely dry. If he put on trousers, you would laugh. But he was a big man; he had his own car.

The only one I have seen like that was that Biafran[1] man in Togo. I think I talked about it, the time when I was at Royal Hotel.[2] He had a very big prick. Anyway, he didn't make sexing with me, but I was following him as a friend because of his money. I knew that if I go to his place, he will give me everything, but he won't sex me. Even I think he couldn't sex. I think so because all the girls were giving me the same complaint. If I asked, "When you went with him," then the girl would say, "Ah, when I went with him, he just fell asleep." But I followed him. Morning time, I will have my money.

So this big prick, and the girls are running away, if you go to Togo, Benin, and Côte d'Ivoire, and Ouagadougou-side, Niger-side, you will hear these talks plenty from the girls. I have been hearing it, because you know my habit is that I don't follow our people much, so I can't know much about them. But many of my girlfriends used to tell me about this.

As I told you, any time our African men are following you like that, then they will be seeing you outside telling you something foolish. And I used to be suffering some places because I don't like to follow them. But I don't feel like following them, you know. Yeah, because you know — especially we Africans — we have this habit. He can go with a girl, and to-morrow, if the girl doesn't want him, or if he doesn't want the girl again, if he sees the girl with somebody, he will be trying to talk something about the girl. You know? Maybe to show the fellow who is walking with the girl, that he has already known the girl, that the girl is that and this. And this kind of life, I don't used to have much feeling for that.

: OUAGADOUGOU :

Limata's Boyfriend

Even Limata had a boyfriend like that at our house. The boy was called Ajax. It is funny, huh? This boy was a son of our landlord. This boy also had a wife, at Kaya. When Limata saw the boy, she said, "Hey! What a black beauty is this! This boy is very beautiful."

So when she said this, this boy also spoke a little English. Limata didn't

1. Igbo; also, Ibo; cultural group in southeastern Nigeria
2. small hotel in Lomé, where many Ghanaian women lodged

know. So after, he came to greet us. At that time the wife was not there. So Limata agreed with this boy and went with him. And then Limata: *every* night, Limata didn't go out. That time Limata had the old man I told you about. If the old man came and left, Limata would just *cha-cha-cha-cha* and go to this boy. I didn't know what was happening. And once Limata gave me a check, five thousand, to take to cash for her at the bank. It was the boy who gave her.

OK? So Limata was in the room the day when the boy's wife came. The husband didn't know that the wife was going to come that day, you know, and he left Limata in the room, and he was going to the bank. And the wife came and knocked the window. And Limata opened, and she met this woman, with her daughter and a small boy. So this woman started fucking Limata, abusing Limata, *"Ta-ta-ta-ta!"*

Limata! Every day when Limata wakes up, she will sweep this *whole* house! If Limata slept with this man, about five o'clock in the morning, she is already awake, sweeping the whole compound. Beautiful! Up to the gates, outside, burning all the rubbish. Twelve o'clock, this boy's chop is ready; she has covered it with a nice tablecloth. And she was with her old man, too! I told you this old man had a wife, so she couldn't sleep there. So if the old man came to visit and went, then she was for this boy.

OK. When this wife came and then had a problem with Limata, Limata said, *"Pfft, tweaa!* Even this boy, with a big prick, when he's fucking me, I used to discharge. But the next day, until I sit on hot water, because of this big prick."

Then I said, *Ah!* So this boy was having this thing and she was suffering with this every time! She used to wake up early in the morning and sweep the whole place, and then she would boil hot water. So sometimes me and Mama used to say, "Ah, Limata. Hot weather like this? And you are keeping fire in your room?" Do you know that Limata didn't want to do all this in front of us? The way she liked the boy, she felt the way the boy sexed her, but if she finished sexing, she used to feel pains. You see? So in this case, if she did this hot water outside, me and Mama would get to know what she was doing. So she used to boil the water and then put this medicine in and sit on it in her room. She was hiding herself, not to let us know. But when the boy's wife came and abused her, then she was trying to disgrace the boy.

Then I said, "Oh, but don't talk this one loudly. It's between me and you. I hear it. Somebody won't hear it. If Mama hears it too, I think it is the same thing. But don't try to be loud with it, because people will laugh at you, because you have been with him many times, many days—*weeks.*" So: *ha!* The way she liked it, that is the way the wife also liked it! But some women used to give complaint about it because they used to suffer from it. So sexing with the big pricks, there are differences. If somebody sexes you and tomorrow you are feeling pains, is this not different? It is different.

Ginger for Sex Workers

Look. What about these people who are sitting outside? You know, in Ghana too, they used to have that kind of ashawo, the women who are sitting outside a room for the men to come and sex them there. I think it was two shillings. In Ouagadougou there are some, the young ones, some of them charge one hundred francs, and the old ones charge fifty francs. The last young one,[1] maybe one hundred fifty or two hundred. You will see *nice* Ashanti girls who are doing that. OK. Every time they have hot water in the corner. Why do they have it? They put this hot water on the fire until they close their work. Anybody who comes to them, when he goes away, they take this hot water: I think they used to put some small medicine inside and wash themselves. Somebody can have a big prick or all this, so every time they used to get many things to treat themselves. In day time, they're all in the house, making a pump to douche, putting ginger in their vaginas, and doing many things. They do this business; they have treatment.

So this ginger is treatment for them. Even when they were young. You know, when we Africans, when we have a baby — OK? I think it's not for all Africans, because in my village, when I go there, I don't find these things, but in Ghana, if you have a baby, and maybe this baby is starting to be eating sweets, and all this, then every week, if he's a boy or a girl, you have to put ginger in his ass. Yeah, in his ass. They used to do the boys like this up to the time when they are about twelve years old, before the mothers think they can't feel to do this to them. But growing up, they do it for the girls, they do it for the boys. So these girls, they have been training you with this thing since you are young. OK? And when you are a woman, you will do it for yourself. Even some Ashanti men, especially Ashanti, if a man doesn't go to toilet today, instead of taking medicine, he will just let the wife grind ginger and make it into a ball, and he put it in his ass and go to the toilet.

Yeah, so the girls, OK? The girls who come to sit in the doors and make ashawo. Since you were a baby, huh? If a baby is eating many sweets, they

1. the youngest one

have been treating you with this. And we have some kinds of sickness. There is some kind of sickness for the women, and all your vagina used to have small-small white water. If you get this ginger, it's good medicine for it: if you can take patience to have it inside you. It will *pain* you. But it's medicine for this thing. If you put the ginger in your vagina in the morning, then you will leave it, up to the evening. And then you will take another bath again. If you wash yourself at that time, if you don't want to spoil your pants, you will put cotton, and when you take it out, you see how you are wet. This thing: all of it is dropping. So if you put the ginger, then in three days, you will see all the inside of you is dry. So it takes three days' time, and if you have patience, when you do it, you don't go with a man. Yeah, you will see that everything is dry. You won't see how you were feeling the first time.

At our place, Upper Volta, I think there are many women who have this sickness, because they don't know many treatments. You can see a woman who has white panties, and that place used to have some color. Even if you wash it, it can't come out. It is this thing which brought it all, that sickness. So this is why many girls used to put ginger, and all these things, inside the vagina.

So these girls who are doing this hundred-hundred business, this is what they do. Yeah. They clean themselves. They think that this is better than to go to hospital where they will charge them plenty.

: LOMÉ :

The Italian Man with a Prick Problem

So we girls, when we are sitting outside, you will hear many stories from the different girls. You can go with somebody, and then maybe you will see something from the man, or he has some kind of prick, or else he has something and you will think he's sick.

Yeah, when we were in Togo, once I went with one Italian man. When we were getting to this man's place, then he said I should sleep in the car. *Agh!* A big woman like me? To sleep in the car? I said, "No, I can't."

He said, Eh, his wife's sister is upstairs with the husband. So then I said, "OK, then you better drop me back."

Then he said, "OK, let's go to your place."

So he brought me to my house, OK? When this man took off his dress, you know, it's not that he had something bad, but I think this thing was a sickness. He had a *big* —oh, something like a boil, but it wasn't a boil. A *big* one here, on one side. Then I said, "Hey, what is this?" You know, when we were dancing in the nightclub, I was feeling it, but I didn't believe it. I thought maybe the way he put on his trousers, or it was because he was fat, so he had this kind of skin like that. But when this man took the thing, I looked, and I was afraid! I said, "Hey! What is this? It doesn't pain you? Didn't you go to hospital?"

He said, no, it doesn't pain him.

And I said, "OK, get on your dress."

He said, "Why?"

I said, "No."

He said, "What?"

I said, *"No-o!"*

So this man was a very bad, wicked man. In my house, can you do me something? You know? He said, why should I say so? Then he held my neck. *Ha!* He said why should I let him take off all his clothes, and then I will tell him to put his clothes on.

Then I said, "What! But here is my house." You know, such a man, suppose I slept in his car, or he took me to his home, he could kill me, isn't it?

Yeah! So: in my own house! He said I shouldn't fool him. Why should I tell him to put all his clothes on? Then I said, "No. I'm afraid of this. I haven't seen that before. I don't know what kind of sickness it is. If you give it to me, whatever money you are going to give me wouldn't take care of it. Even I think you are rich, but you still have it because there is no medicine for it. And if I get it, I have spoiled my life. I can't have this."

So he held my *neck!* Then I was trying to swell up my throat, but it was not coming. Then I said, *"Kae!!"* I shouted! And you know, our small-small rooms at that house, the room I went with this man was Afi's room, the second door to Vélé's room. So when I shouted, Vélé just came out and pushed the door, and then he got hold of the man. The man was serious! *Hey!* So when Vélé got the man away from me, then I said, *"Out!"* I wouldn't shut up my mouth. *Oh!* "Out! Out! A sickness man like you!" *Ha!* "I don't want! You want to give me sickness? Can it—? Do you think—? How much are you going to give me? Because of ten thousand, you are going to give me this sickness? Do you think ten thousand can do this? Come on! Out!"

So this man said, "You are very lucky. You are very lucky." Then he went away.

You know, the time at the nightclub when he was drinking with me, he left his five thousand with me; he forgot it. So he was annoyed. So after he went away, then in three days' time I saw him, and he said I should give him that five thousand. I said, "You! You haven't got sense? Why should you ask me for that five thousand? Don't you think that the day when you held my neck, I'm the right girl to report you to police? Do you know how many medicines I paid for that?"

Then he said, "No, you know, you are a nice girl, but that day I was drunk. You have talked to me rough," and that and this.

I said, "Yes, because what I saw from you, I haven't seen it before, and I was afraid. Because if I'm falling sick now, I have nobody here. I have no boyfriend. I have no anything. I have no brother, no sister. That's what I'm looking at."

Then he said, if he were sick, could he marry and get children with his wife?

Then I said, "Ah, maybe you were with your wife before you got it. I think if your wife saw you the first time with this, she wouldn't marry you."

So he said, OK. So did I understand him now?

Then I said, "Yes, I have understood you that it's not something bad. But that day, you know that you have wounded me."

And so he said, "How much did the pharmacy cost you?"

Then I said, "Ah — the pharmacy — even the five thousand, your money you are asking about, you know, if you like it I can give it to you." You know, that time when I was saying this, I had only five hundred in my bag. "But this five thousand, it's doing me nothing, you know, but that day, when I went and paid for the medicine at pharmacy, it was more than five thousand. If you like, I can call one of my friends to ask her. Or if you go to my place, you can see the receipt."

Then he said, "OK." So, did I forget about what he did to me?

Then I said, "Yes, I forgot about it."

Then he said, OK.

It's now I know that he was not sick. One day he brought two children — girls. The girls were *nice* girls. So he said, "You see my children?"

Then I said, "OK. I believe you." But I didn't go with him, you know.

He said, "OK. What do you think?"

Then I said, "You know, the way — that time — what I have done, even I am ashamed to take you to my place. And I don't want to sleep in the car to go to your place. So I think, the best thing: I will go and book some hotel. And then, when we meet in the night, we will go there."

He said, OK. So: how much did I think the hotel will cost?

So I said, "Oh, we can take a cheap hotel — about three thousand or four thousand. It's OK."

So he said OK. He gave me ten thousand. So — *ha!* — I took the ten thousand to go to Royal Hotel to ask for the room with fan. They said there is no room with fan remaining. OK. Then I asked for another room, where you also have a small toilet inside and everything, upstairs. Then they said, that room too, there's no room. So I had one of my girlfriends who lived in the Royal Hotel. And I made an arrangement with her that, "Look, there is a white man who wants to come here, and this man wants a girl. He is a friend of my boyfriend, and he wants a girl."

You see? Huh? I was about to get a room for him, then I would go and boss some girl to follow him. But I didn't get the room. So it's better I boss a girl who already had a room: "So I want to bring this man here. He will pay you. I will tell him that I am the one who took the room for you, and that I have paid for it. So I will give you that money to keep, and if this man comes to you, before he goes, you can ask him for any money you want."

This girl was called Adisa. She was my girlfriend. So she said OK. Adisa had a nice room in the Royal Hotel. She paid fifteen hundred a day. She had a fan; she had a toilet; upstairs. OK. So I went and told this man that, OK, I have the room, but, you know, I have to go home and change myself. So he should relax in the room with my younger sister. *Ha!* So we took a taxi and went to the hotel, and then I gave him to the girl, and then I told the girl in Ashanti language, "You know, this man wants me, but it is because of his friend that I know him. I don't want two friends to be using me. So if I go, you can just be making a way to play love with this man so that he will make something with you, and you will get your money."

So I got seven thousand. I paid the room — three thousand — for the girl. I gave her that money. So I had my seven thousand, and then I went away. Do you know, it's a funny thing: this man, *all* his last money which he was giving me was that ten thousand. I didn't know anything about it. So he finished with the girl and he wanted to go, and the girl said, no, he has to give her five thousand. He said, "What? How come five thousand? I wanted Hawa; I didn't see her. You started playing love with me. What kind of five thousand? I have given all my money to Hawa." *Ha!* "So OK, if you want money, then you can go and ask her."

So this girl came to my place, full speed! She was annoyed! "What?! You think I'm so stupid, for you to go and collect the white people and collect their money and bring them to fuck me free?"

And I said, "Shut up. People used to fuck you in your room. How much do they pay? I paid the room bill today. Three thousand. The people who fuck you, if all of them are paying three thousand, you would be rich. I have paid three thousand, isn't it?" *Ha!*

"Hey, but you must tell me the truth!"

Then I said, "What kind of truth? What kind of truth do you want again? Didn't I tell the truth? I told you to catch the man, to take the money from him. I know that the man has money. OK?"

Then she said, "Eh-h, the man said he had given you all his money."

I said, "What! Given who? Where is the man?"

She said the man had gone.

I said, "Yeah, you did yourself. He was just bossing you. Do you think I can collect your money like that and eat it? But what kind of fool are you? He gave me money to search for the room. Did I give it to you or not? I know that you are living there, and I have given that three thousand to you. Maybe you don't pay three thousand a day, isn't it? But how much money is he going to give me to give you, and then I will collect that money and chop it? So you don't believe me?"

So she said, "This man, the day when I will see him —!"

Then I said, "Yeah. It's better you see the man."

So, it was about a week, and then this girl was at Le Rêve,[1] and this man was sitting there. She didn't see the man. And I came after both of them, and I saw the man, and I went and greeted him. He said I should go and drink what I want and bring the receipt to him. So I went and took one drink, and then I took the receipt to him. Then I said, "How did you finish with my younger sister? When I came back from the market, my younger sister told me that you had gone. But I told you I was going to eat and come. And you had sex with my younger sister, and you didn't want to give her money. What is this?"

Then he said, "That day I had ten thousand. I gave it to you, and she was not nice. She just — she was the one who started playing romance to me. I don't want her. It's you I want."

Then I said, "But you shamed me. She came and talked all this in public. Do you think it's good? You disgraced me. So I had to give her three thousand again."

Then he said, "OK. OK. Then let's forget it."

Then I said, "Even she wanted to take five thousand from you, but for this case, I didn't have a lot of money. I gave her three thousand."

So he said, "Where is she?"

Then I said, "Don't you see her there?"

He said, "Ah." The girl was passing. He was looking at her like he knew her, but he didn't know where he knew her from.

So I said, "Yeah, she is the one."

So he called Adisa, then she came and sat there. He said, "What will you drink?"

1. discotheque in Lomé

She ordered her drink and drank, and he took three thousand and gave to the girl. And he also gave me five thousand. So I didn't want the girl to know. Then I said, "This time, we have become serious. OK. This girl is my younger sister. You have had sex with her. Even if we are going to do something, you know, I don't want this girl to know anything about it, because she will think that we are sexing the same man. As we are sisters, it's not good for us. So we have to hide it."

So that day we had a full promise. Then I said, "OK, I'm going to lead my sister, my younger sister, to go home. Then I will come back."

So he was sitting to wait for me, and I went away with the girl. We went to another club. When we got this money, we went to another nightclub, you know, so maybe we will see somebody there, too, and also teach him a little.

14 THE GAME

: *Something like a Thief*
: *The Poor Man Who Tore Limata's Dress*
: *Customer Relations*
: *Popularity Party*
: *Revenge of the Men*
: *The Price of Champagne*

: OUAGADOUGOU :

Something like a Thief

You know, when you don't work, when you are just hanging in this business, and you don't want to be going with people to be sexing before you get your money, you used to be somebody like — what they say? — somebody just like a thief. You know? You go here and there, and then you lie to somebody and take his money. It's because you don't want too much sexing. OK? And maybe you don't have money, but you need money, too. OK? You go to some place — somebody likes you — you play him some way. "OK, I have agreed with you," or something like that. "But I want money to buy something," or something like that. You know, some people, if they are poor, maybe they will take one thousand out of their pocket. Maybe the rich ones, when they will touch their pocket, it's maybe five or ten thousand, and they say, "Go and buy it, and bring me the change."

You know, sometimes, you can be a good girl to go and find the change. If it's big money, you will know that if you chop the money, the day they will ask you for the change, you won't have it to pay, and you will be in trouble, you know. So you will go and find the balance and keep the amount of the thing you asked the fellow for, and you will give him the balance. You see? And sometimes, you can collect this money and say, "Oh, as for this kind of person, if he challenges me, I will challenge him. What? Because today is hot."

You will just collect the money and take your bag, and then you will get outside, and you call a taxi like a rich man, you know. *Ha!* You will get in the taxi. And what is a *big* shame, you know, if you do somebody like that: some people are proud. If you do him like that, he will see you and then be shouting, "Hey! You have done me that day! *Dat-dat-dat-dat!*" That kind of people: they are easy to boss. The people who used to shout, to show themselves, if you boss them, they are cool. They are just like ice blocks.[1] So if you chop somebody's money and he just sees you, and then he starts to shout at once: "*Eh-heh!* Today we will see. Today —!" That person is *cool,* you know, just like an ice block.

But somebody wouldn't say anything. When he sees you: "Hello, how are you? How do you do? What do you want to drink?" You know? The people who want to do you bad, they have patience for that.

Then you will say, "Maybe I will drink this." You know, he wouldn't even say something about this thing you have done to him. Then maybe if you are stupid, if you didn't meet such a problem before, you will think, "Ah! This fellow is a nice fellow." Isn't it? But he knows the way he is going to treat you.

But someone who sees you, "*Hey! E-ee!* Is that so? You, woman, this time — the women who are coming up now — is this how you people's life is? So you think you can lie to me and chop my money like that? What?!" Maybe you just got his money about two or three thousand. It's not big money. He will shout on you: "You think I went and stole that five thousand?!" Maybe it's two thousand or three thousand, but he is calling more on top of it.

That kind of person, you know, when I get them like that, I used to like them. I just talk slowly. I will say, "Five thousand? Five thousand. I chopped your five thousand. OK? And I'm going to pay you ten thousand. OK? You: how much do they pay you for a month? How much do you work for a day? And to give a woman five thousand a day? Ah! I will give you ten thousand. I chopped your five thousand, isn't it?"

---

1. ice cubes

You see? You will shout on me, and then I will call you seriously! I will say, "Even if you are saying this, you should look at all these people here. They are looking at you. Are you not ashamed of it? You have been talking this. Everybody is taking you like a stupid idiot. Don't you know that? That you have five thousand — a good five thousand — to give to a woman for a day, for one night. Do you think your father did so? So that he could marry your mother and get you? And you will be growing, and he will send you to school?"

So, you know, our people, they used to say that I'm *naughty!* They don't know what kind of person I am. *Ha!*

The Poor Man Who Tore Limata's Dress

Look. Somebody's three thousand. Limata went to Cabane Bambou. This man just held Limata and tore her dress. *Oh!* She was wearing cloth,[1] so she had to take the other cloth to cover herself. Then they called me. I had gone to the toilet, and I came and saw this man holding Limata there. Then I said, "What?! What is wrong?"

He said, "Eh, look at this ashawo woman like this! Even she's an old woman, all with her big stomach, and the shit is full up inside! She can't fool me and chop my three thousand!"

I said, "Look, how did she chop it? She chopped your three thousand? Oh! My sister! Why? A nice girl like you. You can't get money? To go and steal this man's three thousand?"

He said, "Oh, no. She was not stealing."

Then I said, "Ah! You didn't steal it? But how did you get it?" *Ha-ha!* You know? He thought he was clever, isn't it? So I said, "How did you get it?"

Then Limata said, "One day I was talking to him, and he said, 'Oh, take this.'"

So then the man said, "She wanted five thousand to go with me. Yeah. So I didn't have five thousand, so I told her that I would give her three thousand. And then she said that I should bring the money. When I gave her the money, at that moment, she said she was going to buy bread and come back, and we would go home. Since then I was sitting there, up to the morning time, and I didn't see her."

So I said, "*Aha!* Is that the case?"

He said, "Yes."

1. African-style dress with wax-print cloth

"But when you saw her, did you call her?"

He said, "Eh-h, I saw her when she was going to the toilet. And then I thought it's better to go and ask her by the toilet."

Then I said, "When you asked her at the toilet, did she say something to you?"

He said when he was asking her, she was trying to say that he shouldn't hold her.

Then I said, "Did you hold her before asking her?"

He said, "Yes."

I said, "But why did you hold her before asking her?"

He said he was annoyed too much.

"Then you are annoyed?"

He said, "Yes."

I said, "OK. Three thousand is money, isn't it?"

He said, "Yes."

"Maybe you can take two or three weeks to get three thousand, isn't it?"

He said, "Yes."

"OK. And this girl chopped it."

He said, "Yes."

I said, "OK, I'm going to pay for it, OK? Three thousand: I'm paying for it. But I'm charging you for this cloth and all that dress you tore down. She is my younger sister. I bought it for her. And I'm charging you for eight thousand five hundred. If you want, we can go to the market. I will show you the cloth. You will see the cloth, and then you can ask the price and buy it for me. OK?"

"No. Why should you say that?"

I said, "Why shouldn't I say that? Somebody chopped your three thousand. You haven't got patience to ask her, and you come and tear her dress! Suppose you asked her: you don't hold her, and you ask her, 'Hey, sister, oh, come here. Why? Yesterday I gave you three thousand.' Maybe she is holding your money, and she will give it you. But you have come to ask somebody a question, at the same time you are holding her."

Then he said, "*Eeh!* My heart was annoyed too much."

Then I said, "Your heart is not too much on me. Your three thousand is hurting you. And this cloth which this girl was wearing, I bought it. Eight thousand five hundred. And it is in the market. So if your three thousand is hurting your heart, then as for my eight thousand five hundred, if I were you, I would be dead! So you should know that it pains me, too." So then, you know, I wouldn't leave it. I said, "OK, if you like, here is your three thousand." I took three thousand and gave to him.

Then he said he wouldn't take it.

Then I said, "OK. But this cloth: whether you take the three thousand or you don't take the three thousand, you will pay for it. If you like, we will go to the police station."

So then Limata said, "No, *camarade,* leave him. I'm going home to change."

Then I said, "Look, you don't move! Stay here. Let all Ouagadougou come and see you. You are ashawo. Are you ashamed that you are doing ashawo? You don't shame to be ashawo. OK? Then don't be ashamed to let people look at you. You are beautiful. You are not some ugly woman."

So: *dat-dat-dat-dat!* Then this man wanted to go to police station. If not that, he said he was going to tear my dress to add to Limata's one. Then everything will finish. Then he will knock my head on the wall and go away.

But I wouldn't leave him. I held his dress. Then topics were coming, and the people were coming one by one, one by one: all the place got full up. Then they called the bar man at Cabane Bambou. This bar man, when I went to Ouagadougou, I think he was the first fellow I knew. He was called Apollo. We were working together at La Tringle. He was the bar man there. So then he came and said, "Oh, Hawa, everybody is begging you."

I said, "Apollo. You know our Madame." Madame Colette, the one who had La Tringle, she was the one who had this bar. "Madame Colette can't say *anything* to me here to listen to her. This cloth: I *bought* it. Only yesterday I took it from the tailor to give to my younger sister. This man tore it because of his three thousand. Here is the three thousand, but I want this cloth — a new one. He can take me to police station, or he can take my head to knock on the wall because he's a man, he's strong. He can kill me and go his way, and God will bless him. It's better."

So, you know what happened? *Everything* that was happening: this Apollo had to tell the man that, truly, he knows me, and since I was in Ouagadougou, he hasn't seen me doing something like this in a bar. Never in his life. Even if Madame Colette were here, Madame would stand by me, because every time, if something like that happened, if they said I was inside, Madame used to refuse: "No. Hawawu is inside? No." You know, sometimes I can be a crook to do something. But if they come to the night-club and ask of me, this woman will never allow it. She will say, "No, no, no, no. This girl doesn't know how to talk. Eh, what? This girl doesn't care about anything. She jokes with anybody. She dances with anyone. If she doesn't know a kind of dance, she will be trying to dance it, and people will be laughing. She's jovial. She is not the girl who is doing this."

She would never agree. So this case, too, even if I took this man to the police station, the inspector is the brother of the Madame of our nightclub.
Then I would go and give Madame this story, and Madame would come
and tell the brother to charge him more.

So then Apollo told this man: "So the best thing, you should beg this
girl, and then, if you have money, you will pay for the dress. Or if you
don't have money, you should tell her the day you will come and give me
the money to give her. As for me, I can stand and talk, and this girl will
listen to me. Because this girl has never boiled up like that. It's my first
time to see her like that. And if she is boiled up, I don't think that if anybody else talks to her, she will hear it. Even if Madame herself comes
here, this girl wouldn't mind her. But I can talk to her. So you should understand me."

So this man said, OK, if that will be the case, he has four thousand, so
that adding to the three thousand I was going to pay him, then four thousand plus three thousand is seven thousand. So I should take the seven
thousand, and the next day he would bring the one thousand five hundred and add it to it. So Apollo said OK.

Then I said, "OK. Tomorrow, I am going to bring the whole cloth, with
all the dresses, with the one he tore, and with the other parts,[1] to give it
all to him. When he pays, I will give him the cloth."

So you know, we took this cloth and left it there for about one week.
This man didn't come. We didn't see him. When we went there, Apollo
said, "Ah, take your cloth to the house. Go and keep it. The day he comes
and gives me the one thousand five hundred, I will give you the money,
and then you can bring the cloth. If the cloth is here, it will be dirty."

Since then, up to today, it's now getting to a year: we didn't see this
man again. Huh? From that time. So we chopped him. Seven thousand.
He said his eyes were open. The cloth, Limata took it, OK? It was only the
top one he tore. But the two parts were there. We could have bought one
section to sew another blouse, but we didn't. Limata said she wanted a
different blouse for it, so she just got a blouse, and then she didn't even
want to wear this dress again.

And since then, this man was afraid to come to that place, because if
he comes, then maybe they will ask of the one thousand five hundred he
owes. So this is why, sometimes, if you go to someplace, to say your eyes
are open, or you know anything, you can get into some easy trouble, and
they will get you like something. Look. This man thought he was going to

---

1. the remaining six yards. The dress is made from six yards: two for the blouse, two
for the skirt, two to wrap around the waist, with the extra pieces sewn for a head-tie.

hold Limata and start beating her like the way they used to get some girls
and beat them, you know. Free. Even he can tear all the cloth, or he can
remove all the cloth. At some places, when they get the chance, they used
to do this to the girls. So he just held her.

And Limata, this time, she has been taking some medicine to grow fat,
and I think this medicine made her heart big, because any time, if any
small thing comes, the heart used to go fast: *bo-bo-bo-bo!* And you know,
when this man held her, she was forcing herself, "Leave my dress! Leave
my dress!" And then, that was when some place got torn. So this man had
to pay his seven thousand.

This poor man, you know. I used to pity for him. Sometimes, when we
were sitting down, then I would say, "Oh, Limata, you know, sometimes — let us pray and beg God — we have done some bad."

Then she asked me, "What is that?"

I said, "We took this boy's seven thousand. He didn't get the cloth. And
since then we didn't see him. Maybe he went and stole the money, and
they caught him to prison. That four thousand that he gave to us, maybe
the day when he gave us, it was his last money, and he walked on the
road, and then he fell in some way and died. Maybe he took a broken
heart to go and fall somewhere to die. So we did some bad. Let's pray for
God."

Then Limata said, "*Pfft!* This kind of fellow, even if you kill him, if you
take a knife and stick him, God will never punish you!" *Ha-ha!*

Then I said, "Oh? So it's not God who makes the fellow?"

Then she said, "God made the fellow. But God makes some of them by
mistake, you know. So he came from a mistake. Even if you kill him with
a knife, God won't punish you. Let's forget about this." *Ha!*

Customer Relations

Sometimes, when we go out in Ouaga, I used to meet nice people, "Oh-h,
hello. I'm that and this." You can meet nice ones who like to talk to
people. Sometimes somebody, like the man I told you about with the
trucks — Pierre — when he sees you, he will try start speaking English:
"*Me no sprink English, eh? Me Français. Me Inglais, sprinkie small-small-
oh. Me school Inglaish. Écris, mais, parle pas, mais no sprink.*" This kind of
people, when you meet them, it's nice. Some of them are even big, big
people. When they drink, when they see you like that, they try to make
something like joking. Then you will happy and laugh. They say, "*Mademoiselle, tu peux danser?*"

And the way we used to do them, you know, when we hear this *"Mademoiselle,"* we say, "Me, I no speak French."

"Oh! You sprink English! Oh good, good, good, good!" *Ha!* "Nice! You sprink English. *Me — Français. École. L'école français. Me Voltaique. Moi no sprink Inglaish. Mais moi sprink small-small. L'école. Moi j'ai fait l'école anglais. Mais je peux pas parler, eh? Me. Comme ça je peux pas parler. Mais je peux écrire.*" Then he makes his hand so, like he's writing. Ha-ha! *"Je peux bien écrire anglais mais je peux pas parler. Écrire. Écrire."*

"Can you write?"

"Oui, oui, écrire. Oui. J'écris, mais je parle pas. Je peux pas comprendre. Mais je peux bien écrire. Je peux bien read. *Mais prononcer, c'est pas possible."* He can read well, he can write, and he cannot speak. He cannot try. So when we see a guy like this, I say, *"Agh!* I dey for home. Na dis, na be cool one-o." [1]

Yeah, when it's like that, then we have to drink — *heavy one!* We will drink all of your money. If you have a car, we can boss you to take us to our house, drop everybody free, and then we give you another day to meet us. *Ha!*

But sometimes, you can see somebody who will say, "OK, I don't care about anything. I'm waiting for you." OK? Maybe he waits for you to the closing time.

So I used to think about the way I was a fool to the people. I think about how I could be going with somebody without saying how much. When I went to Ouagadougou, I used to take some people as gentlemen. Sometimes I think, in Ghana, the girls who are clever, they are high-class to charge. They can get some amount. And some girls are fools, but they can get some amount which the high-class girls can't get. Because to say the price, there is somebody: you can say the price to him, and he will be annoyed. Even he won't go with you. And there is someone, you can say the price to him: he will answer, and he'll go with you, but he wouldn't give you the price. And there is somebody, you say the price to him: he will give you the money, but when he takes you home, he will also feel like, "Suppose this girl wasn't charging me, I would give her more." There are some people like that. OK?

So some people in Ouagadougou, if they want to go with a girl, they will be trying to ask, "How much are you going to take?" Because they don't want a problem in the morning time. And some won't ask you any-thing. They will go with you. And morning time, he will ask you, "How much do you want?" You see? So the kind of people who ask you in the

---

1. (Pidgin): I'm at home; this is an easy time.

nightclub, "How much do you want?" some girls can say, "I want this," and they will give you the amount straight. Or someone will say, "OK, we will go. Tomorrow morning, I will give you. I haven't got any money here."

But if you go to him, maybe you won't get anything. In the morning time you will find that he has gone to work. You won't even find any cook in the house to talk to, to ask him where the master has gone. If you wait, you are wasting your time. Yeah. Maybe you will think you can seize something from the place. You will say, "I will carry this thing to my place." You know, we have the kind of people like that.

So when you see these kinds of things about two or three times, you have to try to change your mind, so that, "OK, this time: 'money wɔ ha;[1] ass in the bed.'" *Ha! Ha-ha!* Yeah, the money must be there before you will stay with that person.

So then when anyone will ask you, you have to say your price. Whether it's good, or it's not good, you have to say your price. If it is good, he can hold the rest of the amount he was going to give you. He can use the rest by his own self.

Yeah, you know, I told you that there are problems in the nightclub. OK. Maybe. A man goes to the nightclub. Maybe he goes to Triomphe or Bataclan or Flamboyant or any nightclub. OK? Any nightclub he goes, there are girls who are working there. And there are girls who are doing nothing; they just come like that to the nightclub. OK? Maybe when he goes around the town, he will know that maybe this nightclub is the best for a man who likes the girls. He will choose one of the nightclubs that is good. And there are some men who don't want to be with one girl every day. OK? Every time he wants to change the girls. Maybe he sees a girl. He thinks that this girl resembles somebody, or that girl is that and this. He wants to see what is inside all of them. There are men like that who used to come to the nightclub like that.

You know, it's very funny. When he gets one girl today, the way he will deal with the girl, then tomorrow if he comes, if he doesn't say "Hello" to you, maybe you will say "Hello" to him. There are some girls who are like that. And there are some men, too, who are like that.

And hey, a man can come because of one girl. He wants that girl. He can buy drinks for all the girls in the nightclub. Maybe the girls are about fifteen or eighteen or twenty: he will buy for all, everybody, just because of one girl. OK? And the way he is doing with the girl, maybe you will

---

1. (Asante Twi): money is there. The full phrase is like a joking proverbial slogan about the ashawo life.

think, "Ah! This girl has this man?" There are some girls who will think of this. And the girl will also be happy, that, "Yeah. I have bluffed them. Even, my boyfriend came and bought drinks for all of them."

Some girls can sit from nine o'clock to four o'clock in the morning, and they won't get anybody to buy them a drink. So they just sit like they are sick. *Ha-ha!* Yeah, they are just like sick people in the hospital. Somebody will be sitting like this, and open her eyes, but if there is not much light, you will think she is sleeping. And then you walk in front of her. She sees you. Then she will tell you, "I'm not sleeping." *Ha!* But she is feeling sick. Yeah. So if you have somebody who will get all these people who are sleeping, and be waking them up, buying them drinks, trying to be dancing with them, then you will be *happy.* So: "Hey! My man has come."

Maybe you go with him: he will do *good* for you! He doesn't care even to give you twenty thousand, because he knows that tomorrow he will be coming to the same place, and he wouldn't mind you. *Ha-ha!* He can give you about twenty thousand, or some of them give *thirty.* They don't care. But: you know what is he going to do? Tomorrow, when he comes to the nightclub, you the girl will rush on him, "Hey, hello! Hello! How are you? Are you all right?"

He will say, "Yes. Do you want to drink something?"

You say, "Yes."

He will say, "OK, you drink something, and you bring me the receipt over there. I'm going to sit down."

Maybe you work in the counter, you know. And the people who bluff like that come straight to the counter. They know that the counter girls are the girls who are heavy. If you take a girl from the counter, you know, to ask her how much she wants for the night, she can ask you for thirty or forty thousand. So when people are bluffing like that, they come straight to the counter first.

And you at the counter, maybe you will think he wants you to come and sit with him. *Ha!* And maybe you will think, "Ah, yesterday he was nice, so — he has told me to drink what I want. So maybe I can ask my manager, as he's a good man, he can buy many drinks for people." You can think of that. Then you will tell the manager, "OK, *Patron,* you know, this fellow is the one who did this yesterday. Even — all his receipts were this amount. He was buying for anyone. But today, he doesn't want to stay at the counter." You will go to play some game like that with your master, and go out to the table, and be bringing your paper with your glass, to come and sit down.

And maybe, you know, the girls who have seen you with that man, you people all are working together. Maybe he will catch some chicken in his hand. So when you come, at once you will see that the chicken will just take herself sharp, and move to some place. Then maybe you will come and sit at the place. You think you are the one. And the man will tell you, "Excuse me. Did you take your drink?"

You will say, "Yes."

"Do you want more?"

As for me, Hawa, I will say, "Yes." Some people say, "No-o." But as for me, if you ask me, "Do you want more drink?" I know what you mean, you know, because I have been seeing these things for a long time, so I try to know them. So if you say, "You want more drink?" then I will say, "Yes."

"OK. And what is your paper?"

I say, "*Voilà,* this is my paper. This is what made me come, to give you your receipt." And then I can tell you, "Cheers." And then I'm going. Anything I drink, I will bring you the paper. I will get up because I'm clever. I don't want you to shame me.

But there is some girl who can sit down, and then he will say, "Did you bring your paper?"

She will say, "*Oui,* I am in counter."

He will say, "OK. Are you all right with this?"

Maybe somebody will say, *"Yes."* She thinks that she is going to sit with the person, but when she wants to force and sit with him, he just says, "You are working in counter?"

She will say, "Yes."

"OK. Go and do your work. And you can drink whatever you want. And you bring me the paper. I will pay. But I don't want to bring you out from your work, your heavy work, to come and sit with me. But I can be joking with your younger sisters. And then I think this girl is nice. She is young. *Toute petite,*[1] eh? She is very beautiful. She is very young. What do you think about that? Are you annoyed?"

You see? Then some girls will say, *"Yes!"* Straight. And that will turn to this. In the nightclub, even if the manager doesn't want to close, this palaver will close the nightclub.

But, as for me, Hawa, as I was coming to you, I saw that some girl was behind you, and she got up and I came and sat at the same place. I have been seeing it a lot of times, so when I just come, I know. But the first time, when I didn't know it, I didn't know the way to do. Before, I didn't read well. I did it like the others, how they do. But I didn't make trouble.

1. (French): very small; delicate

I used to say, "OK, OK, if you want to go with this girl. But until the closing time, I'm going to sit with you. You will buy what I want." I used to
force like that before. But when I saw this many times, I don't force again.

So in the nightclub, some girls can fight. I don't fight, because I know
that I'm not strong. If I fight, they will beat me every time. And I don't
want them to shame me.

Everything, you know, in this ashawo — OK, the first time when I
started to be ashawo, before going with somebody, I didn't watch the man
well. I didn't look at the man well. Somebody can come and lie: "Look, I
can give you ten cedis, huh? OK. If you want to come with me, tonight I
will give you ten cedis. OK?" But this time we have known all this. The
man who says he will give me the ten cedis, when I look at the person, I
will know that this man can give me ten cedis. I can know. If he can't
give, I can also know. Then maybe I will say, "OK. You say you will give
me ten cedis. OK. You give me here, before we will go."

But before, when I started, I didn't know all these things. Somebody
will just call the name of the money, and then I will think, tomorrow I'm
going to have it. You know? *Ha!* So it was just like that. And then maybe
tomorrow, even maybe you had your twenty pesewas, and then that one
too will be lost. You wouldn't see even your twenty pesewas which you
brought to that place. *Mm-hm.* They just — yeah.

So from the starting it was like that, but when you are getting grown
up, then you have to study what you have seen: the time when you didn't
know these things, and that and this. You have to know the differences in
it. When we came to this place, Ouaga, I started working in the bar. I have
tried. First time, when I was there, they were nice people. And every
time, as for me, in French country, you know, I'm Voltaique. I am from
Ouagadougou. But people, many white people used to tell me that, "Aren't
you ashamed that here is your country? Voltaique girls don't do that."

And I say, "Yes, I am *Voltaique façon.*" You see? Voltaique in some manner. I'm different. I'm Voltaique, but I'm different from them. So I have to
charge. *Ha!*

I used to charge people, you know. When I go with someone the first
time, I think this is the best way, to charge them. So OK, maybe you will
be lucky. You will charge somebody, then he will say, "OK. Do you want it
now?"

When you answer, then he will give it to you. And you will charge
somebody, then he will say, "OK, OK. Tomorrow I will give you that, because I have spent a lot here, I can't — I have not got enough here. So let's
get home. I will give you."

And home, before you reach home, he will bring another conversation, so he will forget. You think that tomorrow morning you are going to collect it. And maybe tomorrow morning, you will wake up, you are alone in the house! *Ha!* You have to find a way to piss![1]

So since I have seen that with them, every time, they think I'm so clever. And I'm not much clever, too, you know. Every time, they used to take me like some toy. I have many people in Ouagadougou I have known as friends. But they all become as brothers — these white people. I used to serve them the girls.

Maybe the first time, they have met me like this, as a friend, and maybe they had me free like that. But the second time, when they're going to bring themselves, there I will start to tell them, "You know, I'm not busy for a boyfriend. I am not busying myself to get a boyfriend. I don't need a boyfriend. I feel that the day when I'm happy, I'm happy. The day I'm happy to make my love —" and all this.

I used to give them many problems. So they ask me, "OK, so do you want to tell me that today you are not going with me?"

Then I will say, "Oh, no. It's just that today is not the day. But if you like, I can serve you a girl. But don't think I'm annoyed with you, eh? Any time, when I need you, I will sack the girl out and come in. OK?"

Then he will say, "*OK! Hey!* A good girl! You are a good girl!"

I will say, "OK. Will you give me one thousand?" He knows that he has been with me. He didn't give me anything. This is the time when I am going to collect all that he has owed me. You know? *Ha-ha!* Uh-*huh!* So: "I can give you this girl. but you know, today, my brother, how can I go home? I am telling you everything plain. So can you give me a thousand to take a taxi?"

Some people say, "Oh, Hawa, *tu es gentille. Je n'ai jamais vu une fille comme toi.* I haven't seen any girl like you! You are a *nice* girl. Oh-h-h! Can you do that for me?"

I say, "Yes! Because I know you are a man. The women are not pressing like a man. I know that you are a man. I can — I know that as you have come and asked me, you feel something like that. You haven't got a wife. You feel like going with a woman. And maybe *I* can go with you, but you wouldn't feel happy, because today I have no feeling. So I can give you a happy girl, who will be happy with you for the whole night, and you will enjoy it. But I will never forget about you, you know. Only today I don't feel it, so please, can you help me a thousand?"

1. There is no one around to show you where to piss.

Some people give me a thousand, some people give me two! Oh, some people give me even five thousand. *Ha!* I get them like that.

So any nightclub where I work, do you know why the managers used to like me? The kind of people I know like that, when they come to meet me where I'm working, they try to do their *best,* to buy me something, some drink which is costly. Any drink which is costly, if I call it, they will buy for me. Maybe one person will stand and buy about three or four, for me. So this is the way. When I know somebody like that, if he is a thick person, he can buy me drinks like that. I used to take him to the counter: always the manager is there. When they see me like that, then when I want to leave their work,[1] they are following me. Then I say, "No. Don't walk with me." They think I'm a fool. But I'm so stupid. They don't know how these people got me, before I knew them, before I will start drinking with them like this. *Mm-hm.* First time they showed me, but after that, the way they showed me, I used to drink them. And then be getting thousand-thousand-thousand. Sometimes I used to collect — Look, I'll tell you something.

Popularity Party

The time I traveled to Ghana with Limata, the day before we left Ouagadougou here, we didn't work. We stayed at home, up to two o'clock in the night. Then I told Limata that I was going to buy bread. So Limata was waiting for me. I was wearing knickers, with one of my blouses on top. So it was looking like I was wearing a maternity dress. So when I reached the boulangerie,[2] somebody said, "*Ey-y-y!* Look at this old lady. She is conceived and she is walking on the street." OK, the time this man said that, there was a car coming, and this car came and stopped and asked me where I was going, so I told him that I was going to La Tringle. Then he got me to La Tringle, and he asked me, "Should I come inside with you?"

I said, "If you like."

He said, "What are you going to do in La Tringle?"

I said, "I'm working in La Tringle. And I have slept. I was tired, and now I have come out to see La Tringle."

When we got inside, I knew many people there, about seven people. Yeah. They were all at the counter. They were two groups. These French

---

1. quit the job there
2. (French): bakery for baguettes or French baked goods; bake shop

people. They were all not my boyfriends. There were three people I had known as a boyfriend, and the others were all friends I knew because of them. So: "Hey, Hawa! *Et qu'est-ce qu'il y a? Tu ne travailles plus ici, non?* What is happening? You don't work here anymore?"

So I said, "Oh, *mais je travaille;* I'm working."

Then they said, "But we came tonight. We didn't see you."

Then the other group also said, "Hey, Hawa! Why? Tonight you don't say hello to us? Can you have a drink with us?"

Then the first people were annoyed, you know. So I said, "Oh, let me say hello to them."

Then they said, "Yes, but if you have to say hello to them, we don't refuse. But ask for what you are going to drink," and, "We want you, to drink with you," and, "Why didn't we see you tonight? Because today is a day to work. You don't work on Sundays, we know, but today is not Sunday. Because of what did you leave work?"

So this man who was following me, he became like a toy, you know. He was one African man. I think he was a driver. He was driving the car of the master, so he thought he had picked a cheap girl from the road, so I said, "Oh, but sorry. This is my brother."

So they bought him one drink. When he finished it, then he said that he was going.

Then they asked me what I was going to drink. Then I said, "You know, I'm going to travel tomorrow."

"Why? You are going to travel?"

I said, "Yes."

"You are going to leave us? You are going to spend Christmas there?"

I said, "Maybe I will spend the Christmas, or maybe I will come and spend the Christmas here. I don't know yet."

"But what is wrong? What is wrong?"

I said, "I want to see my family." *Ha!*

They said, "Oh-h-h. So you can stay in that small village for all these days?"

I said, "Why not? I have stayed in it to grow up, no?"

They said, "Ah, yes. Maybe, but we didn't think—"

I said, "Yes, I'm going to stay there."

So: "OK, then we will make a party."

You know: a party is coming.

So: "OK, we didn't know that you are going to travel. We have met you; you are going to travel, so we will make the party. We will pay for it. When you come back, you will pay."

I said, "OK."

Then: "Take something to drink."

Then I said, "You know, I have drunk a lot of champagne. So I don't want to mix up."

I had just come out from my place. I didn't taste anything! So: *ha!*

"Oh! OK! One bottle of champagne!"

Then I said, "OK, excuse me. I'm going to the toilet."

So I went to the toilet. I had to pass to greet the others who were calling me, you know, because I hadn't answered them. So I went to them, too, and then: "Oh, you know, I'm going to travel tomorrow."

"Where? Where are you going?"

I said, "I am going to my village."

"So what day are you coming back?"

I said, "Oh, maybe I will take about one month, or —"

"*C'est vrai?* Truly? Are you going to spend your Christmas there?"

I said, "Maybe. Maybe I will spend my Christmas, or maybe I will spend the Christmas here in Ouagadougou. I don't know yet, until I reach the place."

"Oh, Hawa, you are a good girl. You are going to leave us. Oh-h, let's drink together. What are you going to drink?"

I said, "Champagne." *Ha! Hee!* So I had two bottles of champagne.

And the first group who had called me, I didn't like them, because I knew two people in that group, OK? So I didn't feel their life. The second group, I felt the way: only one person I knew. So I felt we were all right. All of them were talking to me nicely. So I was feeling that group. Then I also lied to the first group and left them. You know, I had just woken up from sleep. I didn't drink anything, and my stomach was empty, to have a drink. Champagne, the cup — when I drank two times, it was finished. We finished all the bottle of the champagne, then they said, "Can we ask for one more?"

Then I said, "You know, how I'm going to travel, I shouldn't drink much, so I want to go home and sleep."

So: "Oh, but we wish to see you again."

Then I said, "OK."

And you know, I had made a mistake there, because I had told these people different stories: I told one that I have a baby, and then I had told the other one I don't have a baby. OK. *Ha! Hee-hee!* So the one said, "OK, if you go, I'm greeting your baby — he is nice, because — so you can have this ten thousand to buy her some bread," and that and this. So I was happy.

Then the other one said, "OK. I can lead you to the door." The one who I told I haven't got a baby. So —*ha-ha!*— he got up so that he could lead me out to outside, and he said, "Ah, Hawa, you haven't told me the truth. I didn't know that you have a baby. So I think all this is that I have. You can have this three thousand to pay your passage." Then I didn't say anything. "So this man is your boyfriend too? He knows your baby?" *Ha!*

So I was very ashamed. So when I went out, the second people who had the bottle of champagne, I had to send the watchman from the gate to tell them that they shouldn't be annoyed — I'm not going — I'm going to hide some way — I would like these people from the counter to go because I know them, and they are good people, and they want to buy me more drinks, but I don't want to stay with them, so I know that if I go out, they will also go out — but they are the special people I need to talk to, so they should wait for me. They shouldn't be annoyed. I'm going to wait at someplace. If the first people go, the watchman will come and tell me. So the watchman went and told them, and they understood. So when these people went out, I was in Cabane Bambou. Cabane Bambou and La Tringle are just near. So I went and sat down at that place, and when these first people went out, the watchman came and called me, and then I went inside with these second people. We were drinking, and then I said that I was going, "Good night."

And Limata was waiting, making Quaker Oats. Limata was cooking that, waiting for me. When I left Limata, I was going to bring bread and milk. And then I was someplace, so Limata got tired and then carried this Quaker Oats inside and then slept. So I also told these people that we were going to get up at four o'clock. And when we left the nightclub, it was a quarter to four. So they said, "OK, we will take you home and wait for you and drop you at the station."

So when we reached our place, then I said, "Hey, *camarade,* we have some people to drop us."

Then she said, "How?"

I said, "But it's quarter to four. If we go to the lorry station, you know, we will get the first car."

Limata said, "Ah, you told me you are going to buy me milk, when I'm hungry like this!" *Ha!* "You bring people to drop us, because we can't pay for taxi?"

Then I said, "No! Not because we can't pay the taxi. But if you keep that money, it's better." You know, I only had one bag, but she had many things. "If we are from our place to go to the lorry park in Ouagadougou with all these things, they will take us for nine hundred. Yeah. But suppose these people drop us, we won't pay this."

Then Limata said, "Hey! Don't talk this to me. You have *wasted* all my time. You didn't want me to sleep. I was hungry and waiting for you, and all this, so that you — you will come and tell me this. Even if these people bring an airplane, and they are going to Ghana straight, let them go. Tomorrow I will rent another airplane to go with you."

So I went out and told these people that, "My sister isn't ready yet, because she was sleeping. So she has to take time."

And then they said, "OK, then if that will be the case, we will leave you."

Then they also gave me six thousand. So I got plenty money! Suppose that night I slept, or suppose that night, when I went to that place to buy the bread, when these boys were starting to abuse me with my conceive dress, suppose I started to be annoyed with them, this man would have come and stopped his car, and he would have met me being annoyed with him. Isn't it? This man would have passed with his car. He wouldn't have stopped.

Revenge of the Men

So that is why I say the men who like shouting, they are not difficult. But yeah, the ones who are quiet, they know what they are going to do to you. Somebody who is bossing you like that, he wouldn't say anything about the thing you ate, about all his money you spent. He can take about one week, and he will still be spending for you. When he sees you: "Oh! Hello! How are you?" And then one day, he will just take you.

You too, you will trust that, "Ah, *pfft!*" Even you will think that he is good, eh? You will say, "Ah, I have spent his — maybe it's two thousand or it's ten thousand or five thousand — he didn't say anything." And even, every time, you will be getting his thing like that. When you come home, you used to tell your friends: "You know, I have a fucking, stupid man. He doesn't know what to do with his money. That day I chopped him this amount of money, he didn't get me. And now he's trying his best again. Even today I was with him. He was buying me drinks like that, and even he has given me two thousand or three thousand. He thinks his eyes are open, and he's going to get me. Fuck you."

You think you have got him cheap. He will be following you for about a week. And then he will just say something like inviting you, like he has a party — he has some friends who are making a party — and they invited him to come — and you know, they are going to have music — so everybody will be with a girlfriend, and he doesn't have a girlfriend — and this and that. So he wanted to ask you if you can be excused from your work so that he can go with you, because he wouldn't feel like going to the party alone. And the friends, too, he will introduce you to the friends, because he thinks they are nice. Maybe sometimes, if you don't see him in town, you can ask of the friends. You see? This kind of life, *heh? Ha!* Then maybe you will go to that party. They will be mixing drinks for you *fine.* You will be feeling *good,* and you will start to be happy. Then he will start bossing you. And maybe sometimes, you know, we women, when we drink, sometimes we don't have our own sense. So when he starts bossing you this way, you have agreed with him already, and maybe he will get you home with him.

And then, morning time, if he gives you even forty pesewas, you are lucky! This is the way he is going to show you. And he wouldn't go out; he wouldn't do anything. He will be sleeping his sleep. When you wake him, that you want to go, he will say, "OK, bye-bye." So: *ha!* He will not run away and leave you in the room. No. He is there. When you wake him, "I want to go," he will say, "OK, bye-bye. I will see you in evening time."

"How can I manage to go?"

He will say, "Oh, if you pass this place, just there, the main road there, you will get a taxi."

"But how can I take a taxi?"

He'll say, "Oh, a taxi is not plenty money. How much? It's only one hundred or two hundred. You can pay it. Evening time I will see you, because I can't get up now. And, you know, I can't go to town now. We have spent all the money that I had yesterday. So unless I go to the bank."

Then, you know, you will just look at this fellow. You can't beat him; you can't do him anything. And if you try to talk something which will let him annoyed, then he will wake up, and he will say, "Look, that day, maybe that money you took from me, you went and slept with some man, your boyfriend you love. He fucks you well, and you like it, and even you will take out of my money and dash him because he knows how to fuck." *Ha-ha!* You know? "So don't think I am a fool. I have nothing to give you. I thought you were somebody who respects yourself a lot. That's why I have been talking to you. Suppose you go away, maybe in the evening, I can give you something. But the way you are talking, if you want to show that your eyes are open, if my eyes are not open, too, I wouldn't give you that money. You know, if you see a man who is looking for a girl, and he is spending a lot, it is because his eyes are open and he wants his girlfriend to look beautiful. That's why he has been giving her money." So: *ha! Hee-hee!* You know? He will just fuck you out like that. So if you get a kind of man like that, you know, he will show you something.

The Price of Champagne

Look, when I was in La Tringle, I had one friend, a *nice,* handsome boy. Every time he came to La Tringle, I would say, "Champagne," and he would buy. Maybe he would buy two or three bottles. He never asked me to go home with him.

So one Saturday, he came. Then he said, "Oh, tomorrow is Sunday. I won't travel. So I want that we should go home." So we went to his place and we slept there till the morning time.

Morning time I said I wanted to go home. He said, oh no, he has a swimming pool and all these things at his house, so we should relax there.

Then I said, OK if that will be the case, he should take me home, then I would change my dress for the night; I would take another dress, because I didn't want to go with the same dress to the nightclub. So we went home, and then I took my dress and my swimming pants, and we came to the swimming pool. We were sitting there and drinking tea and coffee. There were some friends who came. We mixed together. We were enjoying there nicely. OK? Up to five-thirty in the evening. So I called him, that I wanted to go home.

Then he said, "Put on your dress."

Then I dressed finish.

Then he said, "OK. Can I drop you?"

Then I said, "Yes, if you can drop me. And what about your friends?"

He said, "Oh, never mind. I can drop you. I can give them an excuse to go and drop you."

So when we got to my place, I thought that when we got there, he would give me some money. So when we got there, I was sitting in the car. And he also opened the door for me. Then I said, "*Mais, qu'est-ce qu'il y a?* But what is that? Why?"

Then he said, "Why why?"

Then I said, "But, I haven't got money today, so you should try to give me something, you know?" I didn't say how much. "Oh, you have to try to give me something."

So he gave me two thousand, then I said, "What? What do you think I am? Two thousand? Two thousand? You think I am a two-thousand woman?"

Then he said, "Why? Why do you say that?"

Then I said, "Why should you give me two thousand? It's the first time to know me, isn't it? It's the first time when I have gone to your house. Why should you give me two thousand? OK, what do you mean by that?"

Then he said, "It is not the first time to know you. I have known you
many times from La Tringle. I have been drinking with you. Every time
you want to drink champagne. Every time you want cigarettes, I give
you one thousand, and you don't give me balance." *Ha! Hee-hee-hee-hee!*
"Sometimes I buy champagne. I know the champagne is twelve thousand.
Sometimes I give you fifteen thousand, and you don't give me balance.
But I used to think maybe you were drunk." So I—I—I—*ha!* I didn't
know that he was making all these accounts, you know! "So the first time
I know you? It's the first time you know my house, yes. I understand that.
But even the girls who are coming to my house, who know my house
every day, they don't get profit more than you. You have more profit than
them. Champagne, and your master has been marking you, too: 'Hawa,
you are drinking champagne. Hawa drinks champagne.' Every month
when this woman sees you, she sees you like gold. When they are talking
about Hawa, she will say, 'Yeah, Hawa is a good girl! She's a good girl!' Because of your champagne. And I have been giving you this good name. So
if I give you two thousand, are you not all right with that? By evening
time, if I come, I can get more to buy you champagne. Fifteen thousand.
Because your champagne, your master sells it for twelve thousand, and
you are selling it for fifteen thousand." *Ha-ha! Hee-hee!*

So I didn't say anything to him. I threw the two thousand in his car,
and he went away. Yeah. I don't want it. It's better I give him a gift. So he
went away with his two thousand.

That very night, he came to the nightclub. I didn't mind him. Then he
came: "Hawa, *tu es fâchée?* Are you annoyed?"

I didn't mind him. I didn't talk to him.

Then he said, "Oh, let's go and drink champagne. Even if I don't give
you anything, your master will mark you *more*. You will get more than
what I'm going to give you. Let's go and drink champagne. Hey! Bring one
bottle of champagne. I will drink with Hawa."

I didn't talk to him. So they served me the champagne. I said I wouldn't
drink. Then my manager came, she said, "Hawa, why?"

Then I said, "Madame, no, it's nothing. This man has played some
rough way which I haven't seen in my life. So I don't want to take any
drink from him."

Then the Madame called me to the toilet to boss me. She said, "Oh, no,
you just drink with him. Never mind about this and that."

Then I said, "Oh, no. This man, what he did to me, truly, I can't drink
with him."

So this woman tried to know what this thing was, and I was ashamed
too much to tell this woman what happened.

She said, "What has this man done to you? Tell me. You know, these white people, many of them, it's because of this nightclub I know them. So I can call him and talk to him, and you people will get understanding, and then it will be finished. You know? He is a good customer. Every time he used to come here and buy three or four bottles of champagne. You know, he is a good customer for you. It's because of you he's coming here. You shouldn't be annoyed with him." *Ha! Shit!!*

No, I couldn't help it. I would disturb this woman. So I said, "Do you know: this man, yesterday, he lied to me to go with me, and this morning he came and dropped me in my door, and he was trying to tell me what expenses he was making here. Because of that, he didn't give me money."

And this fucking idiot, do you know what this woman also said? "OK, I will give you five thousand for that. Don't say anything. Go and drink with him."

And I said, "I don't want it. I don't want your five thousand. If you can sack me tonight, sack me. I won't drink with this man."

So this woman got up. She didn't know what to do. So she called Limata to boss Limata, so that Limata would also come and boss me. And when Limata called me, *"Camarade."*

Then I said, *"Camarade,* I don't want trouble today. You people can pay me off. You are the cashier. You are the accountant. You can pay me off if you want to!"

Then Limata said, "Oh, *camarade,* but why are you annoyed with anybody like that?"

I said, "I don't want talk today. I told Madame I wouldn't drink with this man."

So this man said, "Oh-h-h, my sister —"

But, you know, he didn't speak English well. If he speaks English, you will laugh. "My sister"— he was talking to Limata —"My sister, you good! This girl no good. You — this girl make big big. You no big. You make so. My sister big. No make so."

So when he was talking, he made this kind of English. When I looked at him, he made me laugh. So I laughed. Then he said, "You laugh? You laugh me? You laugh me? You laugh? Me no drink. Limata. Give her one bottle champagne. Me no drink. Me no drink."

So Limata went and brought the champagne in front of me, a full bottle, and then opened it —*poff!* Then I said, *"Eh-heh!* This time I will drink!"

Ha! You see? I refused the five thousand of this woman. OK? And now I'm starting drinking with the man. *Ha!* So she had one bottle of champagne with him, and she had one bottle of champagne with me.

So when they served me, he was standing there. "Eh! My sister is drinking champagne. Is good my sister. Hey! This my sister — is good. *Hawa est gentille, eh? Et c'est pas problème, eh? Ah, tu vois comme elle boit le champagne là. C'est jolie, eh?*" He started bossing me: "You see how she's drinking. She is nice. Even it's beautiful if you see her mouth with the cup of champagne."

So I was annoyed because of that. I took my champagne and went and sat at a table, some distance away. Then this man carried his glass and came. Then he said, "Look, you are a fool, you know? I was about to give you money, but your heart is *too* much." —*Ha-ha!*— "So I can't give you much money. But next time, if somebody is good for you, try to be good for him. Don't do like the last time when you asked me for money. I was testing you. Suppose you dropped and you didn't ask me for any money, evening time when I came, I would know how much I am going to give you. But the way you asked me, I don't want the girls who will make a price with me."

Then I said, "What kind of price did I make? I didn't make a price with you. I said, 'Give me money because I haven't got money.' Then you said, 'OK, I will give you two thousand. I think you can use that for your expenses for the day time.' No. As for me, I don't want teaching. I don't want somebody to be seeing me on a *first* day, then he will be giving me two thousand. Even if he sees me a first day, and gives me twenty thousand, and the next time or second or third time, if he doesn't give me anything, I will never mind. You know. But I don't want this kind of teaching."

Then he said, "OK, I understand you. So take ten thousand. Don't be annoyed. But if I'm talking to you, don't make — if you are making your face like this, you know, I wouldn't be happy to be coming here to see you. I used to like to see you, you know. So don't be annoyed."

So then I took the ten thousand. I went to the counter, then I said to Limata, "See? *Aboa!* Suppose he didn't pay, where would he pass to go home?" *Ha!* Suppose he didn't give me anything, do you think I could hold him? But I was telling Limata: "Look at this stupid man. If suppose he didn't give me this money, where will he pass to go out?" Look-o! How big I am, and how tall I am — to hold somebody at the gate that he shouldn't go out, because he went with me yesterday, and he didn't give me money.

So we were joking and laughing. Then the man said, "Ah — you see? My sister is happy now. My sister — don't be annoyed with me. We dance?"

He liked this record, "One for You and One for Me." That time, they used to play it in Ouagadougou on the wireless. So we went and danced that dance and came back. And we drank, and when he paid for the drink, he had a balance of about three thousand and eight hundred, so he said Limata and I should share it. So we shared that one. And he bought me two packets of St. Moritz. He bought Limata the same — two packets. Then he went.

The next day he didn't come. The third day, he came. This man was not a real Frenchman. I think he was a German, or something like French-German. He spoke French nicely. He had a big shoe store. He gave us a paper with his name, that if we are going there to buy shoes, if we have this paper, if the shoe is ten thousand, they will give it to us for five thousand. *Ha!* So he is a good friend to me now, but we don't keep a friendship like boyfriend or girlfriend. From that day, I didn't go with him again. Every time he buys me a drink. And when he's going home, maybe two thousand, or three thousand. Then he will say, "Take this for your taxi." Sometimes he drops us home, me and Limata. But from that first time, he said I have bad character. He likes the girls who have character like that, but he doesn't want to keep a friendship with them. *Ha-ha!*

GLOSSARY

abi (Yoruba, also Pidgin). or. The word is used for emphasis, like saying, "Or what?!" or "Isn't it?"

aboa (Asante Twi). an exclamation of contempt or scorn, literally, an animal; comparable to the French expression, *"Ta gueule!"* or the English, "In your face!"

Akan. cultural group in central and southern Ghana, comprising Ashanti, Fanti, Akuapem, Akyem, Ahafo, Kwahu, and other groups

akpeteshie (Ga). Akpeteshie *(akpɛtɛshi)* is locally distilled spirits, usually made from sugar cane or palm wine. Akpeteshie was illegal during colonial times, and the name has two applicable Ga meanings, one from "hide-out" and the other from "lean over or against."

all. *at all:* not at all (from Asante Twi: *koraa*); *all the house:* the whole house

Amariya (Hausa). title of the most recently married wife in a Muslim household; a woman without cowives who was married in a Muslim ceremony; also, the marriage ceremony itself

APC. an analgesic tablet, no longer used, containing aspirin, phenacetin, and caffeine

area. neighborhood or section of a town or village

Asante Twi. the Ashanti dialect of the Akan language

Ashanti. cultural group in central Ghana, centered in Kumasi. "Ashanti" is the English form of "Asante."

ashawo (Yoruba). a "loose" or "free" woman dependent on men outside of a family situation; literally, money changer

bagatelle (French): a trifle, a flirt; an easy or loose woman, a woman who sleeps around, an ashawo

balance. *n.:* change

beg. to apologize; to ask forgiveness, often with a sacrifice or gift. *I beg:* Please.

blow. *v.:* to give a blow; to hit; *n.:* a punch

bluff. to take oneself high, to boast, to present oneself as better than others

bobo. a large embroidered gown, worn by men or women

Bobo. short name for Bobo-Dioulasso; also, name for cultural group from Bobo-Dioulasso and its environs; also, *bobo:* a large embroidered gown

boil. to give medicine or juju to; *boil up:* to become furious, to become very angry

Bolga. short name for Bolgatanga

borne. to have given birth to. The idiom is used for both men and women, and it is normal for a man to say he has borne his children.

boss. to persuade or convince; to talk nicely or gently to, sometimes but not necessarily with a connotation of insincerity; to trick; to cool someone out, to calm someone

bosun (Pidgin). a tough guy. The bosun (boatswain) is a warrant officer or petty officer on a boat, a rank below commissioned officers; the bosun would normally be the ranking sailor in a group of seamen hanging out in port.

bottom. buttocks; underside

buroni-wawu (Asante Twi). *See* **Oburoni w'awu.** The pronunciation is "broni-wawu."

bush. any wild or uncivilized area; *from bush:* an abuse, that a person has no sense or manners

cadeau, cadeaux (French): gift, tip, dash

camarade (French): mate, friend, comrade

car. a taxi or minibus; any transport

cedi. unit of currency in Ghana. One cedi is one hundred *pesewas* or ten shillings. Decimal currency was introduced in Ghana in 1965, replacing and phasing out the Ghanaian pound that had replaced British West African currency in 1958. The old or Nkrumah cedis were originally valued at eight shillings and fourpence; for ease of calculation, the New Cedi was introduced in 1966, valued at ten shillings, with two new cedis being a pound. The New Cedi was aligned with the U.S. dollar but was progressively devalued, slowly in official trading, radically in black market trading.

The actual value of the cedi, and by extension the actual cost of goods in hard currency, could only be known via the black market rate. In 1970, the cedi was trading at 1.15 to the dollar officially and 1.50 unofficially. In 1977, when most of the interviews for this book took place, a dollar bought 4.00 to 4.50 black-market cedis; in 1979, when additional interviews were conducted, the figure was 12–14 cedis. Eventually, the currency was floated under a "structural adjustment" program of the World Bank, and in early 2001, a dollar was about 7,500 cedis.

For a rough calculation of cedi values, one can divide the black-market value of a dollar in cedis into the inflation factor for a given year. For example, in 1974, a dollar bought 1.80 cedis, and a 1974 dollar would be worth about $3.60 in 2001, so in 1974 a cedi was worth about two 2001 dollars. Generally for this book, from the late 1960s to the early 1970s, when Hawa was in Accra and Tamale, one cedi would be equivalent to between two and four dollars after adjusting for inflation. In 1971, when I knew Hawa in Accra, a bottle of beer was fifty-five pesewas; an orange was threepence; a trotro ride across town might have been sixpence; a short taxi ride from one area to another cost two shillings. By 1977, in 2001 terms, a cedi was worth about seventy-five cents.

CFA. francs. Francophone African currency indexed to French francs. CFA stands for la Communauté Financière Africaine. 50 CFA were previously equal to one French franc; in 1994, the currency was devalued to 100 francs CFA to 1 French franc, or 1 centime. In 1999, CFA francs were pegged to the euro at just under 656 francs per euro. In this book, U.S. dollar prices for CFA therefore directly reflect the prices for French francs. In the 1970s, with the dollar generally between 4 and 5 French francs, CFA varied between 200 and 250 to the dollar, only occasionally pushing 300 or above. Generally in this book, one can use 250 CFA per dollar to calculate amounts.

cheap. easy; easy to get, easy to learn

chicken. a young woman or girl

chop (Pidgin). to eat, consume, use, spend; also, to get money from; also, to have sex with; also, to kill; *chop money:* money for cooking or food

C.I.D. detective. The detectives on a British police force are the C.I.D., or Criminal Investigation Department.

cinema. movie, movie theater

cloth. normally refers to wax-print cotton cloth. Wax-print cloth made in local factories in West Africa is regarded as lower quality than cloth from overseas. Quality is judged by how fast the colors are and by whether the printing is done on both sides. Particular print designs from various manufacturers can become fads, but in general wax-print cloth from different countries is ranked and priced accordingly, with "Hollandais" at the top, followed by English and then specific African countries, headed by Côte d'Ivoire and Senegal; local factories also produce different "qualities" or grades. Saying "different kinds" of cloth generally refers to different patterns.

cola. a type of bitter seed about the size of a chestnut. Used for soft drinks in the West, in Africa cola is chewed as a mild stimulant.

comedies. short subjects or ads or diversions before the main film at a movie theater

coming. coming back. *I'm coming:* I'll be right back.

conceive. *v.:* to become pregnant, to make someone pregnant; *n.:* pregnancy; also, the fetus; *conceived, adj.:* pregnant

corner. *corner-corner, adj.:* dodging; moving in a hidden or secret way; *corner ways:* shortcuts or indirect ways; back ways, as behind or between the houses

counter. the bar; *on counter, in counter:* behind the bar; *counter girls:* girls who serve from behind the bar

country. traditional area, cultural area

craze. go crazy; suffer a mental breakdown

cut. to take; to pull away a bit of something; to drink

Dagbamba. cultural group in northern Ghana, around Tamale and Yendi; singular: *Dagbana*

dash. *n.:* gift, tip; *v.:* to give, to tip

dawadawa. a seasoning, used mainly by northerners, prepared from the seeds of the dawadawa tree, *Parkia clapertiniana,* a type of locust tree

Dioula. also Jula, Djula, Dyula; cultural group in western Burkina Faso and northern Côte d'Ivoire

do. *do someone something:* to do something to someone; to make medicine against someone

dodge. to elude, avoid

dress, dresses. clothes, any outer garment; applies to both men's and women's clothing

drink. *n.:* any alcoholic beverage, generally hard liquor but also beer

eat. *See* **chop.**

European. any white person, including Americans

every. *every time, every day:* all the time; always

Ewe (*pr.* eh-ʊ eh). cultural group in southeastern Ghana and southern Togo

experience. intelligence; also, ideas, sense, wisdom

eyes. *whose eyes are red:* who is serious, who is angry; *whose eyes are strong:* who is proud, connoting stubborn pride; *whose eyes are open:* who is experienced or intelligent, who is modern; *whose eyes are good:* who is satisfied

face. *give face:* to respond to; to relate to; to give respect to; *squeeze (one's) face:* to frown; *tie (one's) face:* to tighten (one's) face; *show face (that):* indicate by one's expression; *make (something) on face:* act concerned but without sincerity

Fanti. cultural group in south central Ghana, around Cape Coast and Takoradi

feel. to have a feeling for; to like; to want; to enjoy

find. to look for; to get

finish. and finished; *die finish:* be dead. The word "finish" at the end of a phrase signifies the conclusion of the action.

first-time. at first

force. to make a hard effort

Frafra. cultural group in northern Ghana, around Bolgatanga

franc. *See* **CFA.**

fuck. to abuse verbally

fuck off. *exclam.:* Get away! Piss off!; also, *fuck (someone) off:* drive away, sack

fufu. a pounded, starchy food, eaten with soup. Fufu is a staple food of Akan people. It is pounded with a heavy pestle in a large mortar. The ingredients are generally boiled cassava blended with plantain, but fufu can be made with cassava alone, or occasionally cocoyam can be substituted for plantain. Fufu can also be made from yam, and yam fufu is more common (and is preferred) in savanna regions where cassava and plantain are not grown. Generally two people prepare fufu, one pounding and the other turning the fufu in the mortar.

Fulani. cultural group, widely dispersed across the savanna region from Senegal to the Cameroons, with concentrations in northern Nigeria and Niger; known in French as Peul

full. *are full up in:* to be filled up

Ga. cultural group in Accra area. The pronunciation is nasalized as "Gã."

gendarmerie (French). police station; barracks or administrative offices of armed forces militia or armed police

groove. *v.:* to smoke marijuana; *groove, grooving, n.:* marijuana; also, Indian hemp, wee; *groover, groovier:* marijuana smoker; *groovy:* high

groundnuts. peanuts

Guruma. cultural group in southeastern Burkina Faso

Gurunsi. generic name applied to any of the small but distinct cultural groups in the Volta Basin (northern Ghana, northeastern Côte d'Ivoire, southern Burkina Faso)

guy. a term that can apply to men or women; a person who is modern in every way, but is unpretentious and easygoing; someone who fits in with the other young people in a place

habit. way of living, character; also, culture

harmattan. a dry dust-laden wind that blows south from the Sahara desert during late November, December, January, and into February. The word can also refer to the season.

Hausa. cultural group in northern Nigeria

hear. *hear a language:* to understand a language, to speak a language

heart. *by heart:* senselessly, roughly, for no reason, without sense of purpose, carelessly; also, *adj.:* careless

hot. easily annoyed, angry, worried, broke; *to heat:* to become annoyed or angry; *to be hot on:* to trouble, disturb; *a hot time:* a difficult time

join. *join a car:* to board a passenger vehicle; *join a case:* to judge a case, to hear a case

juju. The word "juju" is no longer generally used by anthropologists because it has derogatory connotations, but the word is still used in common parlance to refer to animist (or pagan) religious activities, to medicine for herbal or sympathetic treatment of sickness if administered in an animist context, to animist religious or superstitious practices, to the animist deity or spirit it-self, or to the shrine of that spirit. *Make juju:* to make a sacrifice for medi-cine; *make the juju:* to do a sacrifice to the spirit; *beg the juju:* to do a sacrifice; *show the juju:* to make the juju manifest; to become possessed

Kaɛ (Asante Twi). an exclamation of objection, rejecting a situation or state-ment as useless. It can also be used as an affirmation, like saying "No!" or "No way!"

kalabule. corrupt, lying, trickish, bullshit

Kanjaga. town in northern Ghana; also, Builsa cultural group

keep. to manage; to hold; to stay, take (time); *keep long:* to take a long time

knickers. wide-legged shorts; for a woman, culottes

Koo *or* **Ko.** nickname for any "guy," short for Kofi; also used as an exclamation, like "Hey, man!"

Kotokoli. cultural group in northern Togo

kɔnkɔnsa. *Kɔnkɔnsa* (Asante Twi) refers to talking about people, often in a manipulative or distorting way, to meddling, or to gossip that causes trouble between people. Gossiper: *kɔnkɔnsani* (s.); *kɔnkɔnsafoɔ* (pl.). *Make kɔnkɔnsa:* to talk about people, to gossip, to cause trouble between people; *make kɔnkɔnsa on:* to tell on; *adj.:* fake, bullshit, lying, indirect, hypocritical

Krobo. cultural group in southeastern Ghana

lead. to accompany someone part of the way when that person leaves your place, a custom in many African societies; occasionally, to drop off

leave. to let something be, to stop doing something, to let go of something or someone; to let someone be free. *Leave me:* Let me go.

light. electricity; any light

life. way of living, lifestyle, character

lorry. any motor transport, including passenger buses

maalam (Hausa). Muslim scholar or cleric

mean. *to mean somebody:* to intend something toward somebody

Mina. alternate name for Gen, a cultural group in southern Togo

Mm. yes

Mossi. large cultural group in Burkina Faso, centered in Ouagadougou

naming. a small (occasionally large) ceremony formally giving a newborn a name, usually done a week or so after the birth; also called an **outdooring.** Muslim boys are circumcised on their naming day.

North. *the North:* northern Ghana, former colonial Northern Territories; *Northerners:* people from the North, the savanna area north of the coastal forest, about 150–200 miles inland, i.e., northern Ghana; people to the north of the Akan traditional area; also sometimes used to refer to Muslims; also sometimes applied to people from Muslim cultures in northern Togo, Burk-ina Faso, northern Nigeria, Mali, etc.

now-now. just now; at this very moment

nyama-nyama (Hausa). general word for anything of low quality or messed up; pathetic, lousy, cheap, poor, dirty, messy, run-down, worn-out, torn, nasty; literally, a pile or assortment of "stuff"

-o. *suffix:* adds emphasis to a word

Ouaga. short name for Ouagadougou

Oburoni w'awu (Asante Twi). second-hand clothing from overseas; literally, "White man, you died." The noun form is shortened to *buroni-wawu.*

pack. to gather; to take and set down

palaver. problem, case, argument, matter, worrisome or troubling talk, quarrel, dispute

palm wine. the sap of a type of palm tree, which rapidly ferments into a slightly sweet drink. Palm wine is made and drunk in the coastal forest regions.

pants. underpants

pass. to be more than; also, to go, go by or through; *pass menstruation:* to menstruate

patron, patronne (French). owner, manager, boss; also a form of address: sir, big man, boss, mistress

pesewa. unit of Ghanaian currency like a penny; one hundred pesewas to a cedi

piece. A *piece* of cloth is twelve yards. A half-piece (six yards) is used for women's traditional dresses with skirt, blouse, scarf or head-tie, and waist-wrap; two yards is used by men for shirts.

pick. to take; to carry

pito. a fermented drink generally brewed over three days from malted sorghum or sometimes from millet, reddish-brown in color with a somewhat sour taste; *pito house:* normally a brewing house, with an area or a room with benches where people come to buy and drink pito

play. *play with:* to joke with; to be free with; also, to mess with, to bother; to do (something) to

pocket lawyer. an argumentative person, someone who acts as if he carries around a law degree in his pocket in order to be able to bring it out at any time

proper. *adv.:* really, well; generally used simply to emphasize a verb

quarters. the rooms for cooks or stewards or other servants, generally a separate small building behind a house

quick. *make quick:* to hurry

rough. *make rough, do (someone) rough:* to quarrel with, to hassle; *do rough:* to be careless, do something without much thought

sack. to drive away, make someone go away; also, to fire (from a job)

seize. to take possession of

self (Pidgin). even

shit. to get rid of, ignore; to dismiss, snub

show. to teach; also, to take advantage of, cheat; *show oneself:* to boast, to bluff, to act proud; *show to:* to introduce; to let someone be known to

size. age; also, in some contexts, standard, status

small. *adj.:* little; also, "some small"; *adv.:* a little; *small-small, adj.:* doubled for emphasis, i.e., very small; *adv.:* little by little, bit by bit

smart. fast, quick; fast-moving, on top of things, hip

stranger. visitor, guest. In many African languages, the same word refers to stranger or guest; you would call your visitor a "stranger" even if you knew him or her very well, and you would introduce the person to your friends as "This is my stranger I have brought to greet you."

sweet. tasty, delicious (not necessarily sweet); pleasing, good

tam-tam (from French). drum; drumming

tawa (Asante Twi). tobacco

teach. to cheat; to show someone about life or give someone experience, with the implication of taking advantage of the person. The idea is of somebody opening one's eyes to something one didn't think or know about.

tey (Pidgin). continuing on and on; the same like that

tigernut. a kind of dried tuber, slightly sweet. One chews it for the juices and then spits out the roughage. Its juice (tigernut milk) is also extracted and made into a kind of pudding. Tigernuts have the reputation of being an aphrodisiac, and sometimes people refer to them as "charge-your-battery," as in "I want to buy some charge-your-battery."

too. very. "Too" as a modifier normally means "very," without implying comparison or excess.

tot. a shot of liquor

torch. flashlight

tough. heavily built, heavy-set, thick and large-framed; also, strong

tuwo (Hausa). food; staple hot food of savanna region, made from boiled flour of sorghum or occasionally other grain, eaten with sauce or soup. See **T-Zed.**

Tweaa (Asante Twi). an exclamation of disgust

type. age, standard, size

T-Zed. staple hot food of the savanna region, made from boiled flour of sorghum or occasionally other grain, eaten with sauce or soup. T-Zed is a conversational acronym for T-Z, which is Hausa for *tuwon zafi,* literally, a linked form of "hot *(zafi)* food *(tuwo).*" See **tuwo.**

up. *up and down, adv.:* around, here and there; *up-and-down, n.:* an outfit that uses the same material or cloth for blouse and skirt, or shirt and trousers; *upstairs:* upper story

waist. lower back and hips

wake up. to get up; to stand up

watchman. a private watchman guarding a residence. Many bungalows in residential areas have such an employee.

way. *which kind way, what kind way:* which kind of way, what kind of way; also, *some kind way.* The phrase usually is meant to question an unacceptable or unknown alternative.

wonder. to be surprised

Yoruba. cultural group in southwestern Nigeria and southern Benin

Zambarima. also *Zaberma:* cultural group in western Niger

zongo. (Hausa): a section of any town where people from other African cultures, generally savanna cultures, live; also, the name for the neighborhood